Conspiracy Theories in Eastern Europe

This collection of state-of-the-art essays explores conspiracy cultures in post-socialist Eastern Europe, ranging from the nineteenth century to contemporary manifestations.

Conspiracy theories about Freemasons, Communists and Jews, about the Chernobyl disaster, and about George Soros and the globalist elite have been particularly influential in Eastern Europe, but they have also been among the most prominent worldwide. This volume explores such conspiracy theories in the context of local Eastern European histories and discourses. The chapters identify four major factors that have influenced cultures of conspiracy in Eastern Europe: nationalism (including ethnocentrism and antisemitism), the socialist past, the transition period, and globalization. The research focuses on the impact of imperial legacies, nation-building, and the Cold War in the creation of conspiracy theories in Eastern Europe; the effects of the fall of the Iron Curtain and conspiracism in a new democratic setting; and manifestations of viral conspiracy theories in contemporary Eastern Europe and their worldwide circulation with the global rise of populism. Bringing together a diverse landscape of Eastern European conspiracism that is a result of repeated exchange with the "West," the book includes case studies that examine the history, legacy, and impact of conspiracy cultures of Bulgaria, Estonia, Hungary, Moldova, Poland, Romania, Russia, Slovakia, Ukraine, the former Yugoslav countries, and the former Soviet Union.

The book will appeal to scholars and students of conspiracy theories as well as those in the areas of political science, area studies, media studies, cultural studies, psychology, philosophy, and history, among others. Politicians, educators, and journalists will find this book a useful resource in countering disinformation in and about the region.

Anastasiya Astapova is a research fellow at the Department of Estonian and Comparative Folklore at the University of Tartu, Estonia.

Onoriu Colăcel is a senior lecturer in English at *Ştefan cel Mare* University of Suceava, Romania.

Corneliu Pintilescu is a researcher at the *George Baritiu* History Institute (in Cluj-Napoca) of the Romanian Academy.

Tamás Scheibner is an assistant professor in literary and cultural studies at the University of Budapest (ELTE), Hungary, and a senior research fellow in contemporary history at the Research Centre for the Humanities, Hungarian Academy of Sciences Institute of Excellence.

Conspiracy Theories
Series Editors:
Peter Knight
University of Manchester
Michael Butter
University of Tübingen

Conspiracy theories have a long history and exist in all modern societies. However, their visibility and significance are increasing today. Conspiracy theories can no longer be simply dismissed as the product of a pathological mind-set located on the political margins.

This series provides a nuanced and scholarly approach to this most contentious of subjects. It draws on a range of disciplinary perspectives including political science, sociology, history, media and cultural studies, area studies and behavioural sciences. Issues covered include the psychology of conspiracy theories, changes in conspiratorial thinking over time, the role of the Internet, regional and political variations and the social and political impact of conspiracy theories.

The series will include edited collections, single-authored monographs and short-form books.

Routledge Handbook of Conspiracy Theories
Edited by Michael Butter and Peter Knight

Contemporary Conspiracy Culture
Truth and Knowledge in an Era of Epistemic Instability
Jaron Harambam

Strategic Conspiracy Narratives
A Semiotic Approach
Mari-Liis Madisson and Andreas Ventsel

Conspiracy Narratives from South of the Border
Bad Hombres do the Twist
Gonzalo Soltero

Conspiracy Theories in Eastern Europe
Tropes and Trends
Edited by Anastasiya Astapova, Onoriu Colăcel, Corneliu Pintilescu, and Tamás Scheibner

For a full list of titles in this series please visit www.routledge.com

Conspiracy Theories in Eastern Europe
Tropes and Trends

Edited by Anastasiya Astapova,
Onoriu Colăcel, Corneliu Pintilescu,
and Tamás Scheibner

LONDON AND NEW YORK

First published 2021
by Routledge
2 Park Square, Milton Park, Abingdon, Oxon OX14 4RN

and by Routledge
52 Vanderbilt Avenue, New York, NY 10017

Routledge is an imprint of the Taylor & Francis Group, an informa business

© 2021 selection and editorial matter, Anastasiya Astapova, Onoriu Colăcel, Corneliu Pintilescu and Tamás Scheibner; individual chapters, the contributors

The right of Anastasiya Astapova, Onoriu Colăcel, Corneliu Pintilescu and Tamás Scheibner to be identified as the authors of the editorial material, and of the authors for their individual chapters, has been asserted in accordance with sections 77 and 78 of the Copyright, Designs and Patents Act 1988.

All rights reserved. No part of this book may be reprinted or reproduced or utilised in any form or by any electronic, mechanical, or other means, now known or hereafter invented, including photocopying and recording, or in any information storage or retrieval system, without permission in writing from the publishers.

Trademark notice: Product or corporate names may be trademarks or registered trademarks, and are used only for identification and explanation without intent to infringe.

British Library Cataloguing-in-Publication Data
A catalogue record for this book is available from the British Library

Library of Congress Cataloging-in-Publication Data
Names: Astapova, Anastasiya, editor.
Title: Conspiracy theories in Eastern Europe : tropes and trends / edited by Anastasiya Astapova, Onoriu Colăcel, Corneliu Pintilescu and Tamás Scheibner.
Description: Abingdon, Oxon ; New York, NY : Routledge, 2021. | Series: Conspiracy theories | Includes bibliographical references and index.
Identifiers: LCCN 2020023573 (print) | LCCN 2020023574 (ebook) | ISBN 9780367344771 (hardback) | ISBN 9780429326073 (ebook)
Subjects: LCSH: Conspiracy theories—Europe, Eastern. | Political culture—Europe, Eastern. | Post-communism—Europe, Eastern. | Populism—Europe, Eastern. | Europe, Eastern—Social conditions—1989–
Classification: LCC HV6295.E87 C66 2021 (print) | LCC HV6295.E87 (ebook) | DDC 001.90947—dc23
LC record available at https://lccn.loc.gov/2020023573
LC ebook record available at https://lccn.loc.gov/2020023574

ISBN: 978-0-367-34477-1 (hbk)
ISBN: 978-0-429-32607-3 (ebk)

Typeset in Times New Roman
by Apex CoVantage, LLC

Contents

List of figures	viii
List of tables	ix
Acknowledgments	x
List of abbreviations	xi
List of contributors	xiv

**Introduction: Eastern Europe in the global traffic
of conspiracy theories**   1

ANASTASIYA ASTAPOVA, ONORIU COLĂCEL, CORNELIU
PINTILESCU, AND TAMÁS SCHEIBNER

PART I
**Conspiracy culture under Socialism and its afterlife
in Eastern Europe**   27

1 **Chernobyl conspiracy theories: from American sabotage
to the biggest hoax of the century**   29

ANASTASIYA ASTAPOVA

2 **Stalinist conspiracy theories in France and Italy: the limits
of postwar Communist conspiracy culture**   48

PASCAL GIRARD

3 **"By the order of their foreign masters": Soviet dissidents,
anti-Western conspiracy, and the deprivation of agency**   67

ANNA KIRZIUK

vi *Contents*

PART II
"The enemy within": Jews and Freemasons
87

4 **The myth of a Judeo-Bolshevik conspiracy in Hungary, within and beyond the far right** 89
PÉTER CSUNDERLIK AND TAMÁS SCHEIBNER

5 **An open secret: Freemasonry and justice in post-socialist Bulgaria** 110
TODOR HRISTOV AND IVELINA IVANOVA

6 **From Judeo-Polonia to Act 447: how and why did the Jewish conspiracy myth become a central issue in Polish political discourse?** 125
DOMINIKA BULSKA, AGNIESZKA HASKA, MIKOŁAJ WINIEWSKI, AND MICHAŁ BILEWICZ

PART III
After independence: nation-building and victimhood narratives
145

7 **Dissolution of Yugoslavia as a conspiracy and its haunting returns: narratives of internal and external *othering*** 147
NEBOJŠA BLANUŠA

8 **The dangerous Russian other in Ukrainian conspiratorial discourse: media representations of the Odessa tragedy** 167
OLGA BAYSHA

9 **The victims, the guilty, and "us": notions of victimhood in Slovakian conspiracy theories** 186
ZUZANA PANCZOVÁ

PART IV
Eastern Europe goes global: conspiracy theories and the rise of populism
205

10 **Soros conspiracy theories and the rise of populism in post-socialist Hungary and Romania** 207
CORNELIU PINTILESCU AND ATTILA KUSTÁN MAGYARI

Contents vii

11 **Conspiracy theories on Moldovan commercial TV** 232

ONORIU COLĂCEL

12 **North Macedonia goes global: pro-EU aspiration and
anti-EU sentiment as a basis for EU-related conspiracy theories** 250

BILJANA GJONESKA, KRISTIJAN FIDANOVSKI, AND ANDRÉ
KROUWEL

13 **Conspiracy theory, epistemology, and Eastern Europe** 268

M R. X. DENTITH

Index 289

Figures

6.1.	Differences in means for scales of belief in Jewish conspiracy theories in years 2009, 2013, and 2017, with error bars representing standard error of the mean	131
6.2.	Correlations between various conspiracy beliefs and conspiracy mentality in Poland, controlling for political stands	132
6.3.	Percentage of Jews in various countries who heard a statement that Jews have too much power	134
7.1.	Pandemonium of enemies of socialist Yugoslavia in the 1980s	157

Tables

6.1. Percentage of agreements to the questions indicating the belief in Jewish conspiracy in Europe   134

8.1. Number of news stories on Odessa in selected media, May 3–4, 2014   173

8.2. Coding key: frames of reference in Odessa coverage   174

8.3. Frame employment across news media   175

Acknowledgments

This edited volume is one of the results of the work within COST Action CA15101 (Comparative Analysis of Conspiracy Theories). The work was also supported by personal research funding from the Estonian Research Council PSG48 "Performative Negotiations of Belonging in Contemporary Estonia" (1.01.2018−31.12.2021). The editors wish to thank COST Action CA15101 colleagues for their feedback (provided during many conferences and meetings) on some chapters and Lindsay Porter for her invaluable help in putting together this book.

Abbreviations

ADL	Anti-Defamation League
AFCP	Archives of the French Communist Party
AIG	Archives of the "Istituto Gramsci"
ANOVA	Analysis of variance
ATO	Anti-terrorist military operation
BBC	British Broadcasting Corporation
CDDDABCSSISBPA	Commission for the Disclosure of Documents and Declaration of Affiliation of Bulgarian Citizens with State Security and the Intelligence Service of the Bulgarian People's Army
CEDIM	Center for the Study of Ethnicity, Citizenship and Migration
CEU	Central European University
CIA	Central Intelligence Agency
COMPACT	Comparative Analysis of Conspiracy Theories
COST	European Cooperation in Science and Technology
CPU	Communist Party of Ukraine
CPI	Corruption Perceptions Index
CPSU	Communist Party of the Soviet Union
CRULH	Centre de Recherche Universitaire Lorrain d' Histoire
DGSI	Direction générale de la sécurité intérieure (General Directorate for Internal Security)
DNA	Direcția Națională Anticorupție (National Anti-Corruption Directorate)
EEA	European Economic Area
EEU	Eurasian Economic Union
EU	European Union
FBI	Federal Bureau of Investigation
FIDESZ-MPP	Fiatal Demokraták Szövetsége – Magyar Polgári Párt (Hungarian Civic Alliance)
FNA	French National Archives
FRG	Federal Republic of Germany
FSS	Federal Security Service
GDCOC	General Directorate Combating Organized Crime (Bulgaria)

xii *Abbreviations*

GERB	Grazhdani za Evropeisko Razvitie Balgariya (Citizens for European Development of Bulgaria)
GL AFAM	Grand Lodge of Ancient Free and Accepted Masons of Germany
GMG	General Media Group (Republic of Moldova)
GMO	Genetically modified organism
HHC	Hungarian Helsinki Committee
HIV	Human immunodeficiency virus
HPV	Human papillomavirus
HSS	Hrvatska seljačka stranka (The Croatian Peasant Party)
HUF	Hungarian forint
ICTV	International Commercial Television (Ukraine)
ICTY	International Criminal Tribunal for the former Yugoslavia
ILS	Istituto Luigi Sturzo (Luigi Sturzo Institute)
IMF	International Monetary Fund
IRES	Institutul Român pentru Evaluare și Strategie (Romanian Institute for Evaluation and Strategy)
IRI	International Republican Institute
IRH-ICUB	Institute for Research in the Humanities – Research Institute of the University of Bucharest
KGB	Komitet Gosudarstvennoy Bezopasnosti (Committee for State Security)
LGBTI	Lesbian, gay, bisexual, transgender, intersex
LW	Left wing
MANSZ	Magyar Asszonyok Nemzeti Szövetsége (National Association of Hungarian Women)
MDF	Magyar Demokrata Fórum (Hungarian Democratic Forum)
MGB	Ministerstvo gosudarstvennoy bezopasnosti SSSR (Ministry for State Security)
MK	Republic of North Macedonia
MMR	Measles, mumps, rubella
MP	Member of Parliament
MSI	Movimento Sociale Italiano (Social Italian Movement)
MTI	Magyar Távirati Iroda (Hungarian News Agency Corporation)
NATO	North Atlantic Treaty Organization
NGO	Nongovernmental organization
NKVD	Naródnyiy Komissariát Vnútrennikh Del (People's Commissariat for Internal Affairs)
NTS	Narodnno-Trudovoj Sojuz rossijskix solidaristov (National Alliance of Russian Solidarists)
OHCHR	Office of the High Commissioner for Human Rights
OSF	Open Society Foundations
PiS	Prawo i Sprawiedliwość (Law and Justice)

Abbreviations xiii

PRM	Partidul România Mare (Greater Romania Party)
PSD	Partidul Social Democrat (Social-Democratic Party, Romania)
PSI	Partito Socialista Italiano (Italian Socialist Party)
PUNR	Partidul Unității Naționale Române (Romanian National Unity Party)
RM	Republic of Moldova
RMBK	Reaktor Bolshoy Moshchnosti Kanalniy (High power channel-type reactor)
RPF	Rassemblement du Peuple Français (The Rally of the French People)
RW	Right wing
RWA	Right-Wing Authoritarianism
SANU	Serbian Academy of Science and Arts
SAS	Slovak Academy of Sciences
SBU	Sluzhba bezpeky Ukrayiny (Security Service of Ukraine)
SD	Standard deviation
SRI	Serviciul Român de Informații (Romanian Intelligence Service)
SWAT	Special Weapons and Tactics
TI	Transparency International
UFO	Unidentified flying object
UK	United Kingdom
UN	United Nations
UNSCEAR	United Nations Scientific Committee on the Effects of Atomic Radiation
US/USA	United States/United States of America
USAID	United States Agency for International Development
USL	Uniunea Social Liberală (Social Liberal Union)
USSR	Union of Soviet Socialist Republics
VMRO-DPMNE	Vnatrešno–Makedonska Revolucionerna Organizacija–Demokratska Partija za Makedonsko Nacionalno Edinstvo (Internal Macedonian Revolutionary Organization–Democratic Party for Macedonian National Unity)
VOA	Voice of America
WHO	World Health Organization

Contributors

Anastasiya Astapova is a research fellow at the Department of Estonian and Comparative Folklore at the University of Tartu, Estonia. She has defended her PhDs on student humor (Academy of Sciences, Russia, 2016) and Belarusian political folklore and nationalism (University of Tartu, Estonia, 2015). She has published over 30 peer-reviewed works on these issues.

Olga Baysha is an associate professor at the National Research University Higher School of Economics in Moscow, Russia. Her research centers mainly on the political and cultural aspects of globalization with an emphasis on new media and global social movements for justice and democratization.

Michał Bilewicz is a professor at the Faculty of Psychology and director of the Center for Research on Prejudice at the University of Warsaw, Poland. He is interested in the social psychology of intergroup relations, dehumanization and infrahumanization processes, contact hypothesis, and prejudice reduction as well as the linguistic aspects of discrimination.

Nebojša Blanuša is an associate professor and director of the Center for the Study of Ethnicity, Citizenship and Migration (CEDIM) at the Faculty of Political Science at the University of Zagreb, Croatia. In his work he deals with the formation of conspiracy theories as collective narratives related to cultural traumas and provoked by crises and wars, with a special focus on conspiratorial culture in the Balkans.

Dominika Bulska is a doctoral candidate at the Center for Research on Prejudice at the Faculty of Psychology at the University of Warsaw, Poland. Her scientific interests lie at the crossroads of the psychology of intergroup relations—namely, prejudice—and the psychology of conflict. She is interested in the various expressions of antisemitism and their behavioral consequences.

Onoriu Colăcel is a senior lecturer in English at *Ştefan cel Mare* University of Suceava, Romania. He has written on the contemporary English novel and on Romanian and Moldovan literary cultures and visual media.

Péter Csunderlik is an assistant professor at Eötvös Loránd University, Hungary, and a research fellow at the Institute of Political History in Budapest,

Contributors xv

Hungary. He is interested in the history of left-wing radical movements, in the remembrance of the Hungarian Soviet Republic, and in the theory of history.

M R. X. Dentith is a philosopher who specializes in the epistemic analysis of conspiracy theory as well as writing on rumors, fake news, and the epistemology of secrecy. He is co-host, along with Josh Addison, of *The Podcaster's Guide to the Conspiracy*.

Kristijan Fidanovski is an early-career scholar based in Skopje, North Macedonia, where he is currently working as a monitoring and evaluation assistant at USAID's Office for Transition Initiatives. His research interests include strategic communication, identity politics, and public health in the ex-Yugoslav and Eastern Europe countries.

Pascal Girard is an associate research fellow of history at the Centre de Recherche Universitaire Lorrain d' Histoire (CRULH) at the University of Lorraine (Nancy-Metz), France. His main research topics are postwar political history (with a focus on the spread and impact of conspiracy theories) and domestic political violence (Communist Party, far right, trade unions).

Biljana Gjoneska works as a research associate at the Macedonian Academy of Sciences and Arts on cognitive and social neuroscience topics, with emphasis on neuroethics and neuropolitics. She investigates the neurophysiological and behavioral correlations of ideological division and group distinction, which may be at the core of conspiratorial beliefs.

Agnieszka Haska is a cultural anthropologist and sociologist and an assistant professor at the Polish Center for Holocaust Research at the Institute of Philosophy and Sociology at the Polish Academy of Sciences. In her work she is interested in researching the Holocaust in Poland, especially regarding the problem of collaboration, witnesses, social networks, and the memory of World War II in contemporary public discourse.

Todor Hristov teaches critical theory and cultural studies at the University of Sofia, Bulgaria, and sociology at the University of Plovdiv, Bulgaria. He has published a number of books on governmentality, social movements, cultural studies, and practical rationalities.

Ivelina Ivanova is a fellow of the Institute for the Study of Societies and Knowledge of the Bulgarian Academy of Sciences and a visiting research fellow of the University of Bologna, Italy. She is an author of a number of articles and books in the field of philosophy of history and political theory.

Anna Kirziuk is a specialist in folklore studies and social anthropology. She is the author of works on Soviet and post-Soviet rumors, urban legends, and conspiracy theories. She is a research fellow at the Laboratory of Theoretical Folkloristics at the Russian Presidential Academy of National Economy and Public Administration (Moscow).

xvi *Contributors*

André Krouwel teaches comparative political science and communication science at the Vrije Universiteit Amsterdam, the Netherlands. His research focuses on public opinion and politically relevant sentiments, voting behavior, political parties, and social movements. His most recent research has investigated the impact of information on political attitudes and opinions, (negative) political emotions, and belief in conspiracy theories.

Attila Kustán Magyari is a journalist, who since 2006 has published broadly on topics such as populism, far-right movements, and conspiracy theories in Hungary and Romania. He has also published a large number of interviews with cultural personalities such as Judith Butler, G. M. Tamás, George Ritzer, Saskia Sassen, and Ruth Wodak.

Zuzana Panczová is a senior research fellow at the Institute of Ethnology and Social Anthropology of the Slovak Academy of Sciences (SAS). She studied history and ethnology at Comenius University in Bratislava, Slovakia. Her research is focused mainly on narrative folklore (traditional and contemporary legends, rumors, theory of humor) but also on social stereotypes, caricatures, discourse, and ideology.

Corneliu Pintilescu is a researcher at the *George Baritiu* History Institute (in Cluj-Napoca) of the Romanian Academy. His research interests include state coercion and dissent in Eastern Europe during the Cold War period, state of siege and conspiracy theories in interwar Romania, and nationalities policies in postwar Romania.

Tamás Scheibner is an assistant professor in literary and cultural Studies at the University of Budapest (ELTE), Hungary, and a senior research fellow in contemporary history at the Research Centre for the Humanities, Hungarian Academy of Sciences Institute of Excellence.

Mikołaj Winiewski is an assistant professor at the Center for Research on Prejudice at the Faculty of Psychology at the University of Warsaw, Poland. He is mainly interested in the phenomenon of collective violence, the psychology of intergroup relations, and antisemitism. His latest research deals with the complexity of anti-Jewish and anti-Roma stereotypes.

Introduction

Eastern Europe in the global traffic of conspiracy theories

Anastasiya Astapova, Onoriu Colăcel, Corneliu Pintilescu, and Tamás Scheibner

After the fall of the Iron Curtain, expectations about the rapid democratization, smooth transition to market economy, and integration into the global flux of goods, people, and ideas of Eastern European countries ran high. Over three decades after 1989, the political trends in Eastern Europe, such as the rise of populism, reveal that the democratic transition is easily reversible. Moreover, the region has emerged as a propitious place for inventing, adapting, mediating, and redistributing conspiracy theories. What was initially viewed as a source of all virtues is now seen as evil: the European Union has become the primary target of conspiratorial narratives in the region (and beyond), often being perceived as a plot of hidden powers bent on dominating the continent and drastically changing the world as we know it. These conspiracy theories are hardly marginal, since leading political figures such as Viktor Orbán, Jarosław Kaczyński, and Liviu Dragnea have been disseminating them for a long time now. Their conspiratorial narratives depict Brussels as the "new Moscow" (Bridge 2017, 48), thus comparing the EU to the Soviet Union or, alternatively, portraying the European project as a German plot to colonize Eastern Europe. These narratives revive twentieth-century experiences all too familiar to the locals: the Soviet effort to limit state sovereignties across Eastern and Central Europe and the German imperial aspirations known as *Drang nach Osten*. The new narratives also resonate well with the traditional self-perceptions of the nations of the region as victims of great powers whose "very existence may be put in question at any moment" (Kundera 1984, 35).

Another historical experience the area commonly draws on when constructing conspiratorial narratives is the historical Jewish presence and long-standing antisemitism in Eastern Europe. While larger Jewish communities in the region did not survive World War II outside Russia and a few Southeastern European countries, it has been proven that antisemitism actually requires no Jews (Lendvai 1971): contemporary Poland is a striking example (Bilewicz et al. 2013). As it is well known, one of the most influential conspiracy theories, *The Protocols of the Elders of Zion*, originated in Eastern Europe and was mediated to the West mostly by White Russian émigrés in the late 1910s and 1920s (Marks 2003, 172–73). For example, the Russian "white émigrés" disseminated a conspiracy theory in interwar Germany depicting Jews as operating "a seamless web of conniving finance capitalists and murderous Bolsheviks, threaten[ing] to conquer the world"

(Kellogg 2005, 1–2). Although it was unveiled as a forgery a hundred years ago, it survived and has been widely circulated on the internet and reprinted by publishers spreading neo-Nazi ideology.

With the recent populist revival and the rise of authoritarian leaders in Eastern Europe, however, antisemitic discourse reached mainstream politics and surfaced in campaigns against the American-Jewish billionaire George Soros across the region. The Soros campaign revived old antisemitic tropes and iconography. Effectively, it scapegoated Soros as an embodiment of an alleged hidden global network of ruthless capitalists. The novelty of the campaign was that it added human rights activists, refugees, and migrants to the old antisemitic conspiracy theories. Since Donald Trump's victory in the US presidential elections, anti-Soros conspiracy theories have gained special popularity. For example, there were claims that Soros aims to bring Mexicans back to the United States—due to some antipatriotic money hustle resulting in the conscious destabilization of the country. Affirmative reporting on such ideas has also helped to establish anti-Soros conspiracy theories in Eastern Europe. Ironically, in the United Kingdom, they reversed the geography of conspiracism and looked for scapegoats in the East: there, migrants and migrant communities from Eastern Europe were depicted as major threats and fueled conspiracy theories against a European Union, blamed for allowing the free movement of the workforce.

Anti-EU and anti-Soros narratives are just two examples of conspiracy theories that have received a great impetus from Eastern Europe in the past decade. The ruling techniques that authoritarian politics employ globally are roughly the same, and conspiracy theories are parts of a common toolbox. Far-right subcultures, with extensive online presence, have effectively spread such theories across borders, while rightist radical parties are well connected and emulate each other. However, it is safe to argue that some of the best-known international conspiracy theories are co-created by American, Western, and Eastern European actors.

This volume aims to corroborate this view and challenge the public and academic consensus on conspiracy theories as a primary product of the United States or, generally, Western political culture. This consensus is partly a result of the very history of conspiracy theory research, which has developed at the conjunction of American studies, political science, and psychology and, consequently, has focused on US sources and phenomena. Undoubtedly, due to a set of historical conditions (Goldberg 2003), the United States proved to be a particularly rich soil for the development of a conspiracy culture. Moreover, with English being a *lingua franca* and US culture having worldwide impact, conspiracy theories that originated in the United States set the main trends of conspiracism. The primary focus on the United States and, somewhat later, on Western conspiracy thinking (Butter and Knight 2016, 8) has shaped the perception of the United States and the West as the primary sources of conspiracy theories. Also, most of the influential works on conspiracy theories have been written based on US materials, with the United States often understood as the ultimate case of conspiratorial paranoia (Knight 2003; Butter and Reinkowski 2014). Conspiracy theory research, however, hardly profits from an exclusivist attention to English sources,

Introduction 3

and continuing on this beaten path is likely to relegate the global phenomenon of conspiracism to the confines of Western-style democracies.

Consequently, this edited volume aims to bridge yet another "great divide" in conspiracy theory research (Butter and Knight 2016) by highlighting some of the most widespread or particularly telling conspiracy narratives of Eastern Europe. Our focus is on a region that, in spite of its major significance in both the history of some of the best-known conspiracy theories and their contemporary circulation, has rarely made it into the mainstream of conspiracy theory research. We argue that the overview of these particular conspiracy theories can help us to better grasp not only their specificities, as they emerged, reshaped, or just recirculated in Eastern Europe, but also the diversity of the conspiracy narratives across the region and beyond.

Definitions and approaches

Even though research into conspiracy theories has been dominated by representatives of political science, psychologists, and American studies, interest in this field has been growing at such a large pace across a wide range of disciplines that it has arguably become a discipline in its own right (Boltanski [2012] 2014, 196). However, while defining what a conspiracy is does not constitute a subject of disputation (see M R. X. Dentith's chapter in this volume), what constitutes a conspiracy theory remains a big issue. There are, however, several key characteristics of conspiracy theories scholars agree on. One of the most synthetic is the definition provided by Michael Barkun, who argues that "a conspiracy belief is the belief that an organization made up of individuals or groups was or is acting covertly to achieve some malevolent end" (2003, 3). A similar one is proposed by Cass R. Sunstein and Adrian Vermeule, who claim that any attempt to explain an "event or practice by reference to the machinations of powerful people" acting in secret is a conspiracy theory (2009, 205). These definitions point at two essential characteristics of conspiracy theories: that of secrecy and the assumption of the existence of a clandestine group with specific interests. It is also important that the latter has a broad action radius; it is a "gigantic and yet subtle machinery of influence set in motion to undermine and destroy a way of life" (Hofstadter 1964, 29). The third common feature concerns not the content of the claim, but rather, its epistemological status: conspiracy theories are presented as "fundamental, unshakeable principle[s]" that are "by [their] very nature irrefutable" (Byford 2011, 36). In its sometimes complicated structures of causes and consequences, conspiracism imitates genuine intellectual inquiry, but in contrast to the latter, it indulges in a mode of questioning that does not allow for the reconsideration of original causes. The result is "a closed system of ideas about a plot," and this system dismisses all attempts at criticism and relativization as actions by the very powerful conspirators that take information management under their control (Barkun 2003, 7). What follows is that any piece of criticism is yet another argument in favor of the conspiracy theory. This regime of inquiry is so essential to conspiracism that Brian L. Keeley even defined conspiracy theories as theories "for which evidence against them is actually construed as evidence in favor of them" (1999, 120). The discursive regime that governs conspiracy theories is closely linked to their obsessive character: as Mark Fenster argued, conspiracy theorists are "driven by a circular, inexhaustible desire for more information" of which carefully selected pieces on the expense of other types of evidence could be mounted to prove the existence of a conspiracy ([1999] 2008, 13).

Approaches to conspiracy theory discourses vary greatly in academic scholarship, and it is difficult to bridge the gap between two basic attitudes toward conspiracism (Butter and Knight 2016). One approach treats conspiracy theories as pathological and strongly related to paranoia and irrationality (Hofstadter 1964; Pipes 1997; Robins and Post 1997), while another growing body of research rejects this pejorative connotation and argues for viewing conspiracy theories as "a cultural practice of interpretation," "a narrative form" (Fenster [1999] 2008, 13) or a sort of "stigmatized knowledge" (Barkun 2003, 12). The first approach relates conspiracism to normative constructs of knowledge production being interested in revealing either the universal logical flaws of conspiracist thinking or some psychological flaws irreconcilable with an imagined liberal subject. The second approach takes a functionalist view and tries to identify how conspiracy theories are conditioned by the social and cultural milieu in which they appear and in what ways conspiracism ultimately affects that very environment (e.g., Butter 2014; Byford 2011). While the rationalist-universalist approach has provided strong arguments against certain forms of conspiracy theories and proved its potential to add valuable input when it comes to fight actual malign conspiracy theories in the political and social arena, it could also hinder research by oversimplifying complex discursive phenomena (Fenster [1999] 2008, 11). There is no doubt that conspiracy theory is "an evaluative term with significant pejorative connotations" (Byford 2011, 21) and has long been a "routinized strategy of exclusion," of "stripping the claimant of the status of reasonable interlocutor" (Husting and Orr 2007, 127) both in the mass media and academia. The catchphrase "conspiracy theory" has become a tool of delegitimization, which "confer[s] stigma on certain knowledge claims" (Barkun 2003, 13, 71) and switches off the modus interpretandi. However, recent changes in forms and discourses of global politics suggest that stigmatization does not even keep conspiracism out of the social-political agora. Rather, assertions of any sort could be labeled as conspiracy theory no matter how well grounded their truth claims are. Therefore, the primary task of the volume is to seek to understand the function that conspiracy theories fulfill in societies and cultures, both right now and in the long term.

As mentioned previously, however, the "great divide" in this area of research has also formed due to its regional focus on the United States and the West more generally, which is why the definitions above often formed by taking into account only limited cases and contexts. This is why one of the questions raised by this edited volume is this: How do these definitions operate outside of the Western world? Conspiracy theories in Eastern Europe provide a compelling answer to this research question.

Introduction 5

An introduction to a volume that features the term "Eastern Europe" in its title has to grapple with the issue of "the East of Europe," which is far from being a self-explanatory one. There has been a plethora of concepts developed in various languages to describe more or less the same geographical area on various grounds. Other than cultural and political traditions and agendas that have a say in the issue, there are also specific academic disciplines that have their own preferred options. There is hardly a choice that could be satisfactorily applied to all historical and contemporary contexts and that is suitable to all approaches within an interdisciplinary project (Mishkova and Trencsényi 2017). No doubt, "Eastern Europe" is a historically loaded term that has rarely been taken up as a self-description in the region itself that it is supposed to designate, and the notion is historically closely associated with a cultural grade where the "East" is always already backward (Wolff 1994; Schenk 2017). In the second half of the twentieth century, "Eastern Europe" was applied to the Soviet Bloc in the English-speaking world and was often accompanied by a simplifying approach that presumed the existence of a unified culture in the Soviet satellite states (Autio and Miklóssy 2011), although it was less common after the anti-Stalinist uprisings, and the diverging political routes elevated the political significance on the international arena of each socialist state that did not belong to the Soviet Union. From the 1990s, however, the epistemological crisis of area studies, which in a large part resulted from a policy-oriented approach motivated by an imperial conduct (Dale, Miklóssy, and Segert 2015), was joined by a dramatic decrease of interest in European states between Germany and Russia. These two related factors resulted in a gradual refashioning of Eastern European Studies within academia. By now, many centers, departments, and institutes specializing in Eastern Europe lack subsidies to maintain a geographically and linguistically diverse academic portfolio, and the remaining funds are usually channeled toward Russian Studies, or the programs are shut down entirely. As far as remaining projects in area studies are concerned, Eastern Europe as a geographic reference has mostly been replaced by East Central and/ or Southeastern Europe. However, no choice is actually free of geopolitical underpinnings, since they all reflect the advance of the EU or the NATO enlargement process.

First, there have been political developments that from our perspective rather connect than divide the broad region. The way populist authoritarian leaders in government are instrumentalizing conspiracy theories as part of their political propaganda is not (yet) a pan-European phenomenon and also cannot be restricted to either East Central or Southeastern Europe. Political systems, institutions, and practices in these countries may vary greatly, but the transformation of liberal democracies into illiberal states is a political tendency that links both sides of the Eastern borders of the European Union. An unmistakable concomitant of such tendencies is the increasing emphasis conspiracy theories get in the political campaigns of ruling political forces. By now, conspiracy theories are clear underpinnings to state policies at an unprecedented extent elsewhere in Europe. The term "Eastern Europe," therefore, appeared a practical choice that reflected both our specific interest in conspiracy theories in a historical context marked

6 *Astapova, Colăcel, Pintilescu, and Scheibner*

by the socialist period and post-socialist transition, and still kept the distinction from a Central Asia with a considerably different political, economic, and cultural history.

Second, a loosely defined Eastern Europe makes sense for a region where large minority groups, though represented in nation-states, have frequently been the target of conspiracism perpetrated against them by ethnic majorities. For instance, Germans, Russians, Poles, Romanians, Hungarians, Armenians, Ukrainians, the Roma, and first and foremost, the Jews formed communities that provoked conspiracy theories from Russia to the former Yugoslavia, with no real alternatives to the label of Eastern Europe. As Benjamin Schenk (2017) pointed out, in Jewish studies, there seems to be a renaissance of the term, exactly on the basis of a massive Jewish historical presence across these lands.

Conspiracy theories in Eastern Europe

Conspiracy theorizing has a long history in Eastern Europe, but scholarship started to reflect on this legacy relatively recently, in a large part as a result of current global political trends and the growing impact of such theories on social imaginaries. In the past two decades, social sciences and, in particular, political science contributed the most to research in conspiracy theories converging, naturally, on contemporary phenomena in most cases. In the past few years, historians also started to investigate the prehistory of today's discourses, but most other disciplines within the humanities, such as literary studies, have not shown considerable interest in conspiracy theories so far, even though in related fields, such as semiology, groundbreaking research has been done in countries where semiotics has a strong tradition (e.g., Estonia; see Madisson and Ventsel 2020). Even though research on conspiracy theories in Eastern Europe is scattered and fragmented, it is still possible to identify certain major patterns that stand out as focal points.

Conspiracy theories in Eastern Europe are predominantly interpreted as political techniques to overcome rival social or political forces. In this respect, the region resembles most other areas, but it is important to point out that the relative significance of directly politically related conspiracism is even higher in Eastern Europe than in the United States. This has a lot to do with the history of the peoples living in the region and the way conspiracy theorizing emerged as an effective technique both to rule and to challenge the ruler. Toward the end of this section, we will consider a series of other reasons as well, but the legacies of empires and nation-states, as well as related xenophobic attitudes, deserve particular attention from the perspective of contemporary authoritarian employment of conspiracism.

Although conspiracy thinking is deeply embedded in the human character and is reflected in centuries-old practices, such as witch hunts and trials (Rabo 2020), according to a wide consensus, modern conspiracy theories emerged in Europe as a reaction to the spread of the ideas of the Enlightenment and the 1789 French Revolution (Groh 1987, 23–24; Cubitt 1989, 144–46; Byford 2011, 44–45). In Eastern and Central Europe, the striving for social and national emancipation destabilized the great powers dominating the region—German, Austrian, Russian,

Introduction 7

and Ottoman Empires—from within. Their conservative elites—made up mainly of the aristocracy and the clergy—deferred liberal reforms and showcased alleged or moderately significant conspiracies (such as the Hungarian Jacobin conspiracy in 1794–95) as major threats to the throne in order to introduce stricter social control or even terror. As such, conspiracism entered the usual repertoire of court politics. In such circumstances, secrecy became a main ingredient of political activism, because, as Dieter Groh argues, "under the conditions of the Ancien Regime," any kind of oppositional activity "was only possible in secret" (1987, 24). Freemasons or later, Italian *Carbonari*-inspired secret societies became common forms of sociability across the region during the late eighteenth and nineteenth centuries (ibid.). Consequently, the idea of secret societies plotting against the "Throne and Altar" traveled from Western Europe eastward (Rogalla von Bieberstein 1977, 5–6).

While conspiracy theories continued to serve as political tools for rulers to limit the chances of being seriously challenged, such theories were also twisted in the new context to serve the opposition. The emerging national movements seeking national independence—from under what was (re)conceptualized then as foreign oppression—elaborated narratives of martyrdom and suffering caused by the aforementioned empires. Suspicion was redirected toward real and perceived social actors who were supposed to advance the interests of the court. This inspired a rich variety of tropes, from the empire's hidden tentacles reaching everywhere to precursory concepts of a "deep state." Narratives of victimhood also flourished in a context where great powers continued to pose challenges to the emerging nation states' sovereignty and territorial integrity (Byford and Billig 2001; Blanuša 2013; Panczová 2017). Accordingly, Poland was presented by the local nineteenth-century Romantic writer Adam Mickiewicz as the "Christ of Europe" following the three partitions of the country (1772–95) (Rosman 2017, 29). Religious martyrdom and suffering served as a central trope for self-representation in a series of other Eastern European cultures as well. Such deep-rooted imagery reinforced the allegorical nature of self-identification, and new calamities or crises, which were often incredibly severe and violent, were usually understood in terms of historical precedents, suggesting that the same external forces prevented the nation from regaining its agency. We need to recall this in order not to claim that such interpretations are necessarily wrong or lie far from a realist account of international relations, but to point out that there is a historically conditioned mindset that is receptive to any explanation based on strictly limited collective agencies being overruled by the coordinated action of mighty powers. For conspiracy theorizing, such conditions provide excellent opportunities and certainly figure as an important factor in the emergence of conspiracy cultures in the region.

Apart from conspiracy theories related to an "external" enemy that could be identified with an actually existing state or political entity, the same context inspired a plethora of conspiracy theories about "the enemy within." Among the internal enemies that supposedly undermined national cultural and political fulfillment, the heterogeneous and politically varying lodges of Freemasons, oppressed religious groups, various minorities (e.g., the Roma, ethnic Germans,

8 *Astapova, Colăcel, Pintilescu, and Scheibner*

Hungarians, Polish, Ukrainians, and Russians), and a particularly elusive social construct, "the Jewry," all played a prominent role. The Jewish minorities, largely due to their significant roles in an often extremely rapid economic and social modernization, received outstanding emphasis in Eastern European conspiracy theories throughout the nineteenth and twentieth centuries. Accordingly, discussions of antisemitic conspiracism provide a substantive part of conspiracy theory research: for the most part, this research discusses antisemitic conspiracy theories in the context of authoritarian regimes or dictatorships (Cohn [1967] 1996; Gerrits 1995; Michlic 2006; Gibson and Howard 2007), but attention was paid to the effects of old religious beliefs (Poliakov 1987; Patai 1996) and to the phenomenon of "antisemitism without Jews" (Lendvai 1971; Bilewicz and Krzeminski 2010; Bilewicz et al. 2013) as well.

Clearly, antisemitism in Western Europe was widespread, and conspiracism often relied on centuries-old prejudices against "the Jewry." It is well known that religious antisemitism contained a strong conspiracist component ever since the Middle Ages (Maccoby 2006, 2–3), and the legend of the blood libel (the idea that Jews kidnap Christian children and use their blood for Jewish ritual food) received repeated attention and credit up until the mid-twentieth century, being a pan-European phenomenon (Dundes 1991). Still, the pace of modernization in Western Europe was less intense, and social tensions did not fuel "othering" that much, which found all too easy a subject in Eastern Europe, given the proportion of Jews in most societies in the latter part of the continent. Either in rapid course of assimilation (as in Austro-Hungary) or less assimilation (as in the communities from the Russian Empire), Jews were largely (although not exclusively) perceived in the region as strong promoters of the capitalist economy and liberalizing reforms. Within the modern urban society, Jews were able to enjoy "anonymity" and assert themselves, especially in various areas of the tertiary sector (Bronner [2000] 2019, 45). Besides, Jews became associated with emerging new cultural and intellectual currents and were "identified with avant-garde trends in literature and painting" (ibid., 49). Some of them were involved in the most diverse (national) liberal or socialist political settings that sought emancipation on multiple levels. In sum, Jews were perceived "as a symbol of the modern world by those who most detested this world" (Cohn [1967] 1996, 28). All these developments created by the turn of the twentieth century a particularly favorable context for the flourishing of various antisemitic conspiracy theories in Eastern Europe.

The outstanding text that made a major impact on antisemitic conspiracism worldwide was born in this context. *The Protocols of the Elders of Zion* was first published in Imperial Russia in 1903, and it was disseminated, and possibly fabricated, by Okhrana (the secret police of the late tsarist period) in order to fuel state-endorsed antisemitism (De Michelis 2004; Hagemeister 2008). This was the first conspiracy theory emerging in the region that enjoyed global impact following its translation into many languages (Webman 2011, 2–3). *The Protocols* merged old forms of "Judeophobia" with a "distinctly modern form of political antimodernism" (Bronner [2000] 2019, 48). It is difficult to measure the impact of religious cultures on modern antisemitism, but it could be that Greek Orthodox Christianity

Introduction 9

provided an even more hostile context for both Jewry and modernism than Roman Catholicism westward (Poliakov 1987). Drawing on this dual-originated antisemitism, Jews were identified as those who were plotting to overthrow the tsarist "feudal despotism in order to set up their own far worse form of tyranny," in which their control of the world was allegedly installed through their gradual takeover of the universities, the newspapers, and all spheres of public space (Bronner [2000] 2019, 48–49).

The Protocols illustrate how top-down disseminated conspiracy theories became a key instrument of twentieth-century authoritarian or dictatorial regimes to mobilize support and legitimize violence against various groups perceived as enemies from within (Byford 2011, 144). *The Protocols* also provided context for a new conspiracy theory: that of Jewish Communism or Judeo-Bolshevism. This was instrumentalized in the region for explaining the abrupt dismantling of the multinational empires after World War I and the Russian Revolution of 1917 and still is. In this conspiracy theory, which was very popular in the interwar period and resurfaced after 1989, Jews—who were equaled with Communists—were found guilty of the dramatic fall of these empires and the revolutions that followed (Gerwarth 2016, 89; Hanebrink 2018, 34–35). The potency of this conspiracy theory, which became a "cliché of counter-revolutionary," rested on a combination of sentiments, which, due to cultural, political, and geographic factors, was felt most acutely in East-Central Europe—antisemitism and anti-Communism (Gerrits 1995, 60). Hitler's rise to power boosted the emerging Fascist movements in the region and their antisemitism. For example, the Legion of the Archangel Michael, founded in Romania in 1927, or the Arrow Cross Party, established in Hungary in 1935—at that time under the name "the Party of National Will"—gained momentum in the late 1930s (Payne 1995, 273). In Romania, Fascist conspiracist narratives "conflated Freemasons with Jews and communists as perpetrators of a global plot against Christianity and national self-determination" (Clark 2012, 41). Later on, during World War II, the myth of Judeo-Communism turned into a key element of the anti-Soviet official propaganda of the East European satellite countries or puppet-states of Nazi Germany, especially in Hungary, Romania, Slovakia, and Croatia (Voicu 2004).

The emergence of the Cold War brought yet another shift in the conspiratorial narratives of the region targeting the Jews: under Communist rule clearcut antisemitic public discourse was generally not allowed (it always had to be wrapped), which provided yet another reason for adherents of the myth of Judeo-Bolshevism to stick to their belief, and the myth remained a main component of the local underground anti-Communist narratives. Various groups within the leadership of the Communist parties, however, continued to rely on Jewish stereotypes in their political practice (especially by linking capitalism with Jews). They did not refrain from the use of antisemitic coded language and abused antisemitic conspiracy theories in their struggle for power. Such conduct gained momentum during the Stalinist anti-Jewish purges of the early 1950s, reaching its climax with the Slánský trial in Czechoslovakia in November 1952 (Hodos 1987, 84). Another important example would be the anti-Zionist campaign in Poland in 1968

10   *Astapova, Colăcel, Pintilescu, and Scheibner*

(Stola 2006), but the idea of a Zionist conspiracy was employed as a political tool throughout the entire era.

In general, the early Cold War was undoubtedly one of the "golden ages" of conspiracy theories. On both sides of the Iron Curtain, conspiracy narratives in their McCarthyist or Stalinist versions were key features of political life in the late 1940s and 1950s. During the first decade of the Cold War, Stalinist conspiracy culture was transferred to the satellite states and also informed the political choices and practices of Western European Communist parties (Girard 2012). Cold War conspiratorial tropes marked also the post-1989 conspiracy landscape (Melley 2011), and these reverberations were intensified by the new tensions between the West and Russia following the 2014 Ukrainian crisis (Kuzio 2017).

The roots of Stalinist conspiracy culture could be identified in the profound vulnerability of the regime in the aftermath of the October 1917 Revolution. At that time, the Bolsheviks developed a strong disposition to perceive both the inner and the outer world as inexhaustible sources of counter-revolutionary conspiracies. This disposition became an essential part of Soviet political culture under Stalin and a component of the powerful syndrome of the "siege mentality" (Viola 1993, 98). Furthermore, the Soviet Union experienced radical economic and social transformations during early Stalinism. This created an "unpredictable world," in which conspiracy theories had been turned into "central paradigms by which the [Soviet] regime sought to explain undesirable political processes," while "behind-the-scenes intrigues" became everyday practices within all echelons of the party hierarchy (Rittersporn 2014, 13, 25). What might be called Stalinist conspiracy culture entailed various political and cultural practices of identifying and punishing the imagined or real conspirators mainly through purges. The latter were carried out in a performative way (Wood 2005; Caumanns 2016) and instrumentalized by the official propaganda for legitimizing state violence, mobilizing the population, or explaining the failures of some state policies. Although much more reduced in intensity compared with the Stalinist period, some of these conspiracy theories continued to frame the way party elites looked at political dissent during the 1970s and 1980s, when these narratives portrayed dissidents as tools of Western plots undermining the stability of the Soviet regime (see Anna Kirziuk's chapter in this volume).

The role of authoritarian or dictatorial regimes in contributing to the emergence of a conspiracy culture in Eastern Europe, whether historical or contemporaneous, features as a primary concern of scholarship on conspiracy theories in Eastern Europe. It is still contested as to what extent such non-democratic regimes added to the proliferation of conspiracy theories in Eastern Europe over the last century. According to Ilya Yablokov, who compared conspiracy cultures in the United States and Russia, there are significant differences between these two cases apart from the common elements. While in the United States (and in the West, in general) conspiracy theories usually "emerge from grassroots movements and are kept at the margins of official political discourse," in Russia "the political and intellectual elites are major producers and disseminators" of conspiracist narratives (Yablokov 2018, 2). In order to explain this feature, Yablokov draws on

Introduction 11

Matthew Gray's research, which argues that in most of the countries of the Arab world, "the state is a conspiracist narrator, aided by state monopolization, control or influence over the mass media, strong governing party structures, and the direction of a charismatic or domineering leader" (Gray 2010, 119).

This leads us to the already classic debate about the relationship between authoritarianism and conspiracy theories. As many observed, conspiracy theories have been a key tool of dictatorships: Nazi Germany and the Soviet Union under Stalin are the best examples (Cohn [1967] 1996; Byford 2011; Rittersporn 2014). Arguably, conspiracy theories have been "the refuge of every dictator and authoritarian leader in the world" because real or imagined conspiracies represent useful tools "for legitimizing tyranny and oppression," taking into account that their alleged existence makes people believe that they "need a strong leader to guide them and protect them from malign outside influences" (Byford 2011, 144). In this context, the question of how conspiracism conditioned the politics of fear gained particular attention (Humphrey 2002; Rittersporn 2014; Stojanov 2015; Caumanns 2016).

Consequently, it does not come as a surprise that the argument of a connection between authoritarianism (especially right-wing) and conspiracist beliefs (Abalakina-Paap et al. 1999; Grzesiak-Feldman and Irzycka 2009) is strong. In this respect, the recent extensive instrumentalization of conspiracy theories by populist authoritarian leaders in Eastern Europe could be seen as yet another chapter in the same story. Although these tendencies have a history in the region, the recent success of populist leaders in the West suggests that these trends are also connected with global phenomena. Namely, it seems to be linked to what Ruth Wodak interpreted as the process of "taking advantage" of the "media-democracy" (Grande 2000) by right-wing populist leaders who managed to "on the one hand, [appear] unusual and populist, or anti-establishment, and on the other, authoritative and legitimate" (Wodak 2015, 11).

There are reasons to think that the legacy of dictatorships continues to impact how people react to conspiracy theories. In Eastern Europe, the secret police have been a much more feared agency in the everyday life of citizens than in any democratic state: while research proved that the United States intelligence agencies spied on domestic individuals to a much greater extent than previously thought (Theoharis 2004; Culleton and Leick 2008; Charles 2015), they generally did not form an integral part of the citizens' perception of what constitutes the state. In contrast, the potential presence of the secret police triggered suspicion and secrecy in a way that could be conceptualized in retrospect today as part of the "deep state." Such impressions were reinforced by the opaque ways state institutions functioned before 1989/1991 and also by the unclear legacy of these after the transition period to democracy. In Belarus, for instance, the experience of living under dictatorships lives on in folk memory and still stirs fear of the secret services, and not without reason (Astapova 2017). In Romania, the 1989 revolution is frequently portrayed by conspiracy theories as the outcome of coordinated actions by a group of party members and secret police leaders seeking to overthrow Ceaușescu and his close collaborators (Voicu 2000; Roth 2016). In

12 *Astapova, Colăcel, Pintilescu, and Scheibner*

Bulgaria, it is believed that Freemasons secretly took power during State Socialism and kept their influence on state institutions such as the Bulgarian courts (Medarov 2017). These conspiracy theories could find a relatively wide audience, fitting in with the citizens' previous experience under dictatorships. Ultimately, this entails an empathic disposition to the interpreter: conspiratorial thinking should not necessarily be dismissed as something irrational.

Ethnic conflicts have also risen along with extreme nationalism and antisemitism, which in turn, proved to be a further source of conspiracy theorizing: former conspiratorial tropes resurfaced in new forms, adjusted to the post-1989 contexts. Conspiracy theories about Freemasons, Jews, or about great powers plotting against the nation's sovereignty and territorial integrity, most of them suppressed by censorship under State Socialism, became particularly popular after 1989. For example, the conspiracy theory of Judeo-Communism reemerged in Poland, Romania, and Hungary intertwining with the anti-Communist ethos (Shafir 1994, 80; Hanebrink 2018, 2–3).

Conspiracism was further boosted in the entire region by disappointments with the post-socialist transition caused by disturbing economic and social outcomes, which have increased economic inequalities and a feeling of powerlessness (Ortmann and Heathershaw 2012). Many scholars argue that belief in conspiracy theories rises in political, economic, and social turmoil (Grzesiak-Feldman 2013; van Prooijen and Acker 2015; Swami et al. 2016). Those feeling powerless when facing large-scale turbulences are predisposed to explain away their difficulties as effects of the machinations of evil conspiratorial forces (Hofstadter 1964; Abalakina-Paap et al. 1999; Darwin, Neave, and Holmes 2011; van Prooijen and Jostmann 2013). Thus, by "simplifying and by linking a series of events in relation to its supposed causes and effects, conspiracy theories may offer seemingly coherent explanations for distressing phenomena" (Swami et al. 2016, 74) and have the function of restoring the feeling of control over an environment disturbed by "distressing societal events" (van Prooijen and Acker 2015, 753).

Two kinds of conspiracy theories made particularly salient marks on the post-socialist transition. On the one side, former Communist elites disseminated narratives that presented the fall of the regimes as effects of Western or Jewish plots or, in some cases, as we have seen, the coordinated action of secret police institutions (Byford and Billig 2001; Yablokov 2018). Many of these conspiracy theories in the region aspire to explain the sudden fall of what was previously perceived as stable regimes. On the other side, different kinds of conspiracy theories were spread from below. Someone had to be blamed for the billions of lost jobs in the region and the general feeling of insecurity in the 1990s. A theory was formulated, for instance, that the former *nomenklatura* conspired to acquire the economic positions and wealth in the emerging capitalist societies. From the fact that some members of the post-Communist elite greatly benefited from the privatization of national firms thanks to the unequal distribution of information, networks, and access to state infrastructure, not to mention questionable legislation (Eyal, Szelényi, and Townsley 1998, 4–5), accordingly, it was concluded

Introduction 13

that a hidden statewide agenda was executed step by step in a well-coordinated manner.

The post-1989 democratization led to the acceleration of the globalization of Eastern European societies with an immense impact on conspiracy theorizing. Not only did old conspiracist tropes resurface to be reshaped to fit the new post-socialist context, but the region rapidly integrated into the global exchange of conspiracy theories. Very often age-old conspiratorial tropes were blended with new global ones. One of the most popular conspiracy theories in Eastern Europe, which we mentioned above, is precisely like that: the case against the entre-preneur George Soros has relied on old antisemitic stereotypes and was further inspired by New World Order–type conspiracism. The latter found a large audi-ence in the region since the political and economic transition did not provide the expected prosperity to all. Global plots embodied by international institutions such as the International Monetary Fund, the World Bank, or the European Union were found guilty. The dramatic economic and social effects of the ravaging neo-liberal reforms promoted in the region by these institutions after 1989 fueled the spread of such conspiracy theories. One of the most harmful consequences of such conspiracy theories has been that due criticism of some transnational actors and institutions became politically loaded and stigmatized, which essentially under-mined critical discourse worldwide.

The wider context of such conspiracy theories that make effective tools of explaining the world is found in an emerging anti-elitism. Distrust in the political, economic, cultural, and intellectual elite has been a core feature of global politics from Donald Trump to Viktor Orbán. While there is little doubt that anti-elitism has popular roots, a significant part of the elite capitalized on these tendencies and used them to defend their privileges vis-à-vis the very people they were sup-posed to act for. In turn, as global humanitarianism opened career opportunities for the privileged, self-proclaimed representatives appeared to speak for the dis-possessed with little knowledge of the real interests and specific contexts of those they claimed to represent. This created complicated political dynamics in which anti-imperial and anti-elitist sentiments played a role. It is not rare for the Euro-pean Union (aligned with the Habsburg Monarchy or the Soviet Union in histori-cal allegories) to be seen as an instrument of the elite to undermine traditional values with the help of liberal policies.

Anti-elitism translated to international relations, however, is not specific to small states. Some great powers also employ narratives about national victim-hood, and Russia is a particularly interesting case complicated by a self-colonizing twist. For centuries, Russia has portrayed the West as a plotting oppressor (Yablokov 2018), and growing anti-Western attitudes among the Russians in the 2000s are far from a novelty. Concentrating on popular nostalgia about a lost para-dise and growing anti-Western attitudes among Russians in the 2000s, Serguei Alex Oushakine showed that conspiracy theories could be an efficient tool for achieving social cohesion and defining the collective identities of newly emerging communities (Oushakine 2009). In some countries, these antisemitic conspiracy narratives involved the revival of religious beliefs and the growth of new religious

14 *Astapova, Colăcel, Pintilescu, and Scheibner*

movements that involved frequent references to the struggle with "Western subversion," on behalf of the principles of the Orthodox Church (Melnikova 2004; Verkhovsky 2006; Akhmetova 2010; Astapova et al. 2021). The most recent book on conspiracy theories in Russia by Elliot Borenstein shows how this paranoid fantasy—which, until recently, characterized only the marginal and the irrelevant—now, through its embodiment in pop culture, has spread everywhere (2019). Borenstein focuses on the role of the folk in this respect and argues that in the Russian example, none of the ideological stances that have become prominent in Putin's rule is simply top-down propaganda. The leaders nearly always build the fantasy from what they already have to work with—what people readily provide and circulate (ibid., xi).

Although marked by the legacy of past dictatorships and the post-socialist transition, Eastern European countries are hardly unique and isolated nowadays, which is also true for their conspiracy theories. Scholars have shown how recent conspiracy narratives repeat the concerns from all over the world, such as the ones about food safety (Kormina 2016), vaccination (Craciun and Baban 2012; Pop 2016), genomic technologies (Kalmre 2016), and natural and technological disasters (Kalmre 1998). In some countries of the region, including but not only Hungary and Poland, there has emerged a recent thread of Islamophobia and the Eurabia conspiracy theory, in particular—the idea that there is a secret plan to Islamize and Arabize Europe, although these countries do not have (yet) a significant number of immigrants coming from outside Europe (Goździak and Márton 2018; Krekó and Enyedi 2018). This could be seen as a recent ideological shift from fears of the "Western conspiracy" to fears of the "Eastern conspiracy"—migrants from the Middle and Far East seeking to destroy European nations by infiltrating them (Astapova 2020).

Since Eastern Europe became clearly integrated into the global flux of conspiracy theories, there is no point in speaking about Eastern European exceptionalism. However, it makes sense to start to map Eastern European conspiracism to identify major patterns, which are either specific to the region or could be compared to other semi-peripheral regions, and to explore the shifts and local varieties of existing conspiracy theories. Further, issues like fake news and post-truth, currently researched in the Anglophone cultures, have been embedded in Eastern European politics for decades and still persist. The use of conspiracy theories by Eastern European populist politicians as well as contemporary authoritarian leaders is obvious according to many scholars (e.g., Kuzio 2011; Ortmann and Heathershaw 2012; Stojanov 2015; Colăcel and Pintilescu 2017; Kasekamp, Madisson, and Wieringa 2018; Yablokov 2018; Borenstein 2019). Thus, a significant part of the contributions dealing with the conspiracy theories in various countries of the region focus on these recent trends marked by the rapid globalization of the conspiracy landscape.

This overview of the contributions on conspiracy theories in Eastern Europe lead us to the conclusion that most of them focus on four thematic areas: (1) conspiracy theories and their relationship with dictatorships or authoritarian regimes in the region, including the recent authoritarian drift of some East European countries;

Introduction 15

(2) antisemitic conspiracy theories (this category overlaps with the first one, since the Soviet Union, but especially Nazi Germany and its satellite countries, heavily instrumentalized anti-Jewish conspiracy theories); (3) conspiracy theories that are strongly entangled with national victimhood narratives, presenting the countries of the region as victims of great powers; (4) new trends or emerging conspiracy tropes in the region framed by the globalization process. This volume is the first systematic collective attempt to provide an overview of the most prolific and influential conspiracy theories in Eastern Europe. These topics are exemplified in terms of the main trends and tropes of conspiracy theories in the region and by presenting their variety from different countries. The volume aims also to cover the gaps of previous research, often written in national languages with limited international academic circulation or concentrating on some countries that are bigger players in the region (Russia, in particular) rather than others. As a first step, our objective was to bring together scholars of cultural studies, ethnology, folklore, history, media studies, political science, and philosophy to present case studies from a variety of countries that either are of significance to the analysis of the entire region or apply an approach that transcends national boundaries.

There are several lines of investigation guiding the inquiry along this edited volume: (1) the historical conditions of the popularity of conspiracy theories in the region, with a focus on how the interwar, Cold War, and post–Cold War periods framed the conspiracy landscape of the region; in this respect, particular attention will be paid to continuities and discontinuities of some key conspiratorial tropes during the twentieth century and beyond; (2) the relation between conspiracy theorizing in the region and broader phenomena such as authoritarianism, national-identity building, antisemitism, populism, and globalization; (3) the modes of circulation from the Cold War to the post–Cold War period, with a focus on the integration of the conspiracy culture of the region in the global flux of conspiracy theories; thus, some of the chapters included in this volume tackle the issue of what particular conspiratorial tropes circulated and how and challenge the previous assumptions such as those related to Cold War conspiracy culture; (4) how an assessment of the conspiracy landscape in Eastern Europe could help us better understand what conspiracy theories are, why people endorse them, and what their functions are within societies.

Structure of the volume

Starting from the main trends displayed by the conspiracy landscape of the region, this edited volume is divided into four sections: the first one focusing on how the experience of recent dictatorships marked the content and dissemination of conspiracy theories in the Cold War and in post–Cold War contexts; the second section dealing with two of the most influential conspiratorial tropes related to "the enemy within" from the nineteenth century up to today—namely, the anti-Jewish conspiracy theories and those related to Freemasons; the third part, which outlines some key conspiracist narratives in the countries of the region within the broader framework of the national victimhood narratives; and the fourth part focusing on

16 *Astapova, Colăcel, Pintilescu, and Scheibner*

the rapid integration of the region into the global flux of conspiracy theories and the rise of populism.

The first section consists of three chapters dealing with some of the most prominent manifestations of conspiracism under Socialism and their reverberations either in other spaces (Western Europe) or in the post-socialist period. This part aims to provide insights into less-researched parts of the landscape of conspiracy theories of the Cold War period. We also hope to enrich the previous contributions on conspiracy theories in the Eastern bloc that focused mainly on Stalinist conspiracy culture. The chapters of this part provide new arguments for challenging the image of the Iron Curtain as an impenetrable barrier (Péteri 2004) and contribute to a better understanding of the aftermath of Cold War conspiracy culture.

The opening chapter of the volume, authored by Anastasiya Astapova, deals with Chernobyl-related conspiracy theories. She investigates storytelling about the tragedy, highly significant for understanding the background of conspiracy theorizing going on in the Soviet and post-Soviet world. This chapter shifts the focus from the most invoked approach of conspiracy theories in the post-Soviet space as mainly top-down disseminated narratives. It brings to the fore the importance played by rumors in shaping and spreading them. Astapova argues that despite their dissemination for more than three decades, the forge of these conspiracy narratives is still an ongoing process. The latter reflects ethnic and ideological clashes, conspiracist elements of popular culture, and the Cold War–like tensions between Russia and the West, heavily deepened after 2014.

In his chapter, Pascal Girard elaborates on the transfer of Stalinist conspiracy culture to the Western Communist parties during the early Cold War period. He argues that Stalinist conspiracy culture played a key role in shaping the mindset of the members of the French and Italian Communist Parties and influenced the domestic political life in the two countries where these parties activated a phenomenon that was previously underestimated by scholars focusing on the history of the two Communist parties. Drawing on the archives of the French and Italian Communist Parties, Girard provides us a view contesting the impermeability of the Iron Curtain in the early Cold War period and helps us to better understand the entanglements between the inflated conspiracy narratives in the socialist bloc and those in the West. He concludes that this transfer, which was part of building a "Western *homo sovieticus*," largely failed.

Anna Kirziuk discusses in her chapter the nature and the function of anti-Western conspiracy theories mentioned in secret documents circulated within the KGB and CPSU leadership during the late Soviet period. In her view, conspiracy theories were instrumental for the late Soviet regime when dealing with dissidents after the Helsinki agreements. Kirziuk argues that in these secret documents there were three main intertwined "narrative strategies" aimed at depriving dissidents of agency: one presenting their activity as a result of a Western conspiracy to undermine the Soviet regime; the trope of presenting dissent as a form of "mental illness"; and the so-called Jewish wives conspiracy theory, interpreting the activity of the dissidents as an evil influence of their alleged Jewish spouses. These conspiracist beliefs endorsed by leaders among the KGB and Party elite provided

Introduction 17

"a coping mechanism" to protect their self-esteem and their worldview when facing vivid criticism targeting the official ideology and way the Soviet system functioned.

The second section covers two of the most widely circulated conspiracy theories in the region about "the internal enemy": Jews and Freemasons. Besides the external plotting enemies coming from the West or from the East, among those conspiracy theories enjoying a long-term impact in Eastern Europe are those featuring Jews and Freemasons as "enemies" from within. Due to their past significant share of the urban population and the key role played by Jews in the modernization process in Eastern Europe, anti-Jewish conspiracy theories enjoyed and still enjoy a prominent place within the conspiracy landscape of the region. As in other parts of the world, the conspiracist narratives about Jews were related to those about Communists. This connection was accentuated within the conspiracy theories in Eastern Europe by the deep effects of the 1917 Russian Revolution on its history. The conspiratorial tropes related to Freemasons and Jews share also the legacy of the anti-modernity and anti-liberal ethos, which emerged within the conservative circles of the region by the end of the eighteenth and early nineteenth centuries and continued in different forms up to the present.

The second section is opened by the chapter authored by Péter Csunderlik and Tamás Scheibner on a highly influential conspiracy theory in Eastern Europe during the twentieth century and beyond: the myth of the Judeo-Bolshevik conspiracy. The authors argue that this myth has a long history in Hungary, quite revealing of the discursive context within which the tide of illiberal politics is growing across present-day Eastern Europe. As an alleged plot against the people, the self-effacing strategies of Judeo-Bolshevism are indicative of both the myth's use over time and of its value for Viktor Orbán's brand of populism.

Todor Hristov and Ivelina Ivanova's chapter shifts the focus from Jews to Freemasons by dealing with the conspiracist narratives about Freemasonry and the judiciary in post-socialist Bulgaria. After 1989, Bulgarian secret societies had recruited many former secret police members. Hristov and Ivanova argue that the latter turned their networks, created under Socialism, into forms of capital to be used in other social fields. Several media scandals surrounding the issue reverberated across the country and revealed a web of relationships between Freemasons, magistrates, and the former secret police. Ultimately, the conspiracy theories related to the rule of law brought together contradictory rationalities that, according to Hristov and Ivanova, helped local audiences come to terms with post-socialist transition. Drawing on this case study, they argue that "the psychoanalytic concept of overdetermination" should be reconsidered as an epistemic tool in the research of conspiracy theories.

Dominika Bulska, Agnieszka Haska, Mikołaj Winiewski, and Michał Bilewicz deal with the antisemitic conspiracy theories in Poland. Jewish-related conspiracy theories are deeply rooted in the history of this country. Even if nowadays the number of Jews living in the country is dwindling, antisemitic attitudes, especially antisemitic conspiracist beliefs, are widespread within Polish society. This chapter aims to measure the popularity of conspiracy theories about Jews and to

18 *Astapova, Colăcel, Pintilescu, and Scheibner*

assess their function within contemporary Polish society. The authors conclude that belief in antisemitic conspiracy theories was constant in Poland during the last decade. These conspiracy theories reshape old antisemitic conspiracist tropes that have been popular among the Poles since the nineteenth century. The function of these conspiracy theories is to provide simple explanations for complex social and economic phenomena or the failures of one's own group, thus restoring feelings of control over the situation.

The third section of the volume deals with the relationship between conspiracy theories, national-identity building, and victimhood narratives in the context of the upsurge of nationalism and populism in post-socialist Eastern Europe. From the violent dissolution of Yugoslavia to the emergence of post-2014 Cold War–like narratives, the chapters of this part provide insights into how conspiracy narratives have been instrumentalized in ethnic conflicts or fueled narratives of national victimhood that had already enjoyed deep historical roots in the region.

Nebojša Blanuša analyzes various conspiracy theories related to the dissolution of Yugoslavia before and after the breakup of the Yugoslav federation in the early 1990s by paying special attention to their genealogies. Most of these conspiracy theories developed before the dissolution of Yugoslavia and outlived the Yugoslav way of life, although taking new shapes and being instrumentalized in new contexts. If before the dissolution of Yugoslavia the legitimacy of the federal state was partially based on popularizing conspiracy theories about enemies from within and abroad plotting against the Yugoslav people, after the dissolution, various local conspiracy narratives explained this process by blaming states such as the United States, Germany, Hungary, or Italy. Blanuša argues that, although displaying significant differences from one post-Yugoslav country to another, most of the widespread conspiracy theories related to the dissolution of Yugoslavia share a similar function: that of blaming the other in order to elude coping with the traumatic, violent past.

Olga Baysha analyzes the anti-Russian conspiracy theories within the Ukrainian media in the aftermath of the Euromaidan revolution, with a case study on those conspiracist narratives related to the Odessa street fighting on May 2, 2014. During this tragedy, 48 people died during violent street clashes between groups of Ukrainians supporting the Euromaidan revolution and their opponents. Looking into the possibility that both Russia and Ukraine make use of similar discursive strategies, the author approaches the instrumentalization of conspiracy theories used by Ukrainian politicians to instigate collective fears and shift attention away from ethnic division within the country. Baysha concludes that conspiracist narratives contribute to destroying the symbolic space essential for maintaining communication within a society, and consequently, they deepen divisions and may lead to outbreaks of violence.

Zuzana Panczová deals with the trope of victimhood in Slovakian conspiracy theories, which is conducive to defining a sense of belonging to the nation. The chapter aims to analyze the role played by conspiracy theories in the discursive strategies of self-victimization instrumentalized by political or religious authorities and the media responses to them in the case of the killing of the reporter

Introduction 19

Ján Kuciak in 2018. Panczová argues that this tragic event received media and institutional attention that fed into a broad public assumption that the nation itself was, as a result, under threat. As such, conspiracy theories vehiculated with this occasion tie in with the master narrative of the Slovak nation and their articulation and reception are heavily influenced by deep-rooted stereotypes about external enemies of the nation.

The last section of the edited volume deals with the impact of globalization on the conspiracy theories landscape of the region and how the populist wave fueled the flourishing of conspiracy cultures in Eastern Europe. Two of the chapters in this section deal with conspiracy theories illustrating the full integration of the region into the global flux of conspiracy theories: those related to George Soros and anti-EU conspiracy theories. Finally, by assessing some of the most influential trends of conspiracism in the region, this part aims to contribute to a broader theoretical discussion about conspiracy theories and their function within societies.

Corneliu Pintilescu and Attila Kustán Magyari elaborate on the conspiracy theories about George Soros in Hungary and Romania and their relationship with populism. The chapter focuses on the conspiracist narratives disseminated by two populist leaders, Viktor Orbán and Liviu Dragnea, from 2010 to 2019. Pintilescu and Kustán Magyari argue that post-2010 anti-Soros conspiracy theories have been built on similar narratives endorsed by local far-right circles during the 1990s. Both the old and new versions of anti-Soros conspiracy theories portray the American-Jewish billionaire as the epitome of the evil global financial forces plotting to undermine national sovereignty and values. However, while the Soros-related conspiracy theories of the 1990s were overtly antisemitic and disseminated by extremist groups at the fringes of the political landscape, those emerging in the 2010s display an implicit antisemitism and enjoy a mainstream position. Although these particular conspiracy theories became a key component of the populist rhetoric in both countries, Orbán proved more effective than Dragnea in his endeavor to refuel its populist discourse.

Onoriu Colăcel deals with conspiracy theories on commercial TV and their function within contemporary Moldovan society. The chapter argues that conspiracist narratives come across as a way to legitimate political choices in the former Soviet republic, with conspiracy theories essentially coming from abroad—that is, mostly from Russian and Romanian media. As local political television tends to expose conspiracy theories in order to change or reinforce people's attitudes, the genre offers a compelling case study in the rise of populist politics in the Russian and Romanian-speaking Republic of Moldova. As such, this glimpse into the inner workings of the Moldovan media can help with better understanding of both Brussels- and Kremlin-sponsored news and opinion across Eastern Europe.

Biljana Gjoneska, Kristijan Fidanovski, and André Krouwel elaborate on the emergence of EU-related conspiracy theories in the Republic of North Macedonia in the context of the indefinitely postponed accession negotiations with Brussels, the 2017 political crisis (following the resignation of the conservative leader Nikola Gruevski), and the 2018 change of the official name of the country. All

20   *Astapova, Colăcel, Pintilescu, and Scheibner*

these elements of the international and internal contexts provided fertile ground for the dissemination of EU-related conspiracy theories and challenged the prevailing pro-EU aspirations in North Macedonia. Thus, the chapter provides useful insights into the political, social, and psychological factors affecting the belief in EU-related conspiracy theories in the country. It concludes that the North Macedonian public space became increasingly populated with conspiracy theories about the EU due to the aftermath of a recent turbulent past, a political climate dominated by instability and scandals, and constant support among a part of the local population for the conservative party (VMRO-DPMNE), which turned toward an anti-EU stance.

The closing chapter, authored by M R. X. Dentith, contributes to the theoretical discussion about how to distinguish between warranted and unwarranted conspiracy theories. Drawing on examples from Eastern Europe, with a focus on Romania, Dentith argues that the generalist approach of analyzing conspiracy theories as something that is *prima facie* irrational entails the risk of operating with false assumptions and ignoring the evidence. He claims that this generalist approach was framed mainly taking into account Western political contexts and could be problematic when dealing with other regions. He invokes the case of Eastern European societies where the recent history—especially the experience of living under oppressive regimes—questions the effectiveness of this approach. Dentith concludes that we should favor a particularist approach: investigate case by case based on evidence and pay more attention to the political and historical context in which conspiracy theories occur.

This is precisely the approach we aim to encourage by the publication of this volume. As with every culture, conspiracy cultures, both mainstream and alternative, are complicated sets of theories, tropes, narratives, discourses, images, and practices that could reveal social symptoms; they are likely to provide valuable coping mechanisms and can be easily turned into political tools as well. In all these cases, the local context is decisive in how to interpret them, for very similar conspiracy theories could signal different social dynamics across various social and political structures. The turbulent past of Eastern Europe, from the failed imperial projects through intense national conflicts to the Cold War, created perfect conditions for conspiracy theorizing, and any intervention by any political or social actor, from civil societies to philanthropic organizations or elected political bodies, could be easily portrayed as illegitimate. One of the main reasons for the success of populist governments in the region originates in the fact that the local elites have been divided into two main streams: those who have tried to accommodate local societies to an ideal—an imagined version of Western democracies, a political drive that had its political momentum in the 1990s—and those who have turned underground conspiracism into state policy and, therefore, offered a mistaken but familiar answer for those very real problems that the same conspiracy theories tried to tackle in the first place. As such, conspiracy theories have a mobilizing effect that has shaped political self-awareness. While today it seems that everything happened for questionable reasons, the long-term effects of this mobilization, and all the social conflicts it brought about, are difficult to predict.

Introduction 21

Conspiracy theories have played a key role in building imagined communities and mobilizing citizens against ruling elites at the time nation-states surfaced on the map of Eastern Europe. Thus, conspiracy theories have shaped a sense of identity geared toward contesting (political) authority, while actual engagement in political action suffered from lack of grassroots support. The top-down dissemination of conspiracy theories by members of the establishment is tantamount to the deliberate use of propaganda. Ultimately, distrust in government and various state-building interventions fueled both top-down and bottom-up circulation of conspiracy narratives.

It is important to realize that conspiracy theory research in Eastern Europe almost necessarily needs to go beyond the immediate concerns about the rise of populism: it shall be at least a *moyenne durée* investigation because most popular conspiracy theories are historically embedded. It is quite challenging to understand their contemporary effects without a good sense of their historical scope. The centrality that history occupies in the consciousness of even the less-educated Eastern Europeans is unusual in a large segment of the West. Not only are these histories conditioned by a series of conspiracy theories but also secrecy and actual conspiracies have been integral state practices and core activities to such an extent that they established conspiracy theories as a perfectly legitimate way to make sense of the world. From Prague to Moscow, conspiracy theorists are not stigmatized to the same extent as they commonly are elsewhere, and particularly so in the Western world. The chapters of this edited volume illustrate how the circulation and the transmission modes of similar conspiratorial tropes allow us to approach Eastern Europe as a whole, even though this requires grouping together diverse political, cultural, and linguistic traditions.

Bibliography

Abalakina-Paap, Marina, Walter G. Stephan, Traci Craig, and W. Larry Gregory. 1999. "Beliefs in Conspiracies." *Political Psychology* 20 (3): 637–47.

Akhmetova, Maria. 2010. *Konets sveta v odnoi otdel'no vziatoi strane: Religioznye soobshchestva postsovetskoi Rossii i ikh eskhatologicheskii mif* [The End of the World in One Country: Religious Communities of Post-Soviet Russia and Eschatological Myth]. Moscow: OGI, RGGU.

Astapova, Anastasiya. 2017. "In Search for Truth: Surveillance Rumors and Vernacular Panopticon in Belarus." *Journal of American Folklore* 130 (517): 276–304.

———. 2020. "Ferroconcrete Cases, Sausage Migrants, and Santa Barbara: Self-Reflexive Metaphors among Russian-Speaking Refugees in Estonia." *Journal of Baltic Studies* 51 (1): 87–103.

Astapova, Anastasiya, Eirikur Bergmann, Asbjørn Dyrendal, Andreas Önnerfors, Annika, Rabo, Kasper Grotle, and Hulda Thórisdóttir. 2021. *Conspiracy Theories and the Nordic Countries. Routledge.* New York: Routledge.

Autio, Sari, and Katalin Miklóssy, eds. 2011. *Reassessing Cold War Europe.* New York: Routledge.

Barkun, Michael. 2003. *A Culture of Conspiracy: Apocalyptic Visions in Contemporary America.* Berkeley, CA: University of California Press.

22 Astapova, Colăcel, Pintilescu, and Scheibner

Bergmann, Eirikur. 2018. *Conspiracy and Populism. The Politics of Misinformation*. Basingstoke: Palgrave Macmillan.

Bilewicz, Michał, and Ireneusz Krzemiński. 2010. "Anti-Semitism in Poland and Ukraine: The Belief in Jewish Control as a Mechanism of Scapegoating." *International Journal of Conflict and Violence* 4 (2): 234–43.

Bilewicz, Michał, Mikołaj Winiewski, Mirosław Kofta, and Adrian Wójcik. 2013. "Harmful Ideas, the Structure and Consequences of Anti-Semitic Beliefs in Poland." *Political Psychology* 34 (6): 821–39.

Blanuša, Nebojša. 2013. "Internal Memory Divided: Conspiratorial Thinking, Ideological and Historical Cleavages in Croatia: Lessons for Europe." *European Quarterly of Political Attitudes and Mentalities* 2 (4): 16–33.

Boltanski, Luc. [2012] 2014. *Mysteries and Conspiracies: Detective Stories, Spy Novels, and the Making of Modern Societies*. Translated by Catherine Porter. Cambridge: Polity Press.

Borenstein, Eliot. 2019. *Plots Against Russia, Conspiracy and Fantasy After Socialism*. Ithaca, NY: Cornell University Press.

Bridge, Christopher. 2017. "Orbán's Hungary: The Othering of Liberal Western Europe Art." In *Representing the Other in European Media Discourses*, edited by Jan Chovanec and Katarzyna Molek-Kozakowska, 25–54. Amsterdam: John Benjamins.

Bronner, Stephen Eric. [2000] 2019. *A Rumor about the Jews Conspiracy, Anti-Semitism, and the Protocols of Zion*. London: Palgrave Macmillan.

Butter, Michael. 2014. *Plots, Designs, and Schemes: American Conspiracy Theories from the Puritans to the Present*. Berlin: de Gruyter.

Butter, Michael, and Peter Knight. 2016. "Bridging the Great Divide: Conspiracy Theory Research for the 21st Century." *Diogenes*. https://doi.org/10.1177/0392192116669289.

Butter, Michael, and Mauris Reinkowski, eds. 2014. *Conspiracy Theories in the United States and the Middle East*. Berlin: De Gruyter.

Byford, Jovan. 2011. *Conspiracy Theories: A Critical Introduction*. London: Palgrave Macmillan.

Byford, Jovan, and Michael Billig. 2001. "The Emergence of Antisemitic Conspiracy Theories in Yugoslavia during the War with NATO." *Patterns of Prejudice* 35 (4): 50–63.

Caumanns, Ute. 2016. "Performing and Communicating Conspiracy Theories: Stalinist Show Trials in Eastern Europe during the Cold War." *Lexia. Rivista di semiotica* 23–24: 269–88.

Charles, Douglas. 2015. *M. J. Edgar Hoover and the Anti-Interventionists: FBI Political Surveillance and the Rise of the Domestic Security State, 1939–1945*. Columbus, OH: Ohio State University Press.

Clark, Roland. 2012. "Anti-Masonry as Political Protest: Fascists and Freemasons in Interwar Romania." *Patterns of Prejudice* 46 (1): 40–57.

Cohn, Norman. [1967] 1996. *Warrant for Genocide: The Myth of the Jewish World Conspiracy and the Protocols of the Elders of Zion*. London: Serif 1996.

Colăcel, Oncriu, and Corneliu Pintilescu. 2017. "From Literary Culture to Post-Communist Media: Romanian Conspiracism." *Messages, Sages and Ages* 3 (2): 70–74.

Craciun, Catrinel, and Adriana Baban. 2012. "'Who Will Take the Blame?': Understanding the Reasons Why Romanian Mothers Decline HPV Vaccination for Their Daughters." *Vaccine* 30 (48): 6789–93.

Cubitt, Geoffrey. 1989. "Denouncing Conspiracy in the French Revolution." *Renaissance and Modern Studies* 33 (1): 144–58.

Culleton, Claire A., and Karen Leick, eds. 2008. *Modernism on File: Writers, Artists, and the FBI, 1920–1950*. New York: Palgrave Macmillan US.

Introduction 23

Dale, Gareth, Katalin Miklóssy, and Dieter Segert. 2015. "Introduction to Special Issue on The Politics of East European Area Studies: Disputing Contemporary Identifications." *Debatte: Journal of Contemporary Central and Eastern Europe* 23 (1): 3–8.

Darwin, Hannah, Nick Neave, and Joni Holmes. 2011. "Belief in Conspiracy Theories: The Role of Paranormal Belief, Paranoid Ideation and Schizotypy." *Personality and Individual Differences* 50 (8): 1289–93.

De Michelis, Cesare G. 2004. *The Non-Existent Manuscript: A Study of the Protocols of the Sages of Zion.* Lincoln: University of Nebraska Press.

Dundes, Alan, ed. 1991. *The Blood Libel Legend: A Casebook in Anti-Semitic Folklore.* Madison, WI: University of Wisconsin Press.

Eyal, Gil, Iván Szelényi, and Eleanor R. Townsley. 1998. *Making Capitalism Without Capitalists: Class Formation and Elite Struggles in Post-communist Central Europe.* London: Verso.

Fenster, Mark. [1999] 2008. *Conspiracy Theories: Secrecy and Power in American Culture.* Minneapolis: University of Minnesota Press.

Gerrits, André, 1995. "Antisemitism and Anti-Communism: The Myth of 'Judeo-Communism' in Eastern Europe." *East European Jewish Affairs* 25 (1): 49–72.

Gerwarth, Robert. 2016. *The Vanquished.* London: Penguin Books.

Gibson, James L., and Marc Morjé Howard. 2007. "Russian anti-Semitism and the Scapegoating of Jews." *British Journal of Political Science* 37 (2): 193–223.

Girard, Pascal. 2012. "Les complots politiques en France et en Italie de la fin de la Seconde Guerre mondiale à la fin des années 1950" [Political Conspiracies in France and Italy from the End of World War II to the End of the 1950s]. PhD diss., European University Institute, Florence.

Goldberg, Robert Alan. 2003. "Conspiracy Theories in America: A Historical Overview." In *Conspiracy Theories in American History: An Encyclopedia*, edited by Peter Knight, 1–13. Santa Barbara, CA: ABC-CLIO.

Goździak, Elżbieta M., and Péter Márton. 2018. "Where the Wild Things Are: Fear of Islam and the Anti-Refugee Rhetoric in Hungary and in Poland." *Central and Eastern European Migration Review* 7 (2): 125–51.

Grande, Edgar. 2000. "Charisma und Komplexität: Verhandlungsdemokratie, Mediendemokratie und der Funktionswandel politischer Eliten." *Leviathan* 28: 122–41.

Gray, Matthew. 2010. *Conspiracy Theories in the Arab World: Sources and Politics.* London: Routledge.

Groh, Dieter. 1987. "The Temptation of Conspiracy Theory, or: Why Do Bad Things Happen to Good People? Part II: Case Studies." In *Changing Conceptions of Conspiracy*, edited by Carl F. Graumann and Serge Moscovici, 15–37. New York: Springer.

Grzesiak-Feldman, Monika. 2013. "The Effect of High-anxiety Situations on Conspiracy Thinking." *Current Psychology* 32 (1): 100–18.

Grzesiak-Feldman, Monika, and Monika Irzycka. 2009. "Right-Wing Authoritarianism and Conspiracy Thinking in a Polish Sample." *Psychological Reports* 105 (2): 389–93.

Hagemeister, Michael. 2008. "The Protocols of the Elders of Zion: Between History and Fiction." *New German Critique* 35 (1): 83–95.

Hanebrink, Paul. 2018. *A Specter Haunting Europe: The Myth of Judeo-Bolshevism.* Cambridge, MA: The Belknap Press of Harvard University Press.

Hodos, George H. 1987. *Show Trials: Stalinist Purges in Eastern Europe, 1948–1954.* Westport: Praeger.

Hofstadter, Richard. 1964. *The Paranoid Style in American Politics, and Other Essays.* Cambridge, MA: Harvard University Press.

24 *Astapova, Colăcel, Pintilescu, and Scheibner*

Humphrey, Caroline. 2002. "Stalin and the Blue Elephant: Paranoia and Complicity in Postcommunist Metahistories." *Diogenes* 194/2 (49): 26–34.

Husting, Ginna, and Martin Orr. 2007. "Dangerous Machinery: 'Conspiracy Theorist' as a Transpersonal Strategy of Exclusion." *Symbolic Interaction* 30 (2): 127–50.

Kalmre, Eda. 1998. "Legends Connected with the Sinking of the Ferry Estonia on September 28, 1994." *Fabula* 39: 11–18.

———. 2016. "Salad Rinsing and Baby Carrots: Mercantile Rumors in Contemporary Society." *Contemporary Legend. The Journal of the International Society for Contemporary Legend Research* 6: 1–24.

Kasekamp, Andres, Mari-Liis Madisson, and Louis Wieringa. 2018. "Discursive Opportunities for the Estonian Populist Radical Right in Digital Society." *Problems of Post-Communism* 66 (1): 47–58.

Keeley, Brian L. 1999. "Of Conspiracy Theories." *The Journal of Philosophy* 96 (3): 109–26.

Kellogg, Michael. 2005. *The Russian Roots of Nazism: White Émigrés and the Making of National Socialism, 1917–1945*. Cambridge: Cambridge University Press.

Knight, Peter. 2003. *Conspiracy Theories in American History: An Encyclopedia*. Santa Barbara, CA: ABC-CLIO.

Kormina. Jeanne. 2016. "Killer Yeast: Gastronomic Conspiracy Theories and the Culture of Mistrust in Modern Russia." *Forum for Anthropology and Culture* 2016 (12): 201–29.

Krekó, Péter, and Zsolt Enyedi. 2018. "Explaining Eastern Europe: Orbán's Laboratory of Illiberalism." *Journal of Democracy* 29 (3): 39–51.

Kundera, Milan. 1984. "The Tragedy of Central Europe." *The New York Review of Books* 31 (7): 33–38.

Kuzio, Taras. 2011. "Soviet Conspiracy Theories and Political Culture in Ukraine: Understanding Viktor Yanukovych and the Party of Regions." *Communist and Post-Communist Studies* 44 (3): 221–32.

———. 2017. *Putin's War against Ukraine: Revolution, Nationalism, and Crime*. North Charleston: CreateSpace.

Lendvai, Paul. 1971. *Anti-Semitism without Jews: Communist Eastern Europe*. Garden City, NY: Doubleday.

Maccoby, Hyam. 2006. *Antisemitism and Modernity: Innovation and Continuity*. London: Routledge.

Madisson, Mari-Liis, and Andreas Ventsel. 2020. *Strategic Conspiracy Narratives: A Semiotic Approach*. London: Routledge.

Marks, Steven G. 2003. *How Russia Shaped the Modern World: From Art to Anti-Semitism, Ballet to Bolshevism*. Princeton, NJ: Princeton University Press.

Medarov, Georgi. 2017. "The Freemasons Are in Parliament! Political Economy of Conspiracies in the Judicial Reform Discourses in Bulgaria." *Critique and Humanism* 48 (2): 147–64.

Melley, Timothy. 2011, "Brain Warfare: The Covert Sphere, Terrorism, and the Legacy of the Cold War." *Grey Room* 45: 19–40.

Melnikova, Ekaterina. 2004. "Eskhatologicheskie Ozhidaniia Rubezha 19–20 Vekov: Kontsa Sveta Ne Budet?" [Eschatological Expectations of 19–20th Century: Won't There Be a Doomsday?]. *Antropologicheskii Forum* 1: 250–66.

Michlic, Joanna B. 2006. *Poland's Threatening Other: The Image of the Jew from 1880 to the Present*. Lincoln: University of Nebraska Press.

Mishkova Diana, and Balázs Trencsényi, eds. 2017. *European Regions and Boundaries: A Conceptual History*. New York: Berghahn Books.

Ortmann, Stefanie, and John Heathershaw. 2012. "Conspiracy Theories in the Post-Soviet Space." *The Russian Review* 71 (4): 551–64.

Oushakine, Serguei Alex. 2009. " 'Stop the Invasion!': Money, Patriotism, and Conspiracy In Russia." *Social Research: An International Quarterly of the Social Sciences* 76 (1): 71–116.

Panczová, Zuzana. 2017. "The Image of the West in Conspiracy Theories in Slovakia and Its Historical Context." *Folklore. Electronic Journal of Folklore* 69: 49–68.

Patai, Raphael. 1996. *The Jews of Hungary: History, Culture, Psychology*. Detroit: Wayne State University Press.

Payne, Stanley G. 1995. *A History of Fascism, 1914–1945*. Madison, WI: University of Wisconsin Press.

Péteri, György. 2004. "Nylon Curtain – Transnational And Transsystemic Tendencies In The Cultural Life Of State-Socialist Russia And East-Central Europe." *Slavonica* 10 (2): 113–23.

Pipes, Daniel. 1997. *Conspiracy: How the Paranoid Style Flourishes and Where It Comes from*. New York: Free Press.

Poliakov, Léon. 1987. "The Topic of the Jewish Conspiracy in Russia (1905–1920), and the International Consequences." In *Changing Conceptions of Conspiracy*, edited by C. F. Graumann and S. Moscovici, 105–13. New York: Springer-Verlag.

Pop, Cristina A. 2016. "Locating Purity within Corruption Rumors: Narratives of HPV Vaccination Refusal in a Peri-Urban Community of Southern Romania." *Medical Anthropology Quarterly* 30 (4): 563–81.

Rabo, Annika. 2020. "Conspiracy Theory as Occult Cosmology in Anthropology." In *Routledge Handbook of Conspiracy Theories*, edited by Michael Butter and Peter Knight, 81–93. New York: Routledge.

Rittersporn, Gábor T. 2014. *Anguish, Anger, and Folkways in Soviet Russia*. Pittsburgh, PA: University of Pittsburgh Press.

Robins, Robert S., and Jerrold M. Post. 1997. *Political Paranoia: The Psychopolitics of Hatred*. New Haven, CT: Yale University Press.

Rogalla von Bieberstein, Johannes. 1977. "The story of the Jewish-Masonic Conspiracy, 1776–1945." *Patterns of Prejudice* 11 (6): 1–21.

Rosman, Moshe. 2017. "How Polish Is Polish History? Polish History's Problem of Definition." In *Imaginations and Configurations of Polish Society From the Middle Ages through the Twentieth Century*, edited by Yvonne Kleinmann, Jürgen Heyde, Dietlind Hüchtker, Dobrochna Kałwa, Joanna Nalewajko-Kulikov, Katrin Steffen, and Tomasz Wiślicz, 19–34. Göttingen: Wallstein Verlag.

Roth, Eduard Rudolf. 2016. "The Romanian Revolution of 1989 and the Veracity of the External Subversion Theory." *Journal of Contemporary Central and Eastern Europe* 24 (1): 37–50.

Schenk, Frithjof Benjamin. 2017. "Eastern Europe." In *European Regions and Boundaries: A Conceptual History*, edited by Diana Mishkova and Balázs Trencsényi, 188–209. New York: Berghahn Books.

Shafir, Michael. 1994. "The Inheritors: The Romanian Radical Right since 1989." *East European Jewish Affairs* 24 (1): 71–89.

Stojanov, Ana. 2015. "Reducing Conspiracy Theory Beliefs." *Psihologija* 48 (3): 251–66.

Stola, Dariusz. 2006. "Anti-Zionism as a Multipurpose Policy Instrument: The Anti-Zionist Campaign in Poland, 1967–1968." *Journal of Israeli History* 25 (1): 175–201.

Sunstein, Cass R., and Adrian Vermeule. 2009. "Conspiracy Theories: Causes and Cures." *Journal of Political Philosophy* 17 (2): 202–27.

26 *Astapova, Colăcel, Pintilescu, and Scheibner*

Swami, Viren, Adrian Furnham, Nina Smyth, Laura Weis, Alixe Lay, and Angela Clow. 2016. "Putting the Stress on Conspiracy Theories: Examining Associations Between Psychological Stress, Anxiety, and Belief in Conspiracy Theories." *Personality and Individual Differences* 99: 72–76.

Theoharis, Athan G. 2004. *The FBI & American Democracy: A Brief Critical History.* Lawrence: University Press of Kansas.

van Prooijen, Jan-Willem, and Michele Acker. 2015. "The Influence of Control on Belief in Conspiracy Theories: Conceptual and Applied Extensions." *Applied Cognitive Psychology* 29 (5): 753–61.

van Prooijen, Jan-Willem, and Nils B. Jostmann. 2013. "Belief in Conspiracy Theories: The Influence of Uncertainty and Perceived Morality." *European Journal of Social Psychology* 43 (1): 109–15.

Verkhovsky, Alexander. 2006. "Holy Russia Versus the Fallen World: Conservative Orthodox Mythologies in Contemporary Russia." In *Nationalist Myths and Modern Media: Contested Identities in the Age of Globalization*, edited by Jan Herman Brinks, Stella Rock, and Edward Timms, 229–42. London: Tauris Academic Studies.

Viola, Lynne. 1993. "The Second Coming: Class Enemies in the Soviet Countryside, 1927–1935." In *Stalinist Terror: New Perspectives Stalinist Terror: New Perspectives*, edited by J. Arch Getty and Roberta Thompson Manning, 65–98. Cambridge: Cambridge University Press.

Voicu, George. 2000. *Zeii cei răi. Cultura conspirației în România postcomunistă* [The Evil Gods: the Culture of Conspiracy in Postcommunist Romania]. Iaşi: Polirom.

———. 2004. "The Notion of 'Judeo-Bolshevism' in Romanian Wartime Press." *Studia Hebraica* 4: 55–68.

Webman, Esther. 2011. "Introduction – Hate and Absurdity: The Impact of the Protocols of the Elders of Zion." In *The Global Impact of the Protocols of the Elders of Zion: A Century-Old Myth*, edited by Esther Webman, 1–23. New York: Routledge, 2011.

Wodak, Ruth. 2015. *The Politics of Fear: What Right-Wing Populist Discourses Mean.* London: Sage.

Wolff, Larry. 1994. *Inventing Eastern Europe: The Map of Civilization on the Mind of the Enlightenment.* Stanford, CA: Stanford University Press.

Wood, Elizabeth A. 2005. *Performing Justice: Agitation Trials in Early Soviet Russia.* Ithaca, NY: Cornell University Press.

Yablokov, Ilya. 2018. *Fortress Russia: Conspiracy Theories in the Post-Soviet World.* Cambridge, UK: Polity Press.

Part I

Conspiracy culture under Socialism and its afterlife in Eastern Europe

Part 1

1 Chernobyl conspiracy theories

From American sabotage to the biggest hoax of the century

Anastasiya Astapova

On April 26, 1986, the RMBK reactor exploded in the fourth energy block of the Chernobyl Nuclear Power Station in the Ukrainian Soviet Socialist Republic, next to the Russian and Belarusian borders. A total of 31 people died during or immediately after the accident from the explosion, fire, or radiation exposure (Mould 2000, 29). Subsequently, hundreds of thousands of locals were evacuated from homes polluted with radiation, while hundreds of thousands of so-called liquidators were mobilized from all over the Soviet Union to eliminate the consequences of the radiation releases. Both the evacuees and liquidators are considered to have received large doses of radiation, with Ukraine recognizing almost 90,000 of its citizens as Chernobyl invalids of the most severely affected category; Russia and Belarus recognize 50,000 and 9,000 individuals, respectively (Plokhy 2006, 328). The Soviet Union commission investigation followed by a court trial concluded that human error and problems with the RMBK reactor, which turned out to be unstable at low power, were to blame for the explosion.

These details are perhaps the only elements of Chernobyl history that most journalists, power engineers, writers, historians, healthcare specialists, and ordinary citizens agree on. The rest of the story, which happened just over 30 years ago, remains a point for multiple disagreements. Even the particular numbers of, for instance, liquidators or evacuees varies from one academic publication to another, with a difference of as many as 400,000–800,000 liquidators and 200,000–350,000 evacuees (Bay and Oughton 2005, 239; Ingram 2005, 62). Needless to say, it is not only factual information about the tragedy that remains obscure: theories about the true reasons for the accident have been circulating ever since the day it happened and have been changing in response to historical and ideological needs. This chapter is, to my knowledge, the first attempt to document and catalog alternative explanations and conspiracy theories associated with Chernobyl as they changed throughout recent history.

The major sources for this chapter are (1) academic publications, mainly from the disciplines of history, medicine, and power engineering, but also those from folklore, sociology, and anthropology, all often mentioning alternative explanations for the tragedy; (2) collections of memoirs, interviews with eyewitnesses, oral histories, and accounts of observers and contemporaries of the accident and its aftermath; (3) various writings and manifestos published by nationalist-minded

30 *Anastasiya Astapova*

politicians in Belarus and Ukraine in the 1990s; (4) social media, blogs, and other internet publications on the issue; and (5) mass media publications. I draw from materials published in Russian, Ukrainian, Belarusian, and English to compile a fuller inventory of Chernobyl conspiracy theories. Among the most frequently cited sources are two books: a collection of interviews with Chernobyl survivors compiled by Nobel Prize–winning writer Svetlana Alexievich ([1997] 2016) and what might be the most comprehensive history book on Chernobyl today, written by the historian Serhii Plokhii (2018).

In this chapter, I document the conspiracy theories according to their chronology; however, this is not always possible and should not be considered absolutely accurate. I show how conspiracy theories appeared as a first response to the tragedy and were modified in accordance with dominant and alternative statehood narratives. The expansive mythology and folklore surrounding the Chernobyl accident is worth a description to begin with and will allow us to better understand the context of conspiracy theories as well.

Chernobyl mythology and folklore

Chernobyl exploded only a little more than a year after Mikhail Gorbachev became the head of the Soviet state. For the Soviet government, he was a novel face who had come to power due to the support of many who were tired of economic failure, corruption, and lack of freedom. He won public support by promising to promote openness and eliminate censorship (Plokhii 2018, 9). However, what he promised in theory encountered difficulties in practice, and Chernobyl became, perhaps, the first serious challenge to his program. For decades, the Soviet government had been concealing information about the victims of Joseph Stalin's terror, Gulag camps, and other nuclear accidents (most infamously, the Kyshtym nuclear power plant disaster in 1957 was kept top secret). When news about Chernobyl reached Moscow, it was too hard for Gorbachev alone (even if he wanted this) to act differently and to make the event public (Ingram 2005, 52). There was no precedent in Soviet history of how to deal with such disasters openly.

The first official report on the accident appeared on April 29, only three days after the explosion, in the newspaper *Pravda Ukrainy*; however, neither this nor further brief official announcements showed that there was any real reason to worry. In the meantime, in what would soon become the exclusion zones, people were enjoying the spring warmth and sunbathing; on May 1, clueless citizens participated in the traditional Soviet Parade, spending hours outdoors. It was not until May 14 that Mikhail Gorbachev finally made an official statement about the details of the accident. Even then, people did not get adequate instructions and information about protecting themselves from the radiation.

Due to the lack of comments and the aura of secrecy in official Soviet discourse, rumors were perceived as a better source of information than the Soviet mass media. A widespread narrative theme was that of certain signs people could read from nature, signaling danger while the politicians remained silent. People noticed strangled moles in the garden and the disappearance of bugs, wasps, beetles, or

Chernobyl conspiracy theories   31

worms, which indicated strong radiation. "The radio didn't say anything, the papers weren't either, but the bees knew," some commented (Alexievich 2005, 51–53).

A whole repertoire of folk remedies developed that were believed to cure radiation poisoning, such as cucumbers and fresh milk from the area that many brought to their relatives who had been exposed to radiation and were hospitalized. When people learned that iodine tablets might help as antidotes for radiation poisoning, the tablets immediately sold out, and many bought iodine liquid instead, which sent hundreds to the hospital with serious throat damage (Ingram 2005, 59). Another widely accepted remedy was vodka, which was, in fact, supplied and recommended to firefighters and liquidators. Rumors stated that Stolichnaya vodka was the best antidote to strontium; folk remedies based on vodka with other infusions circulated in recipes (ibid., 43; Alexievich 2016, 106, 138).

Repeatedly, rumors appeared about new explosions, whether in Chernobyl or in other places, directly after the tragedy and years later. Folklorist Larisa Fialkova, who lived in Kyiv at the time of the accident, remembers how she once was walking in a park and was approached by a stranger who urgently told her about an explosion of the reactor at the Kyiv nuclear physics research institute, recommending that she go home (Fialkova 2001, 184–85). Years after, when doing excavations very close to the reactor, military reservists came across two old mines from World War II, and the rumor spread that someone intended to blow up the sarcophagus that had been built over the reactor following the tragedy (Marples 1990, 17). In fact, many questioned the state of the station's sarcophagus, which was allegedly very poorly constructed, with nothing but a few logs as a roof (Bodrunova 2012, 21).

The effects of invisible radiation were hard to imagine, and with the lack of official comment on its impact, the folk imagination developed narratives about grotesque mutations in humans and animals caused by radiation. Rumors developed of three-headed birds, two-headed calves, hens that were pecking foxes to death, bald hedgehogs, mushrooms the size of a human head, birds with two beaks, pikes without heads and fins, giant mosquitoes, and many other mutants in the Chernobyl area (ibid., 21; Alexievich 2016, 124, 137, 141). Similar mutations were soon ascribed to humans: that children from Chernobyl parents have an unknown yellow fluid pulsing through them instead of blood and that they are extremely smart (Alexievich 2016, 142). At the same time, humor appeared, resting on self-reflexivity about such rumors and their oddity.

> A grandfather and his grandson are walking over the ground of Chernobyl.
> "Grandpa, is it true that once there was a beautiful town here?"
> "True, grandson, true," grandfather replies, patting him on his head.
> "Is it true, grandpa, that people lived in it?"
> "True, grandson, true," sighs grandfather, patting him on his other head.
>
> (Fialkova 2001, 191)

> "What is seven times seven?" The answer: "Ask a Chernobyl survivor, they'll count on their fingers."
>
> (Alexievich 2016, 51)

32 *Anastasiya Astapova*

With the liberalization and collapse of the Soviet Union, religious freedom permitted missionaries from abroad to spread the word of their faiths, the influx of New Age beliefs, and the return of Christian practices as legitimate. During this time, imports from the Western New Age mixed together with the concepts of alternative spiritual health and complementary medicine, such as folk healing, which was traditional in a vast part of the Soviet territory (Menzel 2013, 279). A number of folk practices and beliefs developed. People watched hours of TV sessions in which sorcerers who called themselves "psychics" "energized" water, and there were attempts to fix Chernobyl via magic. Svetlana Alexievich presents an account according to which a traditional folk healer, Parashka, signed contracts with several farms and was paid a lot of money upon promising to lower the background gamma radiation and drive away evil spirits in Chernobyl over the course of the summer (Alexievich 2016, 159–60).

Many legends also relied on religion or the supernatural to explain the Chernobyl accident. One claims that the Chernobyl power station was built on the site of a ruined Hasidic cemetery, and this blasphemy caused the catastrophe (Fialkova 2001, 197). Another legend is associated with the meaning of the word "Chernobyl"—"wormwood" in Ukrainian—and the fact that the New Testament book of Revelation refers to the fall from heaven of a great star called Wormwood "burning as it were a lamp." It was as though people had not paid attention to a religious prophecy (Plokhy 2019, 27). With the peak of UFO fascination in the second half of the 1980s (Menzel 2013, 271), many considered a UFO attack to be the true reason for the accident. Witnesses claimed that they had seen a strange light in the sky above the station before the explosion. Someone even took a picture of it and saw an ethereal body in the photograph (Alexievich 2016, 142). Others argued that UFO intervention during the blast saved the disaster from becoming a global nuclear event. The UFO hovered over a newly smoking reactor, stopped the smoke, and sped off (Conroy 2018).

Chernobyl folklore is by no means local and enjoys global proliferation. Initially, this was due to the spontaneous generation of rumors and jokes in different languages, migration by their narrators, phone communication, print media, and television programs; later, popular culture and the internet contributed to its spread and development (Fialkova 2001, 138). Over time, moreover, the folk imagination has constructed more complex narratives: conspiracy theories related to the accident connecting many dots and explaining it in some unexpected ways.

Immediate conspiracy theories: the CIA sabotage

The immediate reaction explaining Chernobyl as the result of sabotage is documented in many written sources. For instance, the main female protagonist of Svetlana Alexievich's collection of interviews, Liudmila, was desperate to save her husband, Vasily—a fireman who had been among the first to arrive at the fire during the Chernobyl accident and thus receive the largest radiation dose. He and other firemen were transported to Moscow, and Liudmila, despite being pregnant, made her way to find her husband. Vasily explained the incident to her as "Most

Chernobyl conspiracy theories 33

likely sabotage. Somebody must have done it deliberately. That's what all the guys [other firemen] reckon" (Alexievich 2016, 11). Various sources suggest that professionals working for the plant, Chernobyl locals, and intelligence services initially believed the accident to be a work of sabotage. Immediately after the tragedy, KGB agents rushed to investigate the plant's files and records and to interrogate survivors dying in their hospital beds (Brown 2019, 7) and increased surveillance over the nearby nuclear plants and the area adjacent to Chernobyl (Plokhii 2018, 183)—all as a result of the suspicion of Western sabotage.

In the meantime, the suspected saboteurs—Westerners—demanded information. On April 28, two days after the accident, a radiation spike was registered at the Forsmark nuclear power plant in Sweden. Unable to find the reason, Sweden contacted the closest states, including the Soviet Union, inquiring about the possible radiation leak. The Soviets denied it, but suspicion from Sweden and other Western countries persisted (Sveriges Radio 2011). As a result, they tried to make their own investigations, the only source of which, with no official information available, could be rumors from anonymous informants, which presented them with difficulty in fact checking (Brown 2019, 156). Little wonder then that the first foreign reports on the accident exaggerated the immediate damage. On April 29, an American correspondent in Moscow reported that 80 people had died on the spot, which was immediately picked up by other foreign newspapers (Whitington 1986). Later, US media sources claimed that 2,000 people died in Chernobyl on the way to the hospital or in the blast (Ingram 2005, 57–58). The Soviets responded, fighting back by broadcasting news reports about previous nuclear accidents in the United States and stating that these had happened due to unsatisfactory equipment and training of personnel (ibid., 57–58).

The vocabulary of the Cold War was revitalized, with phrases like "Western intelligence agents," "arch enemies of Socialism," "spying forays," "sabotage," "a stab in the back," "subverting the inviolable union of Soviet peoples," and so on (Alexievich 2016, 137). On May 6, the deputy foreign minister, Anatoly Kovalev, publicly attacked the United States for organizing "a campaign of hysteria." Even after acknowledging the accident, the Soviet media targeted Western information discourse, blaming Westerners for exploiting the tragedy for political purposes and for using rumors and speculation, which runs counter to elementary moral standards (Plokhii 2018, 233, 238). In the speech Mikhail Gorbachev delivered on May 14, finally breaking the silence, he also blamed the West for spreading misinformation about Chernobyl and for taking people's attention away from real global problems the Americans were uncomfortable to speak about. He inculpated the United States in particular for preventing nuclear disarmament talks by boosting the conflict around Chernobyl (Shkoda 1988, 9).

The background for these accusations is probably the same context that allowed the conspiracy theory about CIA sabotage to thrive, based on a vision of the United States as a villain responsible not only for propaganda but also for the actual explosion. In addition, the sudden collapse of the Soviet Union followed the accident, making many connect the dots. Many historians, in fact, argue that Chernobyl was "a landmark event, the symbolic and de facto beginning of the end

34   *Anastasiya Astapova*

of Soviet communism" (Weeks 2010, 116). While it would be wrong to attribute this to Chernobyl alone, the disaster's impact on the collapse of the Soviet Union can hardly be overstated (Plokhii 2018, xvi).

Undoubtedly, people were not equally happy with the dissolution of the Soviet Union. In the transition economy, many lost their jobs and welfare; with the shutdown of Soviet industrial enterprises in the independent post-Soviet countries, engineers were often among them. Volodymyr Tsymbaliuk, the Chernobyl factory's general manager, told Kate Brown, a historian of Chernobyl, years after the tragedy, "CIA agents . . . sabotaged the plant. I am sure of it. . . . Three thousand people used to work here until Americans brought capitalism and wrecked the USSR" (Brown 2019, 97). Colonel Valery Podsvirov, who had worked as a liquidator in Chernobyl, similarly argued that the accident resulted from the deliberate work of "a foreign agent." "The Chernobyl accident is not an accident, there is a consistent pattern to it. Atomic reactors are highly reliable, which was proven by experiments. The cosmic sputnik of the United States took a photo of the fourth reactor just in time for some reason. The logical analysis shows that this was not an accident, but the large-scale sabotage of the century which undermined the economic basis of the USSR and, with the 'help from the outside,' undermined the whole socialist system as a whole," Podsvirov wrote (2011).

Conspiracy theories noted that a week before the accident, a strange drawing had appeared in a Soviet newspaper unrelated to the text published there: sixteen dots and a symbolic depiction of an explosion—a star—in between two of them. They argued that it was a topographic plan of the Chernobyl station, warning Gorbachev of the upcoming accident in case he did not surrender: it was thought that Americans may have blackmailed him by such secret signs (Poluyan 2016).

Many say that the explosion in Chernobyl was just one accident in a chain of planned attacks by the United States, such as spreading purposeful propaganda against the image of Stalin and making the USSR surrender in Afghanistan when the USSR had in fact won the war (Agranovsky 2013). Needless to say, members of the Communist Party in contemporary Russia are also active proponents of the sabotage version of the Chernobyl accident (Nikitchuk 2012).

Another theme relating to American and Western villains appeared when Western countries offered their aid to children who suffered from health problems after Chernobyl, including the possibility for such children to go for a summer holiday abroad to live with foreign families. One of Svetlana Alexievich's interviewees who coordinated such help in Belarus remembers that the father of one such boy burst into his office and demanded his son's documentation back, saying "They'll take our children's blood! They'll conduct experiments on them!" (Alexievich 2016, 154). In the 1990s, rumors about organ theft persisted in post-Soviet countries, which also could not help but influence this (Astapova 2020).

There is another twist to conspiracy theories about American villains responsible for Chernobyl: many conspiracy theorists now argue that, along with other interested parties, Americans created the apocalyptic and extreme vision of the Chernobyl accident, while the real consequences were not so grave and are being

Chernobyl conspiracy theories   35

exaggerated on purpose. I will examine this very popular (especially recently) conspiracy theory in a separate section.

Americans, however, were not the only villains to blame: conspiracy theories vary according to one's ideological views on the Soviet Union. On the other end of the scale, many thought that Soviets, not Americans, held responsibility for an intentional explosion.

Post-colonial conspiracy theories: Russia to blame

Secrecy about the accident led to theories that the Soviet government might have concealed other facts. Many of those who presumed sabotage or a terrorist attack also suggested that the Soviet government preferred to cover this up so as not to acknowledge its own failure to prevent it (Krishtopa 2011, 62). Other versions suggested the explosion had been caused by an earthquake, which the military had known about in advance but kept top secret (Antoniuk 2019). Some still believe that the Soviet government planned Chernobyl as an experiment to observe the effects of radiation: there seemed to be no feat too daring for the KGB to try during the Cold War, even if it meant thousands of deaths. According to this version, the Soviet leadership was preparing for war against the West, and this experiment was the first stage, which helped to get priceless information about the impact of radiation on humans and on how to handle it (Tuckett 1999). Finally, some think that Chernobyl was planned by the KGB to ensure Western dependency on the USSR for energy by instilling a European fear of nuclear power and thus monopolizing the energy market (Deer 2014).

Blaming the Soviet government had a kernel of truth in it, as secrecy and mismanagement of the tragedy caused more harm than the accident would have had without these complications. Failure to alert residents of the soon-to-be exclusion zone about the impact of the accident and take safety precautions to guard the public's health worsened the situation. Many firefighters and later liquidators lacked equipment to protect them from radioactivity, and they were underinformed about the hazards they faced. Doses accumulated by liquidators were artificially lowered in the paperwork (Resnicoff 2010, 163). These and other similar cases set many to thinking about the Soviets' viler deeds. Rumors spread, stating that the Soviets were organizing camps to keep and observe people sick with radiation and that they would bury them there when they died. Other rumors referred to collective graves similar to those in the Siege of Leningrad during World War II; they might be dug so that corpses from nearby villages could by driven secretly by bus and buried there. Finally, there was a rumor that the authorities were preparing barracks left from Stalinist camps in Siberia to deport people from Minsk who had received high radiation doses there (Alexievich 2005, 128).

Holding Soviet authorities and the Kremlin responsible for the accident and its aftermath, however, acquired very special meaning in the Soviet republics' quest for independence. The Chernobyl tragedy was particularly consequential for Ukraine and Belarus, which suffered most from radiation contamination. In the immediate aftermath of the accident, KGB agents reported to the authorities

36 *Anastasiya Astapova*

about the ethno-national interpretation of the disaster developing among Ukrainian nationalists. In 1986, a former member of the nationalist underground that had fought for the independence of Western Ukraine, I. Z. Shevchuk, allegedly told a KGB agent that he believed "that Russians are deliberately building such [nuclear] stations on Ukrainian territory, knowing that if an accident should happen, it would be basically Ukrainians who would suffer." Another KGB report concerned the niece of a famous Ukrainian writer, Mykhailo Kotsiubynsky, who had been heard to claim that the Ukrainian nation was in danger of dying out, of physical annihilation, and that the Soviet leaders gave the order to build atomic energy stations in densely settled areas of Ukraine on purpose (Plokhii 2018, 286).

What first appeared in the KGB reports became a matter for public discussion with the development of the policy of *glasnost* (openness and transparency) in the Soviet Union. The responsibility of officials in Moscow, and not just of the Chernobyl plant managers, was already an active topic in Ukrainian public discourse in 1987. Plenty of Ukrainian dissidents and nationalists who raised the issue of Chernobyl supported the movement for ecological activism. To give just one example, the writer-turned-activist Volodymyr Yarovsky claimed that "communism, its empire, and militarism, had come together to destroy the Ukrainian nation, ruled as a colony. This was accomplished by placing the reactor with major design flaws 130 kilometers from Kyiv, at the intersection of three Ukrainian rivers" (ibid., 324). Discussion went as far as claiming the deliberate genocide of the Ukrainian nation.

Soon, one of the leaders of the eco-activist movement, Ivan Drach, became the head of *Rukh*, a grassroots organization that would propel Ukraine into a democratic revolution. He and other prominent Ukrainians demanded the punishment of those responsible for the construction of the nuclear power plant, epitomized by Russians. Chernobyl became one of the motivating forces of the awakening of the Ukrainian nation, and anti-nuclear sentiments became a core tenet of the call for Ukrainian independence (ibid., 293–94). Ukraine embraced the Chernobyl accident as a tool of state- and nation-building, a means of mobilizing opposition against the former imperial center. Sergei Plokhy called this phenomenon "eco-nationalism" to describe a political movement "whose leaders linked concerns about environmental protection with ethno-national agendas, presenting their republics as the principal victims" of Moscow politics (ibid., 305). Similar processes took place in nearby Lithuania, where people united to protest against the Ignalina nuclear power station and which became the first republic to declare its independence from the Soviet Union. Ukrainian activists purposefully followed the Lithuanian example.

Accusing Russians of deliberate genocide in Ukraine via Chernobyl radiation was by no means the only conspiracy theory used in political struggle. As in the case of the Soviet-Western competition in holding power over information, the opponents of Ukrainian nationalists did not hesitate to use conspiracy theories for their political purposes. When a Ukrainian environmental activist, Yurii Shcherbak, ran for a seat in the Congress of People's Deputies, party-backed candidates accused him of being both a Ukrainian bourgeois nationalist and a

Chernobyl conspiracy theories 37

Zionist (ibid., 306). Decades later, one of the most infamous conspiracy theorists, the Norwegian far-right terrorist Anders Breivik, who shot dead 69 people in 2011, would also challenge Ukrainian eco-nationalist conspiracy theories with a competing narrative. In his 1,518-page manifesto, he claims that Chernobyl was deliberately blown up by a Ukrainian nationalist military cell who realized how much the explosion could damage the Soviet Union. In so doing, he alleges, they inflicted massive civilian suffering, with tens of thousands dying of cancer; however, at the same time, they may have actually saved millions from suffering from the Soviets, Breivik speculates (Lenta.ru 2011).

In Belarus, to a large extent, Chernobyl conspiracy theories took shape after the success of those in Ukraine and were employed by the Belarusian nationalistically minded elite and their leader, Zianon Pazniak, in the late 1980s to early 1990s. Radical nationalist and anti-Russian claims were a part of his presidential candidacy program in the first independent election in Belarus in 1994. His nationalist radicalism "hardly warranted by the level of national consciousness in the country" (Marples 2003, 28) prevented him from winning; however, years after, his ideas continue to hold sway. In 2002, Pazniak published a collection of short essays exemplary of such thinking in a book titled *The New Age*, which is the most comprehensive list of anti-Russian conspiracy theories. Several essays, are dedicated to the Chernobyl accident, which Pazniak argues is one of many Russian operations deliberately pursuing genocide of the Belarusian nation. He claims that as soon as the Chernobyl accident occurred and radioactive clouds formed, the Soviet military received an order from the authorities to shoot the clouds above the Belarusian Mogilev and Gomiel regions so as to pollute these the most (Pazniak 2002, 49). Russians exploited the situation further in order to exterminate Belarusians in all possible ways, Pazniak further speculates. The state healthcare system was ordered to persuade Belarusian women to have abortions by threatening that their children would be born with mutations due to radiation exposure. This conspiracy theory suggested Russians perpetrated the genocide of Belarusian people through cutting birth rates, as several generations of Belarusians "have been literally flushed into the hospital toilets. . . . Hitler could not have even imagined this in his dream." Those women who managed to bear a child were blackmailed into not giving birth to them, with threats of not being paid the maternity allowance. Due to these restrictions and the illnesses caused by Chernobyl, the Belarusian nation, Pazniak argues, is dying out. He says the Russian state is using the polluted lands of the Mogilev and Gomiel regions, from which Belarusians were forced after the explosion, to settle Russian criminals, drug addicts, migrants, refugees, and the homeless, which he claims is all part of the re-colonization of Belarus by Russia. This is a deliberate Russian policy of destroying the Belarusian nation, Pazniak concludes, which also entailed collectivization, the 1930s Red Terror, eliminating the Belarusian language, destroying works of Belarusian art and literature, and so on (Pazniak 2002, 48–49).

Both Ukraine and Belarus have particular reasons to theorize about a conspiracy by Russia to destroy them. Both countries experienced Russian domination for over two centuries (in addition to speaking East Slavic languages often

38 *Anastasiya Astapova*

perceived as underdeveloped dialects of dominant Russian) and were, perhaps, in greatest need of developing their ethnic identity vis-à-vis Russia. Blaming Russia, an embodiment of Soviet colonial powers, for massacres, manipulations, and nefarious plots developed there was a common practice, and Chernobyl conspiracy theories became part of this repertoire.

The accusations against Russia by Ukrainian and Belarusian nationalist-minded intellectual elites resurface every time there is a political need for them. In Belarus, this relates to the fact that Alexander Lukashenko, the opponent of Zianon Pazniak in the first Belarusian election, still remains in power and keeps many political, economic, and cultural ties with Russia, whom Pazniak and his followers blame for the accident and other atrocities. In Ukraine, Chernobyl attained special significance after Euromaidan (2013–14) and the annexation of Crimea by Russia (2014). The military aggression of Russia as well as Russophobe sentiments, especially strong in certain regions of Ukraine, boosted a formal campaign of de-communization, which also included the uncovering of Soviet KGB crimes. A new law allowed free access to the archives of the repressive Communist agencies, which boosted inquiries into the archives by scholars and amateurs (Marples 2018, 19). One of these investigations led to the 2015 movie *The Russian Woodpecker*, which is based on a project by a Ukrainian artist who tried to discover the real reasons behind the Chernobyl catastrophe and who tells a story of Moscow having organized the accident to conceal a large-scale weaponry project, the Duga over-the-horizon radio antenna (at that time, based in Chernobyl and used as part of the Soviet missile defense early-warning radar network) (Plokhy 2019). Like in 1986, however, there is a Russian patriotic counter-campaign claiming that the Chernobyl accident is nothing more than a great hoax.

The biggest hoax of the twentieth century

Conspiracy theories claiming that a certain phenomenon is a hoax differ according to the extent of their disavowal. On the one hand, they may completely deny such facts as the Moon landing, the Sandy Hook Elementary School shooting in Connecticut, or Ebola and HIV disease outbreaks. On the other hand, they may argue that the effects of certain events, such as the Holocaust, are exaggerated in the interests of certain groups, such as Jews. The conspiracy theory claiming that the Chernobyl accident is a great bluff belong to the second, exaggeration category. It is most reminiscent of conspiracy theories about climate change, which postulate that global warming is exaggerated by people who have something to gain, particularly scientists and governments (Douglas and Sutton 2015, 100). In a similar way, those who are accused of fabricating the Chernobyl hoax in their own interests are most often Ukrainian, Belarusian, and Western scientists and politicians. The conspiracy theory that Chernobyl is a hoax probably originated from accusations that alarmists were spreading false rumors and causing panics in the days following the tragedy, particularly Americans. At the same time, this narrative is in opposition to eco-nationalist conspiracy theories claiming that Russia is to blame.

Chernobyl conspiracy theories 39

One of the major texts used to support the conspiracy theory that the Chernobyl impact has been exaggerated is the report of the United Nations Scientific Committee on the Effects of Atomic Radiation (UNSCEAR). Among other arguments that seem to be drawn from this report, conspiracy theorists circulate the following:

- The liquidators received radiation doses of around 100 mSv, while only a dose above 1,000 mSv is considered to be dangerous for health.
- The liquidators turned out to be healthier than the average population (here, a Polish radiology professor is cited).
- There is no scientific evidence on the increased mortality or disease rates in those who were exposed to radiation. Increased mortality rates have not even been registered generations after the much more serious Hiroshima and Nagasaki atomic bombings.
- There is, however, an increase of psychosomatic diseases caused by fears about Chernobyl (a biophysics professor is quoted).
- The heavily contaminated zone is only within a 500-meter perimeter around Chernobyl. The rest of the territory is safe, and the evacuation was caused by mass panic. The deaths of people living nearby were caused by stress (according to a Polish oncology doctor).

Needless to say, UNSCEAR's assessment of the Chernobyl radiation effects is much more pessimistic than those presented above (UNSCEAR 2012).

The proponents of the idea that Chernobyl is the biggest hoax of the twentieth century often refer to the Chernobyl syndrome, somatic maladies, and uneasiness about the real causes of illnesses (Iarmolenko 2000). In the direct aftermath of Chernobyl, some specialists claimed it was radiophobia that caused people to feel ill, and they tried to prove their point by arguing that children who were too young to have such a phobia did not feel sick (Starovoitova 2001). Many still strive to prove there has been no increase in illnesses. Some say that the Chernobyl accident prompted medical examination of its victims, leading to early diagnoses of many illnesses that had been undetected: this simply had not occurred before and had a heavy impact on the statistics (Sivov 2016). Others claim that the new radiation departments in hospitals, funded through foreign money, were empty, as there was nobody to treat, and that the money was laundered via bonuses to medical doctors and luxurious dinners at medical conferences recorded as aid to Chernobyl victims (Pyhalov 2016).

The idea that the myth about Chernobyl was reiterated for money-laundering purposes is very popular, with many arguing that via self-victimization Ukraine begs for money from the West and steals it. Even those scholars who evaluate the consequences of Chernobyl very pessimistically acknowledge that it is almost impossible to calculate the overall toll of the Chernobyl disaster (Ingram 2005, v). It is unclear as to what extent current death and illness statistics represent an increase over the expected mortality rates and how many deaths are directly (or only) related to radiation exposure (Bay and Oughton 2005, 244). Another

40   *Anastasiya Astapova*

difficulty is that Chernobyl victims' complaints could just as easily result from the lifestyle of those evacuated and those who have lived near the exclusion zone, especially in the transitional, post-Soviet years characterized by a very poor economy. It is hard to say what share of illnesses is due to smoking, drinking, poor diet, and depression rather than radiation (Cheney 2010, 78). What remains unclear is whether the primary effects were caused by radiation exposure or are a result of more complex, psychosocial or psychological factors caused by the general poor health of these poor populations.

Due to such uncertainty, both Ukrainians and Belarusians are accused of boosting Chernobyl for financial reasons only, as the victims of the accident are eligible for additional welfare payments (Romanchuk 2006; Iaroshkin 2019). In 1990, the year that laws on social protection for those affected by the Chernobyl incident were being passed by Ukrainian legislators, there was a sharp increase in clinical registration of presumed Chernobyl-related illnesses. Not surprisingly, observers were skeptical and claimed that Ukrainian scientists had failed to prove (or disprove) these claims on the basis of epidemiological criteria and causality (Bay and Oughton 2005, 246). The conspiracy theory also claims that the Chernobyl campaign has been successfully implemented against nuclear energy in the interests of Greenpeace and other green power lobbies (Romanchuk 2006; Iaroshkin 2019). Some also stress that foreign energy lobby groups played along to install expensive wind turbines instead of nuclear plants (Sivov 2016).

Certain events cause people to revisit the tragedy, reconsider its effects, and return to the theory of Chernobyl as a hoax, and recent times seem to be particularly fruitful for its reiteration. First, following the Maidan Revolution, the Russian annexation of Crimea, and the Russian-Ukrainian war in the Ukrainian east, accusations against the "evil" Ukrainians resurfaced. Many Russian politicians and bloggers immediately connected Chernobyl and Maidan, arguing that both the accident and the revolution were financed by the USA or that the sarcophagus over the atomic station was not actually built, although it was funded (another hoax) (Sulkin 2015).

Second, in 2015, Belarusian writer Svetlana Alexievich won a Nobel Prize in literature. Three of her most well-known books are on Chernobyl (copiously quoted above), women in World War II, and young conscript Soviet soldiers in Afghanistan (*Chernobyl Prayer: A Chronicle of the Future, The Unwomanly Face of War, Zinky Boys: Soviet Voices from the Afghanistan War*). All three are very critical of the Soviet system, which caused vast ideological debates in the post-Soviet space, and Alexievich was accused by many of not being an actual writer (her books are rather collections of interviews) as well as misrepresenting events and overdramatizing Chernobyl in particular. Many accused her of having written the books on Western orders and using American grants (Medvedev 2015). Needless to say, Alexievich was not the first author writing on Chernobyl to be accused of transmitting a view dictated by the West. Ukrainian activist Alla Iaroshinskaia, who presented quite a cheerless view in her book on the consequences of the accident, was also accused of doing so using American money and Western grants (Flibusta 2013). A book by Harvard-based historian Serhii Plokhy, also quoted

Chernobyl conspiracy theories 41

here, is accused of being a Ukrainian nationalist pamphlet, although to a lesser extent: compared to Alexievich's work, it has reached fewer readers due to being written by an academic and in English.

Third, a particular uproar arose following the release and extreme popularity of the HBO semi-documentary miniseries, *Chernobyl* (2019), which was quite critical of the management of the accident by the Soviets. Russian patriots immediately saw the miniseries as an attack on the prestige of the Russian state in its Soviet incarnation or as a Western plot to undermine Rosatom, the Russian monopoly enterprise producing reactors and equipment for the nuclear industry. "And so, all over the world, the creepy and nasty series *Chernobyl* is suddenly shown," wrote journalist Dmitry Steshin in the tabloid *Komsomolskaya Pravda*, "about how wild, confused, and disorderly Russians, with the help of its reactors, created an unprecedented ecological catastrophe in Europe" (Plokhy 2019). The series was blamed for slandering the Soviet liquidators' heroism and the people who had actually granted nuclear energy to the world, as well as for its apocalyptic vision of the consequences of the accident. For some reason, critics wrote, Westerners do not make movies about the Fukushima accident, for which Americans solely were to blame, as it was the US company General Electric that built it (Andreev 2019). Many criticized the series for distortion of what really happened and referred to Robert Peter Gale, the American bone marrow transplant specialist who had been invited to the Soviet Union to perform 19 operations on the people who suffered Chernobyl radiation most, such as firefighters; 11 of the 19 men on which he operated died within one month, and none survived more than a year following the operation (Ingram 2005, 66). However, Gale is an authoritative figure for those who want to criticize the HBO series, as he claims that the radiation contamination was superficial and relatively easily managed by routine procedures. Gale gives a very positive evaluation of the Soviet management of the accident, affirming that the authorities did everything possible to help the victims, agreed to bring all necessary scientists, and did not try to cover up the tragedy as portrayed by HBO (Shellenberger 2019).

As a response to the HBO series and its extreme popularity, at the time of writing this chapter, the Russian State NTV channel was preparing to air its own Chernobyl show that blames the CIA for the meltdown. "There is a theory that the Americans had infiltrated the Chernobyl nuclear power plant, and many historians do not deny that on the day of the explosion an agent of the enemy's intelligence services was present at the station," said the show's director, asserting that the new series "will tell viewers about what really happened back then," promoting a "patriotic" view of the disaster. The series is to follow a CIA agent sent to Chernobyl to gather intelligence on the plant as Soviet agents attempt to counter his efforts (Roth 2019). Like most of the bloggers, politicians, and other actors cited in this chapter, the authors of the series are active advocates of the restoration of the Soviet Union. Blaming the United States for causing the Chernobyl accident and then for slander by constantly revisiting and distorting its impact, they strive to uncover the nefarious plot and reestablish the mourned Soviet Union.

42 *Anastasiya Astapova*

Discussion

The problems with assessing the impact of Chernobyl are, to my mind, perfectly encapsulated by the Soviet joke:

> "How is radiation similar to prostitution?"
> "Neither of them exists in the Soviet Union"

(Bodrunova 2012, 22).

The joke captures three essential peculiarities of the situation: first, the Soviet tradition of denial of inappropriate subjects (whether sex or state failures); second, policies nevertheless changing toward *glasnost* and reflected in the irony of the joke; and third, the invisibility of radiation and its direct effects. All three factors had crucial importance for the development of conspiracy theories around Chernobyl.

This conspiratorial thinking was the first response to the disaster, with the traditional Cold War enemy, Americans, immediately blamed for it. The disaster was too contradictory for the idea imposed by Soviet propaganda about Communist stability, including the safety of the so-called peaceful atom used to produce nuclear energy. Even Gorbachev himself said following the explosion, "After all, the scientists had always assured us, the country's leaders, that the reactor was absolutely safe. Academician Alexandrov said, for example, that an RMBK reactor could be installed even on Red Square, since it was no more dangerous than a samovar" (Plokhii 2018, 121). Needless to say, the general population was more than caught by surprise and could not believe in the failure of the atomic equipment paired with a human mistake. Moreover, the United States was to blame for the following exaggerated rumors about Chernobyl victims and related propaganda, and the border between these accusations and accusations of weaving an actual conspiracy against the USSR was easily transcended.

In contrast to the conspiracy theories about the CIA as the perpetrator of the Chernobyl disaster, narratives blaming the Soviet Union for a deliberate terrorist attack at the power plant arose, most importantly, within the nationalist movements of still-Soviet Ukraine, Belarus, and Lithuania. These rested on accusations of genocide by Russian colonial powers of the non-Russian population of the Soviet Union via radiation exposure and other means (e.g., forcing Belarusian women to have abortions). These conspiracy theories undoubtedly contributed to these countries' national reawakening and independence movements.

In addition, as a follow-up to the conspiracy theories blaming the West for the disaster, narratives developed that the detrimental impact of Chernobyl was purposefully exaggerated for the sake of certain interests. Those accused are Ukrainians and Belarusians (supposedly doing this in order to get foreign aid) as well as the green energy lobby, which was perceived as having implemented its useless energy production models via exaggerating stories about the negative impact of nuclear energy. These conspiracy theories are also closely related to nostalgia about the Soviet republics, formerly united into one country, with the union now betrayed by Ukrainians in particular. All three conspiracy theories presented here

Chernobyl conspiracy theories 43

exemplify how conspiracy narratives "create and reinforce social, political, and scientific alliances, and also enact coherent and powerful epistemologies through which scientific data and evidence are filtered" (Rahder 2015, 301).

It would be a mistake, however, to assume that Chernobyl conspiracy theories are unique; quite the opposite: they take familiar shapes and draw from the repertoires of other conspiracy theories. It is especially with the progressive opening of the borders that the ideas of UFO invasion, explanations based on New Age beliefs, and common conspiracy theory tropes were appropriated. Tropes relating to CIA sabotage, the Soviet intrusion, and the self-serving eco-lobby are among the most popular and are found in major conspiracy theories, such as the "faked" Moon landing, climate change denial, Greta Thunberg hoaxes, John F. Kennedy's assassination, 9/11 conspiracy theories, and even anti-vaccination movements.

The enrichment of the narratives about Chernobyl is still continuing, as tourism, popular culture, and media and internet culture have pitched into what has already been a very complex and subjective debate. Over 30 years after the accident, unforgettable experience tours, Instagrammable photos of the zone, and YouTube videos from dark tourism channels contribute to further mythologization of the Chernobyl accident. One of dozens of tourist companies in Ukraine, Gamma Travel, offers tours to the Chernobyl exclusion zone by vehicles "which have AC, Wi-Fi on board, so you are always safe and in touch with the world even in the middle of nowhere." It promises a visit to the top-secret military complex, meeting the local "babushkas" (elderly female resettlers in the exclusion zone) and trying "Chernobeer" at the local café (Gamma Travel, n.d.). The popularity of the HBO miniseries has brought thousands of tourists to the Lithuanian capital, Vilnius, where some scenes were shot, and Chernobyl tours are now provided. In a similar vein, online games ("Shadow of Chernobyl," "Clear Sky," "Call of Pripiat," "Stalker"), Chernobyl escape rooms, and Chernobyl tours in nearby Belarus warmed up interest for romantics of the place where time stopped (Bodrunova 2012, 23). In these mythologized representations, fantasies and the realities of the accident are hard to separate, as it is hard to separate speculation from truth in the conspiracy theories about Chernobyl.

Chernobyl conspiracy theories went global, and they are no longer owned only by the territories that suffered from the disaster. For instance, the conspiracy theory blaming the CIA for sabotage is not only a part of the Soviet or post-Soviet repertoire. The idea sells well on TV shows popular with Americans too. A 42-minute-long program, *Mysteries of the Abandoned: Chernobyl*, aired on the US-based Science Channel, follows Philip Grossman, an American civil engineer and self-described obsessive about the Chernobyl disaster, as he travels in the exclusion zone. His mission on the trip is to find clues about the true reasons for the accident. In the course of the trip, Grossman notes that the plant has remarkably close physical proximity to a massive Duga anti-missile radar installation. He also visits a nearby manufacturing plant built over a closed-off basement laboratory stocked with chemicals used in the production of nuclear materials. Grossman then connects these dots: Duga radar, production site for nuclear materials, and a massive nuclear power plant that could generate both civilian power and weapons-grade plutonium. He suggests that this complex was a covert weapons

44 *Anastasiya Astapova*

installation ready for activation in the event that the Cold War turned hot. That, he further suggests, might have become the reason for the CIA to sabotage the plant—knowing it had military capability and therefore wanting to neutralize it. The commentators on the show then took the secret conspiracy theory to its limit by noting that Grossman had been granted unmonitored access to this site because he made it known to Russian authorities that he was investigating a potential CIA connection (Hinckley 2017). Chernobyl conspiracy theories thus now proliferate and matter far beyond the Soviet Union.

It is often difficult to decide whom to blame for human disasters: employees managing the plants at the time of an accident's occurrence; people managing accident sites, corporations, or factories as whole entities; construction designers or workers; the state that allowed for their construction; or people who, in the Chernobyl case, believed in the peaceful atom and never questioned the Soviet government's fascination with it (Ingram 2005, viii). Little wonder then that the popular imagination thus comprehends the reasons for the tragedy in a variety of ways based on traditional beliefs, propaganda, novel ideas coming from the West, and a multiplicity of other factors. Chernobyl conspiracy theories have been nurtured by global tropes and have also fed global narratives; however, there is a twist to all three conspiracy theories presented here, which makes them different from many other global plots. What makes Chernobyl conspiracy theories special is their connection to the dissolution of the Soviet Union, which was truly striking for the almost 300 million people who experienced it, whether they were happy about it or not. It is not surprising that Chernobyl is often compared to no less traumatic events from Soviet and post-Soviet history—World War II or the current war in Eastern Ukraine are no less ideologically divisive for post-Soviet populations than Chernobyl. Either Soviet nostalgia or the condemnation of everything Soviet is at the core of these divisions, depending on whether they blame the Americans for the explosion and the following collapse of the Soviet Union, Russians for the deliberate genocide of Belarusians and Ukrainians, or both Westerners and disloyal Ukrainians and Belarusians for contributing to the mystification and bluff around Chernobyl. Stemming from Cold War information warfare, they remain tools for current political and ideological struggles and are no less topical today than they were directly after the accident.

Acknowledgments

This work was supported by personal research funding from the Estonian Research Council PSG48 "Performative Negotiations of Belonging in Contemporary Estonia" (1.01.2018 – 31.12.2021).

Bibliography

7 Days. 1986. "An Assumed Drawing of Chernobyl Sabotage Plan." *7 Days* 17: 12.
Agranovsky. 2013. "Esche Raz o Diversii Na Chernobylskoi AS" [Once Again about the Sabotage at Chernobyl Power Plant]. *Livejournal*, April 27, 2013. https://agranovsky. livejournal.com/814152.html.

Chernobyl conspiracy theories   45

Alexievich, Svetlana. 2005. *Voices from Chernobyl: The Oral History of a Nuclear Disaster*. New York: Picador.

———. 2016. *Chernobyl Prayer. A Chronicle of the Future*. London: Penguin Books.

Andreev, Sergei. 2019. "Chuzhoe Voroshat, a Svoe Ne Pomniat. Zachem Amerikantsy Sniali 'Chernobyl'" [The Touch That Does Not Belong to Them, and They Do Not Want to Remember Their Own One. Why Americans Made the Movie "Chernobyl"]. *Life.ru*. https://life.ru/t/наука/1219833/chuzhoie_voroshat_a_svoio_nie_pomniat_zachiem_amierikantsy_sniali_chiernobyl.

Antoniuk, Evgeny. 2019. "Diversanty, NLO i Zemletriasenie. Alternativnye Versii Avarii v Chernobyle" [Saboteurs, UFO, and Earthquake. The Alternative Versions of an Accident in Chernobyl]. *Life.ru*. https://life.ru/t/чернобыль/1237313/diviersanty_nlo_i_ziemlietriasieniie_altiernativnyie_viersii_avarii_v_chiernobylie.

Astapova, Anastasiya. 2020. "Word of Mouth: Rumours, Urban Legends, and Other Genres Transmitting Conspiracy Theories Verbally." In *Routledge Handbook of Conspiracy Theories*, edited by Michael Butler and Peter Knight. London: Routledge (in print).

Bay, Ingrid A., and Deborah H. Oughton. 2005. "Social and Economic Effects." In *Chernobyl. Catastrophe and Consequences*, edited by Jim Smith and Nicholas A. Beresford, 239–66. Berlin: Springer-Verlag.

Bodrunova, Svetlana. 2012. "Chernobyl in the Eyes: Mythology as a Basis of Individual Memories and Social Imaginaries of a 'Chernobyl Child'." *Anthropology of East Europe Review* 30 (1): 13–24.

Brown, Kate. 2019. *Chernobyl: Manual for Survival*. New York: W. W. Norton & Company.

Cheney, Glenn Alan. 2010. "Radiation Exposure and Negative Health Outcomes Were Underreported and Underestimated." In *Perspectives on Modern World History. Chernobyl*, edited by David Elton Nelson, 70–81. Farmington Hills, MI: Greenhaven Press.

Conroy, Coleen. 2018. "These Conspiracy Theories Suggest Something Even More Sinister Happened At Chernobyl." *Ranker*. www.ranker.com/list/chernobyl-conspiracy-theories/colleen-conroy.

Deer, Rein F. 2014. "Was Chernobyl a Cunning KGB Conspiracy?" *Politico.eu* www.politico.eu/article/was-chernobyl-a-cunning-kgb-conspiracy/.

Douglas, Karen M, and Robbie M Sutton. 2015. "Climate Change: Why the Conspiracy Theories Are Dangerous." *Bulletin of the Atomic Scientists* 71 (2): 98–106.

Fialkova, Larisa. 2001. "Chornobyl's Folklore: Vernacular Commentary on Nuclear Disaster." *Journal of Folklore Research* 38 (3): 181–204.

Flibusta. 2013. "Alla Iaroshinskaia." http://flibusta.site/a/115230/v.

Gamma Travel. n.d. "The Ultimate Trips to Chernobyl and Pripiat." https://gamma-travel.com.

Hinckley, David. 2017. "New Science Channel Doc: Did the CIA Blow Up Chernobyl?" *Huffpost*. www.huffpost.com/entry/new-science-channel-doc-did-the-cia-blow-up-chernobyl_b_59a6c24ae4b0d81379a81c77.

Iarmolenko, Samuil. 2000. "Liudei Brosili Varitsia v Kotle Panicheskih Sluhov" [People Were Thrown to be Cooked in the Pot of Panic Rumors]. *Index* 12. www.index.org.ru/journal/12/yarmon.html.

Iaroshkin, Victor. 2019. "Deversiia Na Chernobylskoi AS" [Sabotage at Chernobyl Nuclear Power Station]. *Blogspot,* April 26, 2019. http://velemudr.blogspot.com/2019/04/.

Ingram, W. Scott. 2005. *The Chernobyl Nuclear Disaster*. New York: Facts On File.

Krishtopa, Oleg. 2011. *Chernobyl: Zona Otchuzhdeniia* [Chernobyl: An Exclusion Zone]. Kharkov: Klub semeinogo dosuga.

Lenta.ru. 2011. "Breivik Pohvalil Ukrainskih Natsionalistov Za Podryv Chernobylia" [Breivik Praised Ukrainian Nationalists for Blowing Up Chernobyl]. *Lenta.Ru*. https://

46 *Anastasiya Astapova*

lenta.ru/news/2011/07/26/chernobyl/ (I deliberately choose to cite secondary source, not Breivik's manifesto).

Marples, David. R. 1990. "Revelations of a Chernobyl Insider. David Marples Interviews Yuri Risovanny." *The Bulletin of the Atomic Scientists* (December): 16–21.

———. 2003. "History and Politics in Post-Soviet Belarus: The Foundations." In *Contemporary Belarus: Between Democracy and Dictatorship*, edited by Elena Korosteleva, Colin W. Lawson, and Rosalind Marsh, 21–36. London: Routledge Curzon.

———. 2018. "Decommunization, Memory Laws, and 'Builders of Ukraine in the 20th Century'." *Acta Slavica Iaponica* 39: 1–22.

Medvedev, Sergei. 2015. "Golos Boli" [The Voice of Pain]. *Radio Svoboda*. www.svoboda.org/a/27307844.html.

Menzel, Birgit. 2013. "The Occult Underground of Late Soviet Russia." *ARIES* 13: 269–88.

Mould, Richard Francis. 2000. *Chernobyl Record: The Definitive History of the Chernobyl Catastrophe*. Bristol: CRC Press.

Nikitchuk, Ivan. 2012. "Diversiia Na Chernobylskoi AS." *YouTube*. www.youtube.com/watch?v=vpCw3K04aoY.

Pazniak, Zianon. 2002. *Novae Stahoddze [New Age]*. Vilnius, Warsaw: Tavarystva belaruskaj kultury u Letuve, Belaruskija Vedamas'ci.

Plokhy, Serhii. 2006. *The Origins of the Slavic Nations. Premodern Identities in Russia, Ukraine and Belarus*. New York: Cambridge University Press.

———. 2018. *Chernobyl: The History of a Nuclear Catastrophe*. New York: Basic Books.

———. 2019. "Spinning Conspiracy Theories Won't Help Us Prevent Another Chernobyl." *The Guardian*. www.theguardian.com/commentisfree/2019/aug/18/spinning-conspiracy-theories-will-not-help-us-prevent-another-chernobyl-nuclear-disaster.

Podsvirov, Valery. 2011. "Chernobyl: Sabotazh Veka" [Chernobyl – The Sabotage of the Century]. *Novyi Peterburg* 18 (485).

Poluyan, Pavel. 2016. "Chernobylskaia Diversiia" [Chernobyl Sabotage]. *Zavtra*. October 17, 2016. http://zavtra.ru/blogs/chernobil_skaya_diversiya.

Pyhalov, Igor. 2016. "Chernobylskaia Katastrofa Kak Krupneishaia Mistifikatsiia Nashego Vremeni." *Livejournal*. Pyhalov. https://pyhalov.livejournal.com/426774.html.

Rahder, Micha. 2015. "But Is It a Basin? Science, Controversy, and Conspiracy in the Fight for Mirador, Guatemala." *Science as Culture* 24 (3): 299–324.

Resnicoff, Mark. 2010. "A Liquidator's Experience at Chernobyl." In *Perspectives on Modern World History. Chernobyl*, edited by David Elton Nelson, 161–71. Farmington Hills, MI: Greenhaven Press.

Romanchuk, Iaroslav. 2006. "Chernobyl: Samyi Bolshoi Blef XX Veka" [Chernobyl: The Greatest Hoax of the 20th Century]. *Nauchno-Issledovatelskii Tsentr Mizesa*. http://liberty-belarus.info/ekonomika-belarusi/sotsialnaya-politika/item/1973-chernobyl-samyj-bolshoj-blef-xxi-veka.

Roth, Andrew. 2019. "Russian TV to Air Its Own Patriotic Retelling of Chernobyl Story." *The Guardian*. www.theguardian.com/world/2019/jun/07/chernobyl-hbo-russian-tv-remake.

Shellenberger, Michael. 2019. "Top UCLA Doctor Denounces HBO's 'Chernobyl' as Wrong and 'Dangerous.'" *Forbes*. www.forbes.com/sites/michaelshellenberger/2019/06/11/top-ucla-doctor-denounces-depiction-of-radiation-in-hbos-chernobyl-as-wrong-and-dangerous/#29ce500c1e07.

Shkoda, Vadim (comp. ed.). 1988. *Chernobyl: Dni Ispytanii* [Chernobyl: The Days of Challenge]. Kyiv: Radianskii pismennik.

Sivov, Alexandr. 2016. "Chernobylskaia Katastrofa – Krupneishaia Mistifikatsiia 20 Veka." *APN Severo-Zapad*. www.apn-spb.ru/opinions/article23672.htm.

Starovoitova, Yelena. 2001. "Chernobyl After 15 Years: More and More Questions." *The Current Digest of the Post-Soviet Press* 53: 9–11.

Sulkin, Oleg. 2015. "Kak 'Russkii Diatel' Dostuchalsia Do Sandensa" [How 'The Russian Woodpecker' Reached Sandens]. *Golos Ameriki.* www.golos-ameriki.ru/a/oleg-sulkin-ukrainian-moviemakers/2653986.html.

Sveriges Radio. 2011. "25 Years after Chernobyl, How Sweden Found Out." https://sverigesradio.se/sida/artikel.aspx?programid=2054&artikel=4468603.

Tuckett, Kate. 1999. "Chernobyl: An Accident or a Conspiracy?" In *Conspiracy Theories*. Moscow: Fair Press. www.e-reading.club/chapter.php/55643/87/Takett_-_Teoriya_zagovora__taiiny_i_sensacii.html.

UNSCEAR. 2012. "The Chernobyl Accident: UNSCEAR's Assessments of the Radiation Effects." *UNSCEAR.* 2012. www.unscear.org/unscear/en/chernobyl.html.

Weeks, Stephen. 2010. "The Chernobyl Disaster Was the Fatal Blow to the USSR." In *Perspectives on Modern World History. Chernobyl*, edited by David Elton Nelson, 113–18. Farmington Hills, MI: Greenhaven Press.

Whitington, Luther. 1986. "Chernobyl Reactor Still Burning." *United Press International.* www.upi.com/Archives/1986/04/29/Chernobyl-reactorstill-%0Aburning/9981572611428.

2 Stalinist conspiracy theories in France and Italy

The limits of postwar Communist conspiracy culture

Pascal Girard

One of the most significant conspiracy theories during the early Cold War in the West was undoubtedly the Red Scare—the fear that Communists secretly infiltrated state institutions, society, and culture, thereby threatening the cohesion and security of democratic states. In the United States, there is a wide agreement that such conspiracy theories were omnipresent in US politics (Heale 1998; Michels 2017), society (Jenkins 1999; Brennan 2008), and culture (Barson and Heller 2001; Doherty 2003; Alwood 2007) in the postwar years. However, extending McCarthyism to Western Europe can be misleading. While anti-Communist sentiments were widespread and conspiracy theories invoking the Red Scare existed, social and political contexts in other countries, notably France and Italy, profoundly differed from those of the United States. French and Italian Communists enjoyed relatively great popularity and established themselves as significant parties on the political scene. Communists in these countries had noteworthy impact on the public sphere. Under the influence and pressure of the Communist Party of the Soviet Union, they were the most active promoters of Soviet-originated conspiracy theories. These conspiracy theories targeted the right wing and, later and more broadly, governments, and they were generally much more widely present in the media of the early Cold War years than any other conspiracy theory associated with an alleged Red Scare.

The conspiracy theories circulated by the French and Italian Communist Parties served to discredit political rivals and form political alliances. But these conspiracy theories, which originated in the Soviet Union, were also pivotal features of a political and cultural transformation affecting internal dynamics within Communist parties. Yet, the presence of conspiracy theories in postwar French and Italian media still does not explain how influential these conspiracy theories were and to what extent and how they could affect domestic politics in these two countries. Answering these questions requires first an analysis of how the Soviet culture of conspiracy was transferred and then an assessment of its function in the given domestic political contexts.

The Soviet culture of conspiracy

Conspiracy had always occupied a prominent place in Soviet political culture. Yet, before the advent of the Soviet Union, tsarist Russia was already a fertile ground for conspiracy theories. *The Protocols of the Elders of Zion* was forged

Stalinist conspiracy theories   49

in 1903 by fanatic nationalist Russians and then circulated within their networks before spreading to the rest of Europe (Cohn 1967). During the Russian Civil War, the Judeo-Bolshevik conspiracy theory was endorsed by the White Russian Army officers who supported the publication and dissemination of *The Protocols* and other fabricated reports (Budnitskii 2012, 187–92). This conspiracy theory claimed Jews were responsible for the war, the fall of the tsar, and the revolution and led to antisemitic atrocities (Gerwarth 2016, 88–89).

With the victory of the Soviets, specific Soviet conspiracy theories emerged. Before the 1917 Revolution, Bolsheviks considered conspiracy a legitimate means to seize power in the context of tsarist repression. After the successful Bolshevik coup d'état, the newly established Soviet regime developed a new discourse about conspiracies, henceforth seen as dangerous political agencies of counter-revolutionary forces. Both the denunciation of conspiracies and the constitution of conspiracy theories served as justification for the repression of political opponents of the newly established regime. Created in December 1917, the Cheka (the secret police) was given responsibility for tracking down the "conspirators," and show trials of alleged conspirators were organized as early as 1921–22 (Leggett 1981, 18, 30–31, 207, 278–92).

During the 1930s, conspiracy theories acquired a new dimension. They became increasingly more central in the political discourse of Stalin's regime (Werth and Moullec 1994, 470–71, 567), which spread the fear of a conspiracy of enemies of the people within the whole Soviet bureaucracy and population (Rittersporn 1993, 99–115, 2014, 15–84). Successive conspiracist narratives were developed to support the repression: the "Trotskyist left" and the "rightist deviation" were the primary targets (Conquest 1989, 48–68, 77–103). Repression culminated in the Great Purge of 1936–38 that helped to eliminate political adversaries through the Moscow show trials and mass repression with a series of arrests and killings. Revisionist historians challenging the totalitarian theoretical model argue that centralization should not be exaggerated. For example, according to this perspective, local show trials are considered to be the result of the population's discontent with party officials, deviating from the Soviet conspiracist narrative (Fitzpatrick 1993). In the case of rural show trials, however, archival materials suggest that these were set up based on directives and even Stalin's personal instructions (Ellman 2001; Werth 2005). In fact, as it was used as a justification for the Great Purge, the official conspiracy theory expanded at a fast pace. It included "traditional" political opponents as well as "spies" and "wreckers" acting in the interests of Western powers but also broad social categories and various ethnic minorities (Werth 2003, 216–39).

The conspiracy theories born during the Stalinist repression had several functions. They served to control the whole of society and to legitimate state violence (Getty and Naumov 1999, 17–21). They were also an educational means to build a *homo sovieticus*, one of whose crucial qualities was the capacity to detect internal enemies (Getty 1985, 113). A functionalist view, however, can hardly give justice to the complex psychological dynamics conspiracy theories set into motion: they were not fully controlled and easily fueled paranoia at the expense of one's own

50   *Pascal Girard*

rational interests. Stalin himself seemed to be convinced that foreign enemy powers had deeply infiltrated his regime (Whitewood 2015, 201–86; Harris 2016). Taking seriously the alarming reports of the political police, he organized staged trials that undermined Soviet economic and political capacities. In the factories, for instance, the campaign against the Trotskyist conspiracy resulted in never-ending denunciations and arrests (Goldman 2007, 80–92, 204–47) that disorganized industrial production (Goldman 2011, 130–35). In other words, Soviet conspiracy theories were far from being versatile tools because they were at the same time beliefs that shaped political action, sometime to the detriment of the regime itself.

Exporting Stalinism and Stalinist conspiracy theories

Ever since the Comintern was established in 1919, Communist parties were expected to make themselves subordinate to the Soviet Communist Party. Comintern became a main vehicle by which the Soviet culture of conspiracy was mediated. The struggle with all the other political forces during the "Third Period" (McDermott and Agnew 1996, 81–98) created a sense of isolation and a siege mentality within Western Communist parties. The growing paranoia and obsession with internal enemies were at the core of the Bolshevik model that they adopted via their affiliation to the Third International. The vast and protean Trotskyist world plot threatening the Soviet Union and Communism provided a ready-made conspiracy theory that conditioned practices of political vigilance and Soviet-inspired internal purges.

In France, with the Stalinization of the party that started at the end of the 1920s, biographies were investigated as part of internal inquiries, denunciations were frequent, and many members were expelled from the Communist Party. In the 1930s, successive blacklists of "crooks, traitors, and Trotskyists" were kept, serving to purge the party at any given moment, to prevent any infiltration of police agents or supposed Trotskyist plotters and also to provide political education to party members (Boulouque and Liaigre 2008, 45–130). These blacklists were the results of a voluntarist political cultural transfer from the Soviet Union to the Communist parties of Europe. This transfer was a top-down and authoritarian process that often provoked grassroots leftist political culture and contributed to a decrease in the number of party members. It was carried out through the instructions of Comintern representatives such as Eugen Fried (Kriegel and Courtois 1997) and the translation of Soviet documents, such as the ones sent to French and British Communist federations (the regional organizations of the party) in 1936–37, warning of the Trotskyist conspiracy (Chase 2001, 158–61, 201–3). The Soviet instructions were spread through direct guidance or regular printed bulletins to the cadres of the party, who implemented the Soviet rules to establish control, educate members, and protect them from enemies.

The political role that conspiracy theories played in French politics, however, changed over time. At first, it was one of the factors that increased the isolation of Communists from other political forces. After 1936, the Comintern's struggle against the world Fascist conspiracy became a cornerstone of Popular Front tactics that managed to integrate Communist parties to the domestic democratic political life. World War II and the German occupation brought yet another shift. Adopting first a wait-and-see policy, the Communist Party went underground and then launched an armed struggle after the German invasion of the Soviet Union. In the fall of 1941, a small group of young Communists established an armed organization (Berlière and Liaigre 2004) to fight against the French police, German troops, and their collaborators. In this context, vigilance was crucial to prevent infiltration by the police and led to executions of former members who had collaborated with the French State and German authorities (Berlière and Liaigre 2007, 53–146). The climate of paranoia within the small clandestine organization was motivated by real threats and was a key for survival.

In Fascist Italy, the situation was different, because the political repression forced the Communist Party, outlawed since 1926, to remain underground until the liberation of the country. There was a clandestine organization, but the leading members of the party were mostly in exile. The secretary of the Communist Party, Palmiro Togliatti, lived for years in the Soviet Union. While other high-ranked Italian Communists were purged in Moscow, Togliatti remained the undisputed leader of his party and was a prominent member of the Comintern as well. It was mainly in the Soviet Union that Togliatti gained his authority over the party and received his Stalinist political education, which he would then try to propagate within the ranks of the party after his return to Italy in 1943 (Agosti 2008, 41–118).

Italy: profiting from the Fascist revival

After World War II, the French and Italian Communist Parties faced similar prospects (Lazar 1992). They were the most prominent political movements in their respective national elections, guided by charismatic leaders trusted by Moscow (to the extent that two new cities were named Thorez and Togliatti) and glorified by their contribution to the Resistance. As a result, their expectations of seizing power were great.

In Italy, after the *ventennio*, the two decades of the Fascist regime that jailed or forced Italian Communists underground or into exile, they set out to rebuild the party according to the Stalinist model. Similarly to France, internal "revolutionary vigilance" and the fear of infiltration of the "enemy" were crucial[1] and resulted in blacklists of spies and traitors expelled from the party.[2] This vigilance extended to the danger of the renewal of Fascism during the immediate postwar years. Indeed, very small groups of young neo-Fascists were formed and engaged in subversion, committing a handful of attacks against Communist buildings. In June 1946, riots provoked by monarchists in Naples led to 15 deaths and tens of injured among protesters and forces of order. Six months later, the Movimento Sociale Italiano (MSI, the Social Italian Movement), a legal neo-Fascist political party, was born and became a stronghold for neo-Fascist activists. This context enabled the Italian Communist Party to build and spread a vast conspiracy theory (Girard 2012a, 215–24).

52 *Pascal Girard*

Driven by the experience of clandestinity and concerns about monarchist and neo-Fascist threats, the Italian Communists organized a political information service based on the reports of the federations.[3] In fact, the peril was rather limited and under governmental control. Among the monarchists and in the military, illegal dissent in the republic was scarce. The neo-Fascists were attempting terrorist attacks, but they were rather desperate and armless. In Rome, they were in great need of even basic supplies (Carioti 2008, 38), and in Milan, they had to hide because of the reprisals of armed Communist groups (Rao 2008, 31–33). In October 1946, a military and monarchist putsch was revealed in the press, but it later proved to be a fake. Worried about the political use that the Communist Party made of this scare, the Italian government set up close surveillance of potential plotters and repressed neo-Fascist agencies.

The exaggeration of the threat, as well as the political use of a far-right conspiracy, was evident. The leaders of the party who publicly denounced the neo-Fascist and monarchist plot were perfectly aware of the innocuous nature of the threat.[4] But in Milan the party printed posters denouncing neo-Fascist agencies with accusations of starting a civil war, on which a space was left blank to write the name of the place where the conspirators were allegedly meeting. In several cities, zealous Communists even staged attacks independent of the direction of the party to give credence to the existence of a neo-Fascist peril (Girard 2012a, 225–52).

Yet, this manufactured conspiracy was apparently less useful than in France. The union against the perceived danger of monarchism and neo-Fascism paved the way for a closer union with the Socialists of the Partito Socialista Italiano (Italian Socialist Party); even if it already had close ties with the Communist Party, it was suspected to be tempted by a collaboration with the Italian government. As a result, the common struggle against the reactionary forces was expected by the Communists to become the basis of an alliance. It might have also been a way to destroy neo-Fascism and enroll isolated neo-Fascists (Dé Medici 1986, 42–47). I consider an alternative explanation, however, also convincing: it was a counterfire to the wave of violence culminating in 1946 and committed by the minority of Communist activists still hoping for a future revolution. While the party was actively fighting internally against the minority of Communist activists, its press publicly claimed that the attacks and assassinations were in fact the work of neo-Fascists aiming at disrupting the party and subverting the young Italian republic (Girard 2012a, 252–57). In the end, alleged conspiracies were used both as a tool to unveil a supposed danger and to hide an uncomfortable truth.

France: magnifying reactionary danger

The French Communist Party, as Philippe Buton has shown, tried to take power through a variety of successive strategies that failed one after another. First, it tried to launch and lead an insurrection of the Resistance, but the country had been liberated by the Allies, leading to the reestablishment of legal French authorities. Then, from the fall of 1944, the Communist Party created a patriotic militia to put pressure on the government. At the same time, it tried to create an exclusive

Stalinist conspiracy theories 53

alliance with Socialists in order to form a government in which they would be eventually diluted (Buton 1993). To achieve these two goals, the French Communist Party disseminated an ever-evolving and growing conspiracy theory. During the months following the liberation of Paris, it intensively denounced agents of the "Fifth Column," in particular the collaborators and German agents remaining on liberated territory or who had come back though infiltration. These agents were alleged to commit sabotage and murder and carry out acts of subversion to undermine France's war effort. Their action was invoked to explain deadly incidents such as the accidental explosions of badly maintained explosives depots. But the action of the "Fifth Column" was also used as an explanation for more petty misadventures, such as the theft of the car of a party cadre or the breakdown of a microphone during a public meeting. In reality, these agents existed, but as accessible documents suggest, they were quite few and very inefficient (Girard 2007a, 66–77, 2012a, 84–115).

For the Communist Party and its satellite organizations, maintaining an atmosphere of constant danger justified the existence and arming of the Communist Patriotic Militias. Posters, newspaper articles, and parliamentary speeches claimed that such paramilitary troops were necessary because the government's regular forces were incapable of handling the threat. Although Communist propaganda managed to generate a kind of psychosis near the front line, legal authorities dissolved the Communist Patriotic Militias in January 1945. But this dissolution did not stop the French Communist Party from voicing the danger of the "Fifth Column."[5] From then on, German agents were simply replaced in Communist propaganda with more traditional enemies, such as corporate trusts, right-wing political forces, and capitalist foreign powers.

As the issue of supplies was henceforth by far the main preoccupation of the population (Rioux 1980, 39–47), Communist leaders accused the reactionary trusts of being responsible for food shortages.[6] Communist organizations implemented a major propaganda campaign, claiming that the trusts, accused of having collaborated with the German occupiers, remained powerful because of an insufficient purge, allowing them to sabotage the economic recovery (Girard 2012a, 116–17, 122–28).

Luckily, in the first months of 1947, the hypothetical danger of the reaction became more credible. General de Gaulle created the Rassemblement du Peuple Français (RPF, the Rally of the French People), a party supporting the change of the Constitution toward a stronger executive power. This aim branded the RPF an antidemocratic and reactionary movement preparing a coup d'état. At the same time, the Ministry of the Interior unveiled the agencies of right-wing activists. For the French Communist Party, these events were a godsend, as they gave substance to the alleged dangers of reactionary forces and Fascism.[7] The propaganda campaign promoting the idea of this reactionary conspiracy intensified through meetings, the press, and posters (Buton and Gervereau 1989, 109). The hope was to discredit the right-wing parties and to scare the leaders of the Socialist Party in order to convince them to unite with the French Communist Party during elections to form a Socialist-Communist government (Girard 2007b, 139–43).

54 *Pascal Girard*

One good example of how Communist parties used conspiracy theories for political purposes was the "Plan Bleu" affair. The "Plan Bleu" (named for the folder in which it was found) was the plan for an armed coup d'état organized by a small network of far-right activists (supposedly linked to the Gaullists), revealed by the Socialist minister of the interior in June 1947, when the plotters had already been arrested. After the discovery of the plot, the Communist press did its best to involve the Gaullists in order to discredit the newly formed RPF, whose leader, General De Gaulle, might have been able to rally anti-Communists. The few members of the plot received light sentences in 1950, commensurate with the ridiculously amateurish conspiracy. In fact, the publicity given by the minister of the interior to this conspiracy was out of proportion with its real significance. Some of the Gaullist militaries suspected of being the leaders of this plot were completely innocent. The minister, as a Socialist and member of the government, was under pressure from the long-lasting Communist campaign about the threat of a right-wing coup, often spread by the Socialist press. Study of the judicial proceedings clearly shows that they were often based on allegations from Communist publications, despite the fact that they were unverified and fanciful (Girard 2012a, 173–89).

Finally, from 1944 to 1947, the successive and ever-growing conspiracy theories propagated by the French and Italian Communist Parties were used in a kind of "salami tactics." The aim was to disrupt anti-Communist political forces to create the conditions for a political alliance with the Socialists to form a government that the Communists could eventually control. The Communists, however, would soon find themselves to be cut off from the Socialists. Thus, their conspiracy theories transformed into a nugatory, if not detrimental, political lever.

The import of the Soviet grand conspiracy theory

During the Sklarska-Poreba meeting of September 1947, during which the Cominform was created, the leaders of the French and Italian Communist Parties received an unpleasant surprise. Satisfied with their electoral results, and still optimistic about the prospect of seizing power, Thorez and Togliatti were taken aback by the violence of the critique expressed by the Yugoslav delegates, on behalf of the Soviets. They were accused of not acknowledging the division of the world into two antagonist blocks (exposed a year before by Zhdanov) and to have been too lenient with their enemies. They were urged to endorse a more confrontational vision of domestic and international politics and to adopt a more aggressive strategy (Fondazione Giangiacomo Feltrinelli 1994). Drawing from the consequences of the Zhdanov doctrine, these parties intensified their denunciation of the alleged anti-Communist conspiracy that, from the fall of 1947, developed to the huge proportions of a "grand conspiracy" (Barkun 2003).

In France, the turn was clear, and these tactics were quickly adopted at the highest level of the Communist Party, immediately emphasizing the idea of governmental conspiracy.[8] The opening speech of Thorez at the Central Committee meeting in late November 1947 set the tone: the conspiracy was an international conspiracy against the Soviet Union, led by the United States and implemented in France by all the non-Communist political forces, including the Socialist Party. As the entire political spectrum was composed of traitors serving a hostile foreign power, the Communists had to fight alone for the preservation of the independence of the country. In this view, American domination was creeping across France thanks to Marshall Plan aid; military material deliveries; and even movies, literature, and beverages accused of purposely "poisoning" the minds and bodies of the population (Thorez 1950; see Girard 2012a, 196–204).

In Italy also, the same kind of conspiracy theory disseminated by the Italian Communist Party expanded to greater proportions, targeting both the MSI and other political movements that were part of the government coalition. This so-called governmental conspiracy was accused of supporting neo-Fascist terrorism as stated by the agenda of the Central Committee of November 1947[9] and to be part of the wider conspiracy led by the United States against Communist parties all over the world (Girard 2012a, 258–74). This international conspiracist vision of domestic politics was supported by propaganda, such as a poster of 1948 depicting the ministers of the Italian government as puppets in the hand of a gigantic and monstrous President Truman (Ventrone 2005, 210–11). The perception of the intentional corruption of minds through American books and movies was very similar to that of the French Communists (Gundle 2000, 49).

In the end, the Communist conspiracy theory reflected and strengthened the deep change of political strategy. Initially limited and broadly targeting the right wing, it was purpose made to isolate anti-Communists and create an alliance with the left wing frightened by the reactionary or Fascist threat. But from the fall of 1947 onward, the conspiracy theory underwent a never-ending expansion, encompassing all political adversaries (considered enemies), themselves the minions of the United States. This grand conspiracy theory reflected Soviet Cold War rhetoric, but it lost on the way its ability and interest as a political tool. Aiming at drawing a clear divide between good and evil, it worsened the gap between Communists and non-Communists. It even created a vicious circle: the conspiracy theory fueled the violence of Communist riots of 1947–48 against supposed plotters (the government), while the harsh repression seemed to confirm the involvement of the government in the American conspiracy against Communism.

The hunt for Trotskyists: a Stalinist obsession

The shift to the "governmental conspiracy theory" underlines the fact that conspiracy theory was not only a "cynical" tool with a political function; it was also a part of Soviet ideology and political culture. Further, conspiracy theories were part of the political education provided by Moscow to party leaders and then by the party to the cadres from the federal to the cell level. This political education was crucial because it conditioned obedience to directives from the Cominform and the top of the party. When lacking directives, leaders as well as grassroots members could rely on this political education as a guide to action.

56 *Pascal Girard*

One channel of transmission of this education within domestic parties were the sessions of the Communist Party schools. Documents found in the archives may give us precious indications about the content of that teaching. First, the schools' courses clearly echoed directions from Moscow. For example, a general course for French local cadres was the pure transfer of the resolution of the political bureau, which itself translated the directions of Zhdanov's speech during the Sklarska-Poreba meeting.[10] Second, the vision of the world promoted by these courses was deeply Manichean and manifested in the frequent use of the word "enemy." The dissemination of this notion could be followed in the debates and motions of the Italian Central Committee meeting of November 1947. Third, the history of the Soviet Communist Party was a significant part of the curriculum, a fact that was very noticeable in the longer teaching programs of the most active party schools held in 1945–47.[11] The *History of the Communist (Bolshevik) Party of the Soviet Union* (1938) was a cornerstone of the curriculum and mediated a profoundly conspiracist worldview with Trotskyists and rightist deviationists as main actors. A conspiracist vision of politics was further encouraged by Stalin's *Concerning Questions of Leninism* (1939) and such pamphlets of fellow travelers as *La guerre d'Hitler continue* (Hitler's War Still Goes On) or *L'internationale des traîtres* (The International of the Traitors), both published in 1948 by the French Communist publishing house. Even an incredulous French Communist making fun of his comrades' obsession with conspiracy testified that his bedside book was the translation of an essay of 1946, "The Great Conspiracy: The Secret War against Soviet Russia" (Daix 1976, 196).

This belief thrived within the Soviet vision of politics; while being impacted by the political context, it had little autonomy from the diegesis generated by the Soviet regime. In other words, when servilely endorsing the Stalinist conspiracy theory, French and Italian Communists were conforming to the Soviet model rather than answering to a real menace. This was particularly true concerning the anti-Trotskyist conspiracy theory.

The Stalinist obsession with the threat of Trotskyist agents led to the assassination of suspected Trotskyists all around the world, including in France (Broué and Vacheron 1997). The debates of the French Communist Political Bureau from 1945 to 1947 show that vigilance against Trotskyists (dubbed "hitlero-trotskists") was a recurring preoccupation that resulted in instructions for gathering information, expanding surveillance, and writing blacklists. The alarmist tone of the instructions signaled a belligerent attitude that was in sharp contrast to the generally friendly disposition of Trotskyists. The transposed Soviet ideological prism led the French Communist Party to believe that the Trotskyists were collaborating with reactionary forces, the government, and the United States within the framework of the anti-Soviet grand conspiracy.

In Italy, Palmiro Togliatti expressed his own concern about Trotskyist infiltration as early as August 1945 (Aga-Rossi and Zaslavsky 1997, 95). Along with other party leaders, he urged the party to thwart the supposed Trotskyist menace. This resulted in vigorous anti-Trotskyist propaganda and a vast campaign of vigilance and information after the summer of 1946. It was grounded on a

Stalinist conspiracy theories 57

questionnaire sent to all the regional Communist federations of Italy.[12] With rare exceptions, the questionnaire revealed that the Trotskyists were few, weak, and not hostile to the party, sometime even voting for it. These conclusions correspond with what can be learned from Italian police reports about Trotskyist activity.[13] In the province of Brescia, for instance, the questionnaire and police reports concur that there were only a handful of innocuous and unorganized Trotskyists. However, after receiving the answers to the questionnaire, in September 1946, the party leaders promptly sent a letter to the federal cadres of Brescia explaining that—given the internal dysfunctions of the federation—it was impossible that there was no Trotskyist organization at work to explain them. In the final account, the Trotskyist "witch hunt" imported from the Soviet Union was completely at odds with the Western context and proved to be not only pointless but also counterproductive with potential allies.

Expansion and decline of Soviet conspiracy theories

Once the Cominform was established in 1947, the groups of enemies referred to in Soviet and, consequently, Communist conspiracy narratives further multiplied because of the geopolitical changes provoked by the decisions of Stalin. In 1948, with the break between the Soviet Union and Yugoslavia, a new group of conspirators was added to the anti-Soviet conspiracy theory: the Titoists. Given the proximity of Yugoslavia, Italian Communists were particularly vigilant about keeping Titoism from emerging in their country. As a consequence, they added it to the already mixed blend of harmful ideologies consisting of Fascism, Americanism, and Trotskyism. The political function of anti-Titoism was different to earlier conspiracy narratives: it did not aim to recruit new adherents but to strengthen discipline within the party.

If anti-Titoism was manifestly a Soviet obsession exported to vulnerable Communist parties of the West, evidence suggests that when struggling against conspiracies, the Western Communist parties did not only obey directives, they also appeared to interpret their own political context and cast their political action through the lens of conspiracism. In France, for instance, the arrest of Duclos, the number two of the Communist Party, in May 1952, resulted in an unprecedented campaign of propaganda against the "government conspiracy." The "struggle against the conspiracy" became a recurrent watchword of the party until the end of 1953. In the instructions to the Communist local sections and cells, it basically encompassed all forms of action, from the international Defense of Peace campaign to the agencies (propaganda, strikes, petitions, meetings, etc.) directed against the French government.[14]

Right before Stalin's death in 1953, a particular new burst of Soviet conspiracism set foot in France and Italy: the "Doctors' Plot," a staged conspiracy with a clear antisemitic background (Brent 2004). The quick embrace of this conspiracy theory was particularly striking in France. This prompt acceptance could be linked to the blind devotion of the French Communist Party, but it also found a favorable preexisting ground with the rampant antisemitism in the party

58 *Pascal Girard*

(Recanati 1980, 10–11, 14–15, 25) that echoed the anti-cosmopolitan campaign initiated in 1949 (Azadovskii and Egorov 2002). The French Communist Party did not merely accept and justify Soviet claims and action; it started to take matching measures within organizations of Communist medics[15] (Daix 1976, 329–33). The fact that this vigilance targeted domestic Communist doctors and Jews confirms that conspiracism was particularly embedded in French Communist political culture, all the more since the Italian Party did not implement comparable measures.

However, after 1953, the theme of conspiracy began to significantly decline within Communist discourse. This was the consequence of the end of the Stalinist era and the decrease of geopolitical conflict of the détente process, which resulted in a decrease in domestic political violence and confrontation. The idea of conspiracy was less likely and credible because the governmental enemy was less hostile and active. While still regularly mentioned in propaganda, it disappeared from the debates of the inner circles of the Communist parties: for instance, the word "conspiracy," formerly so frequent, no longer appeared in the records of the meetings of the French secretary and the political bureau after 1954. Records of meetings of the Italian Communist Party leaders clearly show that the word "enemies" was used less and less frequently in the 1950s and was replaced with "adversaries" to refer to other political movements.[16] In 1958, the Italian Communist Party even published a booklet entitled *Dialogues with the Adversaries* to enable contact with other political forces, including neo-Fascists. The word "enemies" remained in the Communist vocabulary, but it was rather associated with a foreign threat.

It was precisely the international menace in Hungary that awoke the sleeping Communist disposition toward conspiratorial thinking. The official Soviet explanation for the Hungarian insurrection of 1956 was that it was not a popular uprising, but a Fascist and clerical conspiracy orchestrated by the United States. The polls made in Italy (Luzzatto 1956, 1019–39) and France (Institut français de l'opinion publique 1957) show that members of both Communist parties plainly endorsed the Soviet conspiracist explanation of the Hungarian rebellion. In Italy, the elite (leaders and intellectuals) of the Italian party were divided between unwillingness to endorse the Soviet narrative and pressure on party members to show their support. But far from the throes of internal conflict, the majority of Italian Communists claimed to believe the conspiracist explanation of the insurrection spread by party propaganda. This episode underlines that, despite the Twentieth Congress of the Soviet Communist Party and the beginning of de-Stalinization, the culture of conspiracy was still embedded in Western Communist parties. These polls also strikingly demonstrate that this unquestioning acceptance of the conspiracy theory conflicted with French and Italian public opinion generally. A large part of the population of both countries (including Socialists) supported the Hungarian revolution against Soviet invasion, citing the lack of freedom of the Communist system, poverty, and food shortages. This underlines a major issue: the growing inadequacy of Soviet conspiracy theories in the face of the mainstream political culture of postwar France and Italy.

Why were conspiracy narratives so useless?

Immediately after World War II, conspiracy theories seemed a relatively effective tool for Communist parties in Western Europe to increase the atmosphere of mistrust in political adversaries and gain political support. By the beginning of the 1950s, however, it became clear that conspiracism had lost momentum and the attempt of Communist parties to spread conspiracist Soviet propaganda proved to be an inefficient strategy. There were several reasons for this.

First, the media landscape had radically changed. Postwar interest in politics had faded: political publications were read less frequently, and the political content of national and local newspapers decreased, while more entertaining and innovative news magazines began to flourish. This was an unfavorable context for Communist publications, which, especially in France (Delporte, Blandin, and Robinet 2016, 152–58), were unable to adapt and spread conspiracy theories outside of party readership. Modern media, such as radio broadcasting, was even more depoliticized than the press but was also under governmental control and largely inaccessible to Communist parties. From the fall of 1947, Communist journalists in France, for instance, who used public radio for pro-Soviet propaganda were fired one after another by the government.[17] In both France and Italy, television was less common than in the United States or even Great Britain, and the control of the state was complete, with little room for political debate—and none for Communist propaganda.

Second, such changes of the media environment coincided with declining activism on the side of party members. After World War II, Communist parties relied heavily on their relatively large and very active membership, who tirelessly distributed posters and flyers, arranged public discussions and conferences, promoted movies and books, held demonstrations, and so on. Even though such propaganda had its limits, and often failed to surpass satellite organizations and the groups of fellow travelers of the party, at least it kept the existing network of sympathizers together. Persistent mobilization of party members, however, reached its peak in 1947–48 and declined thereafter, to the despair of the leaders of both the French and Italian Communist Parties, whose time-consuming task was simply to try to rally their troops. Conspiracy theories lost their mobilizing force even among party members: in France, the rumored assassination attempt of Thorez while traveling to Moscow in 1950, despite the denunciation of a state-sanctioned plot and the call for strikes and demonstrations, did not lead to any noticeable action.

In addition to poor access to new media and waning party activism, the general political culture was changing in ways that created an increasing gap between Communists and non-Communists. Upon the establishment of Cominform, the use of violence and offensive discourse became normalized within the Communist parties. Communists virtually confronted the entire political spectrum from the right to the center-left. Instances of physical and verbal violence in the streets, in factories, and also in parliament (Bouchet 2010); antipatriotic accusations; and Soviet military oppression in Eastern Europe (especially the Prague coup) created a mistrustful political atmosphere, defined by rejection, hatred, and fear (Luzzatto 1956,

60   Pascal Girard

474–75, 479–81) of rival political forces (Girard 2012a, 382–411, 422–61). It also resulted in a legal state repression, often judicially inefficient in both countries, but more brutal in Italy (Della Porta and Reiter 2003, 11–144). Anti-Communist propaganda was also on the rise. In Italy, the Christian Democracy and the Catholic Church launched widespread anti-Communist campaigns early on, culminating during the general elections in the spring of 1948 (Novelli 2008, 116–64; Casella 1992, 463–85; Mariuzzo 2010, 28–45). In France, an organization dedicated to anti-Communist propaganda, Paix et Liberté, was founded somewhat later, in 1950 (Duhamel 1999). Despite the fear of a Communist insurrection and the suspicion of treason to help a future Soviet invasion, anti-Communist propaganda was targeted more at the Soviet Union itself than domestic Communists (Girard 2012b).

This does not mean that the leaders of governing moderate political parties did not fear a Communist conspiracy. The study of internal debates of the French Socialist Party[18] and of Italian Christian Democracy[19] shows that, during the period of geopolitical tension such as the summer of 1950, there were fears of uprising, a coup d'état, and support for a Soviet invasion. But they were rarely expressed publicly, and mainly downplayed, evoking a hypothetical Fifth Column rather than the Communist Party itself (Girard 2012a, 577–89). In other words, Communist conspiracy theories contrasted with other political discourses not only because they were Communist but also simply because conspiracy theories were not so common in the political speech of the postwar period.

Italian Christian Democracy posters of the 1950s provide a telling example of this contrast as they aimed to present the achievements of the government rather than to denounce the danger of Communism.[20] The Italian Communist Party was portrayed as an obstacle to the march of modernization, revealing another aspect of the failure of Communist propaganda: the incapacity to provide a positive alternative to the process of political, social, and economic transformation of the country. Worse, the catastrophic predictions about the crumble of capitalism matched less and less with everyday reality because Italy was, like France, experiencing their "economic miracle" (Bellassai 2000, 169–71).

In the end, Communist political culture never managed to influence the emerging mass culture. The social and cultural modernization at work in France and Italy was for the most part based on Americanization, capitalism, and mass consumption, so the project to build a Communist counter-society, pure from capitalism and American corruption, could only lead to isolation. However, in Italy, the Communist Party managed to struggle more effectively for cultural hegemony, but the double cost was the appropriation of the values of the republic (Mariuzzo 2010, 150–64) and the adoption of the language and models of—largely Americanized—popular culture (Gundle 2000, 63–82).

In this broad context of deep political, social, and cultural changes, Communist conspiracy theories strengthened the fear of an omnipotent and relentless enemy, sustained the siege mentality among grassroots Communists, and legitimated violence. They were increasingly in conflict with the emergence of the new political culture of the French and Italian republics. Even if the wave of terrorism of the late 1960s and 1970s interferes with the long-term evolution, after 1950, there

Stalinist conspiracy theories 61

was undoubtedly a "civilizing" process. This political pacification resulted in the decrease of all sorts of domestic political violence (Audigier and Girard 2011, 15).

In these conditions, expected to push other political movements (especially Socialists) to conclude a defensive alliance, conspiracy theories were rather fueling Manichean conflictuality and in reality made alliances and compromises less likely. They were, at most, a means to sustain the involvement of Communist members and, as time passed, a mark of the surviving Stalinist political and cultural identity.

Conclusion

Communist conspiracy theories were a tenet of the ideology and political education that was transferred from the 1920s in the Soviet Union to foreign Communist parties. In this view, their endorsement was evidence of a unique and successful process of cultural transfer operated in a far more systematic and methodical way than Fascism or liberalism.

As Communist political culture was a guide for action, conspiracy theories had a direct impact on the decisions of party leaders as well as the behavior of grassroots members. Prospering within the Stalinist Manichean worldview, they were in return contributing to erecting a wall between friends and foes, leading to conflictual politics. That was precisely what made them an inefficient political means in a democratic context. In the Soviet Union, they have been used as a tool of repression; in Western countries, they were expected to unify anti-Fascist left-wing parties against a hypothetical foreign and internal menace. This strategy failed because of the huge gap that appeared between Communist parties and other political forces at the beginning of the Cold War. Manichean and threatening discourse, violent strikes, and deadly riots dug a great political divide, and in this context, conspiracy theories proved to be more and more inefficient, not to say, debilitating.

More broadly, Communist conspiracy theories contrasted with the evolution of the political discourse of the postwar period and lay dormant for some time with the merging of more modern and peaceful forms of political life and media communication. This conclusion suggests that conspiracy theories in Western Europe knew an evolution similar to the one in the United States (Butter 2014) and were pushed to the margins of relatively pacified politics.

Notes

1 Archives of the "Istituto Gramsci" (AIG, Rome): MF 275, Weekly bulletin of instructions of the province of Milan, November 1948.
2 AIG: MF 274–275, Lists of spies, suspects, and expelled members.
3 AIG: MF 314–315, Political parties and movements.
4 AIG: MF 267, Report on the political situation of the Federation of Bologna, March 1946.
5 During the first day of the Central Committee meeting of January 1945 in Ivry, half of the orators mentioned it in their speeches, Archives of the French Communist Party (AFCP, Bobigny): Central Committee meeting, January 21–23, 1945.

62   *Pascal Girard*

6 AFCP: Central Committee meeting, April 20–21, 1946; Political Bureau, October 17, 1946.
7 AFCP: Political Bureau, July 10, 1947; Secretary, July 15 and 28 and September 22, 1947.
8 AFCP: Political Bureau, October 9 and 22 and November 6, 1947; Secretary, October 14 and 20 and November 4 and 10, 1947.
9 AIG: MF 277, Central Committee, November 11–13, 1947.
10 French National Archives (FNA, Paris): 'Ecole centrale de responsables dans le travail municipal, Février 9–28, 1948. Cours général n° 6' in box BB18 4067 (Plot of Toulon, 1952); AFCP: Political Bureau, November 6, 1947.
11 AIG: MF 350, Courses of the Party Schools.
12 AIG: MF 274, Lists of spies, suspects, and expelled members.
13 Italian National Archives (Rome): Box 36, Home Office Minister, Public Order, 1944–46.
14 AFCP: Political Bureau and Secretary, 1952–53.
15 AFCP: Secretary, January 19, 1953.
16 AIG: MF 127 and 262, Records of the Directory, September 1953 and September–October–November 1956.
17 FNA: Papiers Vincent Auriol, Conseil des Ministres, 552 AP 60 and Report « Le PCF en 1950 », Direction Centrale des Renseignements Généraux, 19960325, Article 1.
18 Office Universitaire de Recherche Socialiste (Paris): Comités Directeur, Conseil Nationaux and Congrès Nationaux, 1947–56.
19 Office Universitaire de Recherche Socialiste (Paris): Comités Directeur, Conseil Nationaux, and Congrès Nationaux, 1947–56.
20 Istituto Luigi Sturzo (Rome): Collection of posters of the Christian Democracy.

Bibliography

Aga-Rossi, Elena, and Victor Zaslavsky. 1997. *Togliatti e Stalin. Il PCI e la politica estera staliniana negli archivi di Mosca* [Togliatti and Stalin: The PCI and Stalinist Foreign Policy within the Moscow Archives]. Bologne: Il Mulino.

Agosti, Aldo. 2008. *Palmiro Togliatti: A Biography*. London: IB Tauris.

Alwood, Edward. 2007. *Dark Days in the Newsroom. McCarthyism Aimed at the Press*. Philadelphia, PA: Temple University Press.

Audigier, François, and Pascal Girard, eds. 2011. *Se battre pour ses idées. La violence militante en France des années 1920 aux années 1970* [Fighting for Your Own Ideas: militant violence in France from the 1920s to the 1970s]. Paris: Riveneuve.

Azadovskii, Konstantin, and Boris Egorov. 2002. "From Anti-Westernism to Anti-Semitism." *Journal of Cold War Studies* 4 (1): 66–80.

Barkun, Michael. 2003. *A Culture of Conspiracy. Apocalyptic Visions in Contemporary America*. Berkeley, CA: University of California Press.

Barson, Michael, and Steven Heller. 2001. *Red Scared! The Commie Menace in Propaganda and Popular Culture*. San Francisco, CA: Chronicle Books.

Bellassai, Sandro. 2000. *La morale comunista. Pubblico e privato nella rappresentazione del PCI (1947–1956)* [The Communist Morality: public and private spheres in the representation of the Italian Communist Party (1947–1956)]. Rome: Carocci Editore.

Berlière, Jean-Marc, and Franck Liaigre. 2004. *Le sang des communistes. Les Bataillons de la jeunesse dans la lutte armée* [The Blood of the Communists: Youth Battalions in the Armed Struggle]. Paris: Fayard.

Stalinist conspiracy theories 63

————. 2007. *Liquider les traîtres. La face cachée du PCF 1941–1943* [Liquidate the Traitors: The Hidden Side of the French Communist Party 1941–1943]. Paris: Robert Laffont.

Bouchet, Thomas. 2010. *Noms d'oiseaux. L'insulte en politique, de la Restauration à nos jours* [Names of Birds: Political Insults, from the Restoration to the Present Day]. Paris: Stock: 191–93.

Boulouque, Sylvain, and Franck Liaigre. 2008. *Les listes noires du PCF* [Black Lists of the French Communist Party]. Paris: Calmann-Lévy.

Brennan, Mary. 2008. *Wives, Mothers and The Red Menace. Conservative Women and the Crusade Against Communism*. Boulder, CO: University Press of Colorado.

Brent, Jonathan. 2004. *Stalin's Last Crime: The Plot Against the Jewish Doctors, 1948–1953*. New York: Harper.

Broué, Pierre, and Raymond Vacheron. 1997. *Meurtres au maquis*. Paris: Grasset.

Budnitskii, Oleg. 2012. *Russian Jews Between the Reds and the Whites, 1917–1920*. Philadelphia, PA: University of Pennsylvania Press.

Buton, Philippe.1993. *Les lendemains qui déchantent. Le Parti communiste français à la Libération* [Disappointing Tomorrows: The French Communist Party during the Liberation]. Paris: Presses de la Fondation Nationale de Sciences Politiques.

Buton, Pierre, and Laurent Gervereau. 1989. *Le couteau entre les dents. 100 ans d'affiches communistes et anticommunistes* [The Knife between the Teeth: 100 of Communist and Anticommunist Posters]. Paris: Chêne.

Butter, Michael. 2014. *Plots, Designs, and Schemes: American Conspiracy Theories from the Puritans to the Present*. Berlin: De Gruyter.

Carioti, Antonio. 2008. *Gli orfani di Salò. Il "sessantotto nero" dei giovanni neofascisti nel dopoguerra 1945–1951* [The Orphans of Salò: The "black sixty-eight" of Neo-fascist Youth in the Postwar Period 1945–1951]. Milan: Mursia.

Casella, Mario. 1992. *18 Aprile 1948. La mobilitazione delle organizzazioni cattoliche* [April 18, 1948: The Mobilization of Catholic Organizations]. Galatina: Congedo Editore.

Chase, William. J. 2001. *Enemies within the Gate? The Comintern and the Stalinist Repression, 1934–1939*. New Haven, CT: Yale University Press.

Cohn, Norman. 1967. *Warrant for Genocide*. New York: Harper & Row.

Conquest, Robert. 1989. *Stalin and the Murder of Kirov*. New York: Oxford University Press.

Daix, Pierre. 1976. *J'ai cru au matin* [I had Believed in the Morning]. Paris: Robert Laffont.

Della Porta, Donatella, and Herbert Reiter. 2003. *Polizia e protesta. L'ordine pubblico dalla Liberazione ai "no global"* [Police and Protest: Public Order from Liberation to "No Global"]. Bologne: Il Mulino.

Delporte, Christian, Claire Blandin, and François Robinet. 2016. *Histoire de la presse en France XX – XXIème siècle* [History of the Press in France during the Twentieth and Twenty-first Century]. Paris: Armand Colin.

Dé Medici, Giuliana. 1986. *Le origini del MSI. Dal clandestinismo al primo congresso (1943–1948)* [The Origins of the MSI: From Secrecy to the First Congress (1943–1948)]. Rome: Edizioni ISC.

Doherty, Thomas. 2003. *Cold War, Cool Medium. Television, McCarthyism and American Culture*. New York: Columbia University Press.

Duhamel, Eric. 1999. "Jean-Paul David et le mouvement Paix et Liberté, un anticommunisme radical" [Jean-Paul David and the "Peace and Freedom" Movement, a Radical Anticommunism]. In *Renseignement et propagande pendant la guerre froide*

64 Pascal Girard

(1947–1953) [Information and Propaganda during the Cold War (1947–1953)], edited by Jean Delmas and Jean Kessler, 195–215. Brussels: Editions Complexe.

Ellman, Michael. 2001. "The Soviet 1937 Provincial Show Trials: Carnival or Terror?" *Europe-Asia Studies* 53 (8): 1221–33.

Fitzpatrick, Sheila. 1993. "How the Mice Buried the Cat: Scenes from the Great Purges of 1937 in the Russian Provinces." *Russian Review* 52 (3): 299–320.

Fondazione Giangiacomo Feltrinelli, Russian Centre of Conservation and Study of Records for Modern History. 1994. *The Cominform. Minutes of the Three Conferences 1947/1948/1949*. Milan: Feltrinelli Editore.

Gerwarth, Robert. 2016. *The Vanquished*. London: Penguin Books.

Getty, John A. 1985. *Origins of the Great Purges. The soviet Communist Party Reconsidered, 1933–1938*. New York: Cambridge University Press.

Getty, John A., and Oleg V. Naumov. 1999. *The road to Terror. Stalin and the self-destruction of the Bolsheviks, 1932–1939*. New Haven, CT: Yale University Press.

Girard, Pascal. 2007a. "La cinquième colonne en France 1944–1946" [The Fifth Column in France 1944–1946]. In *Traîtres et trahisons. Guerres, imaginaires sociaux et constructions politiques* [Traitors and Betrayals. Wars, Social Imaginations and Political Constructions], edited by Sylvain Boulouque and Pascal Girard, 65–89. Paris: Seli Arslan.

———. 2007b. "Socialistes et communistes, 1944–1948: des relations fondées sur la peur?" [Socialists and Communists, 1944–1948: Relationships Based on Fear?]. *Recherche Socialiste* 39–40: 135–48.

———. 2012a. "Les complots politiques en France et en Italie de la fin de la Seconde Guerre mondiale à la fin des années 1950" [Political Conspiracies in France and Italy from the End of World War II to the End of the 1950s]. PhD diss., European University Institute, Florence.

———. 2012b. "Une gauche extrême ou une gauche 'de l'étranger'? Représentations et stigmatisation des partis communistes français et italien au début de la guerre froide." [An Extreme Left or a "Foreign" Left? Representation and Stigmatization of the French and Italian Communist Parties at the Beginning of the Cold War]. In *Extrême? Identités partisanes et stigmatisation des gauches en Europe (XVIIIe – XXe siècle)* [Extremes? Partisan Identities and Stigmatization of the Left in Europe (18th – 20th Centuries)], edited by Michel Biard, Bernard Gainot, Paul Pasteur and Pierre Serna, 303–13. Rennes: Presses Universitaires de Rennes.

Goldman, Wendy Z. 2007. *Terror and Democracy in the Age of Stalin. The Social Dynamics of Repression*. New York: Cambridge University Press.

———. 2011. *Inventing the Enemy: Denunciation and Terror in Stalin's Russia*. Cambridge: Cambridge University Press.

Gundle, Stephen. 2000. *Between Hollywood and Moscow. The Italian Communists and the Challenge of Mass Culture, 1943–1991*. Durham, UK: Duke University Press.

Harris, James. 2016. *The Great Fear. Stalin's Terror of the 1930s*. Oxford: Oxford University Press.

Heale, Michael J. 1998. *McCarthy's Americans. Red Scare Politics in State and Nation, 1935–1965*. Basingstoke: McMillan.

Institut française de l'opinion publique. 1957. *Sondages, revue française de l'opinion publique* 19 (3).

Jenkins, Philip. 1999. *Cold War at Home. The Red Scare in Pennsylvania 1945–1960*. Chapel Hill, NC: University of North Carolina Press.

Kriegel, Annie, and Stéphane Courtois. 1997. *Eugen Fried – Le grand secret du PCF* [Eugen Fried: the Big Secret of the French Communist Party]. Paris: Le Seuil.

Stalinist conspiracy theories   65

Lazar, Marc. 1992. *Maisons rouges. Les Partis communistes français et italien de la Libération à nos jours* [Red houses: The French and Italian Communist Parties from the Liberation to the Present]. Paris: Aubier.

Leggett, George. 1981. *The Cheka. Lenin's Political Police. The All-Russian Extraordinary Commission for Combating Counter-Revolution and Sabotage (December 1917 to February 1922)*. Oxford: Clarendon Press.

Luzzatto Fegiz, Pierpaolo. 1956. *Il volto sconosciuto. Dieci anni di sondaggi Doxa, 1946– 1956* [The Unknown Face: Ten years of Doxa (The Italian Institute of Public Opinion) surveys, 1946–1956]. Milan: Giuffrè Editore.

Mariuzzo, Andrea. 2010. *Divergenze parallele. Comunismo e anticomunismo alle origini del linguaggio politico dell'Italia repubblicana (1945–1953)* [Parallel Divergences: Communism and Anticommunism at the Origins of the Political Language of Republican Italy (1945–1953)]. Soveria Mannelli: Rubbettino.

McDermott, Kevin, and Jeremy Agnew. 1996. *The Comintern. A History of International Communism from Lenin to Stalin*. London: MacMillan Press.

Michels, Jonathan. 2017. *McCarthyism: The Realities, Delusions and Politics Behind the 1950s Red Scare*. New York: Routledge.

Novelli, Edoardo. 2008. *Le elezioni del Quarantotto. Storia, strategie e immagini della prima campagne elettorale repubblicana* [The 1948 Elections: History, Strategies and Images of the First Election Campaign in Republican Italy]. Rome: Donzelli Editore.

Rao, Nicola. 2008. *Il sangue e la celtica. Dalle vendette antipartigiane alla strategia della tensione. Storia armata del neofascismo* [Blood and the Celtic: From Anti-partisan Vendettas to the Strategy of Tension. The Armed History of Neo-fascism]. Milan: Sperling e Kupfer Editori.

Recanati, Jean. 1980. *Un gentil stalinien. Récit autobiographique* [A Nice Stalinist: An Autobiographical Story]. Paris: Mazarine.

Rioux, Jean-Pierre. 1980. *La France de la Quatrième République, L'ardeur et la nécessité, 1944–1952* [France of the Fourth Republic: Ardor and Necessity, 1944–1952]. Paris: Seuil.

Rittersporn, Gábor T. 1993. "The Omnipresent Conspiracy: On soviet Imagery of Politics and Social Relations in the 1930's." In *Stalinist Terror. New Perspectives*, edited by John A. Getty and Roberta D. Manning, 99–115. New York: Cambridge University Press.

———. 2014. *Anguish, Anger and Folkways in Soviet Russia*. Pittsburgh: University of Pittsburgh Press.

Secchia, Pietro. 1973. *Il Partito comunista italiano e la guerra di Liberazione, 1943–1945* [The Italian Communist Party and the Liberation War, 1943–1945]. Milan: Feltrinelli Editore.

Thorez, Maurice. 1950. *La lutte pour l'indépendance nationale et pour la paix, XIIème congrès national du PCF, Gennevilliers, 2–6 avril 1950* [The Struggle for National Independence and for Peace, 12th National Congress of the French Communist Party, Gennevilliers, April 2–6, 1950]. Paris: SEDIC.

Ventrone, Angelo. 2005. *Il nemico interno. Immagini e simboli della lotta politica nell'Italia del '900.* [The Internal Enemy: Images and Symbols of the Political Struggle in Italy during the 1900s]. Rome: Donzelli Editore.

Werth, Nicolas. 2003."The Mechanism of a Mass Crime. The Great Terror in the Soviet Union, 1937–1938." In *The Specter of Genocide Mass Murder in Historical Perspective*, edited by Robert Gellately and Ben Kiernan, 215–39. Cambridge: Cambridge University Press.

66 *Pascal Girard*

———. 2005. "Les 'petits procès exemplaires' en URSS durant la Grande Terreur (1937–1938)" [The 'Small Show Trials' in the USSR during the Great Terror (1937–1938)]. *Vingtième Siècle. Revue d'histoire* 86 (2): 5–23.

Werth, Nicolas, and Gaël Moullec. 1994. *Rapports secrets soviétiques, 1921–1991. La société russe dans les documents confidentiels* [Soviet Secret Reports, 1921–1991: Russian Society in Confidential Documents]. Paris: Gallimard.

Whitewood, Peter. 2015. *The Red Army and the Great Terror. Stalin's Purge of the Soviet Military*. Lawrence: University Press of Kansas.

3 "By the order of their foreign masters"

Soviet dissidents, anti-Western conspiracy, and the deprivation of agency

Anna Kirziuk

Introduction

The assertion that the propaganda and secret activities of the hostile West covertly affected the minds of Soviet citizens was the main framework when speaking about dissidents in late Soviet official discourse. The judicial or extrajudicial persecution of dissidents was often accompanied by a media campaign where they were persistently accused of being associated with Western intelligence services and portrayed as obedient puppets of "their foreign masters."

In considering these conspiratorial accusations, researchers usually repeat the opinions of the dissidents themselves. This opinion can be synthesized as follows: the Soviet government represented its opponents as puppets of the Western special services in order to discredit them in the eyes of the people (Vaissié 1999). Ilya Yablokov reaches approximately the same conclusion in his analysis of anti-Western conspiracy narrative in post-Soviet Russia, where it is again directed against the opposition. Relying on the contributions authored by Mark Fenster, who regards conspiracy as an instrument of the struggle for power (Fenster 2008), Yablokov considers post-Soviet conspiracy theories as an instrument that Russian elites tactically use for their political purposes. He shows that the accusations of oppositionists being tied to the West help to rally the people around the current government and discredit the opposition (Yablokov 2018).

I propose that such an instrumental conception of anti-Western conspiracies needs to be corrected and supplemented. It is difficult to deny the effectiveness of conspiracy as a means of discrediting political opponents. But it is important to remember that the conspiratorial idea of a "hostile capitalist environment" was an essential part of Soviet ideology since the very beginning of the USSR. This idea was at the heart of the purges and spy mania of the 1920s and 1930s; it gave legitimacy for the witch hunt of the Great Terror and, at least in part, for the antisemitic campaigns of late Stalinism. It provided a justification for the existence of the institute of secret police (NKVD–MGB–KGB).[1] The notion of an external enemy who seeks by all means to harm the USSR was widely represented in products of Soviet mass culture (novels, movies, songs, etc.). It is logical to assume that in the late Soviet period the idea of a powerful external enemy who tries to damage

68 *Anna Kirziuk*

the USSR through his agents has been somehow internalized—at least by some professional groups, related to special services and political elite.

In the late Soviet period, conspiracy interpretations of political dissent were used not only in propaganda texts but also in the secret documents that circulated between the KGB and the Communist Party's high-ranking officials. It is obvious that such "internal use" of conspiracy interpretations were not aimed at publicly discrediting dissidents. Why was an anti-Western conspiracy needed in this case? What was its role in the system besides the discrediting of political opponents? Were these conspiracy explanations generated by the rules of conventional official language, or were they caused by the inner beliefs of both the addressers and addressees of the secret documents? And what could be the psychological profit of such beliefs in the Soviet context?

This chapter will try to answer these questions by drawing on propaganda texts, published KGB documents, and ego documents (diaries and memoirs) of some high-ranking Soviet officials.

Puppets, masters, and millions of dollars: the structure and message of late Soviet anti-Western conspiracy narratives

The figure of an external enemy always played a very important role in the Soviet political imagination. From the 1920s to the 1950s, Soviet propaganda constantly talked about "wreckers," spies, and "saboteurs" supposedly sent to the USSR from a hostile capitalist environment. The harm they caused to the country was mainly thought of as being physical: they were accused of organizing industrial accidents and killing both Soviet leaders and ordinary citizens (Zaleski 1980; Hoffman 1993; Manning 1993; Rittersporn 2014).

In the late Soviet period, the narratives about the "methods" of the enemy changed. According to late Soviet propaganda, the enemy acts more subtly instead, waging a so-called psychological warfare against the USSR. This war was aimed at making the Soviet people more susceptible to anti-Soviet ideas. The ultimate goal of psychological warfare was to weaken the Soviet state, and its weapons were both unambiguous anti-Soviet propaganda and the attractive attributes of the Western way of life. A description of these methods can be found in a propaganda brochure denunciating the dissidents:

> Attacks are conducted both from the front and from the flanks. Everything is used: from seemingly innocuous music records, entertaining books, and pornographic cards to overtly anti-Soviet brochures and leaflets; from fashionable shirts tinted with stripes and stars of the American flag, to the direct opposition to the norms of a socialist moral with the standards of the "American way of life."
>
> (Antonov et al. 1982, 8)[2]

Soviet propagandists persistently argued that capitalist states spared no effort or money in seeking to defeat the USSR through psychological warfare. According to this propaganda, the capitalist states created a huge network of intelligence

"By the order of their foreign masters"   69

and propaganda services, research institutes, foundations, unions, and anti-Soviet organizations that "day and night spread the poison of anti-communism and anti-Sovietism, trying to spoil people's minds" (Alexandrov 1970). The authors of a propaganda pamphlet about dissidents claimed that, when he was president, Harry Truman had approved $100 million for the CIA to carry out "subversive work" against socialist countries, and since then this sum has been growing steadily (Antonov et al. 1982, 7–14).

Human rights movements had existed in the USSR since 1965 (Alekseeva 1987). The Helsinki Accords of 1975 strengthened the positions of human rights activists in all countries of the Eastern Bloc: with the text in their hands, they were able to charge their governments with human rights violations (Heneghan 1977). At the same time, the Helsinki Accords led to complications (or maybe obstacles) for the Soviet authorities in carrying out propaganda and legal prosecution against the dissidents.

In official Soviet discourse, dissidents were portrayed as a weapon of psychological warfare waged by Western intelligence services against the USSR. Soviet propagandists accused the dissidents of being paid for drafting documents on human rights violations "in large sums in US dollars and Soviet rubles" (Ovcharenko 1968). Allegedly seduced by all these dollars and rubles, dissidents began to collect information on the violation of human rights in the USSR for their "overseas masters." According to official Soviet texts, this information, first, helps the enemies to discredit the Soviet Union and, second, causes "internal conflicts" that should lead to a weakening and decline of the Soviet system (Vakulovskyi 1988, 57). Dissidents were described as "outliers" who fell under the influence of the enemy either in their naivety ("political immaturity") or because of weakness of character or for financial gain.

The narratives based on the idea of Western conspiracy can thus be reduced to two main messages. First, the USSR is the object of sustained attention and constant ideological attacks by Western intelligence agencies. Second, dissidents are not independently acting entities: their statements and actions are just a result of external evil influence and other people's will.

One might say that Cold War circumstances gave real ground for concern about enemy propaganda. During the ideological confrontation between Eastern and Western blocs, both sides were worried about "subversive work" supposedly carried out by the opponent. Moreover, both sides regularly accused each other of waging "psychological warfare" while trying, at the same time, to wage this warfare themselves (Scott-Smith 2011; Risso 2014). Indeed, the methods and techniques used by the two sides were actually quite similar (Risso 2014, 7), and the main reason for this similarity was the close interplay between propaganda and intelligence services (Scott-Smith 2011; Risso 2014).

The aim of this chapter is not to evaluate the extent to which specific official conspiratorial narratives about Soviet dissidents corresponded to reality, but to understand their role in official discourse. I define the Soviet officials' belief in the hidden hand of Western intelligence services behind any dissident activity as conspiratorial not because of an inadequate concept of reality. Such beliefs are

70 *Anna Kirziuk*

conspiratorial by their structure, which includes a super-powerful enemy who is capable of being omnipresent and harming "us" and the idea of someone's invisible evil will that is behind visible phenomena.

The explanation of any opposing activity through an external enemy's will includes another important element. The essential condition for the successful actions of a transcendent enemy is the total passivity of visible "performers" of his will. I will show later that in the discourse of the Soviet authorities on dissidents, the anti-Western conspiracy theory was an effective means (although not the only one) of depriving them of their agency. In order to understand some features and limitations of this tool, I shall examine several cases. These cases will allow us to see how various types of dissident activity were interpreted in different texts designed for different audiences: in propaganda products, in secret documents addressed to high-ranking CPSU officials, and in ego documents of some KGB and party officials.

Anti-Western conspiracy narrative as a tool for depriving agency

The first case is the story of Dmitry Mikheev, a graduate student at Moscow State University. In 1971 Mikheev was detained at Moscow airport while he was trying to fly to Austria using the passport of François de Perrego, a Swiss national. During the arrest, Mikheev said that he wanted to leave the USSR because he did not like the political system of the country (Chronicle n.d., 16). He had planned the escape long before this unsuccessful attempt and had considered various ways to cross the border illegally. Mikheev was an active reader and author of Samizdat,[3] having written both "The Empire of Lie" and "How to Dupe a Population," two texts sharply critical of the Soviet regime.

From this brief description we can see that the attempt at unauthorized emigration was the result of a long period of reflection. However, in the Soviet press, Dmitry's failed escape was presented as "a concert carefully orchestrated by foreign conductors" (Lerov, Pavlov, and Chernyavsky 1971). In several newspaper articles that appeared after the trial, Mikheev was described as a weak and suggestible person, the object of skillful manipulation by several foreign agents who had penetrated Moscow State University under the guise of students and interns. In these accounts, foreigners are active, while Mikheev is totally passive: he is "easily taken by hands of adventurers and provocateurs" (Ignatenko and Kolesnikov 1971). The Soviet journalists convinced their readers that Mikheev's writings were not the products of his own reflection, but a set of ideas, borrowed from anti-Soviet texts, published in the West and secretly thrown in the USSR by "ideological saboteurs" or from foreign radio voices (Lerov, Pavlov, and Chernyavsky 1971, 29).

The pragmatics of the conspiracy narrative is rather clear here: the authorities use it in order to discredit their opponent in the eyes of the people, depriving him of agency and presenting him as a miserable puppet of powerful foreign enemies. But the function of this conspiracy interpretation becomes less evident if we find

"*By the order of their foreign masters*" 71

it not in the media, but in texts that were not intended for the public, such as in secret documents circulating between the KGB and the Central Committee of the Communist Party.

In 1976, Philip Bobkov, the head of the Fifth Department of the KGB,[4] which dealt with dissent, sent an analytical report to the Central Committee of the party titled "On the nature and causes of negative manifestations among pupils and students." This document begins with lengthy speculation about the strong efforts of the enemy in psychological warfare against socialist countries:

> Many intelligence agencies of imperialist states have created special departments to work with the youth of socialist countries. There are also so-called research institutes and research centers that work in the interests of the special services. In the USA alone there are about eighty research centers and departments that on instructions from the CIA work out the tools for an ideological impact on the population of socialist countries, including the youth.
>
> (Makarov 2006, 135)

Then Bobkov mentions the case of Dmitry Mikheev as an example of a successful "ideological sabotage" carried out by the enemy. The attempt to escape from the USSR is described not as Mikheev's own deed, but as a "provocative action" organized by the Swiss Oriental Institute, which "persuaded" the Soviet graduate student "to betray his homeland by fleeing abroad" (ibid., 135).

Such a representation of opposition activity is not unique for secret KGB documents. When it comes to human rights activists, they are described—much like Mikheev—as persons lacking agency. Their deeds are not actually *their own*, but a result of subversive techniques deployed by the enemy. For instance, KGB chief Yuri Andropov, reporting on the work of his bureau for the year 1975, describes the activities of Soviet human rights defenders as the result of "actions by the enemy who tries to speculate by the general principles of the Final Act of the Conference on Security and Cooperation in Helsinki for hostile purposes" (ibid., 112).

In short, in the late Soviet period, conspiratorial narratives became a key tool in the representation of dissent within bureaucratic discourse. If the reasons for using conspiracy theories for explaining dissident activities in public discourse are clear, the question still remaining is this: why were they needed in the texts for internal use? In the following part, I will provide an answer to this question.

Conspiracy interpretations for "internal use": the product of officialese or inner belief?

The first and the most evident explanation for the use of conspiracy interpretations in internal documents is that it was consistent with a conventional discursive frame of the Soviet State Security Committee. This frame implied a set of rhetorical clichés, including references to an external enemy's foreign intelligence services and the "subversive work" that they conducted against the USSR. A conspiracist worldview was incorporated and embedded in the specific language that

72 Anna Kirziuk

KGB officers first adopted during their training at the state security agency and subsequently used both for self-description and for the depiction of political reality. For instance, the task of the Fifth Department was officially formulated as a "fight against the ideological sabotage of the enemy." It was thus framed around an external enemy represented by foreign intelligence services, whereas in practice the department dealt with all sorts of dissent inside the country. Reports and analytical notes on the dissidents compiled by the KGB for the Central Committee, in general, did not report so much about the fight against dissidents themselves. Instead, their authors pondered the "breakdown and exposure of subversive activities of foreign ideological centers and anti-Soviet organizations" (Makarov 2006, 112).

This special language was not only a conventionalized way of representing reality. The idea of the powerful enemy who was steadily trying to destroy the USSR gave meaning to the mere existence of the secret police. When Yuri Andropov convinces the Central Committee to create the Fifth Department of the KGB, he justifies this need for the new department by asserting that imperialistic states will "constantly increase their efforts to intensify subversive actions against the Soviet Union. In so doing, they consider psychological warfare as one of the most important components of the struggle against communism" (Kokurin and Petrov 2003, 712). The party's top leaders found this argument convincing, and the special Fifth Department was created. The logic is quite clear: hostile activities of an enemy (whether perceived or real) require a response. It is not an exaggeration to say that the danger of "subversive work" from an external enemy was a *raison d'être* of the KGB as an institution.[5]

This language also ensured the normal functioning of the institution of the secret police. In particular, the use of conspiracy interpretations allowed KGB officers to justify themselves to the party's leaders, in spite of any acts of opposition some Soviet citizens nevertheless carried out. At the same time, the representation of political reality in terms of a struggle with a super-powerful enemy probably met the expectations of the party's top leaders. The attribution of "anti-Soviet" acts to a powerful external enemy gave an acceptable explanation for these acts to both authors and readers of the reports.

However, I am not sure that this desire to give or receive such a conspiratorial explanation depended exclusively on institutional logic. It might be determined by internalized interpretative frameworks of both the authors and recipients of these reports. Language is not just a way of communication. It provides a specific interpretive lens for describing and understanding reality. Katherine Verdery argues that the Securitate (the secret police in Romania from 1948 to 1989) functioned as a "knowledge-production enterprise" (2014). Since Securitate officers were at the same time both workers and products of this enterprise, a conspiratorial optic became their own way of seeing: they "were convinced that secrets existed among the citizenry, secrets that would unmask a hidden enemy, a saboteur, a spy, a counter-revolutionary, a danger to the state or Party" (ibid., 85). These observations are also pertinent for the cadres of the so-called MGB (later renamed KGB), the institutional model that inspired the creation of the Securitate in 1948.

"*By the order of their foreign masters*"   73

These conspiratorial explanatory patterns not only were produced by the tropes of conventional KGB language but also derived from the inner beliefs of both readers and compilers of the secret documents. It is always difficult to find out to what degree people under socialist regimes internalized narratives of official discourse. Nevertheless, there are ego documents that can bring us closer to understanding Soviet officials' own interpretative patterns. In memoirs written many years after the collapse of the USSR, the chief of the Fifth Department presents the political reality of the Soviet period in the same terms that he used in his service notes. Philipe Bobkov tells about the "centers of psychological warfare" and the Americans who did not spare money to recruit agents among Soviet citizens. He also states that Helsinki Watch groups arose in the USSR "under the aegis of the political department of the USA Embassy in Moscow" (Bobkov 2006, 151). Vladimir Semichastnyi, the head of the KGB from 1961 to 1967, remembers dissident activity in the same terms as Bobkov, claiming that the Moscow human rights activists received "direct instructions from the foreign anti-Soviet organization National Alliance of Russian Solidarists" (NTS)[6] (Semichastnyi 2016, 298).

It was not only KGB officers who had the impulse to see an enemy's hand behind every opposition activity. Piotr Shelest, the Politburo member and the head of the Central Committee of the Communist Party of Ukraine (CPU), was also prone to a conspiratorial explanation of dissent. In 1968, at the time of the so-called Czechoslovak crisis, Shelest noted in his diary: "The entire 'course of action' was felt to be directed by professional CIA hands and intelligence agencies of the FRG [Federal Republic of Germany]" (Shelest 2016). In his eyes, Soviet dissidents—as well as Czechoslovak reformers—are not independent actors who act on their own. Indignant at the activities of Soviet human rights defenders, Shelest believes that it will not stop, since "our special service cannot discover the root where it all comes from" (ibid.).

In brief, some officials apparently preferred to believe that all groups having critical attitudes toward the regime (whether Czechoslovak "revisionists" or Soviet human right activists) were not agents of their own actions. And perhaps the need to deprive the oppositionists of their agency played a more important role in producing conspiracy narratives than the habit of seeing an enemy's hand everywhere. We will see that sometimes this need was satisfied without resorting to the tropes of official ideological discourse.

The insanity and the Jewish wife: other ways to deprive a dissident of agency

Besides the anti-Western conspiracy theory, in the late Soviet period, there were at least two discursive strategies to deprive those displaying a critical stance toward the Soviet regime of their agency. One of them can be traced to antisemitic conspiracy theories, while another is related to the infamous practice of instrumentalizing psychiatry as a repressive tool against dissidents. Jews played an important role in the conspiracy culture of late Stalinism. In the postwar period, such ideological campaigns as the struggle against "rootless cosmopolitans" and the "Doctors'

74 *Anna Kirziuk*

plot" legitimized some folk antisemitic attitudes and beliefs (Kostyrchenko 1995; Bemporad 2012). After Stalin's death, antisemitic campaigns continued: Jews were targeted as agents of "world Zionism" and Western imperialism who allegedly inclined to act for the USA and Israel (Byford 2011, 63–65). However, the official charges against the "cosmopolitans," "Zionists," or "killer-doctors" were fairly different from grassroots narratives on Jewish conspiracies. While in official discourse Jews were suspected of being the spies of foreign intelligence services, in folk conspiracy beliefs, Jews were represented as poisoners and baby-killers (Arkhipova and Kirziuk 2020, 341–63).

One of the Jewish-related folk narratives was the legend of "Kremlin wives." This legend, popular among both the elite and ordinary Soviet citizens, was based on an established belief in a Jewish conspiracy, according to which Jews maliciously influence Kremlin policy through the Jewish wives of Soviet leaders (Mitrokhin 2003, 67–69). This theory suggested that a Jewish wife was able to cleverly and imperceptibly subjugate a Russian husband and realize her evil plans through him. This legend has existed since the 1930s, when the steady rumors about Rosa Kaganovich, Stalin's secret Jewish wife,[7] appeared (Arkhipova 2016). Rosa Kaganovich was presented as a mastermind of all the leader's destructive decisions. In the late Soviet period, hearsay about the Jewish origin of the wives of Brezhnev or Andropov flourished (Voslensky 1991, 414; Mitrokhin 2003, 67). The "Kremlin wives" legend was able to explain the bad decisions of statesmen without changing the generally positive attitude to their personalities and without questioning the political system. But this ability proved to be useful in a completely different context—not to excuse the failures of the leaders, but to explain the behavior of individual dissidents (as will be discussed below).

Another way to deprive dissidents of agency, not related to conspiracy theories, was to label them mentally ill. Of course, this strategy had propaganda goals. First, the existence of political prisoners damaged the international image of the Soviet regime. Overt persecution of dissidents was always at the risk of reputational losses for the regime, and it had become more problematic after the Helsinki Accords. The imprisonment of particularly stubborn oppositionists in mental hospitals allowed the Soviet authorities to isolate them and avoid accusations of political repression. Second, by declaring the dissidents mentally ill, the authorities told the Soviet people: "Don't pay attention to what they say or what they do, they are just crazy." But the functions of the "insanity label" (as well as the functions of conspiratorial accusation) were not limited to these propagandist needs. Our second case will help make this clear.

Andrei Sakharov, the prominent physicist and one of the most well-known defenders of Soviet human rights, was a complex case for Soviet officials.[8] The creator of the Soviet hydrogen bomb and a holder of prestigious state awards, the academic Sakharov held a special place among human rights activists, and it was not only a matter of his international fame. He was too close to the achievements of the regime. His firsthand participation in the creation of the Soviet military complex made it difficult to explain publicly Sakharov's dissident activity through the lens of anti-Western conspiracy: such an explanation would call into question

"By the order of their foreign masters" 75

the country's defense capabilities and show the state's vulnerability. Fortunately, for those who were worried about Sakharov's political activity—namely, party leaders, KGB cadres, and Soviet propagandists—his second wife, Elena Bonner, was Jewish. This fact facilitated the transfer of the "Kremlin wives" legend to the dissident and helped explain Sakharov's "apostasy" without symbolic losses.

Nikolai Yakovlev, a well-known Soviet propagandist, uses the inverted story of "Kremlin wives" to talk about Sakharov in his book *The CIA against the USSR* (Yakovlev 1983, 270–300). He presents Bonner as a Machiavellian woman who manipulated her husband and shamelessly used his money and social status to arrange matters for her relatives. Referring to the testimony of some anonymous students of Sakharov, Yakovlev reports that Bonner turned her husband into a "Zionist hostage." Sakharov himself is described as a "big child" and an "eccentric," completely dependent on his wife in his words and deeds. Yakovlev leads his readers to the idea that such a complete lack of agency does not allow Sakharov to be responsible for his dissident texts:

> I would consider the next "revelations" on behalf of Sakharov transmitted by Western radio voices, bearing in mind this situation. Why "on behalf?" Making a thorough textual analysis of his articles and so on (fortunately, it is a small amount), I cannot shake the feeling that a lot has been dictated or written under pressure of someone else's will.
>
> (ibid., 300)

Yakovlev's book, reprinted several times and published in huge numbers in the USSR, of course had its obvious propaganda purposes. However, Sakharov similarly was deprived of agency not only in this propagandistic text but also in secret documents that were not intended to discredit the academic in the eyes of the people.

In 1980, Andropov sent a secret note to the Central Committee, in which he tries to convince the party's leaders that Sakharov is not the subject of his own actions. For this purpose, he persistently repeats the same idea of the malicious wife: "Sakharov has been under the psychological pressure of his wife for many years. He constantly performs illegal actions that damage the Soviet state at her instructions" (Makarov 2006, 231–32). But it is probably not enough to deprive Sakharov of his agency. Accordingly, Andropov adds two other arguments to the story of a treacherous Jewish wife. He also relies on anti-Western conspiracies, informing the Central Committee members that Elena Bonner receives recommendations from the "US intelligence services and foreign anti-Soviet centers" (ibid., 232). And more, Andropov makes it clear for his high-ranking readers that Sakharov is out of his mind:

> His mental state is notably getting worse. Sakharov's behavior often does not fit into universally recognized norms, it is evidently contrary to common sense and too affected by people around him, especially by his wife. We can see an anomaly in the mood of Sakharov that often changes suddenly from

76 *Anna Kirziuk*

detachment and isolation to vivacity and sociability. According to the greatest Soviet psychiatrists, his profound mental changes suggest that he can be considered a "pathological personality."

(ibid., 231)

The propagandist text uses only one argument to prove Sakharov's lack of agency (his masterful wife), whereas in the secret document, Sakharov is deprived agency by three parameters: as an insane person, as a puppet of his wife, and through her mediation of "foreign masters." This suggests that the KGB officers and their readers in the Central Committee, perhaps, needed more to be convinced of Sakharov's lacking agency than to discredit him in the eyes of the people.

The correspondence about Andrei Sakharov is not the only example of Soviet officials' habit of using several tools at once to deprive agency in order to explain an oppositional activity. It happened in other difficult cases, such as in a note about the opposition rally that the head of the Komsomol organization, Sergey Pavlov, sent to the CPSU Central Committee in December 1965. This meeting, held by Soviet human rights activists on Pushkin Square in Moscow, was the first rally in 27 years not organized by the authorities. Although the protesters were able to hold posters with their slogans for no more than two minutes,[9] for the USSR, where the monopoly on the organization of demonstrations belonged to the state, this was absolutely out of the ordinary. Therefore, in explaining to the members of the Central Committee of the CPSU what had happened, Pavlov reports that most of the organizers of the rally were mentally ill. He adds to this information that the content of the leaflets, through which the organizers gathered people for the rally, "leaves no doubt that more experienced scoundrels stood behind the organizers" (Pavlov 2005, 89).

Thus, we can see that this necessity—to deprive dissidents of their agency—was prior to the requirements of propaganda and not always derived from the clichés of official discourse. While different metaphors of a besieged fortress (including "foreign masters" and "psychological warfare") were a part of official party rhetoric, the "Jewish wife" narrative originated in folklore. It has been recycled for both propagandist and internal use in the very problematic case of Sakharov's dissent. The "insanity label" appeared in secret documents in the mid-1960s, when it had not yet become a common part of official rhetoric. This label also could be used exclusively in secret documents, without being applied in public discourse: Sakharov was never officially labeled as insane in public texts. It may be assumed that the desire to convince—and, especially, to be convinced of—a dissident's absence of agency was due to not only ideological or institutional reasons but also psychological ones.

The psychological profit of conspiracy theories

As I have found, the anti-Western conspiracy theory was one of the tools employed to deprive dissidents of their agency. However, studies in conspiracy theories will help us understand why it was so important for the Soviet authorities to make themselves sure that their critics did not have any agency.

"By the order of their foreign masters" 77

Why are conspiracy theories attractive? Some researchers suggest that people believe in conspiracy theories because they are able to give simple explanations for complex phenomena or for strange or frightening events (Benoist 1992; Campion-Vincent 2005; Ellis and Fine 2010). It is assumed that these explanations are not just epistemologically simple but also psychologically rewarding: "Much of their power lies in the ability to explain large numbers of discrete facts, including those emerging in current events in an efficient and *emotionally satisfying way*" (Ellis and Fine 2010, 55; emphasis added). But how exactly can conspiracy explanations emotionally satisfy their adherents?

To answer this question, we probably should turn to the findings of psychologists. According to some experimental studies in psychology, beliefs in conspiracies are related to frustration, to such uncomfortable feelings as powerlessness, low self-esteem, and guilt. In general terms, the psychological mechanism of conspiracies can be described as follows: conspiratorial interpretations are capable of decreasing emotional discomfort by scapegoating—that is, making an enemy responsible for the uncomfortable feelings and for negative outcomes in an individual's or group's life. More precisely, we can single out two different approaches in the scapegoating mechanism.

One approach focuses on the control-restorative function of scapegoating. The experiments by Marina Abalakina-Paap et al. (1999) show that blaming out-groups for the individual's problems allows one to make strange events, unpleasant feelings, and the whole world more comprehensible. Other series of experiments reveal that the identification of an enemy that can be named, understood, and managed minimizes the anxiety about multiple and indifferent treats existing in the world (Sullivan, Landau, and Rothschild 2010).

In another approach, researchers pay more attention to the function of scapegoating that could be called "self-value-restorative." This approach is based on Gordon Allport's idea of scapegoating as an ego-defense mechanism (1979). Blaming imagined enemies for negative outcomes helps to restore a positive identity (Staub 1989; Glick 2005). Thus, conspiracy theories protect a group's self-esteem from potentially damaging inferences (Kruglanski 1987).

Zachary Rothschild and his colleagues develop the "dual-motive model of scapegoating" and experimentally confirm that both psychological functions of this mechanism—to restore control and to minimize the feeling of guilt—are equally important (Rothschild et al. 2012). So conspiracy interpretations can emotionally satisfy in two ways: they maintain "perceived personal moral value by minimizing feelings of guilt over one's responsibility for a negative outcome," and they keep up "perceived personal control by obtaining a clear explanation for a seemingly inexplicable negative outcome that is otherwise difficult to explain or control" (ibid., 1148).

Scapegoating as an emotionally satisfying way of thinking: from the 1930s to the 1980s

The psychologists mentioned above have demonstrated that conspiracy beliefs arise as a defense reaction to an individual's feelings of a lack of control and as a

78 *Anna Kirziuk*

coping mechanism to protect one's positive self-identity. It seems that in a certain historical context, such sensations of loss of control and weakness become so widespread that conspiracy theories undergo mass distribution and cause large-scale witch hunts. As Gábor T. Rittersporn shows, this is exactly what happened in Stalin's USSR. The system worked in an uncontrollable and unpredictable way: no one knew how the party line would change and who would be declared an enemy tomorrow. Everybody—from party leaders to ordinary citizens—felt unsafe. This unpredictable and treacherous routine made people live with constant anxiety, which, according to Rittersporn, found expression in the imagery of ubiquitous conspiracy (2014, 13–37).

If we apply these psychological findings to Stalinist conspiracy culture, we can say that the mass hunt for "enemies of the people" performed a control-restorative function for the whole of Soviet society. However, or rather, in turn, the self-value-restorative function also played a significant role in the spread of conspiracy beliefs. Scholarship on Stalinism shows that this spread, which eventually led to the Great Terror, occurred against the backdrop of a serious economic crisis (Zaleski 1980; Manning 1993; Fitzpatrick 1999). Belief in conspiracies allowed the Soviet authorities to shift responsibility from themselves to "enemies of the people" and thus preserve a positive self-image in the eyes of ordinary people and in their own eyes (Zaleski 1980; Manning 1993).

But there was another important precondition for the flourishing of conspiracy theories under Stalin. As Rittersporn shows, widespread belief in spies and "wreckers" was strengthened by the "Bolsheviks' innate incapability to attribute the regime's problems to the administration's ordinary mode of operation" (2014, 37). The scapegoats were needed because people could not recognize that the deficiencies of the regime—shortages, failure to fulfill economic plans, low productivity, industrial accidents—were systemic in nature and inevitable. By attributing them to the subversive activities of conspirators, leaders and ordinary people could give an explanation of reality that would not challenge their belief in the rightness of the regime. In other words, the conspiracy theories under Stalin helped Soviet people connect reality with their political belief in a consistent way. They protected their consistent worldview from destruction.

But we should return to the late Soviet conspiracy narratives. The social, economic, and political situation of the "Stagnation era" was relatively stable and safe. At least, everyday life for the majority of people was not on the brink of permanent catastrophe nor under a constant sense of unpredictability and danger.[10] Nevertheless, all the psychological motives discussed above apparently played a role in producing conspiracy interpretations of dissent among the Soviet elite. The scale of the spread of these interpretations had changed significantly, but the mechanism that generated them remained the same.

In psychological terms, the activities of dissidents—their very existence—threatened both the personal moral value and personal control of high-ranking party and KGB officials. And further, they endangered the consistency of their worldview. The political discontent expressed by dissidents was a challenge for Soviet leadership, because this discontent, first, testified to an imperfection of the

"By the order of their foreign masters" 79

system and pointed to problems that required, if not an immediate solution, then at least discussion and analysis. It was an unpleasant reminder of a reality that did not correspond to the slogan of nationwide support for the party and the government. Second, the activity of the dissidents undermined the state's monopoly on public policy. Finally, this activity could hardly fit into the leader's worldview. Altogether, it caused confusion. In 1977, Anatoly Chernyaev, an official of the International Department of the Central Committee of the CPSU, wrote in his diary: "We have no answer to dissent such as Amalrik, Bukovsky, and Sakharov so far. Until now, our actions are explained by surprise: how can it be? That cannot and should not be in our society! I don't know what to do, either" (Chernyaev 2008, 10).

Conspiracy theories about Soviet dissidents provided a psychologically comfortable answer to Chernyaev's question. They can also be invoked for other sorts of dissent, not only for human rights activists like Sakharov or for "betrayers of the motherland" like Mikheev. A strategic deprivation of agency could be applied in almost any case when a Soviet official could tell themselves: "They criticize us/don't like us, and we don't understand why." For example, according to Philip Bobkov's memoirs, the population of the Baltic Republics and Western Ukraine would have been glad to enter the USSR after World War II, and therefore, the USSR was not an occupier. He asserts that, in Latvia, the Soviet authorities had "full contact with the people, it was going without incidents" (Bobkov 2006, 15). However, during the 1940s and 1950s, there was a desperate partisan struggle against the Soviet administration there. Bobkov resolves the contradiction between this annoying fact and his political beliefs through a conspiratorial interpretation. He claims the fighters against the Soviets were just "bandits" led by American and British intelligence services, who sent them instructors, weapons, equipment, and money (ibid.).

Why was it necessary to deprive dissidents of agency? Because if the dissidents are "agentless," it means that their critical statements have no real basis and no legitimacy. According to this narrative, the real authors of these statements are their "foreign masters," who are all enemies of the USSR by definition. Consequently, all these enemies had no positive aims in their criticism of the Soviet realities, and their criticism aimed only at undermining the Soviet regime. Moreover, nobody should take as reasonable the statements of mentally ill people. Finally, social criticism loses any legitimacy if it comes from "agentless" persons, either from mentally ill people or from Soviet citizens manipulated by external enemies. The allegations of oppositionists' complete lack of agency helped KGB and CPSU officials "not to hear" their criticism and, thereby, could restore the officials' self-value that was threatened by the words and actions of dissidents. In this way, the challenging, threatening potential of critical statements was neutralized.

The advantages of anti-Western conspiracy narratives

Although the anti-Western conspiracy theory was only one of several instruments that enabled the State to deprive dissidents of their agency, one can assume that,

80 *Anna Kirziuk*

relative to a label of insanity and other conspiracy narratives, it was more effective in maintaining the self-value of Soviet officials.

First, the conspiracy theories helped not only to deprive agency for individual oppositionists but also to externalize the more serious threat diffused among the Soviet people. For example, in 1981, Semyon Tsvigun, the first deputy head of the KGB, published an article in the journal *Communist* with the following reasoning:

> Until now foreign intelligence services relied on hostile Soviet citizens, on "leaders" who were ready to have an active confrontation with the Soviet power. . . . Now imperialistic intelligence agencies can see that these anti-social elements, disguised as "human rights defenders" and "champions of democracy," were exposed and neutralized, so they begin to search for new disruptive techniques and methods. For example, the ideological saboteurs intensify speculation on the issues of supplying the population with certain types of food products, as well as on certain recent shortcomings in medical and household services for workers.
>
> (Tsvigun 1981, 98)

In 1981, the year Tsvigun published this article, the USSR was experiencing serious economic difficulties. The population suffered from a shortage of food products. The situation was so critical that in some regions there were rumors about the forthcoming introduction of food stamps.[11] Less than a year later, Soviet leaders adopted the so-called Food Program, thereby recognizing the problem. But this process of recognition was not easy: at the beginning it was more comfortable to convince citizens—and, apparently, to believe themselves—that if someone is outraged about the food supply issues, it is the result of the manipulation of "foreign intelligence." This capacity of conspiracies—to relieve the political elite from responsibility for a number of social and economic phenomena—was widely used under Stalin, as we have seen.

Although Tsvigun's statement about food shortages looks like an anachronism by the 1980s, it shows the advantage of anti-Western (or any other) conspiracy theories in comparison with a non-conspiratorial way of depriving agency. The "insanity label" relieves authorities from all responsibility by denying any significance to dissident declarations. A conspiracy theory also proposes a "viable scapegoat" (Rothschild et al. 2012) that is able to bear the responsibility not only for political criticism but also for any failures of the system or the leadership.

Second, conspiracy theories have another important capacity that has not yet been discussed in this chapter. The idea of a powerful enemy, constantly conspiring against "us," props up our self-esteem not only because it provides a "viable scapegoat" but also because any attention, even when hostile, indicates the value of the object of this attention. Eliot Borenstein notes that the narratives of a Western conspiracy in modern Russia supports the illusory notion of the country's important role in the fate of the world, because "victims of conspiracy *matter*" (2019, 238). I think it was also true for Soviet anti-Western conspiracy narratives. The idea of Western conspirators was able to magically transform a painful reality

"By the order of their foreign masters" 81

(a country experiencing major challenges) into a source of pride (the object of envy of the powerful "imperialists"). A confirmation of the magical properties of this idea can be found in the speech of Joseph Stalin, which he made to Red Army commanders in June 1937:

> Comrades, we have so many successes that the USSR has become a temptation for all capitalist predators. We have a huge country, magnificent railways, our fleet is growing, bread production is growing, agriculture is booming and continues to flourish, and industry is on the rise. This is so enticing for imperialist predators that it obliges us to be vigilant.
>
> (Stalin 1997, 224)

In Stalin's speech, the hostile attention by the "imperialist predators" becomes evidence of the prosperity of the Soviet country (in reality, experiencing a severe crisis). The idea of the imperialists' conspiracy could restore the self-esteem of late Soviet leadership in the same way, by turning the country with serious food difficulties into something very enticing for foreign "intelligence centers" and "ideological saboteurs" (see Semyon Tsvigun's statement above).

Conclusions

This chapter contributes to the discussion on the psychological versus the social nature of conspiracy theories (Byford 2011, 120–43). I aim to demonstrate that in certain social contexts (namely, being a part of the Soviet party or intelligence elite), the psychological benefits of conspiracy narratives were of critical importance to both compensate for the lack of control and protect one's positive self-identity and political beliefs. Nevertheless, these psychological benefits played a more important role than the requirements of the official Soviet language.

In the secret documents, circulated between KGB officers and Communist Party officials (as well as in propaganda texts), there are at least three narrative strategies used to deprive dissidents of their agency: the anti-Western conspiracy theory, the labeling of dissent and criticism as "mental illness," and the "Jewish wives" conspiracy theory. These three types of narratives had the same function that could be performed in different ways, depending on the context. The need to deprive the oppositionists of their agency played a more important role in producing conspiracy narratives than the habit of thinking in the categories of official discourse (such as "hostile capitalist forces," "subversive work of foreign intelligence services," "psychological warfare," and so on).

To be sure, Stalinist conspiracy culture seriously affected the late Soviet leadership's patterns of thinking about any oppositionist activity or disturbing events. But if we try to apply the psychologists' findings to the conclusions of historians, we can see that the rise of conspiracy beliefs in the 1920s and 1930s occurred by a psychological mechanism that acted on a mass scale owing to specific social conditions. In the late Soviet period, the social conditions changed, and therefore, the spread of conspiracy beliefs decreased, but the mechanism remains the same:

82　*Anna Kirziuk*

conspiracy beliefs appeared as a defensive reaction to one's feelings of a lack of control and as a coping mechanism to protect one's positive self-identity and consistent worldview. The latter seems to be particularly important. Conspiracy narratives—as well as the other ways of representing the regime's opponents as "agentless" persons—helped late Soviet officials to ignore opposition statements, and, thereby, protect their political beliefs.

Notes

1 The Soviet secret police had different names in different periods of its existence. The most famous of them are *Narkomat Vnutrennih Del* [People's Commissariat of Internal Affairs, 1934–43], *Ministerstvo Gosudarstvennoi Bezopasnosti* [Ministry of the State Security, 1946–53], and *Komitet Gosudarstvennoi Bezopasnosti* [Committee of State Security, 1954–91].
2 All quotations are translated from Russian by the author.
3 The term refers to texts that propagated in handmade copies beyond the eyes of censors among opposition-leaning friends and associates.
4 The Fifth Department was created in 1967 to counter the "ideological sabotage of the enemy."
5 Katherine Verdery comes to a similar conclusion in her analysis of *Securitate*: uncovering of hidden enemies was the *raison d'être* of secret state service in Socialist Romania (Verdery 2014, 85–86).
6 National Alliance of Russian Solidarists (NTS) was an anti-Communist organization founded in the 1930s by Russian émigrés, which aimed to overthrow the Communist regime in their motherland.
7 In reality, this person did not exist.
8 Andrei Sakharov was one of the founders of the non-official Moscow Human Rights Committee, the author of many writings on the issues of human rights, political freedom, free speech, and the dangers of the Cold War arms race. In 1975, Sakharov was awarded the Nobel Peace Prize.
9 As soon as participants opened their posters, plainclothes KGB officers came up to them, tore or seized the posters, and arrested their holders. On the posters there were demands to respect the Soviet Constitution, to release the dissident Vladimir Bukovsky who had been placed in a mental hospital the day before, and to conduct an open trial of the writers Andrei Sinyavsky and Yuri Daniel (both were arrested for publishing their pieces abroad).
10 Knowing the psychological base of belief in conspiracies, we can assume that in the late Soviet period, there were no mass excesses of scapegoating precisely because there was not a widespread, socially determined sense of lacking control.
11 Review of questions received at lectures on the international situation and foreign policy of the USSR, 1981–82, Russian State Archive of Recent History, Fund 5, Inventory 84, Folder 119.

Bibliography

Abalakina-Paap, Marina, Walter G. Stephan, Traci Craig, and W. Larry Gregory. 1999. "Belief in Conspiracies." *Political Psychology* 20: 637–47.
Alekseeva, Ludmila. 1987. *Soviet Dissent: Contemporary Movements for National, Religious, and Human Rights*. Middletown, CT: Wesleyan University Press.
Alexandrov, Ivan. 1970. "Nishcheta Antikommunizma" [The Poverty of Anti-Communism]. *Pravda*, December 17, 1970.
Allport, Gordon. 1979. *The Nature of Prejudice*. Cambridge, MA: Perseus Books.

"By the order of their foreign masters" 83

Antonov, Boris, Alexey Astangov, Alexandre Belov, Timothey Gusev, and Vladimir Mikhailov. 1982. *Schuzhogo golosa* [By Someone Else's Voice]. Moscow: Moskovskiy rabochiy.

Arkhipova, Alexandra. 2016. "How a Legend Turned a Woman: The Story of Rosa Kaganovitch, Stalin's Secret Wife." In *34th International Conference "Perspectives on Contemporary Legend." Abstracts* [Tallinn. June 28 – July 2, 2016], 9–10. Tallinn: ELM Scholarly Press.

Arkhipova, Alexandra, and Anna Kirziuk. 2020. *Opasnye Sovetskie Veshchi. Gorodskie Legendy I strahi v SSSR* [Dangerous Soviet Things. Urban Legends and Fears in the USSR]. Moscow: Novoe Literaturnoe Obozrenie.

Bemporad, Elissa. 2012. "Empowerment, Defiance, and Demise: Jews and the Blood Libel Specter under Stalinism." *Jewish History* 26 (3–4): 343–61.

Benoist, Alain. 1992. "Psychologie de la théorie du complot." *Politica Hermetica* 6: 13–28.

Bobkov, Philip. 2006. *Poslednie Dvadcat Let. Zapiski Nachalnika Politicheskoj Kontrrazvedki* [The Last Twenty Years. Notes by the Head of Political Counterintelligence]. Moscow: Russkoe Slovo.

Borenstein, Eliot. 2019. *Plots against Russia. Conspiracy and Fantasy after Socialism.* Ithaca, NY: Cornell University Press.

Byford, Jovan. 2011. *Conspiracy Theories. A Critical Introduction.* London: Palgrave Macmillan.

Campion-Vincent, Véronique. 2005. "From Evil Others to Evil Elites: A Dominant Pattern in Conspiracy Theories Today." In *Rumor Mills: The Social Impact of Rumor and Legend*, edited by Garry Fine, Véronique Campion-Vincent, and Chip Heath, 103–22. New Brunswick, NJ: Aldine Transaction.

Chernyaev, Anatoli. 2008. *Sovmestnyj iskhod. Dnevniki dvuh epoh. 1972–1991* [Diaries of Two Epochs. 1972]. Moscow: ROSSPEN. http://prozhito.org/notes?date=%221977-01-01%22&diaries=%5B320%5D

Chronicle of Current Events (Informational Bulletin of Soviet Human Rights Activists). n.d. Accessed September 7, 2019. http://hts.memo.ru/.

Ellis, Bill. 2000. *Raising the Devil. Satanism, New Religions and the Media.* Lexington: University Press of Kentucky.

Ellis, Bill, and Garry Fine. 2010. *The Global Grapevine: Why Rumors of Terrorism, Immigration, and Trade Matter.* Oxford: Oxford University Press.

Fenster, Mark. 2008. *Conspiracy Theories: Secrecy and Power in American Culture.* Minneapolis: University of Minnesota Press.

Fitzpatrick, Sheila. 1999. *Everyday Stalinism: Ordinary Life in Extraordinary Times: Soviet Russia in the 1930s.* Oxford: Oxford University Press.

Glick, Peter. 2005. "Choice of Scapegoats." In *On the Nature of Prejudice: Fifty Years after Allport*, edited by John. F. Dovidio, Peter Glick, and Laurie A. Rudman, 244–61. Malden, MA: Blackwell Publishing.

Heneghan, Thomas. 1977. "Human Rights Protests in Eastern Europe." *The World Today* 33 (3): 90–100.

Hoffman, David. 1993. "The Great Terror on the Local Level: Purges in Moscow Factories, 1936–38." In *Stalinist Terror. New Perspectives*, edited by Arch Getty and Roberta Manning, 116–40. Cambridge: Cambridge University Press.

Ignatenko, Victor, and Nikolai Kolesnikov. 1971. "Obmen 'Babochkami'" [Butterfly Exchange]. *Komsomolskaya Pravda*, August 25–27, 1971.

Kokurin, Alexandr and Nikita Petrov, eds. 2003. *Lubyanka. Organy VCHK-OGPU-NKVD-NKGB-MGB-MVD-KGB. 1917–1991.* Moscow. MFD: Materik.

84 *Anna Kirziuk*

Kostyrchenko, Gennadi. 1995. *Out of the Red Shadows: Anti-Semitism in Stalin's Russia*. Amherst, MA: Prometheus Books.

Kruglanski, Arie. 1987. "Blame-placing Schemata and Attributional Research." In *Changing Conceptions of Conspiracy*, edited by Carl Graumann and Serge Moscovici, 219–29. New York: Springer-Verlag.

Lerov, Leonid, Victor Pavlov, and Yuri Chernyavsky. 1971. "Voyage Francois de Perrego" [The Journey of Francois de Perrego]. *Ogonyok* 37: 28–30.

Makarov, Alexey, ed. 2006. *Dissidenty I Vlast'. Iz Dokumentov KGB I-CK KPSS* [Dissidents and Authorities. Documents of the KGB and Central Committee of the CPSU]. Moscow: The Moscow Helsinki Group.

Manning, Roberta. 1993. "The Soviet Economic Crisis and the Great Purges." In *Stalinist Terror. New Perspectives*, edited by Getty, Arch and Roberta Manning, 116–40. Cambridge and New York: Cambridge University Press.

Mitrokhin, Nikolai. 2003. *Russkaya partiya. Dvizhenie russkih nacionalistov v SSSR. 1953–1985* [Russian Party. The Movement of Russian Nationalists in the USSR. 1953–1985]. Moscow: NLO.

Ovcharenko, Fedor. 1968. "V Lakeyh" [Being Footmen]. *Komsomolskaya Pravda*, January 18.

Pavlov, Sergei. 2005. "Zapiska v CK KPSS [A Note to CC CPSU]" (December 8). In *Pyatoe dekabrya 1965 goda v vospominaniyah i dokumentah* [The 5th December, 1965 in memoirs and documents], edited by Alexandre Daniel, 94–98. Moscow: Memorial, Izdatel'stvo "Zvenya."

Risso, Linda. 2014. *Propaganda and Intelligence in the Cold War. The NATO Information Service*. New York: Routledge.

Rittersporn, Gábor. 2014. *Anguish, Anger and Folkways in Soviet Russia*. Pittsburg: Pittsburg University Press.

Rothschild, Zachary K., Mark Landau, Daniel Sullivan, and Lucas A. Keefer. 2012. "A Dual-Motive Model of Scapegoating: Displacing Blame to Reduce Guilt or Increase Control." *Journal of Personality and Social Psychology* 102 (6): 1148–63.

Scott-Smith, Giles. 2011. "Interdoc and West European Psychological Warfare: The American Connection." *Intelligence and National Security* 26 (2–3): 355–76.

Semichastnyi, Vladimir. 2016. *Specsluzhby SSSR v Tainoi Voine* [Special Services of the USSR in a Secret Warfare]. Moscow: Algoritm.

Shelest, Piotr. 2016. *Da Ne Sudimy Budete Dnevniki i Vospominaniya Chlena Politbyuro* [And You Will Not Be Judged: Diaries and Memoirs of a Politburo Member]. Moscow: Centrpoligraph. https://prozhito.org/person/680

Stalin, Joseph. 1997. "Vystuplenie na zasedanii Voennogo Soveta pri Narkome Oborony" [Speech at the Meeting of the Military Council under the People's Commissar of Defense]. In *Compedium of Stalin,* Vol. 14, 214–35. Moscow: Pisatel.

Staub, Ervin. 1989. *The Roots of Evil: The Origins of Genocide and Other Group Violence*. New York: Cambridge University Press.

Sullivan, Daniel, Mark Landau, and Zachary K. Rothschild. 2010. "The Existential Function of Enemyship: Evidence that People Attribute Influence to Personal and Political Enemies to Compensate for Threats to Control." *Journal of Personality and Social Psychology* 98: 434–39.

Tsvigun, Semyon. 1981. "O Proiskah Imperialisticheskih Razvedok" [On the Intrigues of Imperialist Intelligence Services]. *Communist* 14: 88–99.

Vaissié, Cecile. 1999. *Pour Votre Liberté et pour la Notre. Le Combat des Dissedents en Russie*. Paris: Edition Robert Lafront.

"By the order of their foreign masters" 85

Vakulovskyi, Vladimir. 1988. *'Amnesty' v Grime i bez Nego* ['Amnesty' in Disguise and Without It]. Moscow: Moskovskiy rabochiy.

Verdery, Katherine. 2014. *Secrets and Truth: Ethnography in the Archive of Romania's Secret Police*. Budapest: Central European University Press.

Voslensky, Mikhail. 1991. *Nomenklatura* [The Party Elites]. Moscow: Oktyabr.

Yablokov, Ilya. 2018. *Fortress Russia: Conspiracy Theories in the Post-Soviet World*. Cambridge: Polity.

Yakovlev, Nikolai. 1983. *CRU protiv SSSR* [The CIA against the USSR]. Alma-Ata: Kazakchstan.

Zaleski, Eugene. 1980. *Stalinist Planning for Economic Growth, 1933–1952*. Chapel Hill, NC: The University of North Carolina Press.

Part II

"The enemy within"

Jews and Freemasons

4 The myth of a Judeo-Bolshevik conspiracy in Hungary, within and beyond the far right

Péter Csunderlik and Tamás Scheibner

Introduction

The myth of a Judeo-Bolshevik conspiracy is one of the most time-resistant conspiracy theories to conquer the world. From Russia to Australia and from the United States to Japan, it constituted, and often still constitutes, a significant element of antisemitic discourses. With the increasing emergence of authoritarian regimes in former democratic countries, state propaganda discrediting all forms of civil unrest has revived conspiracy theories as an effective means to disinform society. Among others, the idea of the Judeo-Bolshevik threat is making a comeback, especially—and not surprisingly—in countries where both antisemitism and anti-Communism have deep historical roots, such as the United States, the United Kingdom, Scandinavia, Germany, Austria, and virtually all Eastern European states. The increasing popularity of the New Left among the younger generations has added further impetus to the revival of this conspiracy theory.

The Hungarian case is specific, for in no other country in East Central and Southeastern Europe was a Bolshevik regime established with statewide authority during World War I. During the 1919 dictatorship, street violence and state-approved terror were common, all while the regime also had to face the consequences of having lost the war. The Hungarian Soviet Republic did not improve public opinion on Communism, and it was not difficult to establish the identity of the new regime on an anti-Communist basis. Further, the war and the peace treaties severely affected the economic system, creating the ideal conditions for political forces to profit from scapegoating. The long tradition of antisemitism in the Habsburg Empire was easily exploited by such politics. Indeed, both anti-Communism and political antisemitism lay at the heart of the regime established by and named after Miklós Horthy and served as a major source of legitimation.

We are certainly not the first to analyze the myth of a Judeo-Bolshevik conspiracy in Europe, the Habsburg Empire, or Hungary. André Gerrits was the first to devote a book-length study to the myth of Jewish Communism. While Gerrits admitted that the idea was present in the West, he treated the phenomenon as a primarily German and Eastern European concern. There is no doubt that in Eastern Europe the myth has been deeply embedded in public consciousness and appears in contemporary "memory wars" on the state's socialist legacy. Gerrits is largely

90 *Péter Csunderlik and Tamás Scheibner*

right to point out that the myth of Jewish Communism survived only in Eastern Europe after World War II (2009, 21). Certainly, this has a lot to do with the fact that in Eastern Europe Communism was not simply an ideology, but one that dictatorial regimes identified with. However, as Communism appears to reemerge on the global political scene as a potential choice, especially among younger generations, we can no longer state confidently that "Jewish Communism is history" since "Communism is gone, and so too are many of the political emotions, controversies and polemics it caused" (ibid., 192). In these new circumstances, we think it is particularly important to emphasize (as Gerrits himself does in certain passages of his book, e.g., on p. 18) that the conspiracy theory we deal with owes a lot to Western Europeans, among whom appear figures who are generally respected as emblematic members of a pan-European political pantheon. Such a theory can resurface at any time and not necessarily in an explicit, elaborated form, but more as an insinuation, suggesting guilt by association.

Most recently, Paul Hanebrink authored *A Spectre Haunting Europe* (2018), in which he convincingly argued that Judeo-Bolshevik conspiracism continues to exist despite scholars having collected mounting evidence against the related claims. These latter studies might have their value, but our approach is a functionalist one: the purpose of this study is to determine how the myth was used in various political contexts in the twentieth and twenty-first centuries. During this survey, we will not focus on political Catholicism, which was arguably the most effective promoter of the myth. Hanebrink (2008, see also 2006) devoted a separate study for this context, with Ottokár Prohászka, the Catholic bishop in the center, whose ideas developed in the twentieth century were the determinant for political Catholicism in the interwar period and were revived in the 1990s. Instead, we will devote greater attention to the literature that followed the fall of the Hungarian Soviet Republic, of which Cécile Tormay's *An Outlaw's Diary* is particularly significant. By providing a selective overview, our objective is to direct attention to the diversity of political backgrounds of those who subscribed to the myth. The next section focuses on one figure: the writer and public intellectual László Németh. While previously scholars dealt with manifestations of Judeo-Bolshevik conspiracism that were more straightforward and resembled the German Nazi discourse, we would like to call attention to more subtle uses of the myth, to cases when self-contradictions and shifts within a text or a wider corpus do not allow the reader to determine with certainty whether the myth of Judeo-Bolshevism is affirmed or not. We think that in contemporary political discourses, in Eastern Europe and elsewhere, such textual strategies are more common than outright claims. These are also harder to single out and, therefore, more dangerous. At the end of the chapter, we will refer briefly to contemporary uses of the myth, but before that we will analyze how Németh's work determined a stream of Hungarian conservative populism that, in turn, impacted the political vision of the current government.

The Hungarian Soviet Republic as "Jewish Dictatorship"

The idea of the "Judeo-Bolshevik conspiracy" was not as firmly attached to any event in Hungarian history as it was to the 1919 Hungarian Soviet Republic. The

The myth of a Judeo-Bolshevik conspiracy 91

members of the Revolutionary Governing Council that led the dictatorship of the proletariat—which lasted only 133 days—were atheist and internationalist politicians with no "Jewish" identity. An influential tradition associated with right-wing politics, however, maintains that the dictatorship of the proletariat had a "Jewish" face (Gyáni 2003, 49). This tradition started to take shape immediately after the collapse of the Bolshevik regime, first in the form of pamphlets.

A good example of such pamphlets is *A zsidók rémuralma Magyarországon* (The Terror of the Jews in Hungary) that summarized the months of dictatorship as a series of "pogroms against the Christians, accompanied by atrocities never seen in world history" (1919, 3—all quotes are translated by the authors of this article unless otherwise stated). This text contains almost all the typical tropes and interpretive patterns that define far-right political memory of the event up until today. The reference to "world history" is significant, for it stages the Hungarian nation as a victim of uniquely disproportionate suffering, a Christlike figure, a familiar motif when it comes to Eastern European national discourses. The Jews are, in contrast, the orientalized and subhuman "other" ("cruel parasites," more specifically, dodders, nonindigenous parasite plants) that needs to be kept under firm control or entirely liquidated ("put on ice," 4). This control of the Jews appears here as an essential part of the European cultural heritage: the politically stable and prosperous Western states have already shown how to keep the Jewry controlled, and Hungary should follow the example if she wants to recuperate from the economic crisis caused by the war. According to the pamphlet, the moment had come to make things right, for ordinary Jews are now left behind by their "generals." Such claims mirror the author(s)'conviction that the entire revolution was an organized plot, and "the whole Hungarian Jewry is responsible indivisibly and jointly for the catastrophe of the nation" (40). As we shall see below, this and hundreds of similar pamphlets' urge to regulate the Jewry would be put into practice at the dawn of the regime established by the admiral, and soon to be regent, Miklós Horthy.

These pamphlets were not simply manifestations of antisemitic hatred, but additionally often served explicit and very practical social and political purposes beyond the exclusion of Jews from the political body. In particular, the emerging ethnicist (*fajvédő*, literally "race defender") movement tried to frame the Hungarian Soviet Republic in a way that would allow it to counter those middle-class voices that blamed the working class as a source of destructive unrest. An early document of the ethnicist movement, the Hungarian Racialist Guide stated: "Communism should not be called anything other than Jewish communism. Let this expression 'Jewish communism' be at the same time teaching and forgiving our worker brothers-in-race (*munkásfajtestvérek*), who were only blind instruments of the conquest of the Jewry, and if we blame these workers we only take off the heavy burden of responsibility from the shoulders of the Jewry" (Cselekedjünk 1923, 36). The myth of a Judeo-Bolshevik conspiracy was used as a political instrument aiming to smooth class conflicts and help the reintegration of the proletariat to the body of the nation.

This ethnicization of the 1919 revolution, however, was a wider phenomenon than one would suppose: it was also present in some segments of the socialist

92 *Péter Csunderlik and Tamás Scheibner*

movement. Sándor Csizmadia belonged to the pathbreakers of social democracy (in the broad sense): he is remembered as the first poet who promoted proletarian revolution. As a journalist he gained a considerable reputation in the worker's movement for his committed fight for those living in poverty and for himself being a frequent guest in penitentiary institutions. His ideal was a sort of agrarian Socialism based on a combination of private land ownership of the peasantry and cooperatives (Sipos 1997). He became people's commissar for agriculture during the Soviet Republic but resigned due to conflicts within the leadership of the regime. After Horthy's takeover, he chose not to flee the country, but voiced sharp criticism of Béla Kun and other leaders of the Soviet Republic instead, portraying them as traitors of the proletariat, while he insisted that Socialism could not be appropriated by any party. This was useful for the rightist regime, so much so that he was allegedly considered for a high government position in the new cabinet, and the rightist press provided him ample opportunities to elaborate his criticism in public. In 1920, Csizmadia also published his memoirs of the revolutionary times, in which he suggested that a Jewish/non-Jewish fault line existed in the left and that the Soviet Republic was hijacked by the former, who were responsible for terror. This historically untenable thesis led Csizmadia to depict a favorable picture of the leader of one of the terrorist brigades—the protestant, non-Jewish József Cserny, who was contrasted to Tibor Szamuely, who had Jewish ancestors and led the "Lenin boys" (who were also considered usually and counterfactually Jewish). Csizmadia's case cannot simply be disregarded as political opportunism: his ideas show consistency over time. Rather, it suggests that the social democratic movement was very heterogeneous, and some had no difficulty in adding antisemitism to Marxism as an additional framework to explain social inequality, as one could also see in the British, German, and even French workers' movement (Brustein and Roberts 2015).

The interest in the alleged Jewish profile of the Hungarian Soviet Republic was not confined to Hungary: it provoked reactions across Europe. The press disclosed the family backgrounds of members of the governing council, which were Jewish more often than not, and the link was quickly made by the well informed. One of them was secretary of state Winston Churchill, who identified an imagined Jewish agency behind the events. Churchill started the New Year in 1920 by claiming in Sunderland and, in print, in the London *Times* that Bolshevism was a "Jewish movement." A month later he qualified his views in the London *Illustrated Sunday Herald*, where he endorsed Zionism in contrast to Bolshevism, two forces that "struggle for the soul of the Jewish people." Echoing *The Protocols of the Elders of Zion*, a copy of which he possessed at the time (Gilbert 2008, 43), he identified Bolshevism with an evil Jewish plot aiming at world dominance: "From the days of Spartacus-Weishaupt to those of Karl Marx, and down to Trotsky (Russia), Bela Kun (Hungary), Rosa Luxembourg (Germany), and Emma Goldman (United States), this world-wide conspiracy for the overthrow of civilization and for the reconstitution of society on the basis of arrested development, of envious malevolence, and impossible equality, has been steadily growing." He paid particular attention to the Hungarian Soviet Republic: "The same evil prominence was

The myth of a Judeo-Bolshevik conspiracy   93

obtained by Jews in the brief period of terror during which Bela Kun [the leader of the Hungarian Soviet Republic] ruled in Hungary" (Churchill 1920). This article by Churchill has been subject to debate in the context of his general relation to the Jewish people (see, for example, Cohen 2003; Brustein 2003; Gilbert 2008), but for our own purposes, it is enough to note that even such a symbolic person often described as philosemitic occasionally used the idea of a Jewish Communist conspiracy as a political tool.

In any case, Churchill's views, as far as "Jewish Bolshevism" was concerned, were no exception in Great Britain. Churchill's was actually a rather moderate voice, which is in itself revealing: a belief in the Judeo-Bolshevik conspiracy was the standard view in the *Times* and many other high-profile newspapers until the *Protocols* were finally dismissed as forgery in 1921 (Karsai 1994; Brustein 2003, 297–310). The prominence of such views is hardly a surprise if we consider that the *Times'* editor, for instance, was Henry Wickham Steed, former Viennese correspondent, who returned to Britain with well-developed antisemitic convictions that included the identification of Socialism as a "Jewish doctrine" spread by Jews in their efforts to reach world dominance (Steed 1913, 155, et passim). In a similar spirit, the *Morning Post* discussed the Hungarian Soviet Republic in great detail in a series of articles complemented by the British Fascist Nesta Webster (another source of Churchill). Webster was a towering figure in British conspiracism, whose *World Revolution: The Plot against Civilization* also singled out the Jewish character of the Hungarian Soviet Republic (Webster 1921, 295). Such international attention is significant for it immediately found its way back to the Hungarian press, which quoted these sources as evidence that the "Judeo-Bolshevik conspiracy was more prominent in Hungary than anywhere else" (Gwynne 1921, 5, 97). As we previously suggested, this perceived singularity of Hungary was linked to the idea that the country was a primary operative territory for Jews in search of world dominance, a perception now confirmed by the West. Already at that relatively early stage, Judeo-Bolshevik conspiracism was fueled through exchanges across borders and cultures.

The greatest international influence in shaping the views on the Hungarian Soviet Republic was, however, by a French publication. The Tharaud brothers, who traveled to Hungary to experience the country for themselves, reported on the *Bolchevistes de Hongrie* in the pages of the *Revue des Deux Mondes* in the summer of 1920 (Leymarie 2006). By the next year, these articles were out in book form as *Quand Israël est roi* (When Israel Is King) and was immediately contracted for two English translations, closely followed by an American and a Romanian publication, as well as Polish, Swedish, Finnish, German, and Danish editions. The total print run of all editions was over 100,000 copies. The leading figure of *Action Française*, Léon Daudet celebrated the work as a courageous unmasking of the "Jewish war" dressed as revolution (Daudet 1929, 184). It was also translated into Hungarian and appeared in the cultural monthly *Napkelet* (Orient), edited by the writer Cécile Tormay, as a sequel in 1924.

The acknowledged fiction writer and women's movement activist Cécile Tormay was herself the author of the most famous account on the revolution and the

94 Péter Csunderlik and Tamás Scheibner

Soviet Republic. In interwar Hungary, the Horthy regime created a more or less coherent national mythology, and few books better served this mythology than Tormay's extremely popular *Bujdosó könyv* (1920–21, published in English as *An Outlaw's Diary*). She formulated the pseudo-historical explanation known as the "dagger theory" with great erudition, which claimed that the nation was stabbed in the back by the Jewry in the final phase of World War I. According to Tormay, who suggested that the final victory was on the horizon with Russia's exit from the war, "all of a sudden, a shining blade seemed to pierce the air. There was a flash of light, and the light lit up a new wound. What had happened. Who had caused it?" (Tormay 1923 I, 38–39). She was ready with the answer: the Jewish "assassins" and, in particular, the atheist-materialistic student organization, the Galileo Circle, whose members spread antiwar propaganda and acted as agents of Lenin and Trotsky. The main reason for the Circle's association with the Soviet Republic is that several leaders of the Hungarian Bolshevik revolution belonged to or were linked with the group, including such prominent figures as commissars Mátyás Rákosi and György Lukács. Tormay described the proclamation of the proletarian dictatorship on March 21, 1919, as a Good Friday on which the "Jews" crucified Hungary, the latter symbolized with Christ (1923 II, 85). The account is a remarkable collection of fake news, false rumors, and horroristic details, often introduced by the author with expressions like "allegedly," "I was told," or "they say." All in all, it is a source of the "common knowledge" of the bourgeois class on the revolutions and the related Judeo-Bolshevik conspiracy. The genre of the book is difficult to define: many contemporaries read it as a reliable historical account, whereas today it is rather seen in the context of her fictional works.

Tormay was not only a popular novelist but also one of the best-known adversaries of female engagement in public affairs and politics. She was not a progressivist: extending women's voting rights beyond the Christian elite was not her thing. A greater female involvement in higher education made sense for her only if chances for non-Christians and the lower classes were strictly withheld (Pető 2003, 71). As a chair of the National Association of Hungarian Women (MANSZ), her greatest achievement was to redirect the aim of the legislation known as *numerus clausus*. The law was originally intended to limit female involvement in higher education, which was seen by state officials as a factor limiting the chances of former soldiers returning from the war and young refugees arriving from the detached territories of the country upon the peace settlements to acquire a degree. MANSZ made successful efforts to cast Jews instead of women as the real threat. It was nothing else but the Jewish "overrepresentation," they claimed, that would prevent the accommodation of the soldiers' and refugees' needs for a better access to higher education (Kovács 2003, 86–88). Tormay was also concerned that too many Jewish women were getting university degrees, which undermined the prospects of Christian women and diverted the women's movement to a direction that she did not agree with. Her loyalty to the Horthy regime was never shaken, and she always made clear in public statements that female emancipation, even in this limited form, was, for her, always secondary to the national cause. Even though she embodied the figure of an independent woman confidently acting in

The myth of a Judeo-Bolshevik conspiracy   95

the public sphere, which might set an empowering example for a number of privileged females of the time, she never revealed an intention to subvert patriarchy as a whole, only to a limited extent. This stance helped her to rise as a regime-conforming representative of the women's movement despite her rumored homosexuality (Kurimay 2016).

An outstanding writer and literary historian of the interwar period, the Catholic Antal Szerb, who was later murdered during World War II because of his Jewish ancestry, had praised Tormay's novels by observing there was "something we usually do not find in Hungarian historical novels: atmosphere, mystery, fear, and the dark, misty horror of the past centuries" (Szerb 2002, 435). Indeed, even *An Outlaw's Diary* could be seen as a bizarre work of fiction in the Gothic tradition, which itself has historical links to antisemitism (cf. Davison 2004). The book is abundant in images of the horroristic and the *unheimlich*. This was generally true for many pamphlets of the period, but most of these were no different to tabloid journalism, whereas Tormay's literary talent elevated the material to a much higher level. This in turn meant she had a huge impact on her readers, and her book was held as a kind of gold standard of antisemitic literature between the 1920s and the early 1940s. Despite its highly fictional character and the fact that the book was written in a diary form *after* the Soviet Republic, with incomprehensibly exhaustive details, its readers did not consider it fiction. While being fiction does not make it any less distasteful a work, its effect was undoubtedly further enhanced by a certain reality effect. Untroubled by the elusive borders between the real and the imaginary, it was treated as firsthand testimony and unquestionable evidence of Judeo-Bolshevik conspiracy.

From the post-1919 literature on the Judeo-Bolshevik conspiracy, the memoir of the far-right military officer Gyula Gömbös, published in 1920, stands out for the significance of the author in Hungarian history: between 1932 and 1936 he served as prime minister, and it was under his rule that Hungary became a closer ally of Germany. Gömbös was a firm believer in racial theories and endorsed eugenics quite early, when it had already established itself as a discipline (Turda 2014), but was still less common than it was to become in the 1920s and 1930s. In his recollections on the Hungarian Soviet revolution, "blood" featured as a keyword: he tried to explain the failure of the "internationalist (freemasonry) organizations of Jewry" in establishing "red rule" by proving that the Jews are genetically flawed. Gömbös claimed that world domination, the alleged ultimate goal of the Jews, will not ever be reached, for the Jews' tendency of "making great mistakes in great things" (1920, 23) and their inability to build a state (another antisemitic topoi) is not a cultural issue, but the results of inherited character traits. From his perspective, the Hungarian Soviet Republic was destined to fall.

While Gömbös considered a series of factors outside of genetics, another significant pamphlet by physician Béla Szemere (under the pseudonym Progrediéus) interpreted events purely from a racialist and eugenicist perspective. The hospital director Szemere was one of the earliest adherents of National Socialism in Hungary: he joined the movement of Gömbös in the 1920s and became an MP in 1939 as a representative of the Hungarian National Socialist Peasants' and Workers'

96   Péter Csunderlik and Tamás Scheibner

Party. Szemere promoted the application of eugenics and nature sciences in the social sciences, because "society consists of individuals," and therefore human biologists and doctors have to treat the "social illnesses" as well (Progrediéus 1920, 2). According to him, the revolutions of 1918–19 were symptoms of the disease of Hungarian society and resulted from the fact that Hungarians had missed employing eugenicist social engineering in the previous decades. As a result, "the mentally disabled" (ibid., 3)—a term Szemere borrowed from psychiatrist Károly Lechner (1919)—came to dominate the Hungarian political elites, who led the country to catastrophes. "Mentally disabled," to Lechner and Szemere, was a broad, catchall term, which included those "who seek unjust benefits and privileges, without paying any attention to others." These "disabled" people were compared by the author to "cancer cells," which have to be eliminated by the society considered as an "organism" (Progrediéus 1920, 3–8).

Szemere did not hesitate to apply the "disabled" category to the entire Hungarian political elite from the end of the nineteenth century. The evidence was their readiness to offer alliance to genetically "anti-Hungarian" forces such as Jews or other nationalities, and for the sake of their selfish political purposes, these Hungarian politicians let these "anti-Hungarian" forces rise to the top of the Hungarian nation. In this interpretation, the Hungarian Soviet Republic was an attempt by the Jews—who concealed their own "racial aspirations" with the idea of Communism—to achieve their hegemony in Hungary. It is extremely dangerous to the life of a nation, so the argument goes, when "disability" encounters the "aspiration of a foreign interest," so Szemere offered a solution in order to avoid another dictatorship of the proletariat: the replacement of the "disabled" Hungarian political elite and the enactment of strict racial eugenics laws. He emphasized: "In order to secure our racial health, our survival, we do not need Jews living in Hungary" (Progrediéus 1920, 3–8). Cancerous tumor, as it is known, was treated by doctors at that time through excision.

The pamphlets and publications of other genres discussed here, which are only a handful of selected texts from a much larger corpus, not only were manifestations of intolerance, scapegoating, and racist hatred but also had actual political relevance. The omnipresent theme of "Jewish dictatorship," typically framed as Judeo-Bolshevism, embedded and helped to gain social legitimacy for the antisemitic laws after 1919—in particular, the *numerus clausus*, effective from 1921, which ended up suppressing "Jewish intellectuals" (Kovács 1994, 2016). These laws limited the number of persons with minority (in effect: mostly Jewish) origins to study various professions and provoked fierce debates, even within the political right. The pamphlet industry assisted in creating a climate for these laws to be more easily accepted. Since then, the myth of a Judeo-Bolshevik conspiracy was not taken off the agenda until the end of World War II, and it played a central role in justifying the Hungarian holocaust. In July 1944, Prime Minister Döme Sztójay stated: "the racially pure Jews are generally the representatives of destruction, as in 1918 they were the most destructive and were the allies of the Bolsheviks" (Sztójay 2017, 97). It is tragicomic that Döme Sztójay, in his search for the allies of the "Bolsheviks" of 1918–19, would have had to look in the

The myth of a Judeo-Bolshevik conspiracy 97

mirror, because the Nazi collaborator prime minister appointed after the German occupation was the head of the Red Army's secret service under the Hungarian Soviet Republic.

Judeo-Bolshevism and Hungarian conservative revolution: the case of László Németh

By the mid-1920s, the Horthy regime had established itself and the myth of Judeo-Bolshevism became an unquestionable truth: the extensive pamphlet literature, official history writing, and fiction and poetry upholding such views made its impact on public consciousness. In the second half of the decade, however, a great variety of grassroots social initiatives and groups emerged that sought new ideologies that would allow them to challenge the economic and social status quo. The most well known and the most heterogenic was probably the Miklós Bartha Society. Even though some members of such groups subscribed to leftist progressivism, it was more typical, as elsewhere in Europe, to question the tradition of the Enlightenment as an adequate epistemological basis for relating to reality and rethinking the political community. A series of journals and newspapers were launched that usually existed only for a couple of months and rarely lasted longer than a few years. A cohort of young intellectuals with conflicting and not fully distilled views published in these fora, mixing a large diversity of political languages. Racialized rhetoric was by no means absent from these discussions, and political antisemitism was widespread, if not necessarily central to the theories under discussion. Throughout the 1930s, the political field became increasingly more structured as left- and right-leaning political alternatives diverted. One of the key movements to come largely from the Bartha Society, the *népi írók* (populist writers) movement, however, which aspired primarily to emancipate the poor peasantry, institutionalized personal solidarities across the political divide. The major Hungarian novelist and essayist, László Németh (1901–75) belonged to this group.

Németh has been considered one of the most prolific ideologues of the movement, with a profound impact on Hungarian intellectual and political agendas up until today. It is difficult to understand the relationship of the political right to Hungarian Jews of the past 30 years, from the regime change in 1989, without taking into consideration Németh's influence. His intellectual resources were extremely wide ranging, but there is little doubt that German conservative revolutionary thinkers made a lasting impact on him. In 1932, commenting on the anti-capitalist (soon to be National Socialist) economist Ferdinand Fried and the journal *Der Tat*, he urged to align Central European (Polish, Czech, Slovak, Hungarian, and Romanian) intellectuals to create a united front against Bolshevism: "In case in Central Europe the necessary transition to a planned economy and a bound state order does not go according to our plans, Europe will soon be overwhelmed by homunculus culture: Bolshevism. In Germany, young people (not Hitlerists) feel this, and I see it in their journal" (Németh 1993). Németh rejected Hitlerism, and regarded German influence valuable only until the point it did not efface the national characteristics of Central European cultures, but the direct inspiration behind his idea to develop an authoritarian economic and political rule that would lead to a more egalitarian society was Fried's analysis on the death of capitalism and the creation of homunculi by Americanism and Socialism, two sides of the same coin in their view (Németh 1932–1993, 35). Given that alchemy had been traditionally associated with Jews in Europe and was identified as something essentially blasphemous and non-Christian, this metaphor could be regarded as an early indicator of the reemergence of the Judeo-Bolshevik myth in an anti-establishment and anti-Nazi discourse.

The 1920s reverberated with echoes of an alleged Judeo-Bolshevik conspiracy, and no association of Jews and Bolsheviks could escape conspiracist allusions. It is still important to distinguish between explicit claims that Jews intentionally planned a large-scale conspiracy with Bolshevism as one of its vehicles and analyses that attempted to historically understand the role of Jews in Hungarian society and their relationship to capitalism and Communism with an intellectual tool kit of the times. Németh was shifting between the two, and over the 1930s and early 1940s, he came to increasingly attribute specific intentions to "the Jewish people." A single paragraph from a 1934 text by Németh shows very well how a conspiracist mindset takes over, while he argues on grounds notably different to a conspiracy theory:

So what has antisemitism achieved? That a people living next to us who are thrown out of our [national] body and who are particularly sensitive to stigma, are bound together by their wounds, whose relative power is constantly increasing, and the more sanguine part of whom is holding his thirst for revenge behind his clenched teeth. This thirst for revenge must be understood if we are to look into the eyes of Hungarian antinomies; we have to feel it. By 1919, the Jewry had advanced on all fronts. It is natural for people and peoples who are ascending to consider their ascendancy beneficial to the country and beyond that to the whole world, because fulfilling its nature is a mission for all living beings, which mission is believed to serve the purposes of creation. In any case, the Jews, as a strong-minded and thus impatient people, refused to account for the concerns about its outburst. After such a history, the antisemitic wave was a terrible shock to him; a new emergence of the wild beasts extinguished by Theseus that can only be dreaded and never thought about. The Jewry was beaten off with rubber sticks from the inner circles of society; and he became a critical viewer of what Szekfű [a historian of the interwar period, whose 1920 account set the basis for the vision of history during the Horthy regime] described as neo-baroque. He feels his superiority over this society that he could rightly feel, and he feels it even beyond that it is right to feel. All he has to do is fast them out and the moment of paying back would come. It is nationalism, glowing nationalism, under communist, liberal, humanist slogans.

(Németh 1934, 125)

The myth of a Judeo-Bolshevik conspiracy 99

In the view of Németh (also presented in a series of other articles), "the Jewry," as any other *Volk*, is a living organism that naturally aspires for self-realization. This he thought deserving of empathy until a certain point, but if the self-fulfillment confronts similar aspirations by the Hungarian majority, Jewish self-realization needs to be limited. The counter-reaction of Hungarian society in the form of aggressive antisemitism, as the argument goes, traumatized the Jewish people, leading to the emergence of an inner drive, a "thirst for vengeance." This drive in Németh's account is, of course, not a conscious one: it is an instinct of the organism. However, and this is where the key step is taken toward conspiracism, the mentioned instinct affects the way the Jewish people, now cast out from society to a marginal and consequently critical position, reconsider and rationalize their own situation and perspectives and consciously subscribe to a nationalist plot deceivingly masked as Communism, liberalism, and humanism.

No doubt, Németh would categorically reject the idea that he was antisemitic. He would and did refer to his acknowledgment of Jewish virtues here and there and to his outspoken anti-Nazism. The problem with such claims is that these, in effect, veal the context in which the statements are made, and this turns Németh's discursive strategy very efficient and difficult to trace. It is worth to contrast him with the writer and journalist Dezső Szabó (1879–1945), who was a major reference point for populist writers and penned several articles and pamphlets against "anti-Judaism" (the most well known was published in 1938, but earlier versions had been circulated in the late 1920s) only to point out that ethnic Germans living in Hungarian territory were a deadly disease to the nation's "organism" in contrast to the Jews who were "simply" a "curable infection" (Szabó 1926, 1938, 38–39). Németh borrowed a lot from Szabó, but, in contrast to his predecessor, also voiced humanitarian concerns. "The Jew cannot be persecuted by a humanist age because he is Jewish," he asserted (Németh 1935a). In a much less tolerant tone, however, he was usually careful to single out various "types" of Jews and allowed individual trajectories that diverted from the main "type"—that is, the vengeful Shylockian type. He presented such diverting individuals as examples to follow, for they enriched Hungarian culture or have shown the path to a new, non-assimilated Jewish culture that Németh was in favor of (being convinced that assimilation equals Jews masking themselves as Hungarians). But whenever "the Jewry" is referred to as a collective, it is associated with some single-center powerhouse acting behind the scenes: "The Jewry serving worldwide trade is an invisible great power" (Németh 1935b; see also Németh 1935a, 1940) that eventually "was frightened and pushed into sort of semi-ghettos after it unveiled itself in 1919," during the short-lived Hungarian Soviet Republic (Németh 1942).

For Németh, this close association of both global capitalism and Communism with "the Jewry" found its manifestation in a single person: the philosopher and cultural politician György Lukács (1885–1971). This is significant because the figure of Lukács for many embodies the quintessential Judeo-Bolshevik in symbolic politics in contemporary Hungary, as we will briefly discuss in the final part of this chapter. However, the reason he became an ideal person to fulfill this role was, in large part, his prehistory. Lukács came from a wealthy bourgeois family, and his

100 *Péter Csunderlik and Tamás Scheibner*

father was an investment banker. Influenced by the 1917 Bolshevik Revolution, he became a Marxist and joined the Communist Party of Hungary a few months before their takeover in March 1919. Lukács became deputy commissar and then commissar for education. It is worth quoting Tormay's *An Outlaw's Diary* here, who in a critical take on Lukács's cultural policy, did not forget to point out his wealthy background: "George Lukacs-Lowinger, the hydrocephalic little Jewish philosopher, son of a millionaire banker, became a Proletarian apostle through the influence of his Bolshevik wife. As Deputy Educational Commissary of the Soviet [Republic] he had the book and music shops closed down, and after having thus stopped the pulsing literary life, in the midst of Great Silencing he cooked in his alembic the literary homunculus that will never ever get to walk or sing" (Tormay 1923 II, 107; we modified the translation to reflect the original more closely). In Németh's view, the Hungarian Soviet Republic was a betrayal of the 1918 Aster Revolution, for it cut off any chance for land redistribution by opting for collectivization instead. In this respect, he differed from Tormay, who rejected both revolutions. But it is difficult to mistake the resemblance of their views and rhetoric in other respects. Németh explains the betrayal of the poor peasantry and, thus, the revolution, by the lack of the Jews' commitment to national interests but also by a united Jewish response to a sign given by a mysterious actor: "The whistle that was blown over Europe for an international revolution" motivated "hysterical" reaction in favor of "the Jewish cause" (Németh 1942). As such, the international revolution portrayed as inauthentic serves just as a cover for a deeper cause, and all kinds of associated ideologies are secondary and could be easily replaced. "What else could explain the sudden appointment of such an almost conservative scholar like György Lukács as people's commissar?"—Németh asked in his extremely influential 1942 book-length essay, *Kisebbségben* (In Minority). The gap between capitalism and Communism (and even intellectual traditionalism) is bridged. Judeo-Bolshevism is dissolved in a more general antisemitic discourse.

The myth of Judeo-Bolshevism in our times is usually manifested not in full-blown claims but as part of complex discourses specific to various Eastern and Central European politics and cultures. Concerning Hungary, Németh's example is telling precisely because the myth does not take center stage in his works, even though it occurs in his most influential essays. To fully understand the position of the myth in the highly influential ideological design outlined in *Kisebbségben*, one needs to take into account not only ethno-cultural considerations but also the major religious divide between Protestantism and Catholicism in Hungary.

In the essay referred to, the Protestant Németh criticized Catholics for "being more Christian than national" (Németh 1942) and for supporting not the peasantry but the mostly Roman Catholic ethnic Germans in their aspirations to join the ranks of the middle class and the intelligentsia. As Hanebrink (2018) has shown in great detail, the myth of Judeo-Bolshevism was absolutely central for Hungarian Catholicism, Bishop Ottokár Prohászka (1858–1927) being its primary ideologue. The Protestants' stronger identification with the heritage of the Old Testament, however, made the case for them somewhat more complicated. Ever since the sixteenth century, as it was common in a series of other European cultures where

The myth of a Judeo-Bolshevik conspiracy   101

Protestantism played a significant role, there was a well-established parallel between Jews and Hungarians as selected nations. In the mid-1930s, Németh took up this parallelism and claimed that in Central Europe Hungarians are destined to take over the role of the Jews, like Christianity took over the role of the Jewish religion: "The Hungarian call: the realization of Central European socialism. Our history and our diasporic existence destines us for this: we are the people with the most European history here, and we are the new Jews, the omnipresent" (Németh 1935a, 116). Immersed in the characterology discourse so common at the time (cf. Trencsényi 2012), Németh questioned the capacity of Jews to collective self-criticism, a central character flaw he identified that prevented them to be a nation "above History," despite the Jewish people's outstanding qualities that had led them to become the elite of global capitalism. "The Jewry" was the nobility for the age of capitalism, but in a forthcoming age of Socialism, it was the Hungarians' mission to rise above history and connect Central European nations in a unified whole. The way to achieve this was to achieve excellence in cultural and intellectual fields. Thus, in Németh's vision, "the Jewry" was both a contemporary representative of a bygone age, a living anachronism, and a competitor for the Hungarians as a new transnational elite building a rather undefined anti-Nazi Socialism on a renewed left. This new left, integrated in an overarching political movement that transcended the binarism of right and left, was imagined with minimal or no involvement by Jewish people, who nevertheless would be thanked for maintaining the Left during the counter-revolution of the 1920s, even if they "distorted" the Left just to be corrected by Hungarians.

In summary, the significance of such ideas from the perspective of the conspiracy theory of Judeo-Bolshevism is that Jews are deprived here from being representatives of progressivism. In contrast to the most common uses of the Judeo-Bolshevik conspiracy claim, the political value of pointing at the myth serves neither to discredit leftist agendas altogether nor simply to reconfirm Christian (and much less Catholic) conservative or far-right prejudices (although, it does have such an effect in practice). Instead, it reclaims progressivism in the name of conservative revolution with an egalitarian twist based on redistributive practices serving the poor peasantry, a peculiar conservative revolution that places its tokens not in technological or industrial improvement but *Bildung*: the newborn elite shall embrace and stand up for (a selectively defined) European cultural heritage.

This newborn elite shall be, for Németh, the Hungarian people, whose supposed *Volkscharakter* allows itself to turn into such an elite in Central Europe: Hungarians shall achieve an outstanding status in the region by "the revolution of quality," a central term for Németh for the development of a new man via practices of the self that ultimately pave the way to "quality socialism." In contrast, if Jews were running the revolution, claimed Németh, it would lead to Marxist Socialism or Bolshevism, but even that would be betrayed at the first occasion. This is because Jews, it is argued along the usual stereotypes, are guilty of placing an exclusive emphasis on economic interests in changing the world, which necessarily lead to the reemergence of self-serving attitudes without cultural transformation. In

102   *Péter Csunderlik and Tamás Scheibner*

this worldview, "the Jewry," just as the capitalism and Bolshevism associated with it, is a traditionalist force keeping up the status quo. In the final account, this approach positions "Jewish Bolshevism and liberalism" as a *pandante* of the sometimes antisemitic Catholic universalism and suggests that ultimately both work toward the same end. The myth of Judeo-Bolshevism and its related tropes serve here rhetorically to support a peculiar revolutionary project that links social transformation to a nationalist universalism.

State Socialism and the political transition to democracy

It is hard to overestimate the impact of *Kisebbségben* on Hungarian political culture. One may track its influence not only on the political right up until today but also on the thought of István Bibó, an outstanding intellectual who is consensually regarded across political divides as the most elaborate political theorist in twentieth-century Hungary and who has remained a major authority for leftist liberals. Bibó's 1948 essay, *The Jewish Question in Hungary after 1944* urged society to face its own responsibility in persecuting the Jews; however, even Bibó took the opposition of Jews and Hungarians for granted, and in this respect, his thinking remained within the paradigm of Németh (Gyáni 2011). Further, Németh lived long enough to become an influential thinker during State Socialism, and he himself adapted some of his earlier ideas from *Kisebbségben* to the new political conditions.

After the 1956 uprising, new official cultural politics had been forged by the regime of first party secretary, János Kádár. Many writers fled to the West or were imprisoned: their works were not allowed to be published. State officials in the field of culture sought to demonstrate that the new regime was not run by the same old Stalinist guard of Mátyás Rákosi, and it provided greater liberty for writers who did not question but endorsed the legitimacy of the regime. It also allowed a more explicit articulation of Hungarian patriotism (in contrast to nationalism) and addressed the issue of Hungarians living outside the borders of the country. Németh was silenced during Stalinism, and since his involvement in the revolution was occasional and marginal, he seemed to be a potential author to be reintegrated in the literary field. This move was not against the will of Németh either, who always had the urge to address a wide audience not only with his novels but also with his grand schemes of cultural change. His *Karácsonyi üzenet* (Christmas Message) was aired on the Hungarian Radio program *Szülőföldünk* (Our Homeland) in 1962. This propaganda program was directed at Hungarians in the diaspora to improve the image of socialist Hungary in the West and counter the effect of anti-Communist émigré circles (Szabó Juliet 2009). Németh revived the Jewish-modeled Hungarian messianism familiar from *Kisebbségben*. His message urged émigrés to consider repatriation or "at least" to raise their kids as Hungarians, for in the home country, a "new life" had started with all the potential to turn Hungary into something great, and those in the diaspora will soon turn into a system of capillaries just to mediate "the vitally refreshing blood-wave of Hungarian spirit rich in oxygen" (Németh 1961). This overwhelming metaphor

The myth of a Judeo-Bolshevik conspiracy   103

is further explained by a simile that must be familiar by now: Hungarians are like Jews in adding a vitalizing impulse to the world. The difference is that the Hungarian people lacked a mission or lost their way, in contrast to the Jews, who are "triumphant" even in the diaspora. Once again, a unified mission is attributed to the Jewish people. And this is precisely the "triumph" to which Hungarians should aspire, according to Németh. Make no mistake: seeing "the Jewry" as one single, unified entity is actually a projection of Németh's wishful thinking for the Hungarian nation; his creation of an imaginary unified Jewish people could be used as an example for Hungarians. To recast the Jewish people as a role model, they necessarily have to be treated as one single world-encompassing organism: this is the measure of success after all.

This mode of thinking in which antisemitic conspiracism is deeply entangled with appreciation leading to mimetic competition profoundly affected many anti-Communist non-liberals in the late 1980s. Perhaps the most significant event when such attitudes came to the surface and were debated was in 1990, when the poet and widely respected public intellectual Sándor Csoóri published *Nappali hold* (Moon at Daylight), his historical-cultural reflections in a diary form, a few months before the first democratic parliamentary elections. In his cultural pessimist vision that paid tribute to *Kisebbségben*, Csoóri suggested that the 1919 Hungarian Soviet Republic created an unbridgeable divide between "the" Hungarians and "the" Jewry, attributing collective guilt to the latter and implying their coordinated action as a separate collective body. Further, he also linked this collective body to contemporary politics: he portrayed one of the political parties, the liberal Alliance of Free Democrats (Szabad Demokraták Szövetsége), as the force acting in favor of this collective while harming and potentially destroying the Hungarian nation. In Csoóri's words: "these days the tendencies of a reversed assimilation are becoming increasingly and clearly perceptible in the country. The Hungarian Jewry representing liberal principles desires to assimilate Hungarian values to themselves in style and spirit. For this purpose she could build such a great parliamentary jumping board as never before" (Csoóri 1990, 6). The writers Miklós Mészöly and Imre Kertész were among the first who protested against these views, closely followed by Péter Esterházy and a series of others. The *Nappali hold* debate proved to be a major event in the cultural and political history of modern Hungary that catalyzed the fragmentation of the Hungarian intelligentsia and quickly led to a radicalization of public discourse.

These radical voices, including that of Judeo-Bolshevik conspiracism, sometimes came, again, from unexpected sources. In the issue following the debated diary entry of Csoóri in the journal *Hitel*, István Benedek, a psychiatrist and writer with an encyclopedic interest, contributed an essay titled *Nemzetiség és kisebbség* (Nationality and Minority). This, for a change, followed the paradigm of Dezső Szabó and *Kisebbségben* with all the internal tensions of Németh's thinking that categorized "the Jewry" and treated it as a single collective at the same time. In his account, integration of Jewish people went very well until the emergence of Nazism—a peculiar view given the discriminatory legislation of the interwar period—but it was Jewish Communism that really poisoned Hungarian-Jewish

104   Péter Csunderlik and Tamás Scheibner

relations. With an orientalist twist, very familiar in similar contexts, the origin of Jewish sin is identified in an inability to control emotions: like Németh's Shylock discussed above, the argument was that Jews could not keep their thirst for revenge at a tolerable level and so expanded their influence when the Communist party was ruling. In Benedek's reading, reactions to *Nappali hold* was a typical manifestation of "Jewish hysteria" caused by the new political conditions, when "the ministerial and other leading positions are filled not exclusively by Jews" (Benedek 1990, 36) in contrast, supposedly, to the state socialist era. "We are at the point when they silently aspire for Judocracy, and loudly stigmatize everyone as an antisemite, who dares to raise his voice against their tyranny," Benedek concluded. He knew a lot about the discourse of conspiracism and how to use it with stigmatizing effect, for he came from an illustrious Freemason family. His father, literary historian Marcell Benedek, was the grand master of the Grand Symbolic Lodge of Hungary at the time it was outlawed in 1950, and his grandfather and he were also Freemasons (Benedek Sz. 2007). This, however, as one could see, did not prevent Benedek to employ the rhetoric of Judeo-Bolshevik conspiracism.

Csoóri and Benedek are not accidental examples: this entire discourse in the tradition of Németh has been flourishing since the regime change, especially on the political right. It influenced such protagonists of the post-1989 public press and political scene as István Csurka, Gyula Fekete, and Sándor Lezsák, all poets and writers originally, and all founding members of the politically very diverse Hungarian Democratic Forum (*Magyar Demokrata Fórum*, MDF), the party that won the first democratic elections in 1990. Both the refusal to be called an antisemite and repeated favorable references to Jewish individuals that one has developed a good relationship with have been frequent topoi in journalism linked to this tradition. Let alone the important ruptures within the intellectual orbit of MDF, the *spiritus rector* was Csoóri, and when Viktor Orbán's Fidesz inherited the role of an entirely disintegrated MDF as a catchall party on the right, Csoóri became his political advisor.

It is hard to measure to what extent Orbán is influenced by Csoóri and other intellectuals belonging to the populist tradition defined by Dezső Szabó and Németh. But Orbán, who appears as a pragmatist politician and a visionary in one person, likes to think in very similar large cultural-historical patterns as Csoóri and his precursors. No doubt, he read a great deal from this tradition. In contrast to those who believe that Orbán is simply a political entrepreneur, we think that ideology plays an important factor that shapes his policies. And one of the most significant aspects of this ideology is the idea of the people and nation as a unity. The nation does not need to be homogenic. When it comes to "the Jewry," as we have seen before, assimilation is not the preferred option of social integration: only the "visible" Jew is the good Jew. If we translate this to contemporary policy issues, we might come to the conclusion that there is a specific coherent logic behind Orbán's great gestures toward and generous funding of some Jewish organizations (and Christian churches, of course), and the appreciation of Israel as a strategic partner on the one hand (certainly, *similis simile guadet* among illiberals as well) and, on the other hand, the Soros campaign that used antisemitic iconography

The myth of a Judeo-Bolshevik conspiracy 105

or the tacit toleration of antisemitic discourse in the Fidesz-related media. If the Jewish presence is well defined, and it has a specific recognized position within Hungarian society and nation, then it is tolerable, sometimes even recognized as a contributor to the common good and shared culture. At the moment patchwork identities appear, however, the Jewish people become a threat, because this ideology does not tolerate such identities.

Despite this, it must be stated that in the past decade there have been few occasions when the myth of Judeo-Bolshevism was voiced in mainstream media. Even in the daily *Magyar Idők (Hungarian Times)*, which was a primary vehicle of the government to run the anti-Soros campaign, and where antisemitic claims were relatively frequent, the myth did not appear very often, and only then, indirectly, in coded language. For instance, an advisor of the prime minister's office singled out historian and political scientist Charles Gati as a supporter of Soros in an article published in *Magyar Idők* (Tóth Gy. 2018). The article referenced Gati as someone who "believes in his Old Testament mission." Once alleged Jewish stakes are identified, the author could go on to point out that Gáti is a regular contributor to the leftist daily *Népszava*, which was "neocommunist in spirit." The link between Jews and Communism is established; it is up to the reader to sort the rest out. Such occasions, however, are relatively few. Certainly, the refugee crisis and migration issues provided ample opportunities to find different targets than the Jews, not to speak about the Bolsheviks, and the political discourse was further complicated by many prominent Jewish intellectuals in Hungary and Europe elsewhere siding with Orbán and those political forces that supported the closing of borders.

Even if direct claims that explicitly refer to Judeo-Bolshevism are not a regular part of Fidesz's vocabulary, these have been regularly voiced by members of parliament belonging to the far-right Jobbik party. Perhaps, the most memorable incident when Jobbik used such rhetoric happened in 2013, during the World Jewish Congress in Budapest. Then Lóránt Hegedűs Jr., pastor of the Reformed Church in Hungary, and his wife, Mrs Lóránt Hegedűs, MP of Jobbik, organized a demonstration against Bolshevism and Zionism and called upon Congress to "condemn Judeo-Bolshevik anti-Christian and anti-Hungarian terror in 1919 and after 1945." This provocative protest extrapolated ongoing internal conflicts within the Reformed Church, and Hegedűs and his words were publicly denounced by high representatives of the Reformed Church. Fidesz set itself apart of such claims.

The sculpture of philosopher György Lukács was another notable case from 2016–17. Lukács has been a controversial figure in Hungarian history for his involvement in both Communist dictatorships, and a Hungarian law prohibits the raising of monuments to persons who contributed to the maintenance of dictatorial regimes. The issue of his sculpture's removal became a matter of political rivalry between Jobbik and Fidelitas, the youth organization of Fidesz in the 13th district of Budapest, and became a widely followed issue. Neither of these political organizations referred to Judeo-Bolshevism in official statements, but a wide variety of online sources and rightist radical blogs presented the case in such terms. The case was just one stage of a wider campaign against Lukács, during which the closing of the Lukács Archive was initiated, and when even the

106 *Péter Csunderlik and Tamás Scheibner*

legality of the name of György Lukács Foundation was questioned on the basis of a Hungarian law stating that no organization could bear the name of a person who contributed to the establishment and maintenance of dictatorships. Arguably, without Tormay's *An Outlaw's Diary*, which identified the previously mentioned Galileo Circle as a primary source of conspiracy, and without the influence of Németh's *Kisebbségben*, which since the 1940s had made the Circle's recurring lecturer Lukács *the* exemplary figure of the Bolshevik Jew, the philosopher would not have attracted such great attention from the political right. The case of Lukács, however, shows once again that in symbolic politics, precisely because it is symbolic and not elaborated discursively, it is hard to draw a dividing line between anti-Communism/anti-totalitarianism and Judeo-Bolshevik conspiracism. On the one hand, this opens greater possibilities for antisemites to maneuver in the public space, and on the other, this might overcharge scholarly debates with political overtones.

Conclusion

Herf (2008), Gerrits (2009), and Hanebrink (2018) rightly pointed out the danger to democracy of the far right's embrace of the myth of Judeo-Bolshevism. However, even more troubling perhaps are discourses in which the idea is not made explicit or is referred to in an ambivalent way. Such partly veiled uses of the idea make it acceptable for a broader political community beyond the far right. For this reason, we followed the claim that Communism was a Jewish plot in various contexts in Hungarian intellectual history, but with a specific (although, not exclusive) focus on instances where it was manifested in an irregular or unexpected manner or by someone who cannot be called a textbook example of a Nazi. Judeo-Bolshevik conspiracy theories are not exclusive to the far right and have been used as a political weapon by many who found their lifetime mission in fighting for the emancipation of the subjugated, whether (elite) women in a patriarchal society or the poverty-stricken proletariat or the poor peasantry. The use of the myth is not class related, and on occasion, even Freemasons are not immune to it, who themselves have for centuries been the subject of conspiracy theories.

The belief in the Judeo-Bolshevik conspiracy is intimately linked to antisemitism. Therefore, it seems appropriate to reflect on an aspect of discourses that seem to be antisemitic: one that applies historically and today and also explains Judeo-Bolshevik conspiracism. Between Hungarian conservative populists, who follow Németh and Csoóri, and those who criticize them for antisemitism, there is a profound difference that prevents understanding. It has been commonplace for some time that nationalism has religious overtones. However, one aspect has received relatively little attention: for a Christian person, the realization of an evangelical life that aims to be true to Christ is something greater than a life conditioned by the political conditions of this world. These latter are tangential: an environment that does not define in any meaningful and deeper way the life they ought to live. In its secularized version, the realization of an essentialized

The myth of a Judeo-Bolshevik conspiracy 107

Hungarian "way of life," therefore, cannot be defined by anything outside of this historicized ideal: by definition, it cannot be "anti-" anything. Ever since Jews have been defined as the "Other," the realization of an imagined national life overrules all considerations derived from an analysis of the given social-political conditions. The same applies to Communism, defined as alien to this national way of life, not to speak about the combination of the two.

Judeo-Bolshevik conspiracism resembles anti-Semitism in that it is also a genuinely transnational phenomenon, the discursive patterns of which are elaborated through cultural exchanges across borders. It is important for future research to pay greater attention to such aspects: intercultural exchange does not necessarily lead to greater acknowledgment of the other's culture, as is often suggested by idealistic approaches. Such evidence in conspiracy theory research might inform other fields. The memory of the Hungarian Soviet Republic, for instance, was and (as one can see by browsing extreme-right online resources) has been shaped by Western politicians and intellectuals as well, some of whom had previously been affected by Central European antisemitism. An increased attention to such exchanges and influences might shed new light on how the myth of Judeo-Bolshevism was developed.

Bibliography

A zsidók rémuralma Magyarországon 1919. március 21-től augusztus hó 1-ig [The Terror of the Jews in Hungary from 21 March 1919 to 1 August 1919], n. p., n. d. [1919].

Benedek, István. 1990. "Nemzetiség és Kisebbség" [Nationality and Minority]. *Hitel* 3 (19): 34–36.

Benedek, Szabolcs. 2007. "A szabadkőműves Benedek Marcell" [The Freemason Marcell Benedek]. *Új Forrás* 6 (39): 101–4.

Brustein, William. 2003. *Roots of Hate: Anti-Semitism in Europe Before the Holocaust*. Cambridge: Cambridge University Press.

Brustein, William, and Louisa Roberts. 2015. *The Socialism of Fools? Leftist Origins of Modern Anti-Semitism*. New York: Cambridge University Press.

Churchill, Winston S. 1920. "Zionism versus Bolshevism: A Struggle for the Soul of the Jewish People." *Illustrated Sunday Herald* (London), February 8, 1920.

Cohen, Michael Joseph. 2003. *Churchill and the Jews*. 2nd ed. London: Frank Cass.

Cselekedjünk! Magyar fajvédelmi útmutató [Let's Take Action! Hungarian Racialist Guide]. Budapest: A Cél, 1923.

Csoóri, Sándor. 1990. "Nappali hold (2.)" [Moon at Daylight]. *Hitel* 3 (18): 4–7.

Daudet, Léon. 1929. *Ecrivains et artistes*. Vol. 6. Paris: Editions du Capitole.

Davison, Carol Margaret. 2004. *Anti-Semitism and British Gothic Literature*. London: Palgrave Macmillan.

Ferrario, Gabriele. 2010. "The Jews and Alchemy: Notes for a Problematic Approach." In *Chymia: Science and Nature in Medieval and Early Modern Europe*, edited by Miguel López Pérez, Didier Kahn, and Mar Rey Bueno, 19–28. Newcastle upon Tyne: Cambridge Scholars Publishing.

Gerrits, André. 2009. *The Myth of Jewish Communism: A Historical Interpretation*. New York: Peter Lang.

Gilbert, Martin. 2008. *Churchill and the Jews*. New York: Picador.

108 *Péter Csunderlik and Tamás Scheibner*

Gömbös, Gyula. 1920. *Egy magyar vezérkari tiszt bíráló feljegyzései a forradalomról és ellenforradalomról* [Critical Notes on the Revolution and Counter-Revolution by a Hungarian Staff Officer]. Budapest: Budapesti Hírlap Ny.

Gwynne, H. A., ed. 1921. *Földalatti összeesküvők: A Morning Post cikkei a forradalmak okairól* [Underground Conspirators: Articles of the Morning Post on the Causes of the Revolutions]. Budapest: Egyesült Keresztény Nemzeti Liga.

Gyáni, Gábor. 2003. *Posztmodern kánon* [Postmodernist Canon]. Budapest: Nemzeti Tankönyvkiadó.

———. 2011. "Az asszimilációkritika Bibó István gondolkodásában" [The Criticism of Assimilation in István Bibó's Thought]. *Holmi* 23 (8): 1022–35.

Hanebrink, Paul. 2006. *In Defense of Christian Hungary: Religion, Nationalism, and Antisemitism, 1890–1944*. Ithaca, NY: Cornell University Press.

———. 2008. "Transnational Culture War: Christianity, Nation, and the Judeo-Bolshevik Myth in Hungary, 1890–1920." *The Journal of Modern History* 80 (1): 55–80.

———. 2018. *A Specter Haunting Europe: The Myth of Judeo-Bolshevism*. Cambridge, MA: The Belknap Press of Harvard University Press.

Herf, Jeffrey. 2008. *The Jewish Enemy: Nazi Propaganda During World War II and the Holocaust*. Cambridge, MA: The Belknap Press of Harvard University Press.

Karsai, László. 1994. "Zsidók és kommunisták" [Jews and Communists]. *Kommentár* 3 (1): 3–8.

Kovács, Mária M. 1994. *Liberal Professions and Illiberal Politics: Hungary from the Habsburgs to the Holocaust*. Washington, DC: Woodrow Wilson Center Press.

———. 2003. "Hungary." In *Women, Gender and Fascism in Europe, 1919–1945*, edited by Kevin Passmore, 79–90. Manchester: Manchester University Press.

———. 2016. "The Numerus Clausus and the Anti-Jewish Laws." In *The Holocaust in Hungary*, edited by Randolph L. Braham and András Kovács, 37–43. Budapest: CEU Press.

Kurimay, Anita. 2016. "Interrogating the Historical Revisionism of the Hungarian Right: The Queer Case of Cécile Tormay." *East European Politics and Societies* 30: 10–33.

Lechner, Károly. 1919. "Az elmefogyatékosságok szerepe a társadalomban" [The Role of Disabilities in Society]. *Természettudományi Közlöny* 51: 273–86.

Leymarie, Michel. 2006. "Les frères Tharaud: De l'ambiguïté du 'filon juif' dans la littérature des années vingt." *Archives Juives* 1 (39): 89–109.

Németh, László. 1932–1933. "A kapitalizmus vége" [The End of Capitalism]. *Tanu* 1: 25–35.

———. 1934. "A magyar élet antinómiái" [The Antinomies of Hungarian Life]. *Válasz* 1 (2): 117–35.

———. 1935a. "Magyarok Romániában: Útirajz" [Hungarians in Romania: Travelogue]. *Tanu* 3–4: 113–82.

———. 1935b. *Magyarság és Európa* [Hungarianness and Europe]. Budapest: Franklin.

———. 1940. "Töredékek A reformból [1935]" [Excerpts from "The Reform"]. In *A minőség forradalma* [The Revolution of Quality], Vol. 4. Budapest: Magyar Élet.

———. 1942. "A történelem fölé [1935]" [Above History]. In *Kisebbségben* [In Minority]. Budapest: Magyar Élet.

———. 1968. "Karácsonyi üzenet [1961]" [Christmas Message]. In *Kiadatlan tanulmányok* [Unpublished Studies]. Budapest: Magvető.

———. 1993. "Letter from Németh László to Pál Gulyás, Sátorkőpuszta, August 20, 1932." In *Németh László élete levelekben 1914–1948* [The Life of László Németh in Letters]. Budapest: Magvető.

The myth of a Judeo-Bolshevik conspiracy   109

Pető, Andrea. 2003. *Napasszonyok és holdkisasszonyok: A mai magyar női politizálás alaktana* [Women of Sun and Girls of Moon. Morphology of Contemporary Hungarian Women Doing Politics]. Budapest: Balassi.

Progrediéus [Szemere, Béla]. 1920. *Az elmefogyatékosok* [The Disabled]. Budapest: Apostol Ny.

Sipos József. 1997. "Csizmadia Sándor szakítása az MSZDP-vel." In *Múzeumi Kutatások Csongrád Megyében (1995/1996)*, 207–18. Szeged.

Steed, Henry Wickham. 1913. *The Hapsburg Monarchy*. London: Constable & Co.

Szabó, Dezső. 1938. *Az antijúdaizmus bírálata* [The Criticism of Anti-Judaism]. Szabó Dezső Újabb Művei 39. Budapest: Ludas Mátyás.

———. 1996. "A faji probléma: Zsidó – nemzsidó [1926]" [The Racial Problem: Jew – Non-Jew]. In *Két faj harca* [The Fight of Two Races], edited by Szőcs Zoltán, 32–37. Budapest: Szabó Dezső Emléktársaság.

Szabó, Juliet. 2009. "Fellazítási politika a Kádár-rendszerben. Az MSZMP propagandatevékenysége 1958 és 1963 között" [The Politics of Disarrayment in the Kádár Regime: The Propaganda Activities of the Hungarian Socialist Workers' Party between 1958 and 1963]. *Múltunk* 54 (2): 180–221.

Szerb, Antal. 2002. *Mindig lesznek sárkányok: magyar irodalom* [There Will Be Always Dragons: Hungarian Literature]. Összegyűjtött esszék, tanulmányok, kritikák. Vol. 2. Budapest: Magvető.

Sztójay, Döme. 2017. "Napi jelentés [July 6, 1944]" [Daily Report of Prime Minister Döme Sztójay]. In *Vádirat a nácizmus ellen: Dokumentumok a magyarországi zsidóüldözés történetéhez, III, 1944. június 26.–1944. október 15. A budapesti zsidóság deportálásának felfüggesztése* [Indictment Against Nazism: Documents on the History of the Persecution of the Jews in Hungary, Vol. 3, June 26–October 15, 1944: The Suspension of the Deportation of the Budapest Jewry], edited by Elek Karsai. Budapest: Balassi.

Tharaud, Jérôme, and Jean Tharaud. 1921. *Quand Israël Est Roi* [When Israel Is King]. Paris: Plon.

Tormay, Cécile. 1920–1922. *Bujdosó könyv: Feljegyzések 1918–1919-ből* [Outlaw Book: Notes from 1918–1919]. Vol. 1–2. Budapest: Rózsavölgyi, Pallas.

———. 1923. *An Outlaw's Diary*. Vol. 1: *Revolution;* Vol. 2: *The Commune*. London: Philip Allan & Co.

Tóth, Gy. László. 2018. "Egy igazi amerikai: Charles Gati" [A Real American: Charles Gati]. *Magyar Idők*, June 19.

Trencsényi, Balázs. 2012. *The Politics of "National Character": A Study in Interwar East European Thought*. London: Routledge.

Turda, Marius. 2014. *Eugenics and Nation in Early 20th Century Hungary. Science, Technology and Medicine in Modern History*. Basingstoke: Palgrave Macmillan.

Webster, Nesta H. 1921. *World Revolution; the Plot Against Civilization*. Boston, MA: Small, Maynard & Company. http://archive.org/details/worldrevolutionp00webs.

5 An open secret

Freemasonry and justice in post-socialist Bulgaria

Todor Hristov and Ivelina Ivanova

Introduction

A conspiracy theory claims that the Bulgarian judiciary is secretly controlled by the Freemasons. The theory has gained such currency that in 2016 the Bulgarian parliament debated it for 10 long hours. This chapter will examine the reasons for its appeal. The reasons that shape conspiracy theories, however, cannot be deconstructed into individual choices between alternatives, decisions on how to allocate available resources, calculations of potential gains and losses, causal inferences, analogies, predictions, and plans. The rationality of conspiracy theories is, of course, composed of choices, decisions, calculations, and inferences, but just like the cookbook reasonings that shape the trajectories of our everyday lives (Schutz 1964, 73–77), they are too local, too fleeting, too small, perhaps too petty to make sense in and of themselves. They make a difference only if they are accumulated together into a mass. Yet as a mass, they can exert a gravitational force irresistible as fate. We will argue that the appeal of the theory that the Bulgarian judiciary is controlled by the Freemasons is due to its overdetermination by three types of reasons: the practical reason of the former agents of the Communist State Security who tried to preserve and increase the social capital they had accumulated before 1989; the political reason of the small parties trying to compensate for their inadequate resources; and the fantasies about the unthinkable injustice of the post-socialist transition. The first section will map out the context, including the distinguishing features of the post-socialist secret societies. The second section will describe the integration of the former agents of the Communist State Security in the secret societies as a strategy for preserving the social capital they accumulated in the service. The third section will explain how the political entrepreneurs transformed the nexus between the secret police and the post-socialist secret societies into a conspiracy theory. The fourth section will analyze the passionate response provoked by that conspiracy theory in the online forums. The last section is intended to provide a more general account of the rationality of conspiracy theories and on the calculations, choices, and fantasies that make them topical.

The secret societies

The modern Bulgarian state was established in 1878, in the wake of a Russo-Turkish war. A couple of decades later, the country was ravaged by the two Balkan wars and World War I. The tumultuous interwar period witnessed three coups d'état, a civil war, a Fascist regime, a leftist guerrilla movement, and severe poverty. In this context of political instability, secret societies rose in importance. Historians of Bulgarian Freemasonry recently claimed that 17 of the 31 prime ministers of the country between 1878 and 1944 were members of the United Grand Lodge of Bulgaria, including the first prime minister after the Communist coup d'état in 1944 (Ivanov 1992; Andonova 2011). The Communists, however, opposed secret societies and the most internationally renowned among them, Georgi Dimitrov, a general secretary of the Bulgarian Communist Party at the time, even gave a speech about the detrimental effects of secret societies on Socialism, so, after the party managed to depose the king and seize power in 1947, secret societies practically disappeared (Nedev 2008, 391).

Secret societies reappeared after 1989, fed by a nostalgic optimism that if Bulgaria was restored to the state before the Communist coup, it would become a normally developed country. The post-socialist masonic lodges, however, were significantly different from the familiar secret societies. In order to explain the difference, let me briefly summarize the concept developed by one of the founding fathers of modern sociology, Georg Simmel (1964, 356–64): secret societies are social groups constituted by sharing a secret; the shared secret builds up the solidarity between members of the group; in order to protect the secret, the group establishes hierarchical subordination, sanctions, and boundaries that exclude the general public (marked by rituals, oaths, cryptic signs, arcane handshakes, etc.); since the members lead a secret life inaccessible to the other social groups they belong to—for example, their families, communities, or classes—they experience the affiliation with the secret society as a form of autonomy (ibid., 356–60). In contrast to the secret societies described by Simmel, at least in the Bulgarian case, post-socialist secret societies are constituted as open secrets (Birchall 2015). Let us take, for example, the establishment of the Grand Lodge of Bulgaria in 1997. It happened behind a veil of secrecy, of course, but the veil itself transfixed the gaze of the public:

> Sofia. The lobby of the hotel "Fatherland" in the capital is increasingly filled with men uniformly dressed in black tuxedos. The crowd grows any minute. The men speak several different languages at the same time—calmly and softly. Curious eyes grope those solemnly dressed men gathered together in the early hours of the day. They all evoke the feeling that they are so happy to meet each other. They exchange open-hearted handshakes, hugs, brotherly pats on the shoulders, spontaneous exclamations, and despite the differences in language, age and physique the men coming from all around the world seem to be bound together by the bond of a special intimacy. But the curiosity of the bystanders is fully unsatisfied because suddenly, without any explicit signal, the men in black leave the hotel lobby in small groups, and their cars head to an unknown direction.
>
> (Nedkov 2008, 273)[1]

After the ceremony, the grand master gave interviews to almost all national newspapers and appeared at a popular TV show together with all the senior Freemasons in order to lift the veil and declare that the grand lodge, at its inaugural meeting, decided to help the government reform the justice system and the economy in accordance with the founding principles of liberal capitalism as well as to work for the accession of the country to the European Union (ibid., 276–77).

In contrast with the secrets discussed by Simmel, open secrets minimize the risk of disclosure. Imagine that the viewer were to believe the public statements of the grand lodge: the contents of its secret would be banal, in fact, would be indistinguishable from the contents of the policies pursued by the public authorities; in consequence, Freemasonry would seem a contentless secret, a pure secret that has nothing to reveal. On the other hand, if the viewer were to disbelieve the grand lodge, if the viewer wished to penetrate the veil of masonic publicity, the secret she or he revealed would be essentially her or his fantasy. The response of the tabloid press provides a good illustration of that. After the press release of the grand lodge, the press started to search for its temple and soon managed to find it, although the temple looked like a renovated school. Then journalists managed to take pictures from the inside, but the interior looked like a lavishly renovated former gym adorned with masonic symbols. Following this, tabloid journalists started to search for the owner of the building, assuming that he was the mastermind behind the public face of the grand master, but the owner turned to be one of the senior Freemasons (ibid., 276–77). No matter how the journalists tried to disclose the hidden truth of the Bulgarian Freemasonry, any disclosure turned out to be meaningless, just as it would be meaningless to make a film audience watch the screen instead of the images projected on it. In fact, after some time, the grand lodge itself invited the press to the temple, published an official history, and started a website, a Facebook page, and a Twitter account.

Since the constitution of post-socialist Freemasonry as an open secret minimized the risks of disclosure, it made superfluous the means of protection developed in the past—the hierarchical subordination, the rituals, the sanctions. Of course, the lodges were still hierarchical, but the positions of the masters, wardens, treasurers, secretaries, and so on progressively turned into status positions that depended on the recognition of other Freemasons. Without their recognition, any attempt to exert authority was doomed to failure. In 2000, for example, the United Grand Lodge of Bulgaria joined the Ancient and Accepted Scottish Rite of Freemasonry and elected a new grand master, an exceptionally wealthy entrepreneur. But although the entrepreneur had ascended to the highest chair in the grand lodge, he failed to gain the appreciation of his brothers, and the worshipful masters of almost half of all Bulgarian lodges filed a notarized declaration that the election was rigged, accompanied by more than a dozen complaints to the masonic high court. The court decided that the former grand master should be reinstated, but then the new grand master refused to recognize the authority of the high court and, after securing the support of the German AFAM lodge, he excommunicated almost half the lodges. Instead of repenting, the excommunicated Freemasons formed an alternative grand lodge. In the following years, three more grand lodges seceded. Some of the Freemasons also joined another secret society, the Order of the Knights Templar. In consequence, all the masonic factions started a bitter fight for recognition in which even the German AFAM Grand Lodge, which once shed light on the United Grand Lodge of Bulgaria, was no longer able to negotiate a compromise (Nedev 2008, 433–41).

Since, in the post-socialist context, masonic degrees and offices no longer guaranteed authority, the value of lodge membership consisted in the recognition granted by the other Freemasons. Such recognition is a privilege from which the public is excluded, yet it is not hidden from the public; it is displayed as a secret under its prying eyes. Because of that, post-socialist Freemasonry is exclusive in a different sense from the secret societies described by Simmel. Its exclusivity has started to mean excellence. This transformation is illustrated by a comment of the director of the Commission for the Dossiers of the Former State Security, Metodi Andreev: "Every freemason would eventually want to disclose himself, after all, being a mason is prestigious" (Andreev 2016). Yet, although post-socialist lodges seem closer to elite clubs, they nevertheless foster solidarity among their members and evoke a feeling of autonomy from social roles or social groups, as if a loophole in the social order.

The secret police

After World War I, Bulgaria was governed by a leftist party, the Bulgarian Agrarian Popular Union. Since the party could not be defeated in elections, it was brought down in 1923 by a coup d'état led by the army and the secret police called State Security. Between 1924 and 1944, the power of the secret police progressively increased, particularly because it was entrusted to fight the guerrilla movement against the Fascist government. After the Communists came to power in 1944, they took over State Security. In the following decades, the Communist Party extended its prerogatives, and at the beginning of the 1980s State Security investigated criminal offenses ranging from misdemeanors to felonies, fought external and internal enemies of the state, managed its foreign investments, tackled corruption, protected the highest governmental and party officials, and even tried to make sense of trends in the Western Marxism. What was more, the secret services constantly came into conflict with other factions of the Communist Party, conflicts that shaped the party's politics like geological forces forming a seemingly stable landscape (Metodiev 2012).[2] State Security is often portrayed as a clandestine army, but its power depended on a network of agents with positions like "collaborator without a permanent contract" or "manager of a secret meeting place," which shared many features of secret societies: the agents kept their affiliation with State Security secret, because disclosing it would ruin their social lives; the border that separated their group from the general public was closely protected; the shared secret evoked a feeling of intense solidarity. From the point of view of the agents, however, their solidarity was a virtual capital that could be converted into actual advantages in the competition against other social actors. The mechanism of its conversion can be illustrated by the story of Mr. T, a future Freemason.[3] He came from a small town, and as he failed the university exams, he was conscripted into the army. Mr. T was having a hard time there, but one of his commanding officers, Colonel Klyanev, offered him protection if he became a secret agent of military counterintelligence.[4] Mr. T accepted the offer, and soon his military service became a lot easier. After the army, he was admitted to the prestigious Faculty of Law of the University of Sofia. The regulations on higher education stipulated that, in exchange for his free university degree, Mr. T had to take a job allocated by the authorities for a couple of years, usually in a small town or in a village where it would be difficult to find adequately qualified employees without state intervention. Mr. T, however, used his connections in State Security to avoid the regulations and kept on living and working in the capital. Later on, he relied on his connections once again to begin a successful career as a solicitor of almost all the Bulgarian criminal bosses of the 1990s. In sum, Mr. T transformed his affiliation with State Security into advantages in other social fields like special treatment in the army, a law degree, a permit to live in the capital, a job in the Ministry of the Interior, and a very lucrative private practice. Such advantages made a difference that was perceived and recognized by the social actors, and in that sense functioned as symbolic capital (Bourdieu and Wacquant 1992, 118–19). Hoping to gain such capital, agents like T. actively solicited the intervention of State Security. Of course, the secret police was well aware that its agents tried to capitalize on its power; in fact, it encouraged them because in normal circumstances its power depended not so much on open violence than on the enthusiasm of agents like Mr. T who wanted to gain an edge, to repair a vulnerability, to avert a danger, or to satisfy a desire.

After 1989, State Security was reformed once again to turn into a repressive apparatus of the post-socialist state. The network of agents was more or less cut off from its clandestine army, and the identities of all those who were no longer considered assets were disclosed. Nevertheless, the former agents tried to preserve and increase the virtual capital of their solidarity. Mr. T joined a masonic lodge together with one of his commanding State Security officers. Later on, he joined the Order of the Knights Templar founded by another of his commanding officers. This was because, as previously mentioned, post-socialist secret societies constituted an open secret, the open secret of the existence of social groups distinguished by excellence and closed to the general public. Nevertheless, post-socialist secret societies still built up solidarity that functioned as virtual capital, which, in contrast to the affiliation with State Security, could be converted into recognizable advantages at a minimal risk. Its convertibility can be illustrated by the case that formed the real kernel of the conspiracy theory about the Bulgarian judiciary, the litigation between Mr. M and Mr. D.[5]

Mr. M was a district attorney in Sofia since the late 1990s. He was also a Freemason, a wealthy man, and a close friend of a crime lord known as Zlatko the Beret. In 2007, his wife, Ms. M, also a district attorney, filed misleading information in order to be eligible for state housing, although she owned a luxurious house in a posh neighborhood. The prosecution suspected fraud and launched an investigation. Mr. M, however, was soon warned by a prosecutor and masonic brother. Initially Mr. M was not worried because he had been investigated for corruption before, but at the Christmas party of the grand lodge, he was approached by his

An open secret 115

friend Mr. D—a high-ranking prosecutor and Freemason, former "housekeeper" for State Security, and one of the two senior brothers who had recommended Mr. M to the lodge. Mr. D told Mr. M that the SWAT unit of the General Directorate Combating Organized Crime (GDCOC) was planning to carry out a raid on Mr. M's house but that Mr. D would stop them because he was obliged to help Mr. M as a masonic brother. A couple of days later, Mr. D met Mr. M and explained that, in order to help, he had to ask the grand master himself to intervene. The grand master and the minister of the interior were close friends since their school days, so the grand master called the minister, the raid was canceled, and even better, the minister promised that if Mr. M paid €20,000, his problems would disappear. Mr. M did not want to give away that much money, but Mr. D insisted that this was the price for his protection by the lodge and that Mr. M put him and the lodge in a difficult position. Since Mr. T held a very important position in the high court of the grand lodge, both asked him to resolve their argument. Mr. M, however, was dissatisfied with the decision of the high court, and as the authority of the court (as with the authority of any other post-socialist masonic office) depended on recognition, Mr. M simply refused to recognize it. Thus, Mr. M put Mr. T himself in a difficult position because, on one hand, Mr. T did not want to cut ties with two of his very successful protégés, yet on the other hand, he could not tolerate the lack of respect to the high court. At this point, Mr. T simply chose to ignore the conflict. Encouraged by this, Mr. D started to threaten Mr. M that if Mr. M did not deliver the money, the SWAT team would make the raid very violent, beat him and his wife, smash the house, and perhaps even plant some drugs. "They will ruin your life, you will regret it if you do not give them the money," said Mr. D, unaware that Mr. M was recording the conversation, "After all it is not a big deal, a district attorney should be able to make that much money in two months." The phrase uttered by Mr. D was later made famous by the media and resonated through the country where the average monthly salary at the time was about €300. Now Mr. M was frightened. He did not believe that the property fraud committed by his wife was that serious and suspected that the investigation against him was actually a plot between Mr. M and his closest friend, Mr. MM, another high-ranking prosecutor and Freemason who oversaw the work of the GDCOC. At this point, Mr. M considered paying, but his friends advised him that even if he paid, Mr. D would keep on asking for more money. Since Mr. M believed that he needed protection from the legal system itself and his lodge had failed to protect him, he turned to a higher power. He asked for help from his neighbor Mr. R, who would soon become a minister of culture and was a Freemason from a competing grand lodge and a close friend of the future prime minister. Thus, after scores of phone calls, dinners at fashionable restaurants, and coffees at gas stations, Mr. M managed to make contact with the chief prosecutor himself and, after a delivery of dye-pack money, the SWAT team of GDCOC arrested Mr. D In the end, after a six-year trial, Mr. D was sentenced to three years' probation while Mr. M left the judiciary and became a successful private-practice lawyer. The prosecution classified the lawsuit in the hope of minimizing the damage to its reputation, but nevertheless,

116 Todor Hristov and Ivelina Ivanova

the media covered it with enthusiasm, and the Bulgarian website Bivol, modeled after Wikileaks, published the top-secret decision of the court.

If we summarize this rather complicated case, all the actors tried to transform their positions in the secret society into capital in other fields: Mr. D took advantage of his senior position in the masonic lodge to make Mr. M pay the price for his protection from the prosecution, Mr. M used his masonic affiliation in order to protect his wealth from Mr. D, Mr. T used his position in the high court to extend his influence over both Mr. D and Mr. M, while Mr. R exploited his connections at the rival lodge in order to initiate a complex exchange of gifts and services that finally triggered the machinery of justice. In effect, the solidarity between the masonic brothers was converted into economic, social, administrative, and political capital, and quite like the post-socialist masonic lodges, this was all an open secret.

The political entrepreneurs

The nexus between secret societies and the former secret police was transformed from an open secret into a conspiracy theory by small-scale political entrepreneurs trying to gain advantage over the political competition. Although the story is more interesting and intricate than can be relayed here, for the purposes of this chapter, I will focus on two key figures, Tatyana Doncheva and Hristo Ivanov.

In February 2013, Bulgaria was shaken by protests against exorbitant energy prices. The government fell, and as did many other politicians, Tatyana Doncheva hoped to tap into the energy of the protests. In the first decade of the new century, she had been one of the leading figures of one of the biggest Bulgarian political parties, the Bulgarian Socialist Party. Renowned for her temper, after a bitter conflict with the party leadership, Doncheva left the Socialists, returned to her private practice as a lawyer, and started a political party of her own, Movement 21. Her party, however, lacked resources. As with other political parties unrepresented in the parliament, it had a budget subsidy that could buy about 10 minutes on the radio or a dozen billboards. Moreover, Doncheva was unsure if it was worth investing in her movement because it could disappear after the elections, just like hundreds of other smaller Bulgarian parties after 1989. So Doncheva chose to exploit the energy of the lawsuit between Mr. M and Mr. D, whose sentence had just been confirmed by the Court of Appeal of Sofia. Taking advantage of one of her television appearances in March 2013, Doncheva referred to the lawsuit and claimed that the Bulgarian judiciary was controlled by the Freemasons (BTV 2013). "This is the grim reality," nodded a renowned criminal defense lawyer, Marin Markovski, who also participated in the show. The interview went viral. Of course, Doncheva lost the election, but her political movement survives to this day.

A couple of months later, the country was shaken by another wave of protests against the appointment of a media magnate as head of the National Security Agency, against corruption in general, and against the clandestine force that was the reason for it all, which the protesters called "the backstage." Many political

An open secret 117

actors tried to channel the protests, and one of the most successful was the right-wing civil association, Protest Network. After the second wave of protests brought back to power the party that was brought down by the first wave, one of the leaders of Protest Network, Hristo Ivanov, became minister of justice. He promised to fight for a reform of the legal system, but soon his reforms turned into a fight against the chief prosecutor, Sotir Tsatsarov. Protest Network tried to support its minister by organizing a protest that portrayed the chief prosecutor as the face of "the backstage." The energy of the protests had already depleted by this time, so Ivanov lost the fight with the chief prosecutor and had to resign. Protest Network then started a civil movement, Justice for Everyone, registered a nongovernmental organization, organized public discussions and press conferences, and filed a report to the European Commission that claimed that the Bulgarian legal system was controlled by "the backstage" (Pravosudiezavseki 2016). The report received wide media coverage, and the leaders of Justice for Everyone used the opportunity to give a series of interviews in which they accused Tsatsarov of helping the former State Security to orchestrate corruption and sabotage democratic opposition (Velichkov 2016). The members of the movement repeatedly insinuated that Tsatsarov was a Freemason, and after the disclosure of a secret meeting of the chief prosecutor with an investigated tycoon at the office of a very influential politician rumored to be a senior brother, Justice for Everyone, the former minister Ivanov, and even a member of the high judiciary council challenged Tsatsarov to disclose his masonic affiliation (Ivanov 2017; Kalpakchiev 2017).

The attack on the chief prosecutor put the new minister of justice, Tsetska Tsacheva, in a delicate position: on one hand, she promised to continue the reforms of her predecessor, Hristo Ivanov; on the other hand, the next monitoring report of the European Commission on the progress of judicial reform in Bulgaria was approaching, and the report by Justice for Everyone had made the experts of the European Commission suspicious—a negative evaluation would be a serious risk for the government. In addition, the chief prosecutor was a crucial ally of the government, and the right-wing party of the former minister Ivanov was still a junior partner in the governing coalition. So the new minister, Tsacheva, decided to propose a bill that obliged any member of the judiciary to declare her or his affiliations with secret societies.[6]

The bill, however, did not provide for any sanctions if the members of the judiciary failed to do so, and it turned out to be very difficult to define secret societies in legal terms, particularly because the Bulgarian masonic lodges and the Order of the Knights Templar were revealed to be officially registered as nongovernmental organizations. So the parliamentary debates on the bill descended into jokes:

[Speaker Radan Kanev, a member of the right-wing party Democratic Bulgaria] But the question is not what are Bulgarian masons like. The question is not that a significant number of them are just drunkard spooks from State Security who play knights and dress in bedclothes. This is not the problem of the Bulgarian justice system. A huge problem—real, not hypothetical problem of the Bulgarian justice system is some of those bedclothes-dressed spooks, as we very well know, as we have discussed many times, enter in illicit contacts at the level lawyer/prosecutor, lawyer/judge, and judge/prosecutor, and as a result of those illicit contacts we have in Bulgaria an extremely large number of biased court decisions and persecution orders.

(Parliament 2016)

[Speaker Emil Dimitrov, a member of the governing party GERB] Let me first declare that I am a member of the legal association in Gabrovo [a small town], and also a member of a club of the sons-in-law hidden from the public (Laughter and lively mood.) I do not know if we should include the latter in the scope of the law because there are a lot of organizations that are not registered, the people enter contacts, and at the least do not feel guilty if someone in their group, membership, gathering is a bad person.

(ibid.)

After hours of debate, parliament decided that only newly appointed judges should declare their affiliation with secret societies and without any monitoring mechanism. The representatives of Justice for Everyone protested, the media commented that the bill amounted to nothing, the European Commission objected that the legal formulation did not differentiate between permissible and criminal allegiances, and the Freemasons elected new grand masters. Nevertheless, at the end, everybody was happy. The new minister of justice, Tsacheva, managed to convince the European Commission that she was doing the impossible to reform the Bulgarian justice system, the opposition claimed very convincingly that the reform as a whole was a joke, while the Bulgarian Freemasons enjoyed the publicity and used it to advertise the open secret of their power.

Popular fantasies

The strategies of the former secret agents to preserve their virtual capital by joining post-socialist secret societies or the tactics of the political entrepreneurs trying to compensate for their inadequate resources can explain the emergence of the conspiracy theory about the Bulgarian judiciary, but they cannot explain its currency. In fact, Freemasons and former agents were embroiled in at least two more major scandals in the judiciary, and the political entrepreneurs experimented with more conspiracy theories, including the theory that it was all because of the Russians. Yet the other scandals did not develop into conspiracy theories, and the other conspiracy theories failed to gain ground. In order to explain the currency of the conspiracy theory about the Bulgarian judiciary, we should take into account the response it brought forth. This can be illustrated by a couple of forum posts provoked by the media appearances of Tatyana Doncheva (BTV 2014):

[Username "The man of the people"] Doncheva is absolutely right! Even more regrettable is the fact that almost all legal institutions are controlled by

An open secret   119

the Bulgarian mafia. And the last appointments, pardon, transparent elections demonstrate that.

[Username "A citizen"] The corruption at the court and the prosecution is the most obvious, they sentence only small-time crooks. The whole country was stolen, but no investigation of a corrupt politician has ended with a sentence. They stole the money from the banks, they stole the whole industry, the stole the land of Bulgaria, not a word, no scream, no groan! The red coterie fills their mouths with crumbs from the pie so that they do not speak. Until the reds are brought down from power for good, Bulgaria will never be a normal country! I hope this happens in the next elections. God save Bulgaria! Amen!

[Username "Crocosia"] If we had a justice system, I am not talking about the reasons it is lacking, the state would not be a toilet. The court decisions / "In the name of the people"/ destroyed the Bulgarian intellectual elite in the 1940s. Similar decisions allowed the theft of large-scale real estate in the villages and the cities, and murdered the entrepreneurial spirit of the Bulgarian man./"In the name of the people"/ soared above the court orders to sentence/ kill the political opponents of communism. What were the first words of the court decisions that practically legalized the mafia in Bulgaria? Who issued the decisions? How many judges do you want me to point out, with their full names, who are PROVED to have millions (in Euro, not in Mongolian tugriks), and own real estate all over the Mediterranean? There are such specimens in every regional court.

Notwithstanding their agrammatical spontaneity, such forum posts put into play ingenious rhetorical devices. But for the purposes of this chapter, the posts can be summarized as follows: the justice system is a form of organized crime, the whole country has been stolen, the social order is essentially oppressive despite the claims that it acts on behalf of the people. Such phrases are not constatives because they cannot be verified. Indeed, an attempt to verify them would be no less ridiculous than an attempt to verify a hyperbole, and since they cannot be verified, they cannot be debunked. The phrases of the forum users should be interpreted as claims rather than as constatives. Such claims cannot be justified by a reference to norms, concepts, or facts because the norms, the concepts, the facts have validity only as far as they are socially recognized and therefore as far as they are inscribed in the social order. Since the forum users reject the social order in general, they make it impossible to justify their claims. Yet such impossible claims are not meaningless: they articulate an impossibility of at least four dimensions: the unthinkable crimes of stealing a whole country or transforming organized crime into a legal order, the irreparability of such unthinkable crimes, the unacceptability of a social order built on them, and the inconceivability of any alternative social order after the breakdown of Communism.

Why articulate such an intricate impossibility? I believe that it enabled the forum users to represent an object that on one hand, is lacking from the social order, yet on the other hand, without which the social order would be but oppression, and oppression not in the sense of the tyranny of an elite minority over the

120   *Todor Hristov and Ivelina Ivanova*

majority, but rather, in the sense of complete libidinal repression, withdrawal of desire from the social order, and subjective destitution of the social life, which would leave the actors with less than nothing—without anything to desire. Such an inherently contradictory object, whose lack is both impossible to fill and to endure, cannot be represented as we normally describe states of affairs. The forum users stage it as a fantasy of justice, justice for the post-socialist transition that haunts even the scenes of violence imagined by the most infuriated:

> [Username "Crocosia"] You, the representatives of the justice system, destroyed this country morally, socially, economically. You inflicted psychological damage on the psyche of the last generation which impact will be felt in the next forty years. THE PURGE WILL START FROM YOU!!!
>
> (ibid.)

Of course, the contents of such fantasies is appalling, but from a pragmatic point of view, they have the effect of negation, because if injustice is the opposite of justice, then the retributive violence against those that supposedly committed injustice functions as a negation of injustice. From that point of view, void of the moral pathos, of the heroic aesthetics, or the political justifications of a revolution, the sovereign violence of the people imagined by Crocosia is a negation by act (Žižek 2008, 80–81, 200), which notwithstanding its imaginary atrocity, provides the last support for a desire for justice that forecloses the subjective destitution of the social order.

However, are the unthinkable crimes of the post-socialist transition real? To ask if a fantasy is real is an empty question, just like asking what is the literal meaning of a metaphor or how to verify a fiction. If one asks such a question, one does not simply misunderstand, one does not want to understand. Then users like Crocosia start to seem monsters to us and, at least from the point of view of critical theory, this is unacceptable. Because if there is a grounding principle of critical theory, then it would be that, despite the monstrosities we are allegedly witnessing, there are no monsters.

Overdetermination

The conspiracy theory that the Bulgarian judiciary is secretly controlled by the Freemasons has been shaped by multifaceted, heterogeneous reasons that cannot be synchronized into a unity: the practical reason of the former secret agents trying to preserve or improve their social capital, the political reason of the entrepreneurs trying to enter the electoral competition despite their insufficient resources, the imaginary reasons of the forum users weaving fantasies about an impossible justice. If such a conspiracy theory seems unreasonable, this is because it is a condensation of reasons that produce different narratives: a dysfunctional reaction to the socialist past, a devious political strategy, outcry, and rage from the margins. The different versions of the conspiracy theory are irreducible to each other; in fact, they contradict each other. Yet, taken in isolation, none of the accounts can

An open secret 121

explain the social energy of the theory about the Bulgarian judiciary, its currency or its topicality, and even if one would try to disentangle them, they would lead back to each other like ramifying lines of meaning that increasingly intersect and converge (Freud 1976 II, 262–63, 289), like a rhizome (Deleuze and Guattari 1987, 6–7).

We can capture the antithetical rationality of the reasons that shape such conspiracy theories by the psychoanalytic concept of overdetermination. For the purposes of this chapter, overdetermination can be defined as an accumulation of contradictory elements that turns them into a gravitational mass rather than into a cause (Althusser 1969, 101, 106, 113). In that sense, overdetermination is a quantitative phenomenon that cannot be divided into discrete units, just like a traffic jam cannot be divided into individual cars and just like mortality rates cannot be divided into individual deaths. At the same time, overdetermination is a quantitative phenomenon that cannot be synthesized into a unity because it includes elements that are irreducibly external to each other, a multiplicity without one (Deleuze and Guattari 1987, 21). However, perhaps it would be more appropriate to illustrate the concept of overdetermination instead of defining it:

> [A man] was charged by one of his neighbors with having returned a borrowed kettle in a damaged condition. The defendant asserted first, that he had given it back undamaged; secondly, that the kettle had a hole in it when he borrowed it; and thirdly, that he had never borrowed a kettle from his neighbor at all.
>
> (Freud 1976 IV, 619)

This is an example of overdetermination, because each reason could have worked in isolation, but taken together, they turn into a multiplicity that cannot be synthesized into a coherent reasoning and therefore seems unreasonable. Yet precisely because of their incoherence, such reasonings articulate a latent thought, "I do not owe you what you gave to me," an unthinkable thought, which if we take into account the general insignificance or the personal oversignificance of its object, the kettle, makes sense only as a fantasy of saying "no" to the other, of denying the enigmatic question that lurks in the depth of any desire, "what does the Other want" (Lacan 2006, 690).

Conspiracy theories are overdetermined in a similar sense. They aggregate reasons in incoherent combinations in order to articulate impossible claims grounded on fantasies, which at least in the Bulgarian case, often take the form "it should not be like this," "the world is as it should not be," "it is impossible to be like this," "therefore it should be possible to be otherwise," "there should be possible another world." Perhaps conspiracy theories are the poor man's cognitive mapping (Jameson 1988, 357), but they are maps of other worlds. However, if we take into account the concept of overdetermination, then we can explain the social energy of conspiracy theories like the one about the Freemasons in the Bulgarian judiciary by the fact that such theories are overdetermined. If that is the case, then the topical conspiracy theories should be treated as dreams rather than as false

122　Todor Hristov and Ivelina Ivanova

or unverifiable statements about states of affairs, as it is usually done. Instead of appealing to the reason of the conspiracy theorists or decrying their unreasonableness, instead of debunking them, we should learn how to interpret their dreams.

Notes

1 All translations from Bulgarian by the authors.
2 For a detailed analysis of the complex network of resemblances and differences between secret societies and secret police in East European Countries, which also takes into account Simmel's concept of a secret society, see in Verdery (2014, 77–80, 136–38, 148–52).
3 The story of Mr. T as a secret agent is based on his dossier as a secret agent of State Security declassified by the Commission for the Disclosure of Documents and Declaration of Affiliation of Bulgarian Citizens with State Security and the Intelligence Service of the Bulgarian People's Army (CDDDABCSSISBPA 2009). The account of the career of Mr. T after 1989 is based on an interview published in Blitz (2014).
4 See (CDDDABCSSISBPA 2009). The claim that Col. Klyanev offered protection to Mr. T as a conscript is unsupported by documents. However, that seems probable against the background of life stories of secret agents collected in (Angelov 2007) or the typical career of a secret agent described in Metodiev (2012).
5 The account of the case of Mr. D and Mr. M is based on the detailed description of the facts in the ruling of the District Court of Sofia (*Milev v. Donchev* 2007). The case was classified, but it was nevertheless published by an independent website for investigative journalism.
6 The account of the bill and the parliamentary debates is based on the detailed and profound analysis in Medarov (2017).

Bibliography

Althusser, Louis. 1969. *For Marx*. London: Penguin
Andonova, Zoya. 2011. *Masonstvo I masoni v Bulgaria*. [Freemasonry and Freemasons in Bulgaria]. Sofia: "Sv. Kliment Ohridski."
Andreev, Metodi. 2016. "Tajnata vlast na DS prelia v masonskite lozhi" [The Secret Power of State Security Spilled over to the Masonic Lodges]. *Frognews*, July 29. https://frognews.bg/inteviu/andreev-frog-tainata-vlast-prelia-masonskite-loji.html.
Andreev, Veselin. 2007. *Strogo sekretno! Dokumenti za dejnostta na Dyrzhavna sigurnost (1944–1989)* [Top Secret! Documents on the Activities of State Security (1944–1989)]. Sofia: Simolini.
Birchall, Clare. 2015. "Aesthetics of the Secret." *New Formations* 83: 25–46.
Blitz. 2013. "Tatyana Doncheva: Masonite i plevenskiat krag upravliavat sadebnata sistema" [Tatyana Doncheva: Freemasons and the Pleven Circle Control the Justice System]. *Blitz*, March 13, 2013. https://blitz.bg/obshtestvo/tatyana-doncheva-masonite-i-plevenskiyat-krg-upravlyavat-sdebnata-sistema_news189186.html.
———. 2014. "Poly Pantev otvleche zet si otec Totyo I go globi 50000 marki" [Poly Pantev kidnapped his Son-in-law Totyo and Fined him 50000 DM]. *Blitz*, May 21, 2014. https://blitz.bg/obshtestvo/intervyu/advokatt-na-ndrgraunda-toshko-tenev-poli-pantev-otvleche-zet-si-otets-toto-i-go-quotglobiquot-50-000-marki_news268769.html.
Bourdieu, Pierre, and Loïc Wacquant. 1992. *An Invitation to Reflexive Sociology*. Chicago: Chicago University Press.

An open secret 123

BTV. 2013. "Sydebnata vlast e v racete na proatelski kragove i lobita – na masoni I bivshi milicioneri" [The Justice System is in the Hands of Circles of Friends and Lobbies of Freemasons and Former Cops]. *BTV*, March 20, 2013. https://btvnovinite.bg/bulgaria/sadebnata-vlast-e-v-ratsete-na-priyatelski-kragove-i-lobita-na-masoni-i-bivshi-militsioneri.html.

———. 2014. "Doncheva: Pravosadieto e parcelirano mezhdu biznesa, masonite I drugi grupirovki" [Doncheva: The Control of the Justice System is Distributed among Business, the Freemasons and other Groups]. *BTV*, December 15, 2014. https://btvnovinite.bg/videos/tazi-sutrin/tatjana-doncheva-pravosadieto-e-parcelirano-mezhdu-biznesa-masonite-i-drugi-grupirovki.html.

CDDDABCSSISBPA. 2009. "Reshenie No.95/28.10.2019 na Komisiata za razkrivane na dokumentite I obiaviavane na prinadkezhnist na balgarski grazhdani kam Darzhavna sigurnost I razuznavatelnite sluzhbi na BNA" [Decision No.95/28.10.2009 of the Commission for the Disclosure of Documents and Declaration of Affiliation of Bulgarian Citizens with State Security and the Intelligence Service of the Bulgarian Peoples's Army]. *Bivol.* Accessed May 6, 2019. https://agenti.bivol.bg/html/95.html.

Deleuze, Gilles, and Fèlix Guattari. 1987. *A Thousand Plateaus: Capitalism and Schizophrenia*. Minneapolis: Minnesota University Press.

Freud, Sigmund. 1976. *The Complete Psychological Works of Sigmund Freud*. New York: Norton.

Ivanov, Hristo. 2017. "Ostavka na Tsatsarov" [Resignation of Tsatsarov]. *Frognews*, April 22, 2017. https://m.offnews.bg/news/Analizi-i-Komentari_65/Hristo-Ivanov-Ostavka-na-Tcatcarov-Gergov-i-Donchev-go-primamili-ka_653623.html?pagewhich=0.

Ivanov, Mitko. 1992. *Stranici ot istoriata na bylgarskoto masonstvo* [Pages on Bulgarian Freemasonry]. Plovdiv: MKI-1.

Jameson, Frederic. 1988. "Cognitive Mapping." In *Marxism and the Interpretation of Culture*, edited by Cary Nelson and Lawrence Grossberg, 347–57. Urbana: Illinois University Press.

Kalpakchiev, Kalin. 2017. "Dali Tsatsarov I Gergov sa v edna masonska lozha?" [Are Tsatsarov and Gergov in the Same Masonic Lodge?]. *Club Z.* Accessed May 6, 2019. https://clubz.bg/53375-kalpakchiev_dali_cacarov_i_gergov_sa_v_edna_masonska_loja_nqma_otgovor.

Lacan, Jacques. 2006. *Écrits. The First Complete Edition in English. Translated by Bruce Fink*. New York: Norton.

Medarov, Georgi. 2017. "Masonite sa v Parlamenta! Politikonomia na konspiraciite v sadebnata reforma na Balgaria" [The Freemasons are in Parliament! Political Economy of Conspiracies in the Judicial Reform Discourses in Bulgaria]. *Critique and Humanism* 48: 147–64.

Metodiev, Momchil. 2012. *Mashina za legitimnost: Darzhavna sigurnost v komunistich eskata darzhava* [Legitimation Machine: State Security in the Communist State]. Sofia: Ciela.

Milev v Donchev. 2007. "no. C-318/08 Sofijski gradski sad" [Milev versus Donchev. 2007. no. C-318/08 Sofia City Court]. *Bivol.* Accessed May 6, 2019. https://i0.wp.com/bivol.bg/wp-content/uploads/2011/09/Angel_Donchev_Page_01.jpg?fit=596%2C842&ssl=1.

Nedev, Nediu. 2008. *Balgarskoto masonstvo (1807–2007)* [Bulgarian Freemasonry (1807–2007)]. Plovdiv: Hermes.

Nedkov, Dimitar. 2008. *Masonite se varnaha v Balgaria* [The Freemasons Came Back to Bulgaria]. Sofia: Miriam.

124 *Todor Hristov and Ivelina Ivanova*

Parliament. 2016. "44 Narodno Sabranie, 224 zasedanie na 27.07.2016" [44th Parliament, 224th session, 27.07.2016]. Accessed May 6, 2019. www.parliament.bg/bg/plenaryst/ns/51/ID/5687.

Pravosudiezavseki. 2016. "Sadebna reforma po balgarski" [Legal Reform Bulgarian Style]. *Pravosudie za vseki*, July 28. https://pravosadiezavseki.com/2016/07/28/1216/.

Schutz, Alfred. 1964. *Collected Papers. Vol. 2. Studies in Social Theory*. The Hague: Martinus Nijhoff.

Simmel, Georg. 1964. *The Sociology of Georg Simmel*. New York: Free Press.

Velichkov, Velislav. 2016. "Pravosadie za izbranite" [Justice for the Chosen Ones]. *Terminal 3*, June 16. Accessed May 6, 2019. https://pravosadiezavseki.com/2016/06/06/pravosadie-na-izbranite/.

Verdery, Katherine. 2014. *Secrets and Truths: Ethnography in the Archive of Romania's Secret Police*. Budapest: CEU Press.

Žižek, Slavoj. 2008. *Violence*. New York: Picador.

6 From Judeo-Polonia to Act 447

How and why did the Jewish conspiracy myth become a central issue in Polish political discourse?

Dominika Bulska, Agnieszka Haska, Mikołaj Winiewski, and Michał Bilewicz

In spring 2019, the American Congress S.447 Act provoked a public debate in Poland. The bill obligated the US government to offer diplomatic support to actions aimed at the restitution of Jewish property wrongfully seized or transferred during or soon after World War II. In the United States, the act was passed without any wider interest; in Poland, however, it triggered protests and became one of the principal topics of discussion during the European parliamentary elections. Even though the US act does not have any direct legal consequences for Poland, it led to a conspiracy theory suggesting that the bill was a result of anti-Polish policies of Israel that pressured the US government to pass such legislation. As a result of Act S.447, Jewish organizations were said to be able to seize Polish land, property, and assets as well as file financial claims against Poland up to as much as a trillion zlotys (about $25 billion, Zaborowska 2019). The Polish government was also thought to be a part of the conspiracy, since it hushed up the whole issue in order to maintain good relations with Israel and the United States. One of the candidates for the European Parliament and leaders of the extreme-right *Konfederacja* (Confederacy) party, Robert Winnicki, accused Prime Minister Mateusz Morawiecki of taking part in secret negotiations with the Israeli government, and appealed to the ruling Zjednoczona Prawica (United Right) party on Twitter, "Start calling a spade before the Jews start cashing not only your party headquarters, but also the property of all Poles" (Winnicki 2019). The US ambassador Georgette Mosbacher made efforts to disavow the conspiracy narrative of *Konfederacja*. Prime Minister Morawiecki also took a stand, saying: "We [Poles] were the most murdered victims here" and "We will never agree to pay any compensation for this or any other reason" (Fakt 2019). Here, the conspiracy narrative was juxtaposed with the narration of "suffering rivalry" promoted by the ruling party, *Prawo i Sprawiedliwość* (Law and Justice), that aims to challenge the singularity of the Holocaust by pointing at Polish suffering under German occupation during World War II.

The formation of antisemitic attitudes in Poland

The conspiracy theory promoted by *Konfederacja* and the extreme right is exemplary of Polish conspiracy theories and antisemitism. Research on antisemitism in

126　*Dominika Bulska et al.*

Poland distinguishes different forms of anti-Jewish attitudes: (1) traditional anti-semitism, based on historic, Christian anti-Judaic motives of blood-libel accusations (Datner 1996; Tokarska-Bakir 2008); (2) modern antisemitism, more secular in character and based on the idea that Jews aspire to take over a given country or even the entire world; and (3) secondary antisemitism, occurring post-Holocaust and based on the belief that Jews are themselves responsible for antisemitism, that they are using the Holocaust for their personal gain and are abusing other nations' feelings of guilt (Krzemiński 2004; Imhoff and Banse 2009, 1). Those three types of attitudes often occur together in different contexts. It is rare that they can be distinguished in a clear-cut manner, but because they appear in different moments of history and serve different psychological functions, this theoretical distinction helps to navigate the landscape of antisemitism in Poland. As those tropes often influence one another, being conscious of this distinction also helps to understand the specificity of the belief in Jewish conspiracy in Poland. To give an example, the trope of the blood libel was heavily influenced in Poland by the preaching of Saint Giovanni da Capestrano and his subsequent cult in the fifteenth century. It was central to antisemitic culture patterns up to the nineteenth century; rumors about Jews kidnapping children and using their blood for ritual purposes provoked several pogroms after World War I, such as in Strzyzow (1919) and Bialystok (1938). The most well-known example is the pogrom in Kielce in 1946, where the disappearance of an eight-year-old Polish boy named Henryk Blaszczyk set off mob riots resulting in the killing of 36 Jewish people.

Jewish conspiracy theories in Poland are a product of past Polish-Jewish relations and historical social structures. There are several factors that contribute to this. For instance, in medieval times, the Church believed that collecting interest from loaned money was a sin, and therefore, Christians were not allowed to lend money for interest. Jews therefore took on this economic role and became moneylenders, bankers, and tax collectors. This is a partial explanation for the stereotype of the Jew as greedy but also successful in business. Financial competition contributed to the idea that Jews are loyal only to their own group (Poliakov 2003, 14). Furthermore, because of medieval laws specifying where and how many Jews could settle and what occupations were available to them, Jews were placed in direct competition with almost all social groups: serfs and free peasants as well as with the non-Jewish inhabitants of the cities. In the sixteenth and seventeenth centuries, Jews dominated state trade, especially between the village and the city, and were tax collectors, landlords, and artisans (Eisenbach 1988, 1).

In Poland, the groundwork for the notion that Jews aspire to take over a given country or even the world, emerged long before the appearance of the infamous publication, *The Protocols of the Elders of Zion* around the turn of the twentieth century. It began with partition of the Polish state in 1795 between three powers: Austria, Prussia, and Russia. The emerging Polish nationalism—influenced by the antisemitic legislation of the annexing countries, like the Pale of Settlement of the Russian Empire—fueled conspiracy theories in which Jews were seen not only as an economic threat but also, and primarily, as a political one (i.e., as obstacles for regaining Poland's independence). The Pale of Settlement also led to a massive

From Judeo-Polonia to Act 447   127

migration of Jews from the east bringing a sense of threat among non-Jewish populations.

The key idea in the Polish conspiratorial imagination was that of Judeo-Polonia, a vision of Poland secretly controlled by Jews. One of the key figures who contributed to this idea was a playwright, poet, and politician, Julian Ursyn Niemcewicz, who wrote a story, *Rok 3333 czyli sen niesłychany* (Year 3333 or a Dream Unheard Of), also known as *Moškopolis, Warszawa zżydziała* (Moshe-polis, or Jew-dominated Warsaw) (1817). This was one of the earliest Polish science fiction works, in which the author described a vision of Warsaw controlled by Jews (and ruled by King Moshe XII), who embodied primitive characteristics, backwardness, and dirt. Although Niemcewicz's biography and his other writings show that he wrote *Rok 3333* rather as a critique of traditional Judaism (as opposed to the enlightened Haskalah movement) (Domagalska 2015a, 12–15) after its posthumous publication in 1858, the novel became one of the foundations of Polish antisemitism, particularly in the part of Poland that was under Russian control.

Apart from the cultural, social, and economic changes common to the whole of Europe in the mid-nineteenth century—the industrial revolution, gradual modernization, the development of capital economy, emancipation trends, or rapid urban growth—modern Polish antisemitism was primarily a product of the collapse of the feudal order by the abolishing of socage in all three partitions (the last in the Polish Kingdom, which was then a part of the Russian Empire in 1861) and the abortive January Uprising of 1863, which resulted in the confiscations of landed gentry's property and the increasing impoverishment of this social group. At the same time, the processes of emancipation and assimilation were visible among the Jewish population of Poland. As a result of the Haskalah movement (the era of enlightenment) and Jewish participation in the development of industry in Warsaw, Łódź, and smaller cities like Białystok or Radom, Jews were now more often seen as secularized intellectuals, entrepreneurs, members of the working class, and artists (Cała 1989, 12). In this situation, Jews, especially those who had assimilated, not only became competitors for positions in industry, finance, or the professions but also were deemed complicit in the transformation of society as well as a political and economic threat. This led to violent attacks against the Jewish population, such as the pogroms in Warsaw (1881) and Żyrardów (1883). The idea of Judeo-Polonia, outlined in Niemcewicz's book, was revived in the 1880s, especially in the widely read weekly magazine *Rola*, published in the Russia-controlled part of the country between 1882 and 1912. *Rola* was instrumental in the formation of Polish conspiratorial antisemitism. In the articles published by the magazine, Jews epitomized all kinds of evil and allegedly tried to enslave the Poles, by whatever means available—through modernization, capitalism, Socialism, land purchases, assimilation, or collaboration with the partitioners. Their alleged aim was to establish Judeo-Polonia. The *Rola* articles emphasized the religious differences between Poles and Jews and the importance of the Catholic Church in preserving Polishness. Poles were presented as defenders of tradition and the land of their forefathers—as a healthy national "organism" on which "parasites," the Jews, thrived (Domagalska 2015b, 19). In Poland, the *Rola* developed the modern language of antisemitic

128   *Dominika Bulska et al.*

dehumanization, calling the Jews "dirty vermin," "weeds," or "plague" (ibid., 19). The weekly also demanded segregation and emigration of Jews.

The conspiracy theory that Jews are a threat to the Polish nation became fundamental to the programs and rhetoric of the nationalist movement taking shape at that time. The central formation was the *Stronnictwo Narodowo-Demokratyczne* (National-Democratic Party), established in 1897, and headed by Roman Dmowski. In *Myśli nowoczesnego Polaka* (Reflections of a Modern Pole, 1902), Dmowski argued that Jews were internal enemies who polluted Poland's racial purity and weakened it as a state (Dmowski 1933, 202). One of the chief slogans of the National Democrats appealed for political, economic, and social boycott of "the Jewry"; such antisemitic agitation contributed to eruptions of violence.

When Poland regained its independence in 1918, the content of antisemitic stereotypes became sharper and more intense. Violence against the Jewish minority was on the rise. One crucial change was the appearance of a conspiratorial stereotype of *żydokomuna* (Jewish Communism) used as propaganda during the Polish-Soviet war of 1919–20. The National Democrats who strove to build a nation-state campaigned for discriminatory restrictions against Jews, then around 10% of the population. Mostly, these restrictions consisted of exclusion from the national, civic, and economic community and enforced emigration. Right-wing publications featured an internationally well-known theme inspired by *The Protocols of the Elders of Zion*—an antisemitic pamphlet first published in 1903 describing a "global conspiracy" of Jews to take over the world, which in Polish antisemitic discourse was paired with the idea of an "anonymous power," an international league fighting against traditional and Christian values (Nowaczyński 1921). In the 1930s, antisemitism spread quickly, backed by utterly racist ideology and Fascist political slogans and supported by Polish extreme-right organizations, such as *Obóz Wielkiej Polski* (Camp of Great Poland, founded in 1926). They promoted far-reaching racial segregation, which would deprive Jews of political rights, restrict employment opportunities, prohibit the purchase of land, create Jewish districts, or finally, enforce compulsory emigration. After Józef Piłsudski's death in 1935, the ruling Sanation political movement moved to the right of the political spectrum, incorporating much of the ideology of the radical right, as also happened in many other European countries. Antisemitism and anti-Jewish violence rapidly increased; the late 1930s were marked not only by a growth in boycotts, store marking, the popularity of the slogan *"swój do swego po swoje"* (go to your own to get your own), and an increase in pogroms but also in anti-Jewish legislation, including the ban on ritual slaughter, the introduction of "ghetto benches" (a form of official segregation in the seating of students, introduced in 1935 in Lviv), and finally, the idea of forcing mass emigration of Jews to Madagascar. This largely shaped the attitudes of Poles toward Jews during the Holocaust.

Even the evidence of the consequences of the Holocaust, the most drastic in Poland did not eliminate antisemitic sentiments there. In addition to the elements known from traditional and modern antisemitism, after World War II arose the increasingly popular myth of "Jewish communism," reinforced by the presence of people of Jewish origin in prominent positions of the new regime and the security

From Judeo-Polonia to Act 447   129

apparatus. The Communist regime also made use of antisemitic resentment and conspiracy theories, using them as a political instrument in the purges of 1956 and particularly in 1968. After the Six-Day War of 1967, an anti-Israeli campaign was launched in Poland. In March 1968, using as a pretext the student protests, which according to official propaganda, had been inspired by Jews, the government mounted an antisemitic campaign. One of the consequences was mass dismissal of people of Jewish origin and forced emigration, also on a mass scale, to Western Europe, Israel, or the United States without the right to return. To put it simply, the March 1968 campaign was based on a conspiracy theory that accused Israel of "international Zionism," of forging an alliance with the Federal Republic of Germany, and of contributing to the detriment of Poland ("anti-Polonism"). This conspiracy supposedly had several goals: in addition to strengthening the political and military position of Israel, it supposedly aimed to construct a narrative in which Poles were responsible for the Holocaust (Eisler 1991; Osęka 2008). Official propaganda consistently claimed that Poles were the primary victims of Nazi genocide during World War II and that they even helped Jews on a mass scale during German occupation—something the West presumably ignores and the Jewish survivors themselves fail to be grateful for. Furthermore, many official Communist publications insist on the idea of Jewish collaboration with Nazis from within the ghettos and make comparisons with the extent of Polish losses during the war (Eisler 1991; Osęka 2008). First and foremost, however, it was stressed that the Israeli/Jewish-German conspiracy targeted Polish national existence and Socialism.

The Polish narrative of antisemitic conspiracy theories and stereotypes was revisited after the regime change in 1989, with various elements repeated and slightly modified. This was particularly visible after 2001, the year Jan Tomasz Gross's *Neighbours* was published, which proved to be a significant event in the public debate on Polish attitudes during the Holocaust. Gross's book was the first to draw attention to the role of Poles during the mass murder of Jews in Jedwabne on July 10, 1941. Until the publication, the official narrative stated that the massacre was solely the responsibility of the occupying Germans. Gross argued that the pogrom was initiated by the Poles, the neighbors of the title. Conspiracy theories surfaced in reaction to this volume: the accusation that Poles had killed Jews during World War II was deemed to be not only an assault on Poland's positive image but also an international conspiracy aimed at shifting the blame for the Holocaust on to Poland and at downplaying Polish heroism during the occupation (Forecki 2018). This was a discussion mostly about "suffering rivalry": asking, who was more of a victim of World War II—Jews or Poles? The debate on the amendment of the Law on the Institute of National Remembrance provoked comments of the same kind. The amended law passed by the Polish parliament in January 2018 included a fine or imprisonment of up to three years to "whoever publicly and contrary to the facts attributes to the Polish Nation or to the Polish State responsibility or co-responsibility for the Nazi crimes committed by the German Third Reich . . . or for any other offences constituting crimes against peace, humanity or war crimes, or otherwise grossly diminishes the responsibility of the actual perpetrators of these crimes." (Dziennik Ustaw 2018). The diplomatic conflict between

130 *Dominika Bulska et al.*

Poland and the United States and Israel erupted in the wake of the new law and was announced to have been a result of behind-the-scenes intrigue against Poland. For instance, Law and Justice MP, Krystyna Pawłowicz, said in an interview for Republika TV: "Many decisions taken in the Polish interest that are in perfect correspondence with historical facts, are meeting with a massive attack from the outside and by the internal enemy" (A.S. 2018). Ultimately, some of the new provisions were lifted in June 2018.

Before World War II, Jews were one of the largest ethno-religious minorities in Poland. The Holocaust and large postwar waves of migration in the 1940s and 1960s destroyed the Polish-Jewish community almost entirely. The size of the Jewish population fell from around 10% (3 million people) of the population to less than 0.001% (7,000 people [Tomaszewski 1990, 10; Gudaszewski 2015, 31]). And yet, recent public debates about the Institute of National Remembrance or Act S.447 prove that the belief in a Jewish conspiracy still exists and plays an important role in political mobilization, although Jews are almost absent from the social landscape of Poland. In Polish culture, Jews are constructed as a prototype of a conspiring group (Kofta and Sędek 2005, 54), being central to the concept of conspiracy and activating other conspiracy theories when mentioned. Other ethnic groups, such as Germans or Americans, even if they are perceived as power seeking, are not seen as acting "behind the scenes," while Jews often are. For that reason, conspiracy theories about Jews could be considered a key transmitter of "antisemitism without Jews" (Lendvai 1971), a phenomenon well described in post-Communist Eastern Europe.

Belief in Jewish conspiracy in contemporary Poland

The use of Jewish conspiracy narratives in the current political debate is not surprising, given their historical prominence and embeddedness in the culture. However, the occurrence of such attitudes in political debate does not necessarily mean they are shared by the majority of society. In order to verify whether this is the case, we analyzed the data from nationwide Polish Prejudice Surveys organized by the Center for Research on Prejudice and conducted every four years (so far 2009, 2013, and 2017) on a representative sample of Poles.[1] In those surveys beliefs about various groups, such as Jews, Roma, or the LGBT community, are measured among other psychological constructs, such as right-wing authoritarianism or a general tendency to believe in conspiracies. Belief in Jewish conspiracy is measured with a scale applied to statements (Bilewicz et al. 2013, 7) such as "Jews often operate covertly, behind the scenes" or "Jews strive to rule the world." The participants are asked to indicate to what extent they agree with those and similar statements on a scale from 1 (definitely do not agree) to 5 (definitely agree). Our results from the latest, 2017, study show that, depending on the question, 43%–54% of Poles express at least a partial belief in Jewish conspiracy, meaning they marked either a 4 or a 5 on the scale. Interestingly, according to our findings, the likelihood of holding such beliefs is only weakly related to demographic characteristics. Older, less wealthy, and less educated[2] Poles were slightly more likely to indicate that they agree with such statements. Though the strength of relationship was not large, it confirmed our previous results that the belief in Jewish conspiracy is related to age, income, and education of the participants of the studies (Bilewicz et al. 2013, 9; Winiewski and Bilewicz 2015, 24). As for the political attitudes, measured with a question in which we asked the participants to describe their political stance on a scale from 1 (definitely left wing) to 7 (definitely right wing), we observed that people on the right of the political spectrum tended to believe in Jewish conspiracy to a greater extent.[3] Again, this result confirmed the previous findings (based on the Polish Prejudice Survey from the year 2013) on the nature of this relationship in Poland that the belief in Jewish conspiracy is rather a domain of people with right-wing political views (Bilewicz and Winiewski 2015, 24). Notably, the prevalence of anti-Jewish conspiracy attitudes in Poland in the last decade was relatively stable. The comparison of nationwide survey data results from the studies conducted in 2009, 2013, and 2017 (Figure 6.1) showed that the average level of agreement with the statements expressing Jewish conspiracy in Poland did not change significantly through the years (Bulska and Winiewski 2018, 230). This suggests that in the span of the last decade, the belief in Jewish conspiracy in Poland was strong and independent of the ever-changing sociopolitical context.

While this is certainly an important finding in itself, the Jewish conspiracy stereotype seems to be a part of a bigger structure of attitudes composed of various conspiracy beliefs. In the 2017 Polish Prejudice Survey, the Center for Research on Prejudice investigated how specific conspiracy beliefs interact with one another in Polish society and to what extent these beliefs are related to the so-called conspiracy

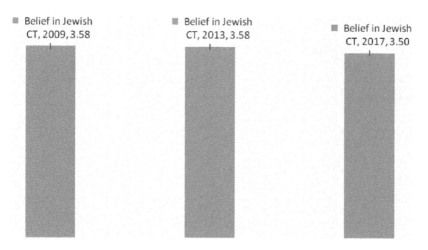

Figure 6.1 Differences in means for scales of belief in Jewish conspiracy theories in years 2009, 2013, and 2017, with error bars representing standard error of the mean. (The bars overlap, which shows that the mean level for scales of belief in Jewish conspiracy theories did not change throughout the years.)

mentality—that is, the general propensity to endorse conspiracy theories (Moscovici 1987, 157), as measured on a scale constructed by Bruder et al. (2013, 5). Two of those theories, specific to the Polish context, were of political nature: the first, the Smoleńsk conspiracy theory, gives an alternative explanation to the Polish presidential plane crash in 2010,[4] suggesting that it was not an accident, but an assassination; the second theory suggests that the various political decisions of then conservative minister of defense Antoni Macierewicz were motivated by the interests of a hostile power—that is, Russia. The third theory was an example of a typical anti-scientific conspiracy theory suggesting that it is better to avoid genetically modified food (GMO), as the consequences of it are hidden from the general public. The last set of beliefs referred to the so-called gender conspiracy—that is, the idea that gender studies are a pseudoscience profiting those who publish within this paradigm and aimed at destroying the Judeo-Christian tradition and at taking control of the media. Having in mind that specific conspiracy theories may be driven by specific political ideologies (Wright and Arbuthnot 1974, 1; Swami 2012, 8), especially when it comes to the theories of a political nature, and that generally those with more extreme political opinions on either end of the political spectrum tend to believe in conspiracy theories to a greater extent (van Prooijen, Krouwel, and Pollet 2015, 575), we analyzed the correlation between various conspiracy theories and their link to the conspiracy mentality, controlling for political attitudes of the participants.

Figure 6.2 shows the correlation between belief in Jewish conspiracy and remaining conspiracy beliefs as well as the correlation between those beliefs and the conspiracy mentality scale (Bruder et al. 2013, 5), measuring the general

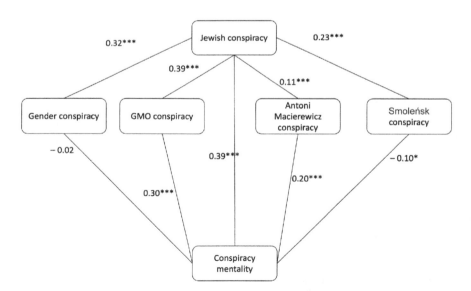

Figure 6.2 Correlations between various conspiracy beliefs and conspiracy mentality in Poland, controlling for political stands.

From *Judeo-Polonia to Act 447*   133

propensity to believe in conspiracy theories. As it demonstrates, the belief in Jewish conspiracy correlated positively with all other conspiracy theories, even the ones that seem to be very distant from antisemitism (i.e., the Antoni Macierewicz conspiracy theory, expressed mostly by liberals). The correlation was the highest when it came to the anti-scientific anti-GMO theory and the gender conspiracy, while political conspiracies were significantly yet not as strongly related. Notably though, the correlation between the belief in Jewish conspiracy and conspiracy mentality was the largest in comparison to the remaining theories. It suggests that the belief in Jewish conspiracy is in a way a central component of the more generalized tendency to explain reality by conspiracy theories. Those results are in line with the aforementioned findings of Kofta and Sędek (2005), which show that in Poland, Jews are considered the prototype of a conspiring group.

Cross-European comparison

Belief in Jewish conspiracy plays a prominent role in Poland, but is this popularity specific only to the Polish context, due to, for instance, historical relationships between Poles and Jews? Or is it a part of a broader trend, present in Eastern European countries? To answer those questions, we decided to analyze the data gathered by the Anti-Defamation League (ADL). This international Jewish non-governmental organization, defining its main goals as struggling against antisemitism, defending democratic ideals, and fighting with all forms of discrimination, has been carrying out public opinion surveys about attitudes toward Jews since 1964. In 2014, the ADL conducted a worldwide survey, called Global 100 Index of Antisemitism, measuring the attitudes toward Jews in 101 countries and the West Bank and Gaza. To the best of our knowledge, this is the most comprehensive system of monitoring hatred toward Jews worldwide, though not without its shortcomings.[5] Because of some methodological problems, the data needs to be treated with some degree of caution (Winiewski and Bilewicz 2013), but it does provide a relatively good overview of anti-Jewish sentiment. In the survey, 11 questions were asked, among them statements suggesting that Jews have too much power over: a) global affairs, b) the business world, c) the international financial markets, d) the United States, and e) the global media. Affirmative answers to all those questions were treated as an indicator of the belief in Jewish conspiracy. The results can be seen in Table 6.1.

The comparison between the chosen European countries shows that generally the participants were most likely to say that Jews have too much power over the business world and international financial markets. Belief in Jewish conspiracy seems to be least prevalent in the Czech Republic and the most common in Hungary. Polish citizens usually are somewhere in the middle: depending on the statement, 30%–57% of Poles were likely to provide an affirmative answer to the questions about the alleged power of Jews. It seems that when it comes to the belief in Jewish conspiracy, Poland might not be the exception to the rule, but rather, part of a general trend in this part of the world. However, even if the popularity of such attitudes in Poland is not the highest in this region, the country

Table 6.1 Percentage of agreements to the questions indicating the belief in Jewish conspiracy in Europe

Country	Business world	International financial markets	Global affairs	the United States	Global media
Poland	57%	55%	42%	30%	35%
Hungary	69%	63%	48%	32%	39%
Ukraine	56%	51%	44%	31%	36%
Belarus	50%	46%	36%	31%	30%
Lithuania	43%	45%	33%	27%	24%
Romania	60%	56%	46%	34%	29%
Czech Republic	35%	30%	20%	16%	15%
France	48%	44%	46%	42%	44%
Italy	32%	45%	30%	26%	18%

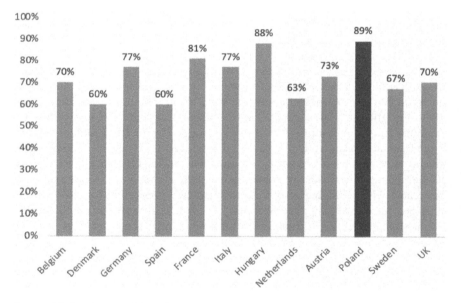

Figure 6.3 Percentage of Jews in various countries who heard a statement that Jews have too much power.

might be outstanding in terms of the willingness to express them. As the study of European Jewish communities, conducted by the EU Agency for Fundamental Rights, shows (Figure 6.3), in the past year almost 90% of Polish Jews have heard from someone of non-Jewish origin that Jews have too much power. Such attitudes are expressed freely by Poles and seem to not be constrained by any social norm.

From *Judeo-Polonia to Act 447*   135

Relative stability over time and relative popularity of the belief in Jewish conspiracy in comparison to other European countries suggests it is a rather solid structure of attitudes in Polish society. Though they are not necessarily present at all times in sociopolitical discourse, they constitute a latent theory, ready to be revealed in a favorable context or when there is a psychological need for them.

Psychological functions of Jewish conspiracy theories

In acknowledging the centrality of the Jewish conspiracy myth in Polish politics, both historically and in the contemporary era, it is essential to explain the roles it might serve in Polish society. We suggest that its psychological functions are essential not only for the proliferation of the myth but also for its recurrence in times of turmoil, crisis, and political instability. There are several psychological functions that the belief in Jewish conspiracy theory might have for an individual. In the forthcoming subsections, we will review its explanatory function, control-restoring function, and identity function.

Explanatory function

Peter Glick (2005, 1) proposed an ideological model of the scapegoat, arguing that times of crisis bring a strong desire to identify those responsible. The belief in Jewish conspiracy is based on the portrayal of Jews as a powerful and influential group that might plausibly be blamed for others' misfortunes. The aggression toward such a group has the potential to provide relief from frustrating conditions.

This process has been observed by sociologist Emile Durkheim (1899), who analyzed the trial of artillery captain Alfred Dreyfus, convicted of espionage during a time of severe political crisis in France, when several assassinations, governmental changes, and bombings created a sense of societal unrest. Durkheim realized that a society in deep political crisis "needs someone to blame, someone upon whom to avenge itself for its disappointments; and those persons whom opinion already disfavors are naturally singled out for this role" (1899, 322). He considered the Dreyfus affair to be a blame-placing process in which the society could blame the times of "moral disturbance" on a minority group that was relatively harmless.

In a similar vein, French sociologist Serge Moscovici, who analyzed antiminority violence occurring during revolutionary situations in Russia, the United States, and India, concluded that "it is in periods of social unrest that minorities are most insistently associated with conspiracy" (Moscovici 1987, 152). The conspiracy theory provides a scheme that puts blame upon and internal enemy and cognitively resolves the problematic, uncertain, and complex situation of social unrest.

This cognitive process is justified also based on the current experimental research on conspiracy beliefs. Van Prooijen and Jostman (2013, 1) suggest that a state of uncertainty creates a heightened need for simplistic explanation. Even an experimentally induced situation of uncertainty increases people's belief in malevolent conspiracies. The complexity and uncertainty of the world motivate

136 *Dominika Bulska et al.*

people to seek simple and coherent explanatory accounts. Polish studies on this topic found that people with the heightened need for cognitive closure were more prone to endorse conspiratorial explanations, for example, of refugee crises and aviation accidents (Marchlewska, Cichocka, and Kossowska 2018, 109).

In Poland, conspiracy theories about Jews became particularly prominent in times of uncertainty. After the end of World War II, when the country faced enormous waves of violence and Soviet power was not yet stabilized, many theories about Jewish conspiracy spread across the country (Zaremba 2012, 585). The Kielce pogrom in 1946, as well as smaller-scale pogroms in Kraków, Tarnów, Rzeszów, shared one characteristic: they were based on theories of Jews intentionally plotting against Poland, kidnapping Christian children, and posing a threat to Polish families. Another situation of uncertainty in Poland occurred in 1956 (after the collapse of Stalinism in Poland, when the totalitarian political system eroded) as well as in 1989 (after the collapse of Communism and state economy). In both these periods of political uncertainty antisemitic voices were particularly visible in public discourse.

Control-restoring function

Times of uncertainty are often associated with shared experiences of control deprivation. Poles suffered from such experiences when living under partition in the nineteenth century, under Nazi and Soviet occupations in the early 1940s and under the Communist regime in the second half of twentieth century. Control deprivation has been experienced on both individual and collective levels. The uncontrollability experiences on a collective level led to individual control deprivation: people losing jobs, having constrained freedom of movement, and risking health and life due to political oppression. As the need to control is a basic human motivation (Deci and Ryan 2000, 228), people tend to engage in many compensatory strategies that subjectively restore their sense of personal control.

Psychological research found that people under control deprivation more often engage in scapegoating (Rothschild et al. 2012, 1148), perceive other groups as powerful and God as controlling (Kay et al. 2008, 264), recognize patterns in random noise and conspiracies among unrelated individuals (Whitson and Galinsky 2008, 115). Numerous studies show that lack of control breeds conspiracy mentality as well as specific conspiracy theories (Sullivan et al. 2010, 434; Imhoff 2015, 122). This is particularly true in people's perception of groups that they consider immoral; under control deprivation people tend to view such groups as conspiring against them (van Proojen and Jostman 2013, 109).

The belief in Jewish conspiracy could also be viewed as a control compensation. When losing control over their lives, people start to engage more systematically in scapegoating. Recently we performed several survey studies in Poland and the United Kingdom, using online research panels, about people's tendency to believe in Jewish conspiracies. We found that control deprivation in the political domain (i.e., political powerlessness) was a key antecedent of such stereotypes about Jewish people. We observed this effect in cross-sectional and longitudinal studies (powerlessness was positively associated with Jewish conspiracy beliefs) as well as in experimental studies (when people were reminded about the uncontrollable nature of contemporary politics, their belief in Jewish conspiracy theories increased (Kofta, Soral, and Bilewicz n.d.).

Sometimes control deprivation is caused by a more general decline in one's economic situation, in addition to the subjective feeling of being in crisis. After the 1989 systemic transition from state economy to capitalism, many in Poland suffered from economic deprivation. At the same time, economic inequalities emerged, and many could see that their living standards were substantially worse than those of elites. When analyzing data obtained in a nationwide representative sample study of 1,098 adult Poles, performed in 2002, we observed that people who considered their economic situation to be worse than the situation of other people, and the situation of their nation to be worse than that of other nations, would declare higher support for Jewish conspiracy theories. This in turn was responsible for their higher levels of prejudice toward Jews as measured by social distance scales (Bilewicz and Krzemiński 2010, 234). The sense of relative deprivation is a well-known antecedent of prejudice and xenophobic attitudes (Smith and Pettigrew 2015, 1). However, some aspects of deprivation specifically cause antisemitic attitudes and not attitudes toward other groups. Research by Becker, Wagner, and Oliver (2011, 871) showed that when Germans were reminded about the responsibility of banks and financiers for the 2008 economic crises, their antisemitic views strengthened, but their attitudes toward other groups (i.e., immigrants) remained unchanged.

A systematic survey of the causes of antisemitic stereotypes in Poland found that relative deprivation correlates strongly with conspiracy-based forms of antisemitism, but its correlation with other forms of antisemitism is weaker (Bilewicz et al. 2013, 10). When people lose their status, the conspiracy theory about Jewish wealth and power can plausibly explain their misfortune and provide a scapegoat to blame.

Identity function

Although conspiracy theories about Jews serve obvious control- and certainty-restoring functions, these functions only partially explain the popularity of such theories in times of prosperity. Recent studies of online communication in Poland after the introduction of the 2018 Holocaust law (Bilewicz et al. 2018, 20) point to such a paradox: after many years of economic prosperity and systematic economic growth, the popularity of Jewish conspiracy theories remains high. When the Polish government introduced a law restricting freedom of speech about the Holocaust and later faced outrage from international Jewish communities, the presence of conspiracy theories about Jews on Polish websites increased noticeably.

A plausible explanation for this phenomenon lies in the specific identity functions of beliefs in Jewish conspiracy. Our studies analyzing the antecedents of beliefs in Jewish conspiracy pointed to the importance of a victim-based identity (Bilewicz et al. 2013, 10). In a study performed in 2002, we compared two

138 *Dominika Bulska et al.*

forms of collective victimhood as potential causes for belief in Jewish conspiracy: relative victimhood (a perception that Poles were more victimized than Jews) and absolute victimhood (a perception that Poles were more frequently victimized than anyone else) (Bilewicz and Stefaniak 2013, 5). The study found that both forms of victimhood were strongly related to the belief in Jewish power. Those who considered their nation to be victimized exaggerated the extent to which Jews have political power. More importantly, regression analysis proved that the sense of absolute victimhood, measured with the question "Do you think the Polish nation was more frequently victimized throughout history than other nations?" significantly predicted the belief in Jewish conspiracy, measured with the scale mentioned earlier in this chapter. This effect was independent of the victimhood competition with Jews. This means that those Poles who felt their nation was victimized throughout history (not relatively to Jews) were more likely to share the belief in Jewish conspiracy. The next study, the Polish Prejudice Survey performed on a representative sample of Poles in 2009, confirmed this finding. It showed that Poles who strongly identify with their nation are more prone to believe in antisemitic conspiracy theories because of their strong sense of national victimhood (Bilewicz and Stefaniak 2013, 7).

The overwhelming sense of victimhood, which is clearly an important component of Polish national identity, puts Jews in an obvious role of potential competitors for the status of unique victims of historical crimes. This is particularly true for those who strive for a strong recognition of their nation. Such a form of identity is known as "collective narcissism," an emotional investment in an unrealistic belief in the group's greatness (Golec de Zavala et al. 2009, 1074). Golec de Zavala and Cichocka (2012, 213) in their surveys performed in Poland on a total sample of 236 undergraduate students showed that such beliefs correlated with Poles' denial of historical crimes against Jews, antisemitic beliefs, and general a sense of unacknowledged victimhood. In a recent study performed on an online research panel in Poland in 2018 on a sample of 1,285 adults, it was found that collective narcissism, as opposed to more secure forms of national identification, is positively related to the belief in Jewish conspiracy (Bilewicz et al. 2018, 35).

Taken together, these findings show that grandiose beliefs about the nation and its past can lead to conspiracy theories about Jews. Jews become a "relevant other"—a competitor to the status of an eternal victim and a figure threatening the uniqueness of national suffering.

Conclusions

The myth of Jewish conspiracy has always been present in modern Polish political discourse, but in certain situations and contexts it manifested more than in others. It has been a political instrument in internal struggles for power, mobilized supporters to action, channeled senses of threat, explained failures, and protected collective self-esteem. Contemporary social studies show that its popularity does not prevail only in Poland but in other Eastern European countries as well. Jewish conspiracy theories are central in the structure of modern conspiracy theorizing and

From *Judeo-Polonia to Act 447* 139

are part of a general tendency toward the belief in conspiracy theories. The results of the 2017 Polish Prejudice Survey show that about half of Poles to some extent believe in Jewish conspiracy and that this belief is only slightly related to demographic variables, such as age or education. The comparison of the studies conducted in 2009, 2013, and 2017 suggests that those attitudes are relatively stable over time. What's crucial, though, is that antisemitic conspiracy theories present in contemporary Poland—like those related to the US Congress S.447 Act— are constructed from the same elements as the first Jewish conspiracy theories: nineteenth-century themes of an international conspiracy, including the takeover of land and purchase of land estates as the main threat to Polish identity, supplemented by the issue of compensation for the Holocaust and "suffering rivalry," characteristic of secondary antisemitism.

Social psychological studies explored several functions of the theory of Jewish conspiracy. First, perceiving Jews as evil conspirators builds in-group identity in opposition to the out-group and boosts collective self-esteem. Second, it provides an easy and clear explanation of the complex world and of the failures of one's own group. Finally, the belief that a powerful Jewish conspiracy is responsible for the misfortunes of one's own group restores people's sense of personal control. Because the belief in Jewish conspiracies fulfills those psychological functions, we see them recurring in times of crisis and political instability. However, even though the sociopolitical context changes, the content of the conspiracies remains the same.

Notes

1 In 2017, 1,019 Poles participated in the study.
2 The r-Pearson correlation between the belief in Jewish conspiracy and age = 0.19, $p > 0.001$; between average income and the belief in Jewish conspiracy the r-Pearson correlation = -0.21, $p > 0.001$; between years of education and the belief in Jewish conspiracy the r-Pearson correlation = -0.16, $p > 0.001$.
3 The r-Pearson correlation between political attitudes and the belief in Jewish conspiracy = 0.32, $p > 0.001$.
4 The Smolensk air disaster occurred on April 10, 2010, when a Polish presidential plane crashed near the city of Smolensk, killing all 96 people on board, including the president of Poland, Lech Kaczynski, and his wife, Maria.
5 One of the problems has to do with the fact that in various countries the data is gathered using different methods (i.e., via telephone interview vs. personal interview). This can be a source of uncontrolled error due to the so-called social desirability bias, according to which participants have a tendency to answer survey questions differently, depending on whether they answer the questions in privately or in the presence of another person. Moreover, ADL only presents data in a form of "percent of participants who agreed with that statement" (League 2014).

Bibliography

A.S. 2018. "Krystyna Pawłowicz: Najważniejsze, Że Uustawa Jest Podpisana" [Krystyna Pawłowicz: Most Importantly the Bill Is Signed]. *TelewizjaRepublika.pl.* Accessed May 6, 2019. http://telewizjarepublika.pl/krystyna-pawlowicz-najwazniejsze-ze-ustawa-jest-podpisana,60281.html.

140 *Dominika Bulska et al.*

Anti-Defamation League. 2014. "ADL global 100: An Index of Anti-semitism." Accessed September 26, 2019. http://global100. adl.org/public/ADL-Global-100-Executive-Summary.pdf.

B.K. 2019. "Protesty Pod Ambasadą USA w Polsce. Powód – Ustawa 447" [Protests Next to the US Embassy in Poland. Reason: Act 447]. *Tysol.pl*. Accessed April 26, 2019. www. tysol.pl/a18484 – video-Protesty-pod-ambasada-USA-w-Polsce-Powod-ustawa-447,

Becker, Julia C., Ulrich Wagner, and Christ Oliver. 2011. "Consequences of the 2008 Financial Crisis for Intergroup Relations: The Role of Perceived Threat and Causal Attributions." *Group Processes & Intergroup Relations* 14 (6): 871–85.

Bilewicz, Michał, Dominika Bulska, Maria Babińska, Agnieszla Haska, and Mikołaj Winiewski. 2018. "Marzec w Lutym? Studium Stosunku Polaków do Żydów i Historii Holokaustu w Kontekście Debaty Wokół Ustawy o IPN" [March in February? Case Study of the Attitudes of Poles to Jews and the History of the Holocaust in the Context of the Debate Around IPN]. *Nauka* 2018 (2): 7–41.

Bilewicz, Michał, and Ireneusz Krzeminski. 2010. "Anti-Semitism in Poland and Ukraine: The Belief in Jewish Control as a Mechanism of Scapegoating." *International Journal of Conflict and Violence (IJCV)* 4 (2): 234–43.

Bilewicz, Michał, and Anna Stefaniak. 2013. "Can a Victim Be Responsible? Antisemitic Consequences of Victimhood-Based Identity and Competitive Victimhood in Poland." In *Responsibility: An Interdisciplinary Perspective*, edited by Barbara Bokus, 1–9. Warsaw: Lexem.

Bilewicz, Michał, and Mikołaj Winiewski. 2015. "Antysemityzm: dynamika i psychologiczne uwarunkowania" [Antisemitism: dynamics and psychological basis]. In *Uprzedzenia w Polsce* [Prejudice in Poland], edited by Anna Stefaniak, Michał Bilewicz, and Mikołaj Winiewski, 15–40. Warsaw: Liberi Libri.

Bilewicz, Michał, Mikołaj Winiewski, Mirosław Kofta, and Adrian Wójcik. 2013. "Harmful Ideas, the Structure and Consequences of Anti-Semitic Beliefs in Poland." *Political Psychology* 34 (6): 821–39.

Bruder, Martin, Peter Haffke, Nick Neave, Nina Nouripanah, and Roland Imhoff. 2013. "Measuring Individual Differences in Generic Beliefs in Conspiracy Theories Across Cultures: Conspiracy Mentality Questionnaire." *Frontiers in Psychology* 2013(4): 225–40.

Bulska, Dominika, and Mikołaj Winiewski. 2018. "Diagnoza i konsekwencje antysemityzmu" [Diagnosis and consequences of Antisemitism]. In *Uprzedzenia w Polsce 2017* [Prejudice in Poland 2017], edited by Anna Stefaniak and Mikołaj Winiewski, 221–52. Warsaw: Liberi Libri.

Cała, Alina. 1989. *Asymilacja Żydów w Królestwie Polskim (1864–1897)* [Assimilation of Jews in the Polish Kingdom (1864–1897)]. Warsaw: PWN.

Datner-Śpiewak, Helena. 1996. "Struktura i wyznaczniki postaw antysemickich" [Structure and Antcedents of antisemitic Attitudes]. In *Czy Polacy Sąantysemitami?* [Are Poles Antisemites?], edited by Ireneusz Krzemiński, 27–64. Warsaw: Oficyna Naukowa.

Deci, Edward, and Ryan Richard. 2000. "The 'What' and 'Why' of Goal Pursuits: Human Needs and the Self-Determination of Behavior." *Psychological Inquiry* 11(4): 227–68.

Dmowski, Roman. 1933. *Myśli Nowoczesnego Polaka* [The Thoughts of a Modern Pole]. Warsaw: Komitet Wydawn. Pism Romana Dmowskiego.

Domagalska, Małgorzata. 2015a. *Zatrute Ziarno. Proza Antysemicka na Lamach "Roli" (1883–1912)* [Poisoned Grain. Antisemitic Prose in the Pages of "Rola" (1883–1912)]. Warsaw: Neriton.

From Judeo-Polonia to Act 447   141

———. 2015b. "Jeszcze Warszawa Czy Już Moszkopolis? Futurystyczny Obraz Stolicy w Polskiej Antysemickiej Prozie Przełomu XIX i XX Wieku" [Still Warsaw or Already Moszkopolic? Futuristic View of the Capital in Polish Antisemitic Literature Between the 19th and 20th Century]. *Kwartalnik Historii Żydów* 1: 12–15.

Durkheim, Emile. 1899/2008. "Anti-Semitism and Social Crisis." *Sociological Theory* 4: 322–24.

Dziennik Ustaw. 2018. Ustawa z dnia 26 stycznia 2018 r. o zmianie ustawy o Instytucie Pamięci Narodowej – Komisji Ścigania Zbrodni przeciwko Narodowi Polskiemu, ustawy o grobach i cmentarzach wojennych, ustawy o muzeach oraz ustawy o odpowiedzialności podmiotów zbiorowych za czyny zabronione pod groźbą kary Dz.U. 2018 poz. 369. [Act from 26 January 2018 amending the Act on the Institute of National Remembrance – Commission for the Prosecution of Crimes against the Polish Nation, the Act on war graves and cemeteries, the Act on museums and the Act on the liability of collective entities for acts punishable by penalty. 2018 item 369]. Poland.

Eisenbach Artur. 1988. *Emancypacja Żydów na Ziemiach Polskich 1785–1870 na Tle Europejskim* [Emancipation of the Jews on Polish Land 1785–1870 in the European Context]. Warsaw: Państwowy Instytut Wydawniczy.

Eisler Jerzy. 1991. *Marzec 1968: Geneza, Przebieg, Konsekwencje* [March 1968: Genesis, Dynamics, Consequences]. Warsaw: Wydawnictwo Naukowe PWN.

Fakt. 2019. "Morawiecki Krótko o Odszkodowaniach dla Żydów" [Morawiecki Briefly about the Repatriations for Jews]. *Fakt.pl*. Accessed May 6, 2019. www.fakt.pl/wydarzenia/polityka/mateusz-morawiecki-o-roszczeniach-zydowskich-nie-ma-zgody/0mzlg3n.

Forecki, Piotr. 2018. *Po Jedwabnem. Anatomia Pamięci Funkcjonalnej* [After Jedwabne. The Anatomy of Functional Memory]. Warsaw: Wydawnictwo IBL PAN.

Glick, Peter. 2005. "Choice of Scapegoats." In *On the Nature of Prejudice: 50 Years After Allport*, edited by John F. Dovidio, Peter Glick, and Laurie A. Rudman, 244–61. Malden, MA: Blackwell.

Golec de Zavala, Agnieszka, and Aleksandra Cichocka. 2012. "Collective Narcissism and Anti-Semitism in Poland." *Group Processes & Intergroup Relations* 15 (2): 213–29.

Golec de Zavala, Agnieszka, Aleksandra Cichocka, Roy Eidelson, and Jayawickreme Nuwan. 2009. "Collective Narcissism and Its Social Consequences." *Journal of Personality and Social Psychology* 97 (6): 1074–96.

Gudaszewski, Grzegorz. 2015. *Struktura Narodowo-Etniczna, Językowa IWyznaniowa Ludności Polski. Narodowy Spis Powszechny Ludności i Mieszkań 2011* [The National-Ethnic, Linguistic and Religious Structure of the Polish Population. National Population and Housing Census 2011]. Warsaw: GUS.

Imhoff, Roland. 2015. "Beyond (Right-Wing) Authoritarianism: Conspiracy Mentality as an Incremental Predictor of Prejudice." In *The Psychology of Conspiracy*, edited by Michał Bilewicz, Aleksandra Cichocka, and Wiktor Soral, 122–41. London: Routledge.

Imhoff, Roland, and Rainer Banse. 2009. "Ongoing Victim Suffering Increases Prejudice. The Case of Secondary Anti-Semitism." *Psychological Science* 20: 1443–47.

Kay, Aaron C., Danielle Gaucher, Jamie L. Napier, Mitchell J. Callan, and Kristin Laurin. 2008. "God and the Government: Testing a Compensatory Control Mechanism for the Support of External Systems." *Journal of Personality and Social Psychology* 95 (1): 18–35.

Kofta, Mirosław, and Sędek Grzegorz. 1992. "Struktura Poznawcza Stereotypu Etnicznego, Bliskosĭcĭ Wyborów Parlamentarnych a Przejawy Antysemityzmu" [Cognitive Structure of Ethnic Stereotype, Closeness of Parliamentary Elections and Signs of Anti-Semitism].

142   Dominika Bulska et al.

In *Stereotypy i Uprzedzenia* [Stereotypes and Prejudice], edited by Zdzisław Chlewiński and Ida Kurcz, 67–86. Warsaw: Wydawnictwo Instytutu Psychologii PAN.

———. 2005. "Conspiracy Stereotypes of Jews During Systemic Transformation in Poland." *International Journal of Sociology* 35 (1): 40–64.

Kofta Mirosław, Wiktor Soral, and Michał Bilewicz. n.d. "What Breeds Conspiracy Antisemitism? The Role of Political Uncontrollability and Uncertainty in the Belief in Jewish Conspiracy." *Journal of Personality and Social Psychology*, in press.

Krzemiński, Ireneusz. 1996. *Czy Polacy Są Antysemitami?: Wyniki Badania Sondażowego* [Are Poles Antisemites? Results of Survey Study]. Warsaw: Oficyna Naukowa.

———. 2004. *Antysemityzm w Polsce i na Ukrainie: Raport z Badań* [Anti-Semitism in Poland and Ukraine: Research Report]. Warsaw: Scholar Books.

Lendvai, Paul. 1971. *Anti-Semitism without Jews: Communist Eastern Europe*. New York: Doubleday.

Marchlewska, Marta, Aleksandra Cichocka, and Małgorzata Kossowska. 2018. "Addicted to Answers: Need for Cognitive Closure and the Endorsement of Conspiracy Beliefs." *European Journal of Social Psychology* 48 (2): 109–17.

Moscovici, Serge. 1987. "The Conspiracy Mentality." In *Changing Conceptions of Conspiracy*, edited by Carl F. Graumann and Serge Moscovici, 151–69. New York: Springer.

Nowaczyński, Adolf. 1921. *Mocarstwo Anonimowe: Ankieta w Sprawie Żydowskiej* [Anonymous Power: the Survey about the Jewish Issue]. Warsaw: Nakład księgarni i składu Nut Perzyński.

Osęka, Piotr. 2008. *Marzec '68* [March '68]. Cracow: SW Znak.

Poliakov, Léon. 2003. *The History of Anti-Semitism, Volume 1: From the Time of Christ to the Court Jews. Vol. 1*. Philadelphia, PA: University of Pennsylvania Press.

Rothschild, Zachary K., Mark J. Landau, David Sullivan, and Lucas Keefer. 2012. "A Dual-Motive Model of Scapegoating: Displacing Blame to Reduce Guilt or Increase Control." *Journal of Personality and Social Psychology* 102 (6): 1148–63.

Smith, Heather J., and Thomas F. Pettigrew. 2015. "Advances in Relative Deprivation Theory and Research." *Social Justice Research* 28 (1): 1–6.

Sullivan, Daniel, Mark. J. Landau, and Zachary K. Rothschild. 2010. "An Existential Function of Enemyship: Evidence that People Attribute Influence to Personal and Political Enemies to Compensate for Threats to Control." *Journal of Personality and Social Psychology* 98 (3): 434–49.

Swami, Viren. 2012. "Social Psychological Origins of Conspiracy Theories: The Case of the Jewish Conspiracy Theory in Malaysia." *Frontiers in Psychology* 3: 280–93.

Tokarska-Bakir, Joanna, 2008. *Legendy o Kkrwi. Antropologia Przesądu* [Legends of Blood. Anthropology of Superstition]. Warsaw: WAB.

Tomaszewski Jerzy. 1990. *Zarys Dziejów Żydów w Polsce w Latach 1918–1939* [Outline of the History of Jews in Poland in the Years 1918–1939]. Warsaw: Wydawnictwo Uniwersytetu Warszawskiego.

van Prooijen, Jan-Willem, André P. M. Krouwel, and Thomas V. Pollet. 2015. "Political Extremism Predicts Belief in Conspiracy Theories." *Social Psychological and Personality Science* 6 (5): 570–78.

van Prooijen, Jan-Willem and Jostmann Nils B. 2013. "Belief in Conspiracy Theories: The Influence of Uncertainty and Perceived Morality." *European Journal of Social Psychology* 43 (1): 109–15.

Whitson, Jennifer A., and Adam, D. Galinsky. 2008. "Lacking control increases illusory pattern perception." *Science* 322 (5898): 115–17.

From Judeo-Polonia to Act 447 143

Winiewski, Mikołaj, and Michał Bilewicz. 2013. "Are Surveys and Opinion Polls Always a Valid Tool to Assess Anti-Semitism? Methodological Considerations." *Jewish Studies at the CEU* 7: 83–97.

———. 2015. "Antysemityzm: Dynamika i Psychologiczne Uwarunkowania" [Anti-Semitism: Its Dynamics and Psychological Conditions]. In *Uprzedzenia w Polsce* [Prejudice in Poland], edited by Anna Stefaniak, Mikołaj Winiewski and Michał Bilewicz, 15–39. Warsaw: Liberi Libri.

Winnicki, Robert (@RobertWinnicki). 2019. "Start Calling a Spade Before the Jews Start Cashing Not Only Your Party Headquarters, but Also the Property of all Poles." *Twitter*. May 15, 2019. Accessed May 26, 2019. https://twitter.com/RobertWinnicki/status/1128708880219951105.

Wright, Thomas L., and Jack Arbuthnot. 1974. "Interpersonal Trust, Political Preference, and Perceptions of the Watergate Affair." *Proceedings of the Division of Personality and Society Psychology* 1 (1): 168–70.

Zaborowska, Malwina. 2019. "Warszawa: Marsz Przeciwko Ustawie 447. Polska Nie ma Zobowiązań" [Warsaw: March Against the 447 Act. Poland Does not Have Duties]. *RMF FM*. Accessed May 12, 2019. www.rmf24.pl/fakty/polska/news-warszawa-marsz-przeciwko-ustawie-447-polska-nie-ma-zobowiaza,nId,2984930.

Zaremba, Marcin. 2012. *Wielka Trwoga* [Great Terror]. Cracow: Znak.

Part III

After independence

Nation-building and victimhood narratives

7 Dissolution of Yugoslavia as a conspiracy and its haunting returns

Narratives of internal and external *othering*

Nebojša Blanuša

Introduction

Conspiracy theories about the dissolution of socialist Yugoslavia did not first appear after its violent breakup in 1991. They were present even before its formation in 1945, burdened by the then fresh experience of World War II atrocities as well as the constant changes of borders throughout the history of the Balkan Peninsula. The most prominent instigators of such anxieties were the memory of occupation and dismemberment of the Kingdom of Yugoslavia by Nazi Germany and neighboring countries in 1941, the bloody civil war from 1941 to 1945 between its constituent nations and political groups, and the Allies' politics of the spheres of influence at the end of World War II. These issues amplified during the existence of socialist Yugoslavia (1945–91) due to its position in the global political arena, internal political dynamics, and structural state features as well as its problematic economic performance.

The major theses of this chapter are that (1) the specter of the dissolution of socialist Yugoslavia has a long history, as evidenced in political discourses after World War II; essentially, the danger of dissolution functioned as the "sword of Damocles" until Yugoslavia's very end. (2) Fears and discussions about political solutions, the so-called national questions, enemies of the state, and possible dissolution intensified after the death of President Josip Broz Tito (1892–1980), who had functioned as social glue and the final arbiter in political disputes between ruling Communist elites of the constituent republics in Yugoslavia. (3) After the real dissolution in 1991, Yugoslav-related conspiracy theories changed, and their content crystallized around the presumed evil intentions and plans of major international political players (such as the USA, NATO, EU), which enabled conspiracy theorists to give a wider meaning to the conflicts during and after the post-Yugoslav wars. (4) Further diversification of conspiracy theories about the dissolution occurred in the newly established post-Yugoslav states, consistent with the official narratives of their status in Yugoslavia and the main reasons attributed to its violent breakup. In that sense, the dissolution of Yugoslavia as a consequence of international conspiracy became a victimizing narrative in Serbia, while the conspiracy theory of Yugoslavia's possible return assumed the same status in Croatia.

148 *Nebojša Blanuša*

In order to corroborate these theses, I will first give a brief history of the formation of the two Yugoslavias, pointing to the sociopolitical roots of the fear of dissolution. Then my analysis will focus on the discursive articulation of these fears expressed in a conspiratorial way by the main political actor of that time, Josip Broz Tito, as well as by the mainstream media of the Soviet bloc. For the last two periods (post-Tito and post-Yugoslav), I will mainly use sources from the prominent political weeklies published in Yugoslavia and international publications, including conspiracy theories and reflections about them as expressed by political leaders, high officials, and intellectuals. I will also briefly refer to recent survey results on beliefs in conspiracy theories conducted in several post-Yugoslav countries.

Contrary to the mainstream approach that treats conspiracy theories as a priori flawed interpretations usually attributed to eccentric personalities, I will consider them as cultural products connected to collective traumas and clearly differentiated from individual pathologies. Conspiracy theories are often unwarranted but sometimes warranted and reasonable, even unavoidable, especially when historical traces point to real conspiracies. To avoid the reductionist trap, I define conspiracy theories formally as an interpretation "that posits a conspiracy" (Pigden 2007, 222). Such theories always include groups with sinister intentions against the state and society. It is impossible to include in this chapter all conspiratorial interpretations. Therefore, I will deal with only the most well-known theories.

A brief history of the formation of the first and second Yugoslavia

On the eve of World War I, there was no Yugoslavia on the political map of the Balkans. The western and central regions of the future state were a part of the Austro-Hungarian Empire, while the eastern part comprised the independent kingdoms of Serbia (including today's North Macedonia) and Montenegro. However, ideas about the creation of the state of all South Slavs were already appearing in the late-seventeenth century, intensifying in the nineteenth century through the Illyrian movement and Yugoslavism, and finally realized after World War I (Roksandić 2017). Gavrilo Princip, a member of the "Black Hand" conspiracy and the assassin of Archduke Franz Ferdinand in Sarajevo in 1914, stated at his trial: "I am a Yugoslav nationalist, aiming for the unification of all Yugoslavs, and I do not care what form of state, but it must be free from Austria" (quoted in Malcolm 1996, 153). During the first two years of the Great War, both the Yugoslav Committee, comprising influential South Slav exiles from the Austro-Hungarian Empire and the government of Serbian Kingdom, commenced planning the creation of the common state, though still without a definitive conception of the form. The Yugoslav Committee intensified its diplomatic actions after they became aware of the secret Treaty of London between the Triple Entente and Italy. The secret treaty promised to Italy central parts of Dalmatia and the whole Istria if Italy entered the war against Germany and the Austro-Hungarian Empire (Lampe 2000, 103). In 1917, both Serbia and the Yugoslav Committee were facing an

Dissolution of Yugoslavia as a conspiracy 149

unenviable situation. Serbia was coping with occupation by the Central Powers, army retreat, and internal political discord. Furthermore, it lost its most significant international support due to the Russian Revolution, while the Yugoslav Committee still lacked support from the West. Another issue for the Yugoslav Committee was the lack of legitimacy caused by South Slav representatives declaring loyalty to the empire in the Austrian parliament. Burdened with such problems, and the still uncertain course of the war, Serbia and the Yugoslav Committee signed the Corfu Declaration on June 20, 1917, which proposed the constitutional monarchy of the "three-named people" (Serbs, Croats, and Slovenes) under the Karađorđević dynasty. This vague document promised democratic rights, freedom of religion, and use of the three people's alphabets, while simultaneously leaving aside issues of internal territorial borders, autonomy, and whether the state should be organized on a federalist or a centralist basis (ibid., 105). The change of war fortune strengthened Serbia's position, while in the southeastern part of the declining Austro-Hungarian Empire, the newly established National Council proclaimed the State of Slovenes, Croats, and Serbs on October 29, 1918. The Italian attack on the newly established country prompted the delegation of the National Council to ask the Serbian king Alexander I to proclaim the Kingdom of Serbs, Croats, and Slovenes, based on Corfu agreement (ibid., 111). The unification, including Montenegro, occurred on December 1, 1918.[1] However, negotiations with neighboring countries about borders lasted until the early 1920s, and disputes about the borders and respective minority rights continued to the very end of socialist Yugoslavia.

As the product of various political conceptions, economically poor, unevenly developed, devastated by the Great War, and comprising ethnic groups living for centuries under the rule of different empires, the Kingdom of Serbs, Croats, and Slovenes was the most complex among all the newly established states in Europe (Coakley 1987, 60; Perović 2015b, 3). It "became a problem the moment it was established, both within its borders, but also outside them" (Roksandić 2017, 55). From its very inception, the country was troubled by constitutional issues, formation of the state, and its internal organization: centralized monarchy or federal republic. The strongly centralist St. Vitus's Day Constitution from 1921 provoked Croatians to question the state's legitimacy, and they accused Serbia of angling for hegemony, and the subsequent destabilization of political life. In 1924, on the anniversary of Bastille Day, after the failed negotiations with the Serbian Radical Party, Stjepan Radić declared that Croatia was a prisoner in Serbia's metaphorical Bastille. The political crisis culminated in 1928 with the conspiratorial assassination of five Croatian MPs in the People's Assembly (including Stjepan Radić as the main target), which may have been ordered by King Alexander himself (Perović 2015a). The king established a dictatorship in 1929 and renamed the state the Kingdom of Yugoslavia. Alexander's dictatorship, backed by the ideology of integral Yugoslavism, provoked separatism in Croatia, Macedonia, Montenegro, and Kosovo, which resulted in his assassination by Macedonian and Croat extremists in 1934 (Perović 2015b). Since Yugoslavia's establishment, the internal organization of state provinces has changed several times, resulting in

150   *Nebojša Blanuša*

the creation of the Banovina of Croatia in 1939, aimed at resolving the "Croatian Question" of autonomy. However, it lasted only briefly.

The Kingdom of Yugoslavia declared itself neutral at the start of World War II, but under pressure from Hitler, the kingdom's representatives signed the Tripartite Pact in 1941. The pact caused mass riots within the kingdom and ultimately a coup d'état. Without declaring war, the Axis powers occupied the Kingdom of Yugoslavia in April 1941 and divided it between Nazi Germany, Fascist Italy, Hungary, and Bulgaria and established the Independent State of Croatia, a puppet state led by the brutal Fascist Ustasha regime. Once the country was occupied, King Peter II and his government fled the country, and the dismemberment virtually destroyed all previously existing institutions (Lampe 2000, 201). Shortly after the occupation began, two resistance movements formed. One was led by Serb royalist Chetniks, who actually collaborated with the Fascist invaders. The other was the anti-Fascist Partisan movement, led by Communists from all ethnicities in the kingdom across ethnic lines and focused on the future of a federal Yugoslavia. The latter gained support from the Allies, and with the limited help of the Red Army, successfully defeated Axis forces and their collaborators, the Ustasha and Chetniks. In that sense, World War II in Yugoslavia was not only a fight against foreign invaders but also a bloody inter-ethnic civil war, including the killing of many civilians, primarily by the Ustasha regime and the Chetniks. On a smaller scale, partisans also committed massacres and executions, especially at the end of the war, against quisling groups and members of their families. Memory and post-memory of these atrocities grew into a significant source of inter-ethnic fear and hatred 50 years later, haunting the second Yugoslavia to the point of its violent dissolution. The Communist-led National Front won the first Constituent Assembly elections after the war. The party abolished the monarchy, deposed the king, and proclaimed the Federal People's Republic of Yugoslavia.

Specters of dissolution after World War II [2]

The fresh experience of occupation and state division by neighboring countries was followed by the civil war, burdened by mass atrocities. These atrocities were fueled by political grievances and inter-ethnic hatred nourished at the time of the Kingdom of Yugoslavia. Faced with the issue of rebuilding a multiethnic country, the violent recent past made Communist nomenclature prone to the conspiracist discourse of inner and outer enemies. Such conspiracism was a part of the policy of inter-ethnic relations, described by Tito in 1942 as "armed brotherhood and unity" but later as the constitutional value "brotherhood and unity" (Godina 1998, 413). In his speech on November 26, 1942, at the first session of the Anti-Fascist Council of People's Liberation of Yugoslavia, in Bihać, Tito said:

> It is necessary to organize the authority, the political power, which will be able to mobilize, to make use of all the latent power possessed by our people and to canalize it in one general direction—into the battle against the criminal fascist invaders, and against their allies, the traitors in our midst—the

Dissolution of Yugoslavia as a conspiracy   151

Ustasha, the Chetniks, and others. . . . You may rest assured that their power in our country is not sufficient to realize and put into practice their diabolical intentions, i.e. to destroy us. . . . I wish you, the great national forum, the Anti-Fascist Council of People's Liberation of Yugoslavia, every success in your future work for the welfare of our peoples, for the welfare of our valiant People's Liberation Army, and in the interests of the unity of all the nationalities in Yugoslavia, for that is the foundation which is now being built, the foundation of brotherhood, unity, and concord, which no one will ever be able to destroy.

(Tito 1959, 36–39)

Another source of threat to the integrity of Yugoslavia appeared in late 1944, after a meeting between Churchill and Stalin in Moscow on October 9, where they agreed on the division of "spheres of influence" in the Balkans between Great Britain and the USSR. On October 27, 1944, in the already liberated city of Belgrade, Tito addressed this issue almost immediately in his speech:

We don't want to be any more a children's ball or bargaining coin, in this struggle we have acquired the right to participate on equal foot with Allies in this war, as well as in building the new and happier Europe, not only Yugoslavia. . . . Spheres of influence end on Yugoslav borders. . . . Our foreign policy is derived from the character of our Socialist state, from the free spirit of our peoples: not the backstage and machiavelistic foreign policy, but open and honest foreign policy which must be based on strict principles and inspired by the spirit of peacefulness.

(ibid, 247)

The same theme appeared in Tito's later speeches. Such an anti-conspiratorial attitude became the symbolic predecessor of future politics of non-alignment as well as one of the reasons for the Tito-Stalin split in 1948. After Tito's speech on May 27, 1945, in Ljubljana, in which he reiterated the same stance, the Soviet government protested, claiming that such discourse equated the Soviet Union with the imperialist Western states. The same accusation was included in Stalin's attack on the Yugoslav Communist Party in 1948 (Stojanović 1980, 129–30). Embedded in the foreign policy of socialist Yugoslavia and its chain of main signifiers, such as anti-imperialism, anti-colonialism, and the peaceful active coexistence, conspiratorial interpretation of "the spheres of influence" became less salient in the political discourse. However, it reappeared in the press after Tito's death, as a memory of his successful resistance to the cynical backstage diplomatic games between the great powers. Evidence of such is corroborated by Churchill's memoirs describing his meeting with Stalin:

I pushed this across to Stalin, who had by then heard the translation. There was a slight pause. Then he took his blue pencil and made a large tick upon it, and passed it back to us. . . . After this there was a long silence. The penciled

152 *Nebojša Blanuša*

> paper lay in the centre of the table. At length I said, "Might it not be thought rather cynical if it seemed we had disposed of these issues, so fateful to millions of people, in such an offhand manner? Let us burn the paper." "No, you keep it," said Stalin.
>
> (Churchill [1953] 2002, 274)

The ultimate purpose of describing Tito in such a way was to represent him as a nodal point of the "open and honest politics" and opposed to various conspiratorial anti-Yugoslav tendencies (Blanuša 2011, 94).

After World War II, the sense of external threat intensified during and after several important political and military events, starting with the Tito-Stalin split in 1948 and the expulsion of Yugoslavia from the Cominform. Following the example set by the Soviet Union, satellite countries in Eastern Europe exited their treaties of friendship and trade with Yugoslavia, which was interpreted as the plot against it (Keesing's Contemporary Archives 1949, 10335). In a series of diplomatic protest notes, Yugoslavia accused several neighboring countries of endangering its independence and territorial integrity. Hungary was also accused of reviving its Fascist expansionist claims toward Vojvodina and granting refuge to Yugoslav traitors and encouraging their terrorist activities, smuggling, espionage, and so on; Bulgaria was suspected of aiming to annex Macedonia and of chauvinistic designs toward this Yugoslav republic; Romania was accused of threatening Yugoslav borders and Albania for aiding Yugoslav deserters and provoking frontier incidents (ibid.). Furthermore, Yugoslavia reoriented its foreign policy to the West and, in doing so, gained political support, significant financial and military assistance, and food relief. It also established the Balkan Pact with Greece and Turkey in 1954. The relationship between Yugoslavia, the Soviet Union, and its satellites slowly improved from 1953 until the 1956 Soviet intervention in Hungary. The Soviet Union then accused Yugoslavia of being an imperialist agent, "infecting" Hungarian intellectuals and working on the destruction of international Communism, especially after it gave political asylum to Imre Nagy's group in the Yugoslav Embassy of Budapest (Granville 1998). Nagy's later kidnapping, trial, and execution were interpreted by the Yugoslav authorities as "another link in the chain of the new anti-Yugoslav campaign, being conducted by the USSR and other bloc countries" (ibid., 507). Another attack on Yugoslavia occurred on May 5, 1958, primarily from China and the Soviet Union. The Peking *People's Daily* claimed that the 1948 Cominform Resolution was basically correct, effectively criticizing Yugoslavia for being a part of the imperialist "sabotage of the world Communist movement." At the same time, during Khrushchev's visit to Sofia, Bulgaria, he condemned Yugoslavia as the "Trojan horse of imperialism" (Keesing's Contemporary Archives 1958, 16229). Albanian leader Enver Hoxha also took part in conspiratorial accusations. On June 29, 1958, he claimed that Yugoslav leaders were "traitors, incorrigible revisionists, enemies of the Soviet Union and Marxism, and hardened agents of American imperialism" (ibid., 16395). This significantly impacted Yugoslav international relations for decades. The rapprochement stopped, but in 1959, such rabid propaganda diminished along

Dissolution of Yugoslavia as a conspiracy 153

with the decline in economic cooperation with the Soviet bloc, and once again, Yugoslavia turned to the West.

Such vitriol outlined above may have been caused in part by Tito's efforts to establish the Non-Alignment Movement. In his speech to the Indian parliament, he highlighted four global issues to be resolved through the anti-bloc policy:

> I think that today there are four basic negative elements which are the cause of all the evils which bring fear and anxiety to mankind today, which are considered by all progressive people today as not only unnecessary but absurd. They are, first: inequality between States and nations; secondly: interference in the internal life of others, and here, those who do the interfering are most often or nearly always great powers or the most developed states; thirdly: the division of the world into spheres of interest and blocs; and fourthly: colonialism. Until these four elements are eliminated from the practical politics of international affairs, mankind will not be free from fear of the future.
>
> (Tito 1963, 29)

The initiative for the establishment of the Non-Alignment Movement began in 1956 on the Brijuni islands in Yugoslavia, at a meeting between Josip Broz Tito, Gamal Abdel Nasser, and Jawaharlal Nehru. At this time, the Hungarian Revolution and the Suez Crisis were both underway. The first conference was held in 1961 in Belgrade in the context of the protracted international crisis involving 25 countries. In the opening of his address, Tito expressed grave concern:

> for the fate of mankind . . . in the existing grave international situation . . . as the Cold War assumed proportions liable to lead to the greatest tragedy at any moment. . . . Overt preparations for war are being made, mobilization is taking place, the manufacture of the most modern weapons is being intensified, hydrogen and atomic tests again being contemplated.
>
> (JFK Presidential Library and Museum n.d.)

Further in his speech, Tito acknowledged that both sides in the Cold War were conspiring against each other, which could have grave consequences for world peace. As a countermeasure, he advocated for a non-violent, anti-conspirational, anti-bloc strategy:

> Actually, constant efforts are being exerted for the purpose of achieving superiority, in order to attain specific goals from a position of strength; that is to say, to solve outstanding questions in one's own favor. In these efforts lie the greatest danger of an outbreak of armed conflict and of a new catastrophe for the entire world. The recent past has shown clearly that the grouping of states into blocs usually leads to a settling of accounts by the force of arms. The history of recent years has also demonstrated that there need not even be two blocs, but that it is sufficient to have only one bloc for war to break out. . . . [I]t is obvious that such a course was most unfortunate and has led to

154 *Nebojša Blanuša*

the present abnormal and perilous situation in the world. . . . The economic arrangements within bloc frameworks have a discriminatory character with regard to other countries. Embargoes are imposed on various products with the aim of exercising pressure upon a given country or several countries. All this and many other characteristic features of blocs are in contradiction with the general interests and views of nonaligned countries and, above all, with the fact that these countries preclude the use of military force for the solution of any dispute.

(ibid.)

Given the global circumstances of nuclear war threat, colonialism, and neo-colonialism, in addition to the economic and international status of nonaligned countries, Tito's conspiracist interpretation of bloc politics, together with the rhetoric of anti-conspiratorial intents, can be considered at least as a form of prudent political rhetoric. Although some other members of the Non-Alignment Movement were sticking to more open conspiracism,[3] such "Titoist" anti-imperialist logic was constantly applied at least to Yugoslav foreign policy, promoting the détente. For example, Tito applied it during the Cuban Missile Crisis in 1962, which brought Yugoslavia closer to the Soviet Union, but without any major ruptures with the West, even after Yugoslavia condemned US policy in Vietnam in 1965 (Hasan 1981a, 117). That changed with the Six-Day War in 1967. Together with six other leaders of Communist states (except Romania), Tito signed a statement denouncing Israeli aggression as "the result of the collusion of certain imperialist forces, and first of all the United States, against the Arab countries. . . [that] would be used for the restoration of the foreign colonial regime" (Keesing's Contemporary Archives 1967–68, 22105). Another shift of Yugoslav foreign policy away from the Communist bloc came with Soviet intervention in Czechoslovakia in 1968. In addition to public condemnation of the intervention, Tito held a secret meeting with Ceaușescu about the possible threat of Soviet invasions in their respective countries. Moscow accused both leaders of giving "active assistance to anti-Socialist forces in Czechoslovakia and of taking the same line as imperialist NATO flowers and the Maoist group in China," along with other accusations of conspiracy (ibid., 22993). A direct consequence of the Czechoslovakian crisis was the Yugoslav development of total national defense (Johnson, cited in Hasan 1981b, 67) and further improvement of economic cooperation with the West (ibid.). Due to its own internal crisis (1968–72), Yugoslav leadership was worried that Brezhnev would start military intervention in the same way as in Czechoslovakia, especially after the critique of the Soviet bloc for the alleged "Tirana-Belgrade-Bucharest axis" in 1971 (ibid., 71). However, plans for joint defense with Romania, the reconciliation with China in 1969, the diplomatic offensive across the globe, and the US support for Yugoslav independence as well as improvement of US-China relations made Soviet intervention unlikely (Lazić 2017). In the following years, the relations between Yugoslavia and the Soviet bloc, as well as other countries, improved.

Dissolution of Yugoslavia as a conspiracy   155

Nonetheless, concerns about the foreign threat were expressed even in primary school education. The best example is perhaps a mnemonic technique taught in geography classes up to the late 1980s, with the purpose of learning the names of the countries neighboring Yugoslavia. Basically, it comprised only one sentence—"Yugoslavia is surrounded by worries" (trans. *Jugoslavija je okružena brigama*). The Serbo-Croatian word for "worries," *brigama*, is actually an acronym made of the first letters of Yugoslavia's neighboring countries: Bulgaria, Romania, Italy, Greece, Austria, Hungary (trans. Mađarska), and Albania. Through this acronym, young children learn that their country is surrounded by enemies who have territorial pretensions to Yugoslavia. This was reinforced in public schools by teaching a narrative of constant South Slav suffering through a tragic history of invasions and violent regimes. The main lesson to be learned was that in order to prevent such occurrences, the Yugoslav peoples should stay together and develop their sense of brotherhood and unity. Another perceived constant threat in socialist Yugoslavia was nationalism, conceived as its internal archenemy (Godina 1998, 415). Until the early 1980s, nationalism was represented in history textbooks by those who had collaborated with Fascists or so-called domestic traitors (e.g., Ustasha, Chetniks), while avoiding any association with a particular ethnic group (Pavasović Trošt 2018, 721) to evade collective stigmatization and endangerment of brotherhood and unity. Taken together with all the previously mentioned political events and accompanied with their conspiracist interpretation, such a mnemonic technique ingrained a siege mentality among Yugoslav youth.

Conspiracy theories about the dissolution of Yugoslavia after Tito's death

The death of Yugoslav president Josip Broz Tito—a charismatic leader who functioned as the central personality and the final "judge" in political disputes—caused a void, which was immediately filled by uncritical reminiscences of his boldness and political wisdom in crucial situations. Examples of his heroism against conspiratorial enemies of the state are found in descriptions of victorious battles of World War II and in narratives of political turmoil in 1948 (Cominform Resolution), in 1966 (clash with the Office of State Security), and in 1971 (removal of nationalists in Croatia and liberals in Serbia). With the liberalization of the press and protracted economic and political crisis, since 1982 this idealized interpretation of Tito's oeuvre has been increasingly criticized and demystified. Especially in Serbia, such a critique was advanced in the process of the de-Titoization in the late 1980s, such as accusing Tito of anti-Yugoslavism, which he, allegedly, institutionalized in the 1974 Constitution (Blanuša 2011, 96–98). In terms of dominant form of conspiracism, we can roughly divide the last decade of socialist Yugoslavia into two overlapping phases. The first one, from 1980 to 1986, may be described as the decay of socialist conspiratorial discourse, while the open rise of nationalist conspiratorial discourse marked the second period, from 1986 to 1991.

156 Nebojša Blanuša

Decline of socialist conspiracism (1980–86)

Throughout this period, Tito functioned as a nodal point of the official discourse, while his concept of Yugoslavia was an ideal against which actual political processes, tendencies, and actors were evaluated and criticized in the mainstream press and politics. In that sense, the pandemonium of counter-revolutionary forces threatening to tear Yugoslavia apart, both from within and without, appeared in public discourse, contributing to the above-mentioned siege mentality. As represented in Figure 7.2, the first circle of enemies comprised "alienated centers of power" or "informal political groups," "clans," or "usurpers" inside of the League of Communists. Their backstage "capillary" activities supposedly corroded Yugoslav self-management and oppressed the working class, trying to establish the "old social relations." These were mostly bureaucrats and politicians, from the local to the federal level, having identified with previously defeated groups, such as Stalinists, centralists, nationalists, liberals, etatists, technocrats, and so on, who comprised the Fifth Column inside the system. The second circle of enemies consisted of open nationalists (mostly Serbian and Croatian) whose proponents were writers, artists, dissidents, and intellectuals who questioned "dark spots" of socialist Yugoslavia, as well as revisionist historians, and Catholic and Orthodox churches, all described as biologically regenerated defeated forces from the past (ibid., 97). A special place in political discourse was given to Albanian irredentists at Kosovo, particularly in the Serbian press. However, the depiction of the crisis in this autonomous province of Serbia would change, especially in the western republics, due to oppressive Serbian politics. From 1981 Kosovar Albanians took to the streets demanding to become a constituent republic, prompting a declaration of a state of emergency. The Kosovar Albanian activities were condemned as a "hybrid war" against Yugoslavia and in collusion with Albania and Western propaganda to ethnically cleanse and ultimately annex it (ibid., 128–30).[4] But, from the mid-1980s, in official Serbian circles, mass counter-protests of Kosovo Serbs were attributed to Serbian nationalists considering Kosovo the explosive device to overthrow the Communist government (ibid., 131). This attitude changed when Slobodan Milošević assumed power and began implementing his oppressive politics toward Kosovo Albanians through the legitimation of nationalist rhetoric. Nationalist enemies within Yugoslavia were often perceived as an extended arm of the extremist diaspora or members of nationalist forces from World War II—namely, Ustasha, Chetniks, and Albanian Ballists. Finally, due to prolonged economic crisis and austerity measures, some intellectuals began to criticize the ruling party as sponsors of the "domestic bourgeoisie" composed of bureaucratic and technocratic groups who betrayed the working class and sold the country to the "occupational regime of the IMF" (ibid., 102). In this discourse, the IMF was only one part of a global "monster of financial capital" with a well-developed exploitative system of deceit, blackmail, and fraud specifically designed for underdeveloped countries (ibid.) (see Figure 7.1).

Dissolution of Yugoslavia as a conspiracy 157

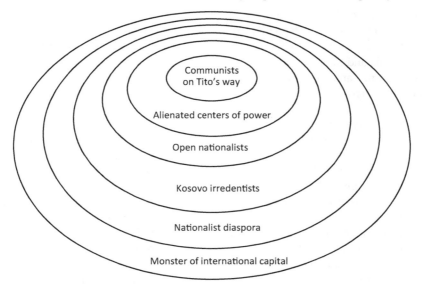

Figure 7.1 Pandemonium of enemies of socialist Yugoslavia in the 1980s.

The rise of nationalist conspiracism (1986–91)

The final years of socialist Yugoslavia were characterized by the acceleration and proliferation of conspiracism with agonizing consequences. Deep economic and political crises, social unrest, divisions between republics and nations, and frequent dissent about the main issues and preferred political solutions as well as the loss of a sense of Yugoslav community were fertile soil for various conspiracist accusations and political actions. The landmark text of this period is the *Memorandum of the Serbian Academy of Science and Arts* (SANU). In 1985, the Serbian League of Communists ordered the academy to write the memorandum as an advisory to the national intelligentsia. After about a year, it was leaked to the mainstream Serbian daily *Večernje novosti*. The Serbian president, Ivan Stambolić, proclaimed it an "in memoriam" of Yugoslavia. The two-part memorandum caused a major scandal, and many politicians, historians, and political scientists across the whole of Yugoslavia severely criticized it (ibid., 132). The first part, titled "Crisis in the Yugoslav Economy and Society," is a largely non-conspiracist economic and political analysis of the Yugoslav long-term crisis that started in the 1960s, including the disintegrative political consequences of the 1974 Constitution, which allegedly betrayed the original idea of Yugoslav federation. The second part, titled "The Status of Serbia and the Serb Nation" develops ideas from the first part in and exclusively conspiracist form. This section addresses three "crucial issues" of Serbs, explicitly attributed to conspiracies of

158 *Nebojša Blanuša*

subterfuge by other Yugoslav republics and their respective leaders. The first two issues—the long-term stagnation of the Serbian economy and Serbian constitutional issues—were interpreted as the result of its exploitation and discrimination by Croatia and Slovenia. The two countries' policies were shaped by the pre-war Cominform's anti-Yugoslav story condemning a hegemonic Serbia that oppressed the other Yugoslav nations and that had to be stopped:

> Consistent discrimination against Serbia's economy . . . cannot be fully explained without insight into the relations among the Yugoslav nations between the two world wars, as seen and assessed by the Communist Party of Yugoslavia. Its views were decisively influenced by the authoritative Cominform, which . . . sought to break up Yugoslavia. . . . [Croatia and Slovenia] also had common economic interests, all of which provided sufficient grounds for a permanent coalition in the endeavor to achieve political dominance. This coalition was cemented by the long years of collaboration between Tito and Kardelj. . . . The watchword of this policy has been "a weak Serbia ensures a strong Yugoslavia," and this idea has been taken a step further in the concept that if the Serbs as the largest national group were allowed rapid economic expansion, they would pose a threat to the other national groups.
>
> (Serbian Academy of Science and Arts 1986)

The third problem, "Genocide at Kosovo against Serbs" is depicted as a drama of suffering, in the form of neo-Fascist and racist aggression in preparation since World War II and supported by those internal political actors who were adhering to the old Cominform policy:

> This open war . . . is being waged with a skillful and carefully orchestrated use of a variety of methods and tactics, with the active and not just tacit support of various political centers in Yugoslavia, which they are taking no pains to conceal and which is more ruinous than the encouragement given by our neighbors. . . . The Ballists' rebellion in Kosovo and Metohija at the very end of the war, which was organized with the collaboration of Nazi units, was militarily put down in 1944–1945, but as we now see, it was not politically quelled. In its present-day physiognomy, disguised with new content, it is being pursued with greater success and is getting close to final victory. . . . The physical, political, legal, and cultural genocide of the Serbian population in Kosovo and Metohija is a worse defeat than any experienced in the liberation wars waged by Serbia from the First Serbian Uprising in 1804 to the uprising of 1941. The reasons for this defeat can primarily be laid at the door of the legacy of the Cominform which is still alive. . . . Conspiracies, which are usually hatched in secret, were planned in Kosovo not just openly but even demonstratively.
>
> (ibid.)

Dissolution of Yugoslavia as a conspiracy 159

According to this document, Serbs were also discriminated in Croatia through the "refined and effective politics of assimilation"; in Vojvodina through secessionist politics; and in Bosnia and Herzegovina through the denial of the political, cultural, and spiritual contribution and integrity of Serbs (ibid., 136–37). In a conclusion of sorts, Serbian academicians claimed that:

> Such trends and the thorough job made of disintegration of the country make one think that Yugoslavia is in danger of further dissolution. The Serbian people cannot stand idly by and wait for the future in such a state of uncertainty. . . . In this event, Serbia would be able to make its own options and define its own national interests. Such a discussion and consultation would have to precede a review of the Constitution.
>
> (ibid.)

The theses of the SANU Memorandum were further expanded by prominent Serbian intellectuals, media, and the Orthodox Church in the following years (ibid., 138). One of these tendencies was expressed in the demonization of Tito and his associates as the archenemies of the Serbian people, whose singular focus was "weak Serbia, strong Yugoslavia." Another notorious theory that gained currency at the time among these circles was about the so-called Vatican-Cominform conspiracy against the Serbs. According to this supposed plot, the Communist Party of Yugoslavia, acting on instructions from the Cominform, conspired against the Kingdom of Yugoslavia between the two world wars. Moreover, the Communist Party collaborated with the Ustasha who were, in turn, receiving instructions from the Vatican, considered the archenemy of Yugoslavia. Allegedly, the Croatian Communists and the Ustasha collaborated during and after World War II, sowing discord through territorial fragmentation and the artificial creation of new national identities of Muslims, Montenegrins, and Macedonians, who were supposedly Serbs. According to this interpretation, the peak of the alleged conspiracy was the 1974 Constitution (ibid., 142–43). Following the logic of these conspiracy theories, the founders of socialist Yugoslavia were actually their biggest enemies. Furthermore, the mainstream Serbian press (e.g., *Duga, Politika, Večernje novosti*) used the same conspiracist framework to interpret the behavior of then prominent politicians and the Catholic Church in Croatia. The conspirationists accused the Croatian Communist leaders of continuing separatist politics, flirting with ideas of the Ustasha, orientation toward Central Europe, discrimination and assimilation of Serbs into Croatian society, and supporting Kosovo Albanians. This peaked in 1989 in the form of a charge of high treason by the Serbian press against Croatian politicians (ibid., 164–66). During this time, Serbian political leaders considered Slovenia openly anti-Yugoslav, and from this belief came the theory about the "Priština-Zagreb-Ljubljana Axis" (ibid.). Meanwhile, the Catholic Church in Croatia was blamed for clerical nationalism and genocidal crimes against Serbs during World War II (ibid., 167–69).

By contrast, in Croatia, Slovenia, and partially in Bosnia and Herzegovina, Slobodan Milošević was largely considered an executor of the SANU Memorandum.

160   *Nebojša Blanuša*

Starting in the late 1980s, it was "common knowledge" that his political designs were to implement a four-step conspiracy to realize the "Greater Serbia" plan. The first step was the internal putsch in the Central Committee of the Serbian League of Communists in 1987. The second step was an anti-bureaucratic revolution targeting the leadership of autonomous provinces of Vojvodina and Kosovo, as well as in Montenegro, through well-organized mass protests, combined with placing constitutional restrictions on autonomous provinces. Croatian and Slovenian leadership perceived these actions as a violent deviation from Yugoslav federative principles. The third step of Milošević's plan was an attempt to export the anti-bureaucratic revolution to Slovenia, Croatia, and Bosnia and Herzegovina. The final step was to instigate a rebellion of the local Serbs in Croatia and Bosnia and Herzegovina, culminating in inter-ethnic war supported by the Yugoslav People's Army (ibid., 146). In that sense, especially in the right-wing Croatian narrative, the war was inevitable, and the only possible outcome was the dissolution of Yugoslavia.

However, another document published in a Slovenian journal, *Nova revija*, in 1987, titled "Contributions to the Slovenian national program," achieved notoriety as the Slovenian parallel of the Serbian Memorandum (ibid., 158). Slovenian Communists condemned it as an attempt to destroy socialist Yugoslavia by denying its cornerstones, such as the People's Liberation Movement, socialist revolution, self-management, and non-alignment policy. Furthermore, they considered it an attack on the Yugoslav People's Army and an unacceptable reconciliation with domestic traitors and the Catholic Church. A series of exchanges between the Slovenian press and the Yugoslav People's Army occurred. The climax occurred when the weekly *Mladina* published the secret plans of the Yugoslav People's Army coup d'état in Slovenia. The subsequent military trial of those who provided the plan to the press provoked mass protests in Ljubljana. Serbia condemned Slovenian constitutional changes as openly separatist and imposed trade sanctions in 1989. This act was in response to the Slovenian obstruction of the overflow of anti-bureaucratic revolution as exemplified by the cancellation of trains scheduled to bring protesters to its territory. Simultaneously, the Croatian League of Communists openly declared that by "an attempt to isolate and silence Slovenia . . . the big scenarists actually contrived the situation to bring Croatia more easily to its knees." The Croatian press disseminated the thesis about "Serbian Cominform conspiracy," which employed Stalinist processes and politics to block whole republics from their usual functioning (ibid., 162). Such a speech act ironically turned back to the sender the message of the SANU Memorandum, whose original logic continued to reveal itself in the following years.

The last step of delegitimization of socialist Yugoslavia before the outbreak of the war was the dissolution of the Yugoslav League of Communists, which held its Fourteenth Congress on January 20–22, 1990. Croatia and Slovenia considered convening the meeting before it was usually held, as a Trojan horse to establish a state of emergency in Yugoslavia. It was perceived as another step in the anti-bureaucratic revolution, a step in Milosevic's "Greater Serbia" project (ibid., 171). After its infamous end and the departure of the Slovenian and Croatian

Dissolution of Yugoslavia as a conspiracy 161

delegates, the Congress was interpreted by these republics as the final unmasking of national majorization in favor of Serbs and the continuation of the neo-Stalinist and nationalistic populism of Milošević, who had already orchestrated a series of coup d'etats in Belgrade, Novi Sad, Titograd, Priština, and Kosovska Mitrovica (ibid., 172–73). As the League of Yugoslav Communists left the historic scene, almost all conditions for a multiparty system and the liberalization of political life were fulfilled. Yet, soon it would lead to the breakout of war, first in Slovenia, then in Croatia, and finally in Bosnia and Herzegovina, leading to the bloody dissolution of socialist Yugoslavia.

After the dissolution

Many scholars agree on several causes of the violent dissolution of Yugoslavia (e.g., Fink-Hafner 1995; Ramet 2007a). The first reason was economic deterioration with high unemployment rates that led to widespread social discontent. The second element was the growing political illegitimacy of the Communist system (and its worldwide downfall in 1989), which led to ideological disillusionment and calls for the Western democratic political order. Another source of discontent was a dysfunctional federal system with its rigid institutions decentralized along ethnic lines. A further factor was the leadership's nationalist agenda, which leaned on the proclivity of a large part of the population toward authoritarianism and the lack of democratic political culture. They built incompatible national grand narratives based on the idea of being exploited by other constituent nations and influenced by the memory of past atrocities, mainly from World War II and the period of the Ottoman Empire. In that sense, both Serbian and Croatian historical narratives accentuate an idea of long-term victimhood and suffering provoked by enemies of the nation. For example, in the Serbian narrative, socialist Yugoslavia was the anti-Serb federal system designed by the Croat, Tito, while in the Croatian historical narrative, it was the anti-Croat Communist system dominated by Serbs at the expense of other nations (Ramet 2007b). In both of these interpretations, the idea of a permanent and institutionalized conspiracy against the whole nation is present at least implicitly.

The international community and its leaders also played a part in the dissolution of Yugoslavia. Their role was usually depicted along the spectrum of being victims of their own prejudices—as was case of the US president Bill Clinton, who changed his policy toward the war in Bosnia and Herzegovina by accepting the thesis of ancient hatreds promoted by journalists, geopolitical analysts, and diplomats in several books[5]—to political manipulation, even in the form of a conspiracy theory. For example, Veljko Kadijević, a general of the Yugoslav People's Army and a minister of defense in the last Yugoslav government, claimed in 1991: "An insidious plan has been drawn up to destroy Yugoslavia. Stage one is civil war. Stage two is foreign intervention. Then puppet regimes will be set up throughout Yugoslavia" (Free Greece 2019). Milošević used the theory of international conspiracy against Yugoslavia in his defense at ICTY: "It existed through the joint forces of the secessionists, Germany, and the Vatican, and also the rest

162 *Nebojša Blanuša*

of the countries of the European Community and the United States" (Gordy 2013, 103), which significantly echoes the previously elaborated Vatican-Cominform conspiracy theory from the 1980s.

As we can see from the above examples, scholarly explanations regarding the dissolution of Yugoslavia were accompanied in the media and political discourse by more ominous conspiratorial interpretations in various ways. In this sense, the myth of ancient hatreds promoted by Western analysts and several important politicians looks compatible with the knowledge of existing national historical narratives. However, it would be an oversimplification to use those conspiratorial narratives as evidence of such hatreds. These narratives are very selective contemporary constructions, which acquired their full forms during and after Yugoslav dissolution. Forged during a period of extremes, they mostly offer Manichean binaries and omit historical evidence that does not fit into such an interpretation. Moreover, political actors from previous examples explained the broader, anonymous processes responsible for the dissolution of Yugoslavia in a conspiratorial way. For example, reasons for the economic deterioration appeared in the Yugoslav nations' grand narratives in the form of mutual blame. Some scholars blamed international financial institutions, Corporate America, the UN, and the EU for provoking the Yugoslav crisis in the 1980s. Alleged conspiracy occurred as the long-term plan to destroy Yugoslavia because of its geopolitical position, richness in minerals, fertile land, cheap labor, coal, and oil reserves on Kosovo, and so on. (Talbot 2000, 104). The nationalistic narratives of imposed political systems by conspirators partially disrupted the political legitimacy of Communist rule and the federal state but also those political actors who were perceived in Communists' eyes as internal and external enemies because of their support of nascent political parties during the late 1980s. Conspiracy theories about the international community's agency, especially among Communist circles, blamed powerful states such as the USA. Its alleged interest was to secure the main routes of oil and strengthen NATO influence, as well as world leadership in the post–Cold War era.[6] A particularly popular theory, especially among left-wing critics of Western politics, is that Germany was one of the main conspirators, who allegedly encouraged Croats and Bosniaks to engage in the war in order to secure German "sphere of influence" (Mahairas 2002; Glaurdić 2011). The same circles sometimes attributed historical reasons and geostrategic interests for the dissolution of Yugoslavia to neighboring countries such as Austria, Hungary, and Italy (ibid.). These ideas about imperialistic attempts further flourished after the creation of post-Yugoslav states. Such theories have changed their content and sinister reasons but not a sense of being an object of conspiracy in each of the former Yugoslav republics, very often among high state officials. Contaminating the political discourse with conspiracy theories, these carriers of influence contributed to the long-enduring culture of fear and made their internal and external politics shortsighted. In order to illustrate the state of the consolidation of conspiracy theories about the dissolution of Yugoslavia, we shall briefly address these issues in the next section by referring to two prominent historians in Serbia and Croatia and our recent survey results.

Divergence of conspiracy theories about the dissolution of socialist Yugoslavia

In an interview for Radio Free Europe in 2015, two prominent historians, Dubravka Stojanović from Serbia and Tvrtko Jakovina from Croatia, were asked to explain why it was so popular to explain the dissolution of Yugoslavia through conspiracy theories as well as which theories prevailed in their countries (Karabeg 2015). Stojanović explained: "The dominant opinion in Serbia blames Germany and the Vatican, together with other Great Powers for breaking down Yugoslavia, together with Slovenia and Croatia who abandoned it" (ibid.). Conversely, Jakovina said, "the prevailing opinion in Croatia is that Serbs are guilty of all the troubles . . . but here we have another story that no one in the world wanted Croatia, but it was established in spite of that" (ibid.). These two opinions correctly describe the divergence in conspiracy theories about the dissolution of Yugoslavia in the two countries that were the major actors in the dissolution. They also reflect the outcome of the development of historically embedded conspiracism described earlier in this chapter. Furthermore, the wartime presidents of these two countries held the very same ideas. As previously mentioned, Milošević used the same theory as a part of his defense strategy during his trial at the ICTY. Franjo Tuđman, on the other hand, stated in a speech in 1996 the theory about "black, green, and yellow devils," or those internal and external enemies who want to reestablish Yugoslavia (Blanuša 2014, 202), which became a mantra of right-wing groups in Croatia. Recent surveys conducted in Serbia and Croatia on nationally representative samples show how widespread such ideas are in the general public. In Serbia, at least 60% of citizens believe the conspiracy theory that the only reason for breaking up the former Yugoslavia was to destroy its up-and-coming market and impose neo-liberalism.[7] Similar surveys in Croatia showed that at least 65% of citizens agree with the statement that in the course of aggression against Croatia, some great powers deliberately tried to undermine Croatian independence in order to preserve Yugoslavia.[8] Recent surveys researching local conspiracy theories in Bosnia and Herzegovina, Croatia, Macedonia, and Serbia (Milošević-Đorđević et al. 2018) have found a strong inclination to believe in contrasting conspiratorial explanations of the causes of post-Yugoslav wars and critical events by those ethnic groups who were a part of the mutual conflict. Croatian citizens mainly believe that the Serbian intellectuals, politicians, and the Yugoslav Peoples' Army started the wars in Croatia and Bosnia with the goal of creating Greater Serbia. They also strongly disbelieve that the Croatian government had a plan of ethnic cleansing of Serbs from Croatian territory in its military operations. Serbian citizens in these matters hold the completely opposite view. An even greater contrast in these views exists between ethnic Serbs and Croats in Bosnia and Herzegovina, showing even more homogenous beliefs in conspiracy theories in alignment with their national grand narratives. Compared to them, Bosniaks (as the third party in the conflict) and Macedonian citizens who were not involved in the conflict do not show such stark differences in their beliefs about war-related conspiracy theories (ibid.).

Conclusion

Conspiracy theories about the dissolution of Yugoslavia are shaped by historical experience and collective perceptions of internal and external threats are held by different constituent political communities that comprised the first and second Yugoslavia. These communities and their leaderships entered both Yugoslav states with different expectations and meanings that they attributed to its existence. The turbulent history of this multiethnic state, with the burden of two world wars and two civil wars, as well as changes in political regimes and dominant ideologies, reshaped the initial enthusiasm into grave worries about internal and external enemies. As we can see, the potential dissolution of Yugoslavia was a permanent concern for Communist elites, whose slogan of brotherhood and unity was too superficial to heal old wounds and collective victimizations. Furthermore, national grand narratives came to be based on the (post)memory of atrocities and cultural traumas used for mutual scapegoating to assure in-group homogenizations. In retrospect, it seems that, after the real dissolution, conspiracy theories that reflect mourning for Yugoslavia exist in Serbia and partially in Bosnia and Herzegovina (Turjačanin, Puhalo, and Šajn 2018). Although further research is necessary in the other former constituent republics to get more conclusive evidence, it appears that in Croatia, the prevailing counter-narrative describes Yugoslavia as the "dungeon of peoples." Nevertheless, both types of conspiracism inherited the circular conception of history and the ominous legacy to blame others, in order to avoid coping with the violent past.

Notes

1 In his speech on November 24, 2018, the prominent Croatian politician and leader of Croatian Peasants Party (HSS), Stjepan Radić warned the National Council delegation that signing the unification will be "an act of conspiracy against people, above all against Croatia and Croats" (Hrvatski sabor n.d.).
2 Parts of this section are based on my research published in the chapter "Conspiracy Theories in and About the Balkans." In *Routledge Handbook of Conspiracy Theories*, edited by Michael Butter and Peter Knight, 596–609. London: Routledge, 2020.
3 Take for example the statement of S. Rajaratnam, second deputy prime minister of Singapore at the Seventh Summit Conference of the Non-Aligned Countries in New Delhi in 1983: "the United States lost the take-over bid primarily because, I suspect, the Americans are not, unlike their more experienced and dedicated Soviet rivals, particularly good at political conspiracy. This may be because, unlike Soviet conspirators, American conspirators tend to talk too much" (cited in Kusumaatmadja et al. 1983, 137).
4 The more nuanced dynamics and primary sources are depicted in Blanuša (2011).
5 For example, Robert D. Kaplan's *Balkan Ghosts* (1993) or Warren Zimmermann's *Origins of a Catastrophe: Yugoslavia and its Destroyers* (1996) (Kaufman 1999).
6 Such conspiracy theories also mentioned the secret US National Security Directive of the Reagan administration as part of its imperialist agenda, which is similar to the already mentioned Yugoslav conspiracy theory about the monster of financial capital (South African Communist Party 1999). Similar ideas of economic destabilization as the first step of dismantling Yugoslavia are also expressed in Talbot (2000).
7 The survey was held by the Department of Psychology, Singidunum University, in Belgrade in 2017.
8 The survey was held by the Faculty of Political Science, University of Zagreb, in 2018.

Bibliography

Blanuša, Nebojša. 2011. *Teorije zavjera i hrvatska politička zbilja 1980–2007* [Conspiracy Theories and Croatian Political Reality 1980–2007]. Zagreb: Plejada, Biblioteka Nova Plejada.

———. 2014. "Political Unconscious of Croatia and the EU: Tracing the Yugoslav Syndrome through Fredric Jameson's Lenses." *Journal of Balkan and Near Eastern Studies* 16 (2): 196–222.

Churchill, Winston. [1953] 2002. *Triumph and Tragedy*. New York: Rosetta Books.

Coakley, John. 1987. "Political Succession during the Transition to Independence: Evidence from Europe." In *The Process of Political Succession*, edited by Peter Calvert, 59–79. New York: Palgrave Macmillan.

Fink-Hafner, Danica. 1995. "The Disintegration of Yugoslavia." *Canadian Slavonic Papers* 37 (3–4): 339–56.

Free Greece. 2019. "Dissolution of Yugoslavia." *You Tube*, February 5, 2019. Video, 0:34. www.youtube.com/watch?v=5UkzHhLMNfg.

Glaurdić, Josip. 2011. *Vrijeme Europe: Zapadne sile i raspad Jugoslavije* [The Hour of Europe: Western Powers and the Breakup of Yugoslavia]. Zagreb: Mate.

Godina, Vesna. 1998. "The Outbreak of Nationalism on Former Yugoslav Territory: A Historical Perspective on the Problem of Supranational Identity." *Nations and Nationalism* 4 (3): 409–22.

Gordy, Eric. 2013. *Guilt, Responsibility, and Denial: The Past at Stake in Post-Milošević Serbia*. Philadelphia, PA: University of Pennsylvania Press.

Granville, Johanna. 1998. "Hungary, 1956: The Yugoslav Connection." *Europe-Asia Studies* 50 (3): 493–517.

Hasan, Sabiha. 1981a. "Yugoslavia's Foreign Policy Under Tito (1945–80) – 1." *Pakistan Horizon* 34 (3): 82–120.

———. 1981b. "Yugoslavia's Foreign Policy Under Tito (1945–80) – 1." *Pakistan Horizon* 3 (4): 62–103.

Hrvatski sabor. n.d. "Govor Stjepana Radića u Saboru 24. studenoga 1918" [The speech of Stjepan Radić in Sabor on November 24, 1918]. *Hrvatski sabor*. Accessed May 3, 2019. www.sabor.hr/hr/o-saboru/povijest-saborovanja/znameniti-govori/govor-stjepana-radica-u-saboru-24-studenoga-1918.

JFK Presidential Library and Museum. n.d. "Non-Aligned Nations Summit Meeting, Belgrade, 1 September 1961." Accessed May 3, 2019. www.jfklibrary.org/asset-viewer/archives/JFKPOF/104/JFKPOF-104-004.

Karabeg, Omer. 2015. "Zašto se raspad Jugoslavije tumači teorijom zavere" [Why the Breakup of Yugoslavia is Explained by Conspiracy Theory]. *Radio Slobodna Europa*. Accessed January 17, 2015. www.slobodnaevropa.org/a/most-rse-zasto-se-raspad-jugoslavije-tumaci-teorijom-zavere/26799348.html.

Kaufman, Michael, T. 1999. "The Dangers of Letting a President Read." *The New York Times*, May 22, 1999. www.nytimes.com/1999/05/22/books/the-dangers-of-letting-a-president-read.html.

Keesing's Contemporary Archives. 1949. (Vol. 7), 1958. (Vol. 11), 1967. (Vol. 16) Cambridge: Longman Group.

Kusumaatmadja, Mochtar, Mahathir bin Mohamad, S. Rajaratnam, and Pham Van Dong. 1983. "Statements by Heads of Delegations from Southeast Asian Countries at the Plenary Meeting of the Seventh Summit Conference of the Non-Aligned Countries in New Delhi, India, on 7–11 March 1983." *Contemporary Southeast Asia* 5 (1): 117–49.

166   Nebojša Blanuša

Lampe, John, R. 2000. *Yugoslavia as History. Twice there was a country.* New York: Cambridge University Press.

Lazić, Milorad. 2017. "The Soviet Intervention that Never Happened." *Wilson Center Blogs: Sources and Methods*, December 4, 2017. www.wilsoncenter.org/blog-post/the-soviet-intervention-never-happened#_ftnref3.

Mahairas, Evangelos. 2002. "The Breakup of Yugoslavia." In *Hidden Agenda. US./NATO Takeover of Yugoslavia*, edited by John Catalinotto, 47–54. New York: International Action Center.

Malcolm, Noel. 1996. *Bosnia: A Short History*. New York: New York University Press.

Milošević-Đorđević, Jasna, Iris Žeželj, Vlado Turjačanin, Petar Lukić, Biljana Gjoneska, and Andre Krouwel. 2018. "Conspiracy Theories about the Conflict: Blaming the Enemy or Finding a Joint Culprit." Paper presented at the Conference: Conspiracy Theories in/about the Balkans, Zagreb, 18 December 2018 (available on request).

Pavasović Trošt, Tamara. 2018. "Ruptures and Continuities in Nationhood Narratives: Reconstructing the Nation through History Textbooks in Serbia and Croatia." *Nations and Nationalism* 24 (3): 716–40.

Perović, Latinka. 2015a. "Croatian MPs Assassinated in the People's Assembly: June 20, 1928." Accessed May 3, 2019. www.yuhistorija.com/yug_first_txt01c2.html.

———. 2015b. "The Kingdom of Serbians, Croatians and Slovenians (1918–1929)/the Kingdom of Yugoslavia (1929–1941): Emergence, Duration and End." Accessed May 3, 2019. www.yuhistorija.com/yug_first_txt01c2.html.

Pigden, Charles. 2007. "Conspiracy Theories and the Conventional Wisdom." *Episteme: A Journal of Social Epistemology* 4 (2): 219–32.

Ramet, Sabrina, P. 2007a. "The Dissolution of Yugoslavia: Competing Narratives of Resentment and Blame." *Südosteuropa. Zeitschrift für Politik und Gesellschaft* 55 (1): 26–69.

———. 2007b. "Srpska i hrvatska povijesna naracija" [Serbian and Croatian Historical Narration]. *Anali Hrvatskog politologškog društva 2006* 15: 299–324.

Roksandić, Drago. 2017. "Yugoslavism before the creation of Yugoslavia." In *Yugoslavia from a Historical Perspective*, edited by Latinka Perović et al., 29–61. Belgrade: Helsinki Committee for Human Rights in Serbia.

Serbian Academy of Science and Arts. 1986. "Memorandum SANU." Accessed May 4, 2019. www.trepca.net/english/2006/serbian_memorandum_1986/serbia_memorandum_1986.html.

South African Communist Party. 1999. "The Real Story behind the Dismembering of Yugoslavia." Accessed May 5, 2019. www.hartford-hwp.com/archives/62/070.html.

Stojanović, Stanislav. 1980. "Titov koncept socijalističke spoljne politike" [Tito's Concept of Socialist International Politics]. *Časopis za suvremenu povijest* 12 (2): 115–40.

Talbot, Karen. 2000. "The Real Reasons for War in Yugoslavia: Backing up Globalization with Military Might." *Social Justice* 27 (4): 94–116.

Tito, Josip, Broz. 1959. *Govori i članci, 1941–1961, knjiga 1* [Speeches and Articles, 1941–1961, Book 1]. Zagreb: Naprijed.

———. 1963. *Govori i članci, 1941–1961, knjiga 10* [Speeches and Articles, 1941–1961, Book 10]. Zagreb: Naprijed.

Turjačanin, Vladimir, Srđan Puhalo, and Šajn Duška. 2018. *Conspiracy Theories in Bosnia and Herzegovina: A Psychological Study of Conspiracy Theory Beliefs in a Post-conflict Society*. Sarajevo: Friedrich-Ebert-Stiftung.

Vukov-Colić, Dražen. 1985. "Različito čitanje 'istočne politike'" [A Different Reading of the 'eastern politics']. *Danas*, February 5, 1985.

8 The dangerous Russian other in Ukrainian conspiratorial discourse

Media representations of the Odessa tragedy

Olga Baysha

Research on the politics of fear gained popularity after the 9/11 terrorist attacks. Predominantly, scholars in this area have concerned themselves with the anti-terrorism policies of the Bush administration (Furedi 2005), often claiming the administration inflated fears of terrorism intentionally, for political reasons (Thrall and Cramer 2009). The term "politics of fear" thus implies that political elites consciously manipulate public anxiety in order to realize policy goals. In this view, elites are unable to process complex social issues and come up with positive political projects for improvement; instead, they tend to rely on negative substitutes like the construction of a dangerous "other" and of the necessity to unite against it (Alexander et al. 2004).

It is here that conspiracy theories come into play, as they help to unite the people against an imagined threatening other, represented as a covert power bloc (Fenster 2008). These menacing others could be "different conspiratorial bodies— The Illuminati, Jews, Communists or a shadow elite within the American establishment" (Byford 2011, 2), but in any case, the fundamental claim of the conspiracy theory is that "there is an occult force operating behind the seemingly real, outward forms of political life" (Roberts 1974, 29–30).

Although conspiracy theories have existed throughout human history, many believed that our contemporaneity can be characterized as the "age of conspiracism" (van Prooijen and Douglas 2017, 324) coexisting with the age of populism: "To make a musical analogy, one could maintain that if populism is the theme, then many conspiracy theories are variations on the theme" (Silva et al. 2017, 425). Both conspiracism and populism require the Manichean division of the social into two antagonistic groups, the people/good us and the other/evil them (Laclau 2005), and both instigate and stoke fear of this evil other (Wodak 2015). In order to establish itself, the discourse of conspiratorial populism needs to ignore social diversity, present its people as a homogeneous unified demos existing beyond social divides and reduce the complexity of social issues to monistic and deterministic explanations exclusively in terms of the other's conspiratorial actions (Clarke 2002).

As a mechanism for simplifying the social to the extreme and dividing the world into clear-cut categories of us versus them, conspiratorial populism knows

168   *Olga Baysha*

no geographical boundaries (de la Torre 2018). It has become a global trend, reflecting a broader cultural logic of postindustrial societies in which the collapse of common sense and purpose (Hammond 2007), the dissolution of collective ideologies (Heins 2007), and the loss of trust in governing institutions (Beck 2010) nourish conspiratorial imagination. These negative developments in what is often called the postmodern condition become especially evident in times of conflict, when all societal contradictions are exacerbated.

This chapter analyzes an anti-Russian conspiratorial discourse within the Ukrainian public sphere in the aftermath of the Euromaidan revolution of 2014. Because it ended with a change of government in Ukraine, the Maidan transformation has provided fertile ground for conspiracy theories of various sorts. The evil West staging revolutions on Russia's borders, surrounding it with a ring of enemies, and thereby undermining the national security of Russia—this has been the strategic narrative employed by the Kremlin in its Maidan-related information war (Hoskins and O'Loughlin 2015). According to this conspiratorial story line, disseminated by Kremlin-controlled media (Khaldarova and Pantti 2016; Oates 2016), Maidan protesters, represented predominantly by neo-Fascists and trained by Westerners, committed "a coup d'etat in the full and classical meaning of the word," as Vladimir Putin (2014) unequivocally put it. Within this fear-provoking conspiratorial construction, Russia was a "besieged fortress" surrounded by foes on all sides. "The effect of the besieged fortress, the image of which propaganda creates" is that "enemies are everywhere; we must unite with the leader," as Russia's *Nezavisimaya Gazeta* sarcastically put it (Garmonenko and Gorbachev 2014).

The Ukrainian government that came to power with the victory of the Maidan also employed conspiracy theories in its own information war against Russia so as to mobilize a patriotic spirit. However, in contrast to Russian propagandistic constructions, Ukrainian conspiratorial discourses have not become a popular subject of analysis in academic research. With the aim of contributing to this research area, this chapter discusses how Ukrainian politicians have exploited conspiratorial theories to incite public fears and shift attention from the internal dimensions of Ukrainian problems to external ones. The case study discussed is the Odessa tragedy that happened on May 2, 2014, when 48 people died as a result of street clashes between two groups of Ukrainians, the opponents and proponents of the Maidan revolution. After presenting the context of the study, the method of research, and its findings, the final part of the chapter will discuss briefly how the collapse of shared meanings, the loss of trust in governing institutions, and the politics of fear reinforced one another to give rise to a conspiratorial populist discourse.

Context

The Maidan revolution

The Maidan revolution started in November of 2013, when protesters gathered in the main square of Kyiv and expressed their disapproval of President Yanukovych's decision not to sign an association agreement with the European Union—a

The dangerous Russian other 169

development many viewed as the result of "Russia's attempt to strong-arm the Ukrainian government into joining the Eurasian Economic Union" (Yekelchyk 2015, 66). Russia's pressure campaign stirred the emotions of Western-looking Ukrainians for whom Yanukovych's refusal to sign the agreement was the last straw: "In 2013, he was the president, who personified a corrupt and inefficient regime and was increasingly subservient to dictatorial Russia" (ibid., 85).

For many of the Maidan protesters who hardly knew the details of the proposed agreement, an idealized Europe served as a symbol of "democracy, rule of law, and economic opportunity" (ibid., 102). In contrast, the Russia-led Eurasian Custom Union signified historical regression: joining Russia instead of Europe was seen as slipping back toward a Soviet despotism (Kuzio 2017). It is here that the positions of Maidan liberals and nationalists converged: The latter supported the revolution not because of democratization but due to its clear anti-Russian stance. It is this paradoxical unity that made the Maidan movement deeply contradictory, alienated Ukrainian Russophones, and finally, transformed the civic protest movement into an armed struggle (Sakwa 2015).

Given that at least half of the country (predominantly its southeastern regions) did not support the revolution (Wilson 2014), the Maidan's victory in February 2014 was far from unanimously cheered. In February and March of that year, a wave of anti-Maidan protests swept across Ukraine's southeastern regions. Crimea, a peninsula in the far south of Ukraine inhabited mainly by ethnic Russians, was then annexed by Russia. In April, the anti-Maidan insurgency in Donbass, a far-eastern region, escalated into armed resistance with help from Russia. Not only did Russia provide the rebels with weapons, but it also supported them with Russian military personnel when the rebels appeared to be facing defeat in August 2014 (Kuzio 2017).

Russia's annexation of Crimea and support for the anti-Maidan insurgency in the east of Ukraine is usually referred to as the Russian invasion by Ukrainian politicians and mainstream commentators. What is often lost in representing the Ukrainian crisis exclusively through this frame is that the majority of residents of Ukraine's southeastern regions opposed the revolution, and the roots of the insurgency were local, despite it being co-opted by Russia for its own geopolitical interests (KIIS 2014; Kull and Ramsay 2015). The opposition in Ukraine's southeast against the Maidan with its agenda of Europeanization has historical origins, beginning with the fact that before all the territories of contemporary Ukraine were unified as a nation-state in the twentieth century, they had been controlled by different state and imperial formations. Prior to World War II, the region of northwestern/western Ukraine was divided among Poland, Hungary, Romania, and Czechoslovakia, while southeastern/eastern Ukraine was under Russia's control. To this day, Ukrainians living in these two mega regions (northwest and southeast) predominantly speak different languages (Ukrainian in the northwest and Russian in the southeast), attend different churches (Greek Catholic or Catholic in the northwest and Orthodox in the southeast), and vote in line with differing geopolitical agendas (Plokhy 2008). Although there is no clear line separating the southeast from the northwest of Ukraine, and although the voting border between

170   *Olga Baysha*

these mega regions is gradually moving eastward, the divide still exists, as borne out by demographics and basic patterns of political affiliation.

Since the declaration of Ukraine's independence in 1991, two opposing visions of national identity have been competing in Ukraine: ethnic Ukrainian nationalist and Eastern Slavic (Shulman 2004). The Eastern Slavic vision, popular in the southeastern regions, "envisages the Ukrainian nation as founded on two primary ethnic groups, languages, and cultures—Ukrainian and Russian" (Shulman 2004, 39). In contrast, the ethnic Ukrainian nationalist idea, popular in the northwestern regions, presents the historical Ukrainian-Russian relationship as one of the colonized and colonizer and explains the presence of Russians in Ukraine as a result of a conscious imperial Russian policy of forced Russification. After the victory of the Maidan, which brought nationalistic forces into power (Sakwa 2015), the discourse of Russia's alleged "unwillingness to accept Ukrainians as a separate people and Ukraine as an independent state" (Kuzio 2017, 249) became hegemonic in the Ukrainian political field. As Petro Poroshenko, the post-Maidan president of Ukraine, put it: "Putin wants the old Russian empire back. . . . As Russian Tsar, as he sees himself, his empire can't function without Ukraine. He sees us as his colony" (Escritt 2018). The fear of Russia reviving its imperial control over its neighbor became inscribed in the hegemonic discourses of the post-Maidan Ukraine.

Although the vast majority of people living in the southeastern territories were against the revolution but not in favor of joining Russia, the new post-Maidan Ukrainian government labeled the whole of the anti-Maidan movement pro-Russian and separatist and later called its participants terrorists (Baysha 2017). In April 2014, the government launched an anti-terrorist military operation (ATO) against Donbass insurgents. In addition to causing thousands of casualties, it also radicalized the societal confrontation and enhanced non-democratic methods of government in both the rebel strongholds and Kiev-controlled territories of Ukraine. Journalists in every region have been attacked, intimidated, and detained (Greenslade 2014). In the Ukrainian mainland, criminal investigations against opposition journalists were based on what the UN later called "the broad interpretation and application of terrorism-related provisions of the Criminal Code" (UN OHCHR 2017, 3). Some opposition journalists were imprisoned (Walker 2015); many left the country to avoid the fate of Oles Buzina, a famous publicist shot dead by nationalists (Carden 2015). Buzina had been deemed an "enemy of the people"—a label pro-Maidan radicals have applied to journalists holding anti-Maidan views. The personal information of such reporters, including their home addresses and passport data, have been published on the nationalistic *Myrotvorets* website launched in 2015 "by a people's deputy holding a position of adviser to the Ministry of Interior of Ukraine" (UN OHCHR 2018, 15). The site was not shut down even after an international scandal when *Myrotvorets* published the personal data of well-known foreign politicians (Deutsche Welle 2018). "National media have adopted a united patriotic agenda following Russia's annexation of Crimea and the armed conflict in the east"—this is how the BBC (2018) presented the issue. The "unified patriotic agenda" in a deeply divided Ukraine was achieved,

The dangerous Russian other 171

at least in part, through the exclusion of alternative voices justified by military expedience, as is typical for societies in a state of war.

The Odessa tragedy

Without knowing the history of the Maidan and post-Maidan civil confrontation, it is impossible to understand the tragedy in Odessa, a Russian-speaking city located on the Black Sea. Here, immediately after the victory of the revolution, pro-Maidan and anti-Maidan groups mobilized; their members armed themselves with shields, bulletproof vests, clubs, and other implements for possible street clashes ("May 2" Group 2015). Over time, as the anti-Maidan movements in the southeastern regions of Ukraine grew, similar forces in Odessa also became strident. According to the "May 2" Group, an independent investigative commission of Odessa journalists and civil society representatives,[1]

> March 1st [2014] was the day when Pavel Gubarev was elected as the "people's governor" in Donetsk. Russian flags were raised above administration offices in Donetsk, Dnipropetrovsk and Kharkiv [regional centers in the southeast]. Meanwhile in Odessa, a "people's meeting" of a few thousand participants happened at Kulikovo Field. Their official position was to hold a referendum and demand federalization within Ukraine. Though one could hear such slogans as "Odessa autonomy" and "Novorossiya" [New Russia] at this meeting. Against the background of the situation in Crimea, it was regarded as evidence that the real target of the "Russian spring" was to violate the territorial integrity of Ukraine, to implement separatism in the country.
>
> (ibid.)[2]

This information is crucial for understanding the ferocity of the confrontation between the opponents and proponents of the Maidan that reached its climax on May 2, 2014. The main demand of anti-Maidan protesters was not separatism but federalization, as reflected in reports by the Council of Europe and the UN describing anti-Maidan insurgents as pro-federalism activists but not separatists (UN OHCHR 2014; Council of Europe 2015). However, in the hegemonic narrative of the revolution, anti-Maidan had acquired the meaning of pro-Russian separatism, extremism, and even terrorism (Baysha 2018).

Here are some typical examples of the discursive transformation of federalists into separatists within the Ukrainian public sphere:

> Luhansk *separatists* organized a referendum right in the street. They asked city dwellers if they supported *federalizing* Ukraine.
>
> (Gordon 2014f, emphasis added)

> In Nikolaev, *separatists* stormed the building of the Regional State Administration demanding a referendum on *federalization*.
>
> (Leviy Bereg 2014, emphasis added)

172   *Olga Baysha*

In Kharkiv, *separatists* demand a referendum on the *federalization* of Ukraine.
(Ukrayinska Pravda 2014, emphasis added)

Because federalization was displaced by separatism in the dominant pro-Maidan discourse, the former came to be juxtaposed not only against the notion of the unitary state but also against the unity of Ukraine. As soon as this transformation of meaning happened, the confrontation appeared to be no longer between political adversaries (the pro-Maidan and anti-Maidan) but between irreconcilable enemies: pro-Russian separatists/extremists/terrorists on the one side and adherents of Ukrainian unity/pro-Ukrainian forces/patriots on the other.

The chronology of the events that occurred on May 2 is now well established; the brief account provided here is based on the investigations conducted by the United Nations (UN OHCHR 2014) and the Council of Europe (2015). The clashes started in the afternoon, after a pro-Maidan rally of soccer fans whose teams were playing that day in Odessa skirmished with anti-Maidan activists; it was the anti-Maidan side that attacked the pro-Maidan rally first. The rally quickly turned into violent street clashes as a result of which six people were shot dead and dozens were wounded. Toward evening, the pro-Maidan side took the offensive and chased the anti-Maidan group in retreat to its base camp at Kulikovo Field. There, the former burned the tents of the latter. The anti-Maidan protesters found shelter in the House of Trade Union building adjacent to the camp, from where they hurled Molotov cocktails at the pro-Maidan group; their adversaries retaliated in kind. One of the bottles containing flammable liquids presumed to have struck a barricade, ignited a fire that quickly engulfed the union building; 42 people died in the incident, including those who burned to death or suffocated and others who fell from high windows in the blaze; more than 200 survived with burns and other injuries.

According to a United Nations report, "some 'Pro-Unity' protesters were beating up 'Pro-Federalism' supporters as they were trying to escape the Trade Union Building, while others were trying to help them" (UN OHCHR 2014, 10). However, for those holding anti-Maidan views, the tragedy acquired the meaning of a mass killing that had been done on purpose, in line with promises to "kill *koloradi*," a phrase spread by pro-Maidan media and social networks leading up to the tragedy. *Kolorad* is a word originally denoting Colorado potato-eating insects distinctive for their bright orange-and-black stripes. Because their colors are reminiscent of the orange-and-black St. George ribbon, a symbol of Russian military glory, the term came to denote Maidan opponents, equated to pro-Russian separatists. In April 2014, it was popular among pro-Maidan users of social media to share posters featuring alerts about the presence of *koloradi* in the cities of southeastern Ukraine and advocating for their extermination (Baysha 2020). The day the tragedy occurred, pro-Maidan social networks were full of posts that cheered the victory over *koloradi*. Here are some immediate reactions posted by members of the EuroMaydan (2014) group that are still publicly visible on Facebook: "extinguish koloradi!" (Ihor Mykhailiv), "kill koloradi!" (Olga Moskovchenko), "koloradi bugs need to be burnt!" (Vitaliy Poronyuk), "to burn

The dangerous Russian other 173

all koloradi!" (Dmytro Marchenko), "death to koloradi!" (Denis Lanetsky), and so forth. These and similar posts indicate that the Odessa tragedy was not simply a horrible accident, no matter whose actions caused the clashes and the fire: When the level of animosity between compatriots is so high, violence of such scale and intensity is highly probable.

Research questions, method, and design

Because fears are constructed and delivered to the public through media channels, as "the mass media rely on governmental news sources and perspectives for most of the information pertaining to social order, internal security and international threats" (Altheide 2006, 150), my analysis was based on media representations of the events in Odessa. The research questions were as follows: How did popular media in Ukraine explain the tragedy? Whom did it identify as the responsible parties? What policy decisions were suggested in media accounts?

To answer these questions, I investigated the coverage of the tragedy by the news programs of three Ukrainian national television networks—ICTV (fakty. com.ua), Inter (podrobnosti.ua), and 1 + 1 (tsn.ua)—and Ukraine's five most popular news websites: Censor (censor.net.ua), Gordon (gordon.ua), Korrespondent (korrespondent.net.ua), Obozrevatel (obozrevatel.com), and Segodnya (segodnya. ua).[3] As I was interested in the most immediate reaction to the tragedy, I analyzed the Odessa coverage posted online by these outlets on May 3 and 4, the two days immediately after the fire.

Within this time frame, the media outlets under study released a total of 179 news stories covering the deaths in Odessa (Table 8.1).

To investigate the contents of these news stories, I employed the method of framing analysis elaborated by William Gamson and Andre Modigliani (1987) as well as Robert Entman (1993). I used Gamson and Modigliani's conception of the media frame as "a central organizing idea or story line" (143) that provides meaning to phenomena or events. I also followed Entman's (1993) elaboration, according to which a story line should promote particular problem definitions, causal interpretations, moral evaluations, and treatment recommendations. In order to identify the recurrent themes or story lines in the news stories under analysis, I sorted them according to my research questions stated earlier.

The result of this qualitative analysis was a classification system with several dominant story lines; they were coded as "Russian conspiracy," "Separatism/ extremism," "Police corruption," "Political responsibility," and "Neutral reporting." The coding key for these frames is presented in Table 8.2.

Table 8.1 Number of news stories on Odessa in selected media, May 3–4, 2014

ICTV	Inter	1+1	Censor	Gordon	Korrespondent	Obozrevatel	Segodnya
9	27	10	39	51	10	17	16

174   *Olga Baysha*

Table 8.2 Coding key: frames of reference in Odessa coverage

Frame	Description

Frame 1: Russian conspiracy	• Russia's Federal Security Service (FSS) or its General Intelligence Agency planned, coordinated, and financed the provocation of mass disturbances in Odessa because it wanted to:
	  ○ Destabilize Ukraine to disrupt its presidential elections.
	  ○ Disrupt the ATO by causing a transfer of military troops from Donbass.
	  ○ Split Ukraine.
	  ○ Provoke a civil war.
	  ○ Destroy Ukraine's statehood.
	• Russian diversion paramilitary groups came to Odessa to provoke the massacre from Russia-controlled Transdnistria—a self-proclaimed republic on the southern border of Ukraine.
	• Among the participants of the unrest, and the arrested, and the victims of the fire at the Trade Union building were Russian citizens.

Frame 2: Separatism/ extremism	• Pro-Russian separatists/terrorists/extremists attacked the unarmed/peaceful participants of a pro-Ukrainian rally of the adherents of the unity of Ukraine by throwing stones or shooting them. • Pro-Russian separatists/terrorists/extremists caused the fire by throwing Molotov cocktails from the upper floors of the building. • Pro-Russian separatists/extremists intentionally set the fire in an act of arson.
Frame 3: Police corruption	• Policemen supported or instructed the pro-Russian separatists/terrorists/extremists who attacked the pro-Ukrainian rally. • Policemen covered the gunmen. • Policemen did nothing to prevent the attack and stop the fighting. • On May 4, police released detained separatists/terrorists/extremists without a trial.

Frame 4: Political responsibility	• Politicians are blamed for the civil conflict in the country.
	• Politicians and officials and public figures are asked to:
	  ○ Start a dialogue to find ways out of the crisis (to stop civil confrontations).
	  ○ Stop using military rhetoric that instigates civil confrontations.
	  ○ Hear the excluded voices and take them into account.
	  ○ Stop playing people against each other for political ends.
	  ○ Investigate the tragedy before making quick judgments.

Frame 5: Neutral reporting	• Nobody is to blame.
	• Both sides of the conflict are described neutrally, as pro-Maidan and anti-Maidan activists.
	• It is acknowledged that both sides of the conflict were:
	  ○ Armed.
	  ○ Throwing stones and Molotov cocktails.
	  ○ Responsible for the tragedy in the Trade Union building.

To account for the presence of more than one frame per story, I coded for both dominant and secondary frames. The dominant frame was the main theme of the story, while the secondary frame appeared as a supplementary idea. All of the frames were eligible to be used in either capacity; the same frame could present the main theme in one story but only contribute a supplementary theme in a

Table 8.3 Frame employment across news media

Medium	Number of stories	Frame 1: Russian conspiracy	Frame 2: Separatism/ extremism	Frame 3: Police corruption	Frame 4: Political responsibility
1+1	8	56.5%	37.5%	6.0%	0.0%
ICTV	9	83.5%	11.0%	0.0%	5.5%
Inter	19	81.5%	8.0%	10.5%	0.0%
Censor	30	55.0%	25.0%	13.0%	7.0%
Gordon	40	51.5%	19.0%	22.5%	7.0%
Korrespondent	8	64.0%	18.0%	6.0%	12.0%
Obozrevatel	16	62.5%	31.5%	6.0%	0.0%
Segodnya	16	56.0%	30.0%	7.0%	7.0%
Average frame employment across media					
All news stories	N=146	63.8%	22.5%	8.9%	4.8%

different story. For every article, I either identified two separate frames or, when only one was present, counted the main theme as both dominant and secondary. After counting the frequencies of all frames in both categories, I calculated the average rate of occurrence for each frame across the media. The results of this analysis are presented in Table 8.3.

Russian conspiracy

As shown in Table 8.3, the main story line of the "Russian conspiracy" frame was the assertion that Russia planned, coordinated, and financed the upheaval in Odessa so as to destabilize Ukraine and undermine its independence through the provocation of a civil war. In order to do this, the frame suggests, Russia had established trained paramilitary groups in Transdnistria, and it was the militants of these groups who provoked the clashes. The main evidence for this claim was the ostensible presence of Russian citizens among the victims of the incident and those arrested after it. The day after the tragedy, all the media were quick to disseminate this information: "There are foreigners among the provokers and the victims" (Korrespondent 2014b), "Most of the participants of the mass disorder are the citizens of Russia and Transdnistria" (Segodnya 2014b), "Most of those detained are the citizens of Russia and Transdnistria" (Gordon 2014c), "Most of the individuals who have been identified so far are the citizens of Russia and Transdnistria" (Obozrevatel 2014), and so on. "Among the victims, there are fifteen Russians and five Transdnistrians," 1+1 (2014) claimed. "Fifteen Russians and ten Transdnistrians," Censor (2014b) echoed. These figures, which turned out to be fake (see below), spread rapidly through social networks.

The information appearing in media reports, sourced from the Ministry of Internal Affairs and the Security Service of Ukraine, resonated with numerous statements made by leading Ukrainian politicians who also framed the incident in Odessa predominantly as a Russian operation. In the representation of Oleksandr Turchynov, then the acting president of Ukraine, the tragedy was "a result

176 *Olga Baysha*

of an external provocation" (Segodnya 2014a). Then–prime minister Arseniy Yatsenyuk called it Russia's "provocation against the people of Ukraine" (Censor 2014a). Petro Poroshenko, soon to become the next president of Ukraine (elected just three weeks after the clash, on May 25, 2014), was confident that "the tragedy in Odessa is part of Russia's plan to split Ukraine" (Censor 2014d). It was "prepared by the Kremlin's secret service," former prime minister Yulia Tymoshenko maintained (Gordon 2014a). For Serhiy Pashinsky, then the head of the presidential administration, the Odessa incident was "a provocation of [Russia's] Federal Security Service" (Inter 2014b). "Putin has started the third world war," Anatoliy Hrytsenko, a former minister of defense, asserted (Gordon 2014d).

This grand conspiracy frame was bolstered by numerous related constructions focused on smaller details, including claims that "a Russian militant [was] shooting peaceful Ukrainian activists" (Censor 2014c), "participants of the rally 'For Ukraine!' were shot by pro-Russian snipers" (Inter 2014a), the majority of "separatists" were "not from Odessa but visitors" (Gordon 2014e). Similarly, articles argued that "there were no Odessa residents among those participating in the fiercest fighting" (ICTVa), all the fighters ("thugs") were brought to Odessa "from Transdnistria and other regions" (Inter 2014c), and so forth. These conspiracy constructions implied that Russia was attempting to destroy the unity of the Ukrainian state where, in Tymoshenko's words, "no confrontation among people exists" (ICTV 2014b). All these discursive constructions ignored social tensions within Ukraine, presented the country as a homogeneous unity existing beyond social divides and reduced the complexity of the situation to a monistic and deterministic explanation solely in terms of Russia's conspiratorial actions.

In repeatedly pointing to a Russian conspiracy against Ukraine, the majority of commentators provided a one-dimensional picture of what had happened and silenced those who called on politicians and public figures to exercise restraint, pending a thorough investigation (Frame 4); the latter perspective came to be marginalized. The scant presence of these alternative voices in the media representations under analysis (see Table 8.3) made the formation of a fully fledged alternative discourse impossible. However, these marginalized voices did enable at least the beginnings of an alternative approach to evaluating the events—one that acknowledged the internal societal split, which was the fundamental reason not only for the Odessa tragedy and the Donbass war but also for Russia's ability to co-opt the situation for its own political agenda.

"A wake-up call"—this is how Frank-Walter Steinmeier, Germany's minister of foreign affairs at the time, reacted to the tragedy in Odessa. "Violence provokes further violence," he argued. "Politicians should not add fuel to the fire. This starts with words. Military rhetoric makes things worse" (Gordon 2014b). Catherine Ashton, first vice president of the European Commission, agreed: "All political forces must now assume their responsibility and engage in a peaceful and inclusive dialogue to find a joint way out of the crisis" (Censor 2014e). Volodymyr Oleinyk, a member of the Ukrainian parliament, similarly believed that "We need to finally understand that conflicts should be transformed into a normal civilized dialogue" (Korrespondent 2014a). "Those in power are unable to establish a

The dangerous Russian other   177

dialogue with citizens; they play citizens against each other"—such was the reaction of Serhiy Abuzov, Ukraine's former first deputy prime minister (Segodnya 2014c). But as Table 8.3 shows, only 4% of all news stories analyzed employed the "Political responsibility" frame to cover the events in Odessa.

Fake news

Importantly, while focusing on Russia's instigation of the crisis, the media under my analysis systematically distorted reality by producing or reproducing fake news. To start with, the news that it was mostly Russian citizens who participated in the street clashes, got arrested, or died as a result of the fire turned out to be false. Every victim of the street clashes and fire on May 2, 2014, in Odessa was later identified as Ukrainian: "According to various sources, all those who died were Ukrainian citizens" (UN OHCHR 2014, 10). Among more than 130 people detained, there were three citizens of the Russian Federation whose involvement in the events was officially proved: "The SBU [Security Service of Ukraine] published the names and passports of three citizens from the Russian Federation allegedly involved in the 2 May violence" (ibid., 14). However, one of them, Andrei Krasilnikov, was fighting on the pro-Maidan side; later, he became a member of a Ukrainian volunteer battalion fighting against Donbass rebels (Swisch 2015). Maksim Sakauov, the second Russian citizen detained in connection with the May 2 events, was released in 2017 after being acquitted (BBC 2017). Yevgeni Mefyodov, accused of violent actions that had aimed to overthrow the government and harm the territorial integrity of Ukraine, was released on bail on August 19, 2019 (Gordon 2019). It is noteworthy that all these Russian citizens moved to Odessa long before May 2, 2014. As Odessa is a Russian-speaking city with close historical connections to Russia, their cases were not exceptional in this sense.

What this information demonstrates is that all the media reports presenting the situation predominantly through the frame of a "Russian conspiracy" were built on false evidence obtained from the Ministry of Internal Affairs and the Security Service of Ukraine. The "news" about (1) the absence of Odessa residents among the participants and victims of the clashes, (2) the Russian diversion put in place with the help of paramilitary groups coming from Transdnistria and other regions, and (3) people shot by a Russian militant or pro-Russian snipers, all turned out to be fake. Today, six years after the tragedy, there is no evidence that any snipers were involved, while the "Russian militant" shooting "peaceful citizens" has been identified as "an activist of 'Kulikovo Field mobile group,' Vitalii Budko, a 40-year-old resident of Odessa, who was shooting, from behind the police cordon" (Council of Europe 2015, 12). Moreover, as it turned out later, there were shooters among the participants of the ostensibly "peaceful" "pro-Ukrainian rally" as well: "On 18 May, a 'Pro-Unity' activist was arrested, accused of firing at, and injuring several people in the city centre on 2 May, including police officers, 'Pro-Federalism' activists and journalists" (UN OHCHR 2014, 12). According to UN reports, the members of the pro-Maidan rally were "wearing helmets and masks,

178   *Olga Baysha*

and armed with shields, axes, wooden/metallic sticks and some with firearms" (ibid., 9). This information was missing from the media accounts. Participants of the pro-Maidan rally were presented in overwhelmingly positive terms: as peaceful patriots attacked by Russia's hirelings. In reality, however, the events represented "a clash of two groups of people armed and prepared in advance for such clashes" (Tkachev 2017), and this is important to recognize even though the anti-Maidan group initiated the actual fighting.

Discussion

As is evident from the case study discussed in this paper, conspiratorial populist discourses related to the Maidan have been employed not only by Russia but also by Ukraine. Of course, it is important to recognize that the anti-Russian conspiratorial discourse analyzed here did not materialize out of thin air: The history of Russia's imperial control over Ukraine, Russia's annexation of Crimea, and the Kremlin's support of Donbass rebels were all factors that undoubtedly contributed to the conspiratorial imagination of many political actors who represented the post-Maidan Ukraine and controlled its public sphere.

However, given that the deep cultural divisions within Ukraine stem not only from imperial history but also from the post-Soviet collapse of collectively shared meanings (Yurchak 2006), it is also important to acknowledge the limits of such discourse; among many citizens of Ukraine, especially those living in the southeastern regions, the anti-Russian conspiratorial discourse never became a common-sense understanding. The population of Odessa responded to the conspiratorial discourse analyzed in this paper with its own conspiracy theories, according to which the tragedy was "a planned mass-murder of Odessians" committed by "the 'junta' (i.e., Kiev) [that] had sent a special group of agents provocateurs to the city" or "military trained elements of the neofascist Right Sector." The apparent fire, in this view, had only been "staged to look like a fire so as to cover up an extensive massacre inside" (Carey 2017, 89–90). If pro-Maidan conspiratorial populism has been informed by a lack of trust toward Russia, anti-Maidan conspiracy theorizing has been fueled by a similar condition of mistrust and skepticism toward supporters of the Maidan.

Commenting on the excessive use of the "Russian conspiracy" narrative by Ukrainian politicians with reference to all aspects of Ukrainian social life, Vadim Karasev, the director of the Ukrainian Institute of Global Strategies, argues: "This is a paranoid policy, when everyone is the agent of Moscow, the agent of the Kremlin, the agent of Russia, the agent of the FSS and so on" (Karasev 2019). According to Karasev, post-Maidan president Poroshenko's crushing defeat in the presidential election of April 2019 (only 24% of Ukrainians voted for him, while 73% supported his opponent) came as a result of people's fatigue with the "paranoid politics of fear" by means of which corrupted elites had been holding on to political power (ibid.). "People want to return to normality" and get out of this "madhouse," Karasev argues (ibid.). The problem, however, is that distinguishing between normal and mad is not so easy: "It is far from clear what distinguishes

The dangerous Russian other 179

the conspiratorial mindset, which sees Reds under every bed, from the simple and undeniable assertion that conspiracies do in fact exist" (Carey 2017, 92). With respect to the subject discussed in this paper, it is logical to ask: Why is it paranoid to suppose that the Odessa tragedy was organized by Russia, but reasonable to suggest that the Kremlin had a lot to do with the radicalization of the Donbass uprising?

One obvious answer is that there is a big difference between "having a lot to do with" and "organizing"; the latter ascribes sole responsibility to one suspected culprit, while the former distributes it among various players. Different discursive choices lead to different policy decisions and outcomes (Entman 1993). As stated in the contextual part of the chapter, the ongoing Ukrainian crisis is multidimensional—"it combines features of a covert foreign invasion with those of a civil conflict," as Serhy Yekelchyk put it (2015, 5)—and cannot be explained exclusively as a result of Russia's provocations. Focusing all of one's attention on Russia alone while ignoring the internal dimensions and causes of the tragedy in Odessa (as well as any other issue), one cannot comprehend the complexity of the situation and cannot, therefore, work out effective solutions to the overarching problem of the country's deep split and animosity between its citizens. The denial of this problem—a tactic employed by post-Maidan politicians and media—is not an effective way to manage the issue. The presentation of Ukraine as a country whose unity is complete and non-problematic, lacking any internal contradictions, does not allow productive analysis of the social situation from within; instead, it only stirs new societal conflicts by repressing, symbolically and physically, those who do not fit into a rosy picture of a homogeneous, unified Ukrainian nation. That which is repressed always comes back, perpetuating a never-ending cycle of animosity.

Conclusion

As stated in the introduction, conspiratorial populism knows no geographical boundaries. Political elites from all corners of the globe may consciously manipulate public anxiety and inflate fears through employing conspiratorial populist discourses. This happens when elites are unable to process complex social issues and come up with positive political projects for improvement; instead, they tend to rely on negative substitutes like the construction of a dangerous "other" and of the necessity to unite against it.

The analysis presented in this chapter shows how important it is in a contemporary interconnected world, where dividing lines run not along but within and across state borders, to recognize and problematize the impossible simplicity of conspiratorial discourses. Articulating complex social issues as plain dichotomies, these discourses destruct shared symbolic space necessary for communication and create the conditions for "maximum separation," to put it in Ernesto Laclau and Chantall Mouffe's terms (1985, 129). When this condition is reached, "two societies" appear in place of one, and the confrontation between these "societies" becomes "fierce, total and indiscriminate" (ibid., 129). As the tragedy of Odessa

180 *Olga Baysha*

shows, such a fierce confrontation may result not only in symbolic but also in physical destruction of the other.

As this chapter also suggests, the destructive potentiality of the conspiratorial imaginary is important to realize not only for politicians and media workers but also for scholars doing research on international wars, social conflicts, and other related fields. By failing to address the complexity of social contradictions, focusing all their attention exclusively on one aspect of the story, siding themselves with "victims" against "culprits" imagined in homogeneous terms, and failing to recognize internal tensions within each of the opposing camps, researchers may inadvertently contribute to the spiraling of animosity between people. As is well known, the battle between good and evil presupposes no political compromise.

Notes

1 More information about the group can be found in the report by the Council of Europe (2015, 20).
2 All translations from Ukrainian and Russian are done by author unless otherwise noted.
3 These three television channels have been leaders in the Ukrainian TV market for decades, which is acknowledged elsewhere (BBC 2018). The situation is more complicated with respect to news sites, as their ratings can be evaluated by many parameters; the sites discussed in this study are recognized as "top popular resources" by different Ukrainian marketing sources (Marketer 2018).

Bibliography

1+1. 2014. "Kryvavi Sutychky v Odesi Zabraly Zhittja 43 Osib, 25 Perebuvajut u Vazhkomu Stani" [Bloody Clashes in Odessa Took the Lives of 43 People, 25 are in Serious Condition]. *TSN.ua*, May 3, 2014. https://tsn.ua/ukrayina/krivavi-sutichki-v-odesi-zabrali-zhittya-43-osib-25-perebuvayut-u-tyazhkomu-stani-347951.html.

Alexander, Jeffrey, Ron Eyerman, Bernard Giesen, Neil Smelsar, and Piotr Sztompka. 2004. *Cultural Trauma and Collective Identity*. Berkeley, CA: University of California Press.

Altheide, David L. 2006. "Terrorism and the Politics of Fear." *Cultural Studies Critical Methodologies* 6 (4): 415–39.

Baysha, Olga. 2017. "In the Name of National Security: Articulating Ethno-Political Struggles as Terrorism." *Journal of Multicultural Discourses* 14 (4): 332–48.

———. 2018. *Miscommunicating Social Change: Lessons from Russia and Ukraine*. Lanham, MD: Lexington.

———. 2020. "Dehumanizing Political Others: A Discursive-Material Perspective." *Critical Discourse Studies* 17 (3): 292–307.

BBC. 2017. "Sud Opravdal Obvinjajemih Po Delu o Sobitijah v Odesse v Maye 2014-go" [The Court Acquitted the Defendants in the Case of Odessa Events in May 2014]. *BBC.com*, September 18, 2017. www.bbc.com/russian/news-41305608

———. 2018. "Ukraine Profile – Media." *BBC.com*, December 10, 2018. www.bbc.com/news/world-europe-18006248

Beck, Ulrich. 2010. *World at Risk*. Cambridge, UK: Polity Press.

Byford, Jovan. 2011. *Conspiracy Theories: A Critical Introduction*. New York: Palgrave Macmillan.

The dangerous Russian other 181

Carden, James. 2015. "At Least 10 Opposition Figures Have Died in Ukraine Just This Year." *The Nation*, April 21, 2015. www.thenation.com/article/least-10-opposition-figures-have-died-ukraine-just-year.

Carey, Matthew. 2017. *Mistrust: An Ethnographic Theory*. Chicago, IL: HAU Books.

Censor. 2014a. "Tragediju v Odesse Budet Rassledovat Specialnaja Sledstvennaja Gruppa Pri GPU" [Odessa Tragedy Will Be Investigated by a Special Group of the Attorney-General's Office]. *Censor.net.ua*, May 3, 2014. https://censor.net.ua/news/283868/tragediyu_v_odesse_budet_rassledovat_spetsialnaya_sledstvennaya_gruppa_pri_gpu_yatsenyuk.

———. 2014b. "Tymoshenko Pribila v Odessu" [Tymoshenko Arrived in Odessa]. *Censor.net.ua*, May 3, 2014. https://censor.net.ua/news/283697/timoshenko_pribyla_v_odessu.

———. 2014c. "Rosijskij Boievik v Odesse Rasstrelivajet Ukrainskih Aktivistov" [A Russian Militant is Shooting Ukrainian Activists]. *Censor.net.ua*, May 3, 2014. https://censor.net.ua/video_news/283765/rossiyiskiyi_boevik_v_odesse_rasstrelivaet_ukrainskih_aktivistov_iz_akm_pod_prikrytiem_militsii_shokiruyuschee.

———. 2014d. "Tragedija v Odesse – Eto Chast Plana Rossii Po Raskolu Ukrainy" [Odessa Tragedy is Part of Russia's Plan to Split Ukraine]. *Censor.net.ua*, May 3, 2014. https://censor.net.ua/news/283775/tragediya_v_odesse_eto_chast_plana_rossii_po_raskolu_ukrainy_poroshenko.

———. 2014e. "EC Prizivajet k Nezavisimomu Rassledovaniju Sobitij v Odesse " [The EU Calls for an Independent Investigation of Odessa Events]. *Censor.net.ua*, May 3, 2014. https://censor.net.ua/news/283819/es_prizyvaet_k_nezavisimomu_rassledovaniyu_sobytiyi_v_odesse.

Clarke, Steve. 2002. "Conspiracy Theories and Conspiracy Theorizing." *Philosophy of the Social Sciences* 32 (2): 131–50.

Council of Europe. 2015. "Report of the International Advisory Panel. Council of Europe." *International Advisory Panel*, November 4, 2015. https://rm.coe.int/CoERMPublicCommonSearchServices/DisplayDCTMContent?documentId=090000168048610f.

de la Torre, Carlos. 2018. *Routledge Handbook of Global Populism*. London, UK: Routledge.

Deutsche Welle. 2018. "Gerhard Schröder Labeled 'Enemy of the State' in Ukraine." *DW.com*, November 15, 2018. www.dw.com/en/gerhard-schr%C3%B6der-labeled-enemy-of-the-state-in-ukraine/a-46319939.

Entman, Robert M. 1993. "Framing: Toward Clarification of a Fractured Paradigm." *Journal of Communication* 43 (4): 51–58. https://doi.org/10.1111/j.1460-2466.1993.tb01304.x.

Escritt, Thomas. 2018. "Ukraine's Poroshenko: Putin Wants My Whole Country." *Reuters.com*, November 29, 2018. www.reuters.com/article/us-ukraine-crisis-germany/ukraines-poroshenko-putin-wants-my-whole-country-idUSKCN1NY03K?il=0.

EuroMaydan. 2014. "Koloradskyh Nametiv Na Kulykovomu Poli Vzhe Maizhe Nemaye" [Kolorado Tents on the Kulikovo Field Are Almost Gone]. *Facebook*, May 2, 2014. Accessed October 1, 2019. www.facebook.com/search/top/?q=%D0%84%D0%B2%D1%80%D0%BE%D0%9C%D0%B0%D0%B9%D0%B4%D0%B0%D0%BD%20%E2%80%93%20EuroMaydan%20%D0%BA%D0%BE%D0%BB%D0%BE%D1%80%D0%B0%D0%B4%D1%81%D1%8C%D0%BA%D0%B8%D1%85%20%D0%BD%D0%B0%D0%BC%D0%B5%D1%82%D1%96%D0%B2&epa=SEARCH_BOX.

Fenster, Mark. 2008. *Conspiracy Theories: Secrecy and Power in American Culture*. Minneapolis, MN: University of Minnesota Press.

Furedi, Frank. 2005. *Politics of Fear*. London: Continuum International Publishing Group.

182 *Olga Baysha*

Gamson, William A., and Andre Modigliani. 1987. "The Changing Culture of Affirmative Action." In *Equal Employment Opportunity: Labor Market Discrimination and Public Policy*, edited by Paul Burstein, 373–94. Piscataway, NJ: Transaction Publishers.

Garmonenko, Daria, and Alexei Gorbachev. 2014. "Rossijane Protestovat Poka Ne Hotjat" [Russian Citizens Do Not Want to Protest Yet]. *Nezavisimaya Gazeta* (Moscow), September 8, 2014. www.ng.ru/politics/2014-09-08/1_protest.html.

Gordon. 2014a. "Tymoshenko Prijehala v Odessu" [Tymoshenko Arrived in Odessa]. *Gordonua.com, May 3, 2014*. https://gordonua.com/news/separatism/timoshenko-priehala-v-odessu-20880.html.

———. 2014b. "Glava Mid Germaniji Shokirovan Sobitijami v Odesse" [The Federal Minister of Foreign Affairs is shocked by Odessa Events]. *Gordonua.com*, May 3, 2014. https://gordonua.com/news/worldnews/glava-mid-germanii-shokirovan-sobytiyami-v-odesse-20919.html.

———. 2014c. "Pozhar v Odesskom Dome Profsojuzov Mog Nachatsa iz-za Broshennih Sverhu 'Koktejlei Molotova'" [The Fire in Odessa House of Trade Unions Might Have Been Started by "Molotov Cocktails" Thrown From Above]. *Gordonua.com*, May 3, 2014. https://gordonua.com/news/separatism/mvd-pozhar-v-odesskom-dome-profsoyuzov-mog-nachatsya-iz-za-broshennyh-sverhu-kokteyley-molotova-20971.html.

———. 2014d. "Tusk o Sobytiyah v Odesse: Eto Neobjavlennaja Vojna Rossiji v Ukraine" [Tusk on Odessa Events: This is an Undeclared Russian War in Ukraine]. *Gordonua.com*, May 3, 2014. https://gordonua.com/news/politics/tusk-o-sobytiyah-v-odesse-eto-neobyavlennaya-rossiey-voyna-v-ukraine-20935.html.

———. 2014e. "Ne Stoit Dazhe Primerivat Na Odessu Tcenarij Donetska ili Luganska" [One Should Not Even Try the Donetsk or Lugansk Scenario in Odessa]. *Gordonus.com*, May 4, 2014. https://gordonua.com/news/separatism/hait-ne-stoit-dazhe-primerivat-na-odessu-scenariy-donecka-ili-luganska-21105.html.

———. 2014f. "Separatisti v Luganske Organizovali 'Referendum' Prjamo na Ulitse" [Lugansk Separatists Organized a Referendum Right in the Street." *Gordonua.com*, March 14, 2014. http://gordonua.com/news/society/separatisty-v-luganske-organizovali-referendum-pryamo-na-ulice-14151.html.

———. 2019. "Mefyodov i Dovzhenkov Vishli Pod Zalog" [Mefyodov and Dovzhenkov Were Released on Bail]. *Gordonua.com*, August 19. 2019. https://gordonua.com/news/politics/figuranty-dela-o-sobytiyah-2-maya-2014-goda-v-odesse-mefedov-i-dolzhenkov-vyshli-pod-zalog-1206188.html.

Greenslade, Roy. 2014. "Journalists Covering the Ukraine Crisis Suffer Intimidation." *The Guardian*, July 23, 2014. www.theguardian.com/media/greenslade/2014/jul/23/journalist-safety-ukraine.

Hammond, Philip. 2007. *Media, War, and Postmodernity*. New York: Routledge.

Heins, Volker. 2007. "Critical Theory and the Traps of Conspiracy Thinking." *Philosophy and Social Criticism* 33 (7): 787–801. https://doi.org/10.1177/0191453707081675.

Hoskins, Andrew, and Ben O'Loughlin. 2015. "Arrested War: The Third Phase of Mediatization." *Information, Communication & Society* 18 (11): 1320–38. https://doi.org/10.1080/1369118X.2015.1068350.

ICTV. 2014a. "Odesa Pislja Tragediji: U Ljudei Zalyshylos Bezlich Zapytan" [Odessa After the Tragedy: People Have Lots of Questions]. *Fakty.com.ua*, May 3. 2014. https://fakty.com.ua/ua/videos/60758.

———. 2014b. "Tymoshenko: My Zdatni Zahystyty Ukrajinu" [Tymoshenko: We Are Able to Defend Ukraine]. *Fakty.com.ua*, May 3, 2014. https://fakty.com.ua/ua/videos/60763/.

Inter. 2014a. "Kolichestvo Pogibsih v Odesse Vozroslo do 43 Chelovek" [The Death Toll in Odessa Increased to 43 People]. *Podrobnosti.ua*, May 3, 2014. https://podrobnosti. ua/974195-kolichestvo-pogibshih-v-odesse-vozroslo-do-43-chelovek-obnovleno-foto. html.

———. 2014b. "Pashynsky Obvinjayet FSB Rossiji v Smertjah v Odesse" [Pashynsky Accuses Russia's Federal Security Service in Odessa Deaths]. *Podrobnosti.ua*, May 3, 2014. https://podrobnosti.ua/974205-pashinskij-obvinjaet-fsb-rossii-v-smertjah-v-odesse.html.

———. 2014c. "Bojnju v Odesse Prorossijskije Boeviki Planirovali Zaraneje" [Pro-Russian Militants Planned the Odessa Slaughter in Advance]. *Podrobnosti.ua*, May 3, 2014. https://podrobnosti.ua/974210-bojnju-v-odesse-prorossijskie-boeviki-planirovali-zaranee-deputat-gorsoveta.html.

Karasev, Vadim. 2019. "Vadim Karasev na 112" [Vadim Karasev on 112]. *YouTube*, April 10, 2019. Accessed October 1, 2019. www.youtube.com/watch?v=L6g443XgNPw.

Khaldarova, Irina, and Mervi Pantti. 2016. "Fake News. The Narrative Battle Over the Ukrainian Conflict." *Journalism Practice* 10 (7): 891–901.

KIIS. 2014. "The Views and Opinions of South-Eastern Regions Residents of Ukraine." *Kiev International Institute of Sociology*, April 14, 2014. Accessed October 1, 2019. www.kiis.com.ua/?lang=eng&cat=reports&id=302&y=2014&page=9.

Korrespondent. 2014a. "Tragedija v Odesse Dolzhna Bit Rassledocana Specialnoj Sledstvennoj Komissiej" [The Tragedy in Odessa Must be Investigated by a Special Investigation Commission]. *Korrespondent.net*, May 3, 2014. https://korrespondent.net/ukraine/politics/3357595-trahedyia-v-odesse-dolzhna-byt-rassledovana-spetsyalnoi-sledstvennoi-komyssyei-verkhovnoi-rady-oleinyk.

———. 2014b. "Sredi Uchastnikov Massovih Besporjadkov i Pogibshih v Odesse Est Inostrantsi" [There Are Foreigners Among the Participants of the Riots and Those Killed in Odessa]. *Korrespondent.* May 3, 2014. https://korrespondent.net/ukraine/politics/3357693-sredy-uchastnykov-massovykh-besporiadkov-y-pohybshykh-v-odesse-est-ynostrantsy.

Kull, Steven, and Clay Ramsay. 2015. "The Ukrainian People on the Current Crisis. *Program for Public Consultation/Kiev International Institute of Sociology*, March 9, 2015. Accessed October 1, 2019. www.publicconsultation.org/wp-content/uploads/2016/03/Ukraine_0315.pdf.

Kuzio, Taras. 2017. *Putin's War against Ukraine: Revolution, Nationalism, and Crime.* Toronto: University of Toronto Press.

Laclau, Ernesto. 2005. *On Populist Reason.* New York: Verso.

Laclau, Ernesto, and Mouffe, Chantal. 1985. *Hegemony and Social Strategy.* New York: Verso.

Leviy Bereg. 2014. "V Nikolajeve Separatisti Pitajutsa Prorvatsa v Zdanije OGA" [In Nikolaev, Separatists Try to Storm the Building of the Regional State Administration]. *LB.ua*, April 7, 2014. http://lb.ua/society/2014/04/07/262274_nikolaeve_separatisti_pitayutsya.html.

Marketer. 2018. "Novostnije Sajti Ukraini: Top Populjarnih Resursov" [New Sites of Ukraine: Top Popular Resources]. *Marketer.ua*, October 6, 2018. https://marketer.ua/ukraine-news-sites-top-popular-resources.

"May 2" Group. 2015. "Predistorija Odesskoj Tragediji" [The Background of the Odessa Tragedy]. *"May 2" Group*, December 7, 2015. Accessed October 1, 2019. http://2maygroup. blogspot.com/2015/12/2-2014_7.html.

184 *Olga Baysha*

Oates, Sarah. 2016. "Russian Media in the Digital Age: Propaganda Rewired." *Russian Politics* 1 (4) (December): 398–417. https://doi.org/10.1163/2451-8921-00104004.

Obozrevatel. 2014. "Posibnyky Terorystiv Sami Pidpalyly Budynok Profsojuziv" [The Accomplices of the Terrorists Set Fire to the House of Trade Unions by Themselves]. *Obozrevatel*, May 3, 2014. www.obozrevatel.com/ukr/crime/94852-mvs-posibniki-teroristiv-sami-pidpalili-budinok-profspilok-kidayuchi-koktejli-molotova.htm.

Plokhy, Serhii. 2008. *Ukraine and Russia: Representations of the Past*. Toronto: University of Toronto Press.

Putin Vladimir. 2014. "Direct Line with Vladimir Putin." *Kremlin Press Release*, April 17, 2014. Accessed October 1, 2019.

Roberts, John M. 1974. *The Mythology of the Secret Societies*. London: Macmillan Pub Co.

Sakwa, Richard. 2015. *Frontline Ukraine: Crisis in Borderlands*. London: I. B. Tauris.

Segodnya. 2014a. "Tragedija v Odesse Proizoshla iz-za Vneshnej Provokacii" [The Tragedy in Odessa Occurred Due to an External Provocation]. *Segodnya*, May 3, 2014. www.segodnya.ua/regions/odessa/tragediya-v-odesse-proizoshla-iz-za-vneshney-provokacii-turchinov-517522.html.

———. 2014b. "Bolshinstvo Uchastnikov Besporyadkov v Odesse – Grazhdane Rosii I Pridnestrovja" [Most of the Participants in Odessa Riots are the Citizens of Russia and Transdnistria]. *Segodnya.ua*, May 3, 2014. www.segodnya.ua/hot/odessa-pozhar-stolkn/bolshinstvo-uchastnikov-besporyadkov-v-odesse-grazhdane-rossii-i-pridnestrovya-miliciya-517552.html.

———. 2014c. "Vlasti Zanimajutsa Ohotoj Na Vedm" [The Authorities are Engaged in a Witch Hunt]. *Segodnya.ua*, May 3, 2014. www.segodnya.ua/regions/odessa/vlasti-zanimayutsya-ohotoy-na-vedm-arbuzov-517563.html.

Shulman, Stephen. 2004. "The Contours of Civic and Ethnic National Identification in Ukraine." *Europe-Asia Studies* 56 (1): 35–56.

Silva, Bruno C., Federico Vegetti, and Levente Littvay. 2017. "The Elite is Up to Something: Exploring the Relation Between Populism and Belief in Conspiracy Theories." *Swiss Political Science Review* 23 (4): 423–43.

Swisch, Ivan. 2015. "Rossijanin s Majdana Zashishajet Ukrainu v Vojne" [A Russian Citizen from the Maidan Defends Ukraine in ATO]. *Odessa Crisis Media Center*, February 25, 2015. Accessed October 1, 2019. www.odcrisis.org/rossiyanin-s-majdana-zashhishhaet-ukrainu-v-ato/.

Thrall, Trevor, and Jane K. Cramer. 2009. *American Foreign Policy and the Politics of Fear*. Abingdon, Oxon: Routledge.

Tkachev, Yuri. 2017. "Sem Mifov ob Odesskoi Tragedii 2014" [Seven Myths About the Odessa Tragedy of 2014]. *Vzglyad*. May 2, 2017. https://vz.ru/opinions/2017/5/2/868624.html.

Ukrayinska Pravda. 2014. "U Kharkovi Separatysty Vymagajut Referendum z Federalizaciji Ukrayini" [In Kharkiv, Separatists Demand a Referendum on the Federalization of Ukraine]. *Ukrainyinska Pradva*, April 6, 2014. www.pravda.com.ua/news/2014/03/16/7019010/.

UN OHCHR. 2014. "Report On the Human Rights Situation in Ukraine." *Office of the United Nations High Commissioner for Human Rights*. June 15, 2014. Accessed October 1, 2019. www.ohchr.org/Documents/Countries/UA/HRMMUReport15June2014.pdf.

———. 2017. "Report on the Human Rights Situation in Ukraine 16 August to 15 November 2017." *Office of the United Nations High Commissioner for Human Rights*, December 12, 2017. Accessed October 1, 2019. www.ohchr.org/Documents/Countries/UA/UAReport20th_EN.pdf.

———. 2018. "Report on the Human Rights Situation in Ukraine16 November 2017 to 15 February 2018." *Office of the United Nations High Commissioner for Human Rights*, February 2018. Accessed October 1, 2019. www.ohchr.org/documents/Countries/uA/reportukraineNov2017-Feb2018_eN.pdf.

van Prooijen, Jan-Willem, and Karen M. Douglas. 2017. "Conspiracy Theories as Part of History: The Role of Societal Crisis Situations." *Memory Studies* 10 (3): 323–33.

Walker, Shaun. 2015. "Ukraine: Draft Dodgers Face Jail as Kiev Struggles to Find New Fighters." *The Guardian*, February 10, 2015. www.theguardian.com/world/2015/feb/10/ukraine-draft-dodgers-jail-kiev-struggle-new-fighters.

Wilson, Andrew. 2014. *Ukraine Crisis: What it Means for the West*. New Haven, CT: Yale University Press.

Wodak, Ruth. 2015. *The Politics of Fear: What Right-Wing Populist Discourses Mean*. London: Sage.

Yekelchyk, Serhy. 2015. *The Conflict in Ukraine: What Everyone Needs to Know*. New York: Oxford University Press.

Yurchak, Alexei. 2006. *Everything Was Forever, Until It Was No More: The Last Soviet Generation*. Princeton, NJ: Princeton University Press.

9 The victims, the guilty, and "us"

Notions of victimhood in Slovakian conspiracy theories

Zuzana Panczová

This text had its genesis during a charged situation in society, when Slovakia was shaken by the death of the young journalist Ján Kuciak and his fiancée, Martina Kušnírová. Apart from the understandable search for an answer to the question of who had murdered them, there was an attempt by the public, the media, and the elites, including the highest representatives of political power, to work with narratives in various versions explaining why such a thing had happened. From the very beginning, it was highly probable (and the investigators too indicated this) that the deaths were connected with the journalist's work, which was uncovering corruption: for a section of the public, this made him a victim of the corrupt representatives of government power. In opposition to this, however, another group of conspiratorially oriented interpretations was created, which found the true target of the conspiracy to be the government or current political system. Among those with strong yet differing political convictions, discussions seemed like the playing out of a contest whose victor would be awarded the status of true victim. Using content analysis of publicly shared texts, this chapter aims to show how this strategy is applied in Slovak public discourse in the rhetoric of the authorities (political and religious), media, and their readers and what role conspiracy theories play in this. The research field entailed public declarations by political and religious authorities, their interpretation, and related discussions on online forums of mainstream and alternative news sources.

Victimhood as part of group identification

A common denominator linking conspiracy theories relating to perceived threats to the nation in Slovak public discourse is the concept of "victimhood." Behind this concept, there is generally the latent (felt or ascribed) status of sacrificial victim; behind "victimization," one may generally understand the process whereby this status is ascribed to or suggested for someone.[1]

The issue of victimhood has been analyzed in detail at the level of individual and social psychology. It is connected with the mentality of the victim in cases of objectively or subjectively felt violence in individuals and societies. At the individual level, the psyche of the victim is characterized by feelings of powerlessness, self-pity, guilt, low self-confidence and also low sense of responsibility,

The victims, the guilty, and "us" 187

a tendency to shift guilt onto others, and so on. Several writers, however, draw attention to related processes in the collective group context (Bar-Tal et al. 2009, 3). Bar-Tal states that victimization may take on a group character through the use of narratives and images shared within the group, which are projected onto individuals as representatives of the given group or onto an object that is a group personification. This usually involves stories describing certain incidents (violence, wrongdoing), which are examples of the subordinated status of one group vis-à-vis another; Bar-Tal emphasizes the following:

> Groups can suffer from collective victimization which, similarly to individual victimization, is not based only on an objective experience but also on the social construction of it. It means that at the collective level of victimization, members of a collective hold shared beliefs about in-group victimization, i.e. of the social group to which they belong. Sharing these beliefs reflects a sense of collective victimhood. In this case the inflicted harm has to be perceived as intentionally directed towards the group, or towards the group members because of their membership in that group.
>
> (ibid., 6)

(Self-)victimization is often a strategy of conspiracy theorizing. Conspiracy theories are stories in which the interests of aggressors/conspirators and their victims stand counterposed. Victimhood may have a social, moral, or physical character. In fact, precisely the moment of persecution and victimization has been identified as one of the cognitive patterns of conspiracist ideation (Lewandowsky, Lloyd, and Brophy 2018, 221).

The introductory section illuminates the thematic rendering of victimhood in the auto-stereotype of the Slovak nation. Evidence is provided of the significance of victimization in creating a positive group self-image. Using the example of Jozef Tiso, I show how the image of the national martyr is instrumentalized, what role conspiracy theories play in this, and what potential there is for updating this image in the contemporary anti-system discourse. The material for this study was acquired principally by following the ongoing public debate on the internet.

Victimhood and nationalism

The concept of "victimhood nationalism" (e.g., Lim 2010) points to the combination of nationalism with victimization, when an "us" versus "them" narrative, creating categories of collective guilt versus collective innocence, is applied in public discourse (ibid., 1). As Jie-Hyun Lim has emphasized, victimhood nationalism, once inserted into the collective dichotomy of victimizers and victims, "becomes hereditary, in order to consolidate the national collective that binds generations together" (ibid., 138). The phenomena highlighted here have been identified, for example, against the background of recent European ethnic conflicts, especially while civil war was in progress in the states of former Yugoslavia during the 1990s (Jalušič 2004; Gödl 2007, etc.).

188   *Zuzana Panczová*

The image of the Slovak nation is also often constructed and symbolically portrayed in the role of victim. It incorporates a memory of real or fabricated national injustices stemming from the recent and distant past, which replicate the idea of the positive self-image of the innocent victim (us) threatened by the incessantly present enemy (them). The image of the nation as victimized is present, for example, in the text of the Slovak national anthem: "There is lightning over the Tatras, thunders loudly sound; let us stop them, brothers—in the end they will disappear; the Slovaks will revive. Slovakia is already rising, tearing off her shackles."); in anthemic religious songs sung during national holidays ("God, after many years of suffering you kindly returned its free home to the Slovak nation so that it can live there, having shaken off the yoke");[2] and in the choice of the national patron, Our Lady of the Seven Sorrows, the patron saint of sufferers. In 1927, Our Lady of the Seven Sorrows was chosen as patroness of Slovakia, in part thanks to the preceding initiative of the priest and politician Ferdinand Juriga (1874–1950). Juriga justified the selection of this national symbol, on the one hand, by the sufferings that the Slovak nation had endured, and on the other hand, by the attempt to separate the Slovak cult from the Hungarian Marian cult of the Great Lady of Hungary (Letz 2014, 66–67). A. Hlinka, a priest and the most conspicuous figure of Slovak nationalist conservatism at the beginning of the twentieth century, made the following statement in 1926 in defiance of the choice of this patroness:

> Our nation has never known joy; there is no other symbol we can decently have but Our Lady of the Seven Sorrows, with the seven-pointed sword in her heart and her son's dead body in her motherly embrace. . . . The fate of Slovakia was always hard, it was full of suffering and struggle.
>
> (ibid., 79)

Legends about national heroes frequently emphasize elements of victimization paralleling the image of the group enemy: Juraj Jánošík, an outlaw sentenced to death in the eighteenth century, was presented as a victim of social injustice; General M. R. Štefánik, a hero of World War I, who died in an air accident in 1919, is interpreted in nationalist conspiracy theories as a victim of Czechs/Freemasons (Panczová and Janeček 2015); Jozef Tiso, president of the wartime state, sentenced to death in 1945 for treason, is seen as a victim of a plot orchestrated by the Czechs and the Communists. There exists, then, a tradition of a collective narrative bound up with the motif of a small, ethnically and socially oppressed nation staunchly facing a mightier external enemy and its conspiratorial accomplices, who are traitors. These include the myth of a 1,000-year oppression of Slovaks in the Hungarian state and the national and religious oppression in interwar Czechoslovakia, whose downfall was marked in 1938 by the Munich Treaty, which was interpreted by Slovaks as treachery by the Western allies, especially Great Britain and France; also seen as a betrayal was the subsequent abandonment of postwar Czechoslovakia to the sphere of Soviet influence. As indicated earlier, it is not only in the national identification of Slovaks that the moment of self-victimization is present. A passive role in traumatizing periods of history,

The victims, the guilty, and "us" 189

experience of geopolitical marginalization—these, according to the political scientist A. Grišinas, are important factors in the creation of identity in the East Central European region:

> The region found itself at the margin but, most importantly, also at the center of the greatest civilizational developments. . . . Over the last century, it has experienced multiple crises, often finding itself at the center of the unfolding dramas, as a marginal and passive object instead of active subject. . . . This marginal character of the region along with violent and turbulent experiences during the world wars and Soviet occupation became the formative factor for regional political identities.
>
> (2017, 70–71)

Historical events create an evaluative framework in collective memory, which in discussions often provides supporting arguments for commentary on the present day. These narratives provide models of heroes, victims, enemies, and traitors.

In certain cases, the nationalist narrative interacts with elements of religious discourse: the myth of the martyr is created. Particular examples of this in Slovak conditions are the narratives about the career of the Catholic priest and Slovak president mentioned above, Jozef Tiso (1887–1947). Tiso became president of the wartime Slovak state in the spring of 1939 on the basis of an offer by Hitler (or an ultimatum, since the alternative was the division of Slovak territory between Hungary and Poland). Slovakia became a satellite of the Third Reich, ruled by an authoritarian regime, which liquidated pluralist parliamentary democracy. Under Tiso's leadership, this state deprived Jews of property and civil rights and later voluntarily requested Germany to transport them to the territory of the Reich. After a rebellion aimed against the ruling regime and German war policy, Slovakia was occupied by German troops, and the regime carried out harsh reprisals. At the end of the war, Tiso was found guilty of treason, war crimes, and crimes against humanity and was sentenced to death by hanging. During the proceedings he did not express any remorse even at reports of the casualties in the extermination camps, and at the place of execution, he declared: "I regard myself as a martyr of the Slovak nation and of the anti-Bolshevik political position" (Rašla and Žabkay 1990, 106).

Indeed, in certain quarters, Tiso's execution was seen as a martyrdom, and ultimately even some figures high up in the Slovak Catholic Church associated themselves with this idea. "I regard his death as martyrdom for the nation," the Košice-based bishop Alojz Tkáč declared in a sermon at a commemoration of Andrej Hlinka in Ružomberok. "He steered the state between Scylla and Charybdis. He was a president who worked for the nation, sacrificed himself for it, loved it. . . . He was an honorable and upstanding man. He was a president with a large degree of responsibility. . . . Therefore I am personally convinced of his innocence." According to the bishop, Tiso was obliged sometimes to choose the lesser evil, but he did so with reluctance and only because "he could not avoid it" (Jancura 2017).

190 *Zuzana Panczová*

An example of the internet diffusion of a positive image of Tiso as martyr is a web page titled *Jozef Tiso. Mučeník viery katolíckej a národa slovenského* [Jozef Tiso. A martyr for the Catholic faith and the Slovak nation] in the domain jozeftiso. org. The web page uses the rhetoric of religious discourse, with frequent images and tropes evoking the struggle with physical or metaphysical enemies. Among other things, it contains a "Prayer for the Beatification of the Martyr Jozef Tiso," which not only aims at exalting Tiso's merits but also targets ideological enemies who must be overcome: including persecutors of the nation and its faithful people, liberalism, relativism, and "the atheistic and inhuman new world order":

> Almighty and eternal God, You, who lit in the heart of Your martyr Jozef Tiso a great and inextinguishable love and fidelity to the faith and to his beloved people. You demanded of him that he offer the highest sacrifice by placing his own life on the altar of the Church and the Fatherland. Fervently we beseech You, through the intercession of our martyr Jozef give back to the Slovak nation our lost freedom and convert those who persecute our nation and its faithful people. We beseech You, convert also all those who blindly propagate and disseminate godless communism, liberalism and relativism. Open their eyes and lead them to the faith. Act so that the atheistic and inhuman new world order shall as soon as possible be overcome, so that you may soon triumph over it definitively.
>
> (Cagáň 2013)

Jozef Tiso is an example of a figure from national history who oscillates between two sharply defined poles: criminal and martyr. Jozef Tiso is regarded by a majority of the inhabitants of Slovakia as one of the most negative figures in Slovak history, according to public surveys. This was confirmed by the most recent survey, taken in 2018, when Tiso was among the top three most negative figures, along with Vladimír Mečiar (Slovak prime minister in the 1990s, often criticized for populism and autocratic tendencies) and Vasil Biľak (high-ranking representative of the Communist regime).[3] At the same time, because of his controversial character, he becomes a symbol of struggle for various nationalistically orientated groups protesting against the contemporary liberal or secularized system (for a more detailed analysis of Jozef Tiso's cult, see Hruboň 2017).

Victimhood among contemporary representatives of state power

Victimhood is also an important component in the rhetoric of contemporary populist politicians. In her study *How Populist Governments Rewrite Sovereignty and Why* E. K. Jenne characterizes populism as "a distinctive discursive style, based on a hard-line Manichean worldview that the people (or nation) are victimized by a set of elites (be it institutions, people or a class), and that a battle must be waged to free the people from the predations of elites" (2016, 5).[4] The essence of populism consists in emphatically distancing itself from the establishment, which

The victims, the guilty, and "us"   191

is presented as the aggressor. The populist politician strives for the image of a non-partisan man or woman of the people, who is just as much a victim of the system as ordinary people, but at the same time is ready to become their protector. In the recent history of Slovakia, probably the most conspicuous example of a nationalist politician using this self-stylization in the dual role of victim of external enemies and protector of the nation was Vladimír Mečiar (Učeň 2004). Equally, critics of the politics of the former premier Robert Fico find parallels between him and Mečiar, precisely because of his stylization as protector of the nation against the West and his tendency to deal with criticism of his government by turning attention to external enemies.

Last year Slovakia found itself in a charged atmosphere, occasioned by the murder of the journalist Ján Kuciak and his fiancée, Martina Kušnírová, which occurred on February 21, 2018. Ján Kuciak was an investigative journalist with the internet daily *Aktuality.sk*. He was intensively concerned with tax evasion and political corruption. His last, uncompleted article revealed possible links between the Italian Mafia and people close to the ruling party SMER-SD. Mária Trošková, assistant to the prime minister and state counselor, had previously been the lover of Antonin Vadala, an alleged member of the Calabrian Mafia ('Ndrangheta) living in eastern Slovakia, whom the murdered journalist had written about in an article in connection with suspected abuse of agricultural grants. The government was accused mainly of corruption related to EU subsidies, specifically the misuse of state power relating to agricultural business, manipulation of investigations into reported cases of corruption, attempts at censorship, and so on. It also came to light that six months before the murder, Ján Kuciak had been threatened by Marián Kočner, who was involved in several suspected cases of financial fraud and was well known as an influential friend of high-ranking politicians and a personal friend of the procurator general. Although Kuciak presented a formal accusation of threat with grave danger to the police, the latter did not find sufficient reason to begin criminal proceedings.[5]

Ján Kuciak and Martina Kušnírová were seen as victims of a corrupt government and provoked a series of mass anti-government protests, the largest since the fall of the Communist regime in 1989. Protests took place in dozens of Slovak towns and cities each Friday in March and April, with the number of participants in Bratislava alone between 20,000 and 65,000 people. Protesters called for the resignation of the minister of the interior, prime minister, and head of the police and for early elections. Some weeks after the journalist's murder, under public pressure, the prime minister and minister of the interior resigned, followed later by the head of police.

President Andrej Kiska declared in his speech of March 4, 2018 (approximately one week after the first large protest), that either a fundamental restructuring of the government was needed or early elections. In justification, he pointed to the social crisis resulting from people's distrust of the state:

> People's distrust of the state is enormous. There are many who do not trust the authorities involved in the criminal proceedings. Many feel this, based

on personal experience. And this kind of distrust is justified. The boundaries have been crossed, things have gone too far and there is no way back. We have reached a moment when we perceive the arrogance of power.

(Prezident.sk 2018)

Prime Minister Róbert Fico, facing accusations of political responsibility for the pair's murder, resolved to put the blame on President Kiska. He chose a conspiracy narrative incorporating the influential financier George Soros, which he presented at a press conference on March 5, 2018:

At this press conference I want to ask Mr. President a single question: September 20, 2017, New York, Fifth Avenue. My question is why the head of the Slovak Republic made a private visit to a person who has a very doubtful reputation and whose name is Mr. Soros. . . . The President's declaration seems to not have been written in Slovakia. . . . What happened after the murder of the journalist and his partner suggests that it is an attempt at total destabilization.

(HNOnline 2018a)

In response to Fico's press conference, the president's administration declared that the prime minister was seeking to use conspiracy theories to divert attention from his share of responsibility for this crisis. In addition to the opposition, his coalition partners from the Most-Híd party also protested against the prime minister's statements (Kern 2018). Indignation at the prime minister's statement was also expressed in the mainstream media and by pro-European domestic and foreign politicians but was met with enthusiasm among alternative, conspiracy-oriented information sources. One such example is the reaction by the daily *Hlavné správy*, which wrote on March 7, 2018, in an article titled "Is George Soros behind the current crisis in Slovakia? Fico is not necessarily a conspiracy theorist":

The crisis which arose in Slovakia after the murder of journalist Ján Kuciak raises a number of questions. Who is this situation good for? Who would benefit from Slovakia's collapse and the removal of the government that rejects immigrants, the LGBT agenda and different kinds of Istanbul conventions aimed at implementing the perverted gender ideology? It is no secret that the controversial billionaire George Soros uses his money to support different colour revolutions and changes of governments that he doesn't like.

(Gdovin 2018)

From the first days when information was published about the murder, suspicions that it was a deliberate anti-government provocation were voiced by certain media.

Many similar ideas were published in the magazine *Zem a vek*. For example, in the blog „Obetný baránok a vzrušujúca príčina" [The Sacrificial Lamb and the Disturbing Cause], the author drew a parallel with the rumor about the murder of

The victims, the guilty, and "us" 193

the student Martin Šmíd in November1989, which roused the indignation of the public and contributed to the anti-government demonstrations and the subsequent overthrow of state power in Communist Czechoslovakia:

> The aim of this intelligence operation, just as in November 1989, was to get people onto the streets and achieve at least structural, if not actually systemic, changes. While in the first case the death was an intelligence agency fiction, in the second case it was a painful reality which moved the feelings even of the most unpolitical person. That was why they chose an ambitious young journalist with his fiancée, so that it would shake up the land of Slovakia, where hitherto the NGOs had been vainly flogging a dead horse for the Open Society.
> (Grečo 2018)

On the very day when the first published information about the murder of the pair appeared, the Czech conspiratorial website *Aeronet* published an article alleging that there were indications of a coup in Slovakia being planned by Soros and broaching the possibility that the murder had been ordered by Soros himself:

> Two hours ago our editors received the information that the right hand of George Soros, Marcello Fabiani, has just arrived at Slovakia. He is one of the architects of the Orange Revolution in Ukraine in 2004. The mysterious Marcello appears always wherever governments and regimes fall. Our editors are working together to produce an exclusive article about this person who travels all over the world and helps to coordinate Facebook crowd events in the streets. The last time he did so was last month, when he organized demonstrations in support of Alexey Navalny in Moscow and St. Petersburg. . . . The Slovak public does want to do something about corruption, which is an enormous problem in Slovakia. However, the medicine against corruption is offered by the master of poison, George Soros, and the non-profit sector and the media in Slovakia, controlled through his funds. If you want to see what Slovakia would look like under the rule of the do-gooders' mainstream and non-governmental organisations, just have a look at Ukraine.
> (Aeronet 2018)

Fears of "maidanization" were enhanced by Prime Minister Fico himself, who warned about alleged plans to attack public buildings on the eve of the announced demonstration in Bratislava. He convoked the State Security Council and declared:

> We have accumulated a huge amount of information which indicates a high probability of attacks against public buildings. I cannot give details. We discussed all the information concerned with the Ministry of the Interior, the Police Force, the Slovak Intelligence Service, the Military Defense Intelligence Service, and also the Prison and Court Guards Service. . . . We have discovered the first piles of paving stones in front of a Government Office building, which were brought there at a time that we haven't identified yet.

194   *Zuzana Panczová*

> They are in the bushes, near the trees, and we're currently searching the camera recordings. We want to find out how they got there.
>
> (HNOnline 2018b)

The attempts to present the protests as a threat to state security was a sham. It turned out that the paving stones came from the reconstruction of a footpath; local residents had stowed them away in the bushes a few months before. Róbert Fico became the target of many jokes in the press and was likened to Viktor Orbán, the Hungarian prime minister, well known for his hatred of George Soros. It was evident that the prime minister's response to the situation, in addition to attempting to place himself and his government in the position of victims of planned attacks, also supported other patterns of conspiracist ideation: overriding suspicion and the idea that nothing is an accident.

The polarization of public debate is apparent in internet discussions also. Criticism of the prime minister and the government is offset, in the spirit of conspiracy theories, with references to manipulation by external forces. One section of those engaged in the discussion regarded Fico's statement as a scandal. Conversely, those who believed the conspiracy theories about Soros financing the subversion of society gave credit to the prime minister for his courage in naming the hidden enemy. For example, one of the contributors to discussion of the above-mentioned article in *Hlavné správy* was heartened by the fact that "thanks mainly to the internet, Slovak society has reached such a level of understanding that even a mainstream politician can afford to express such a 'conspiracy' opinion in public" (Cico Ciciak, March 21, 2018, comment on Gdovin 2018).

It is understandable that the conspiratorial interpretations of Kuciak's murder have not gone unnoticed among Slovak adherents of radical political ideologies. In Slovakia these have their principal platform in the opposition party *Kotleba – Ľudová strana Naše Slovensko* (Kotleba–People's Party Our Slovakia), which openly calls for a radical struggle against the system and also employs dissemination of conspiratorial interpretations of social activity. This party is seen by a section of society and the elites as neo-Fascist, given that its deputies and adherents attempt to spread a positive image of the wartime Slovak state, support the view of President Jozef Tiso as a martyr, and cast doubt on official interpretations of the Holocaust. The Bratislava offshoot of this party published the following declaration on its Facebook page: "Essentially this was the execution of an international criminal who had broken into personal data, emails, and personal bank accounts, which are protected by law. You must understand that Kuciak was only a patsy for the Sorosoid subversive foundations."[6] This standpoint, which attempts to assign to Kuciak's murder the attributes of an internal Mafia-style settling of accounts, where the victim is a co-perpetrator, may again be characterized as an attempt at the argumentative strategy of exchanging victim and perpetrator.

Together with the prime minister's statements and news published by alternative websites, there were allegedly authentic testimonies, of different kinds, about the preparation of a coup. These form another important element of the belief in a conspiracy against the nation. In this view, anti-government demonstrations are only the fulfillment of a carefully prepared malign plan to subvert traditional society. One of these texts is an alleged transcription of an unpublished interview with George Soros, in which he describes his strategy of subversion and disruption of traditional societies (see, for example, Mino6, March 13, 2018, comment on Jaško 2018). This text can be summarized as follows:

- Purpose: disruption and subsequent gain of control over society.
- Motivation: for Soros a kind of "entertainment" (reference to the perverted character of the enemy).
- Means: destruction of traditional in-group values (nation, church, "white race," God, traditional family).
- Executors: nongovernmental organizations, feminist associations, transsexual movements, left-wing groups, homosexual lobby, migrants.

At certain moments the style and form of the "leaked" interview recalls the *Protocols of the Elders of Zion*. Corresponding features are the plans for world government produced by Jewish conspirators (who in Machiavellian fashion dominate the media and the elites), in order to achieve their malignant plans aimed against the traditional Christian order.

The interpretation of anti-government protests as an anti-state conspiracy stage-managed from the West was also voiced at an attempted counter-meeting on March 21, 2018. Around 300 participants expressed their belief in the existence of a planned coup and called for the resignation of President Kiska. In their statement, they formulated the following demands:

1 Let us reject the preparation of an EU-waged war against Russia. We want global peace! Let us say no to NATO military bases in Slovakia.
2 Let us express our rejection of being forced to receive migrants under the Dublin Convention IV.
3 Let us reject the degrading designation of men and women as one of twenty sexes and the threat to families through violent removal of children from families, which is intended to be enforced through the Istanbul Convention!
4 Kiska and the non-governmental political organizations financed from abroad and almost the entire opposition . . . are disrupting the security, economic, and human (family, gender, social) elements of our country.
5 We reject the coup. We demand the resignation of President Kiska, and accountability against all of the culprits in the current situation that threatens our country. We, ordinary citizens, want a civil society that respects our interests (Aktuality.sk 2018).

Elements of victimization in the context of the murder of Ján Kuciak and his fiancée, reflected in anti-liberal religious discourse

The murder of Ján Kuciak and his fiancée was instrumentalized also in a theme that, at first glance, is unconnected: the struggle against liberalism in religious discourse. Let us remember that the Communist regime, which throughout its period

196 *Zuzana Panczová*

of power spread an ideology of militant atheism and had a marked influence on the history of the Christian churches in Slovakia. This brought in its wake new stories of aggressors (the representatives of Communist power) and their victims, often seen through the prism of martyrdom and dissent. However, a section of priests and laity (their numbers are difficult to quantify, due to the lack of relevant surveys) have replaced or compared the image of oppression of Christians under the atheistic Communist regime with the image of oppression of Christianity on the part of liberal democracy or "gender ideology" (on the theme of anti-gender movements in Europe, see further Kováts 2017). The struggle against "gender ideology" has radicalized the activity of pro-life activists abroad. For example, the German sociologist Gabriele Kuby, author of *The Global Sexual Revolution: The Destruction of Freedom in the Name of Freedom* (2015), conducted a lecture tour in Slovakia in 2013, which had a considerable response in Christian circles. She presented disquieting testimonies from families penalized for opposing sexual education in schools. The Christian daily newspaper *Postoj*, reporting on one of her lectures, described her as saying:

> According to G. Kuby, they are driving in the thin end of the wedge, which will lead eventually to this absurd penalization, supported by the legislature. Soft instruments are used at first. The laws will come at the end, when the public no longer notice their key formulations. In this manner, according to her, society is being massaged into accepting the separation of biological sex and social gender, and the "sexualization of children" even in nursery schools. She compared the trampling on basic human nature to the fascist and communist terror. "You in Slovakia have experience of anti-fascist and anti-communist resistance—and resistance is once again necessary," she declared. G. Kuby genuinely comes across as radical in places. She does not care that society is accustomed to regard certain theories as paranoid, and she speaks, for example, of a conspiracy by millionaires such as Rockefeller, Gates, and Soros, who finance the UN's campaigns; or the aim of the "movers and shakers" to depopulate the planet. . . . She praises the new Hungarian constitution for enacting rights to life from conception to natural death, and the reservation of marriage exclusively for a man and a woman; and also the vote by the Russian Duma for a law against anti-family activities in schools. Kuby faces what many avert their eyes from, and she places an issue on the table: the fact of how things are interpreted (by the media), and that what is absurd is not necessarily also incredible.
>
> (Rončáková 2013)

The struggle against "gender ideologies" may, in certain cases, be interpreted as a version of the accusations of imperialism, hence of influence by the negative operations of foreign forces (EU, UN, WHO) aiming to weaken nations and their traditions (Kováts 2017, 176). A common enemy is Western liberalism, which is identified with efforts to subvert traditional values by tolerance of abortions, the "perverted" activities of the LGBTI movement, allegedly

The victims, the guilty, and "us"   197

pornographic methods of sexual education of children, and alarmist reports about the forcible removal of children in the West for the purpose of their adoption by homosexual couples. Responding to growing pressure from Christian pro-life organizations in 2015, a statewide Referendum for the Family was held (Rybar and Sovcikova 2016).

An important issue that stirred up an anti-liberal narrative recently was the attempt at acceptance of the Istanbul Convention. Since it included the concept of gender, it was interpreted in conservative Christian media as a "Trojan horse" of the "gender ideologues," through which this concept would make its way into the Slovak legislative code to achieve legal status. One can trace the power of discursive exclusion in the struggle against allowing the gender concept not only into legislation but also into language. Its very use is interpreted as a threat to Christian doctrine, and the idea that this threat is camouflaged and furtively introduced by respected international institutions is expressed by the image of the "Trojan horse" (see, for example, Ocilková 2015). Again, one finds warnings voiced by Christian preachers, who declare that a time is coming when priests will be imprisoned for their opposition to homosexual marriages, when people will begin arbitrarily to change their sex, when children will be taken away from "normal" parents and given to be raised by homosexual couples, and when the Christian population will gradually be replaced by Muslims. One of the best-known campaigners against liberalism and "gender ideologies" in Slovakia is the Roman Catholic priest Marián Kuffa, who has acquired high moral credit among Christian believers by his care for homeless people and ex-prisoners in eastern Slovakia. His sermons are streamed on the internet through the Masses on Film initiative and have tens of thousands of followers. They are popular in part because of the colorful similes and examples that Kuffa, a successful public speaker, often uses. To discredit liberalism, for example, he uses a comparison that explains why liberalism is a greater danger to the faith than the violent propagation of atheism by the Communist regime:

> Communism is darkness, liberalism is fog. When you put the headlights on you can see in the darkness. In the fog, however, it is not enough to put the headlights on, you must also slow down, be more careful. They use half-truths. . . . Let's keep our religion, our culture, our morals. . . . Do we want bad things from the West? There are good things in the West too, but why do we want the bad ones? So many divorces, so many drugs, so many cases of euthanasia, so many suicides—is this what we want?
>
> (Misiefilmom 2018a)

In his sermons Kuffa calls gender equality "a sick idea" that is spreading like plague or cholera, and he blames it for the most varied perversities of our age— from sex changes and homosexual unions to polygamy, which the migrants from Muslim cultures bring with them (Sdzr 2018). Evoking the feeling of group threat by a conspiracy of the enemies of Christianity, Marián Kuffa has complemented this with a self-stylization in the role of (future) martyr and self-appointed prophet.

198 *Zuzana Panczová*

That is to say, in his sermons he predicts that someone will plan to kill or at least imprison him on account of his opinions:

> And so in Slovakia I can say: "Do you want to kill me? Go ahead! Do you want to lock me up? Here I am! I won't bow down, and I won't stop." Those people are nervous. And so I'm expecting they will do something base. Something vicious. What's in character for them. You'll see yourselves, it'll come to that. But if something should happen, I appeal to you, continue on your present course. Whether they'll succeed or not, I don't know. But I count upon it that they'll do something. . . . That's why I'm saying this beforehand.
> (Misiefilmom 2018b)

Again, in connection with the murder of Ján Kuciak and Martina Kušnírová, he warned that naive participants in the anti-government protests for a decent Slovakia were being misused by "genderists" and "feminists," via the NGOs that were involved:

> Let us look at the people who were in those protests . . . the spirit of Christ was not there . . . there were hate-filled slogans . . . they use us Christians as the ones who naively tear down the wall, and within those crowds, hidden, there are genderists . . . on the social networks I found LGBTI . . . feminists, genderists . . . and they were shouting hate-filled slogans. . . . Among those masses there were also people who wanted to resist evil, they were there genuinely. But there were also LGBTI, feminists . . . NGOs. . . . How are we to prevent that, so that they won't be there?
> (Sdzr 2018)

This speech evoked passionate responses in a charged public discussion. For the most part those responding acknowledged Kuffa's unquestionable moral credit on account of his work with the homeless; however, his position as a campaigner against liberalism and as a martyr was viewed controversially. Here is an extract from the discussion by supporters and opponents of M. Kuffa on the web page of the daily newspaper *SME*, relating to an article criticizing Kuffa's stance (Droppa 2018):

> They need to get rid of him. And so for the moment they just label him, so as to create negative associations with Fr. Kuffa in the minds of the people. He tells the truth to the people, the truth that the Church declares, and for the "Euro-lords" he doesn't fit into the project which they were given to fulfill. This sneering article disappoints me. I would say that the author does not realize that Fr. Kuffa sees farther than the majority of people.
> (jozefpucik77, March 19, 2018, comment on Droppa 2018)

> A fine contribution, excellent foundation for the arguments! I applaud, I am grateful. While I admire and acknowledge Fr. Kuffa for his social work, I am

The victims, the guilty, and "us" 199

ashamed at, and I deplore, the pride and wrong-headedness that he sometimes shows. In my village we have a similar priest. For him, beating the drums for the struggle against LBGTI and praising Kotleba's agenda is more important than love of his neighbor, Christ's first commandment. Alas, that too is an image of our Slovak Church! Fr. Kuffa is no exception. What would Fr. Antonio[7] say about that? . . . His personal story was even more powerful, but he didn't need to preach hate.

(local.sk, March 19, 2018, comment on Droppa 2018)

The case of the murder of Kuciak, his image as a victim of a corrupted system, which mobilized hundreds of thousands of people to a public protest, at the same time became a litmus test for a conflict of world outlooks or values that was ongoing on various levels of social discourse. The controversy over appropriation of the status of "victim" is a dispute that in reality tends to form barriers of group antagonism and is a striking symbol of the crisis of values in contemporary democracy.

Conclusion

The results of group victimization can be seen mainly in societies overcoming "intractable" conflicts that persist for many years and are marked by high losses of life. "Groups encode important experiences, especially extensive suffering, in their collective memory, which can maintain a sense of woundedness and past injustice through generations" (Bar-Tal et al. 2009, 8).

Society in Slovakia is in a different situation. People are not traumatized by personal experience of the violence of war. Nonetheless, they are exposed to a pressure that may be characterized as an information war, which polarizes society, in part by means of conspiratorial apocalyptic visions of the future. Each side in this conflict remains inaccessible to the arguments of the other side. Information is received with a high degree of selectivity. Emphasis is placed not only on differences of opinion but, above all, on the moral differences between adherents of the opposing camps. A process of creating group hero cults, based on victimization, produces a high level of emotional engagement in the group. Although the hero in the position of victim is actually passive (as compared to the warrior hero), he becomes a powerful embodiment of criticism of the opposing/hostile group. Equally, ideological elements are projected onto the image of group martyrs, making an effective instrument of solidarity and confirmation of the ideals of the group. This is further supported by the use of victimhood as part of the group national self-image. In the case of Slovak nationalism, we meet with strategies of the assertion of victimhood both in terms of symbolic national images and in official or unofficial cults of national heroes. It is probable that the presence of a powerful historically transmitted image of victimhood in collective memory, as a legacy of the nationalist sentiment of the last century, facilitates the legitimation of conspiratorial interpretations of contemporary social events.

200 *Zuzana Panczová*

Self-identification with the victims opens up the way to the perception of "the others" as aggressors, including via conspiracy theories. The latter are applied to the rhetoric of populist politicians as well as in anti-establishment radical secular and religious discourses, thus creating effective platforms for an intensification of social tension.

All this is connected with the role of conspiracy theories as an instrument of political struggle. In a situation where the real victim was a journalist and the governing power came under suspicion or was placed in the position of the responsible party, Prime Minister Róbert Fico attempted to use conspiracy theories to shift the government's status from the position of accused to that of victim. The prime minister targeted George Soros, in Central and Eastern Europe, the archetypal enemy (a powerful and amoral Maecenas who manipulates the economy, intellectuals, and the media). He was ably supported in this by the alternative media outlets of the numerous groups of opponents of "western liberalism." In his narrative, the government is a victim of a deliberate attack, which is in preparation for the destabilization of society. Here also we find confirmation of the strategy whereby "the acquisition of the status of victim becomes an institutionalized way of escaping guilt, shame or responsibility" (Bar-Tal et al. 2009, 18).

The above-mentioned processes are not specific to Slovakia. On the contrary, similar employment of the status of victimhood may be found in contemporary populist discourse and debates about the crisis of liberal democracy in various countries around the world. Hitherto, however, in the case of great powers like the USA, populism has often based itself on an attempt to return the country to the position of importance, which it was historically entitled to. In the case of Slovakia, there is a tendency to replicate the image of a politically unimportant, passive player on the field of European politics.

Using the example of the political crisis evoked by the murders of Ján Kuciak and Martina Kušnírová, one can trace the process of the shifting of victimhood on the individual level to a collective dimension—martyrdom for collectively shared values. The image of the victim/martyr is effectively used in public ideological polemics by representatives of various forms of social power (politicians, church, media). In these polemics, the significance of victimization has been principally in its use to discredit the competing/hostile group via conspiracy theories. Furthermore, events in Slovakia have confirmed van Prooijen's observation: "The more strongly people identify with a particular group, the more concerned they are when members of that group are victimized and the less accepting they are of other, competing groups" (van Prooijen 2018). One may also assume that the atmosphere of threat reciprocally heightens feelings of loyalty to one's own group and redoubles the willingness of people to commit themselves actively and publicly in the struggle against "the enemy."

Acknowledgments

This chapter is supported by the Slovak Scientific Grant Agency VEGA no. 2/0107/19 *Folklore, folkloristics and ideology*. Translation from Slovak and proofreading by John Minahane.

Notes

1 This process has a certain gradual progression, with the individual stages developing from the act of aggression, through awareness of injury by the victim and subjective identification with the status of the victim, to acknowledgment of this status by the surroundings (Bar-Tal et al. 2009, 5–6).
2 Pavkovic and Kelem emphasize this point: "Nations singing anthems possess more than rulers, landscapes and homelands, they also have their preferred histories (or rather historical myths) that not only uniquely identify the singing nation but sometimes define it" (Pavkovic and Kelem 2015, 31–32). Victimhood as a component of anthemic lyrics is derived from the poetics of romantic sentiment. The latter drew a contrast between the nation's glorious past and its deplorable present-day suffering. We find this, for example, in the Hungarian anthem, which was composed in the same period as its Slovak equivalent.
3 This survey was carried out by the Institute of Sociology in the Slovak Academy of Sciences in collaboration with the Institute for Public Affairs and the Centre for Research of Public Opinion and the Institute of Sociology in the Czech Academy of Sciences. The collection of data was performed in the first half of March 2018. In Slovakia there were 1,012 respondents, aged 18 and upward (SME 2018).
4 A specific example of contemporary populism that uses the moment of victimization may be found in the rhetoric of Donald Trump (Johnson 2017; Szilágyi 2017).
5 While this paper was being written, Marián Kočner was officially accused of commissioning this murder. Some months previously, other people were accused of performing and facilitating the murder. The presumption of their connection with the Calabrian Mafia was not borne out (The Slovak Spectator 2019).
6 Since the party is attempting to cleanse its public image from accusations of disseminating neo-Fascism, the leading party member and parliamentary deputy Milan Uhrík, responding to the position published here, declared that the murder could not be excused. He said that the Facebook statement was not the official stance of the party or of its Bratislava organization. The statement was later deleted by the administrator of the Facebook page. More about this case at, for example, Kyseľ 2018.
7 Anton Srholec—a priest likewise well known for self-sacrificing work with people on the margins of society, author's comment.

Bibliography

Aeronet. 2018. "Neziskový sektor už naplánoval demonstrace proti vládě Roberta Fica nejen na Slovensku, ale i v celé Evropě!" [The Nonprofit Sector has Already Planned Demonstrations against Robert Fico's Government, not only in Slovakia but also throughout Europe!]. *Aeronet,* February 28, 2018. https://aeronet.cz/news/exkluzivne-slovensky-novinar-a-jeho-pritelkyne-se-nijak-nebranili-vraha-zrejme-pustili-primo-do-domu-teorie-o-italske-mafii-se-hrouti-neziskovy-sektor-uz-naplano val-demonstrace-proti-vlade/.
Aktuality.sk. 2018. "Pred prezidentským palácom bol protest proti 'štátnemu prevratu'" [There was a Protest against the "coup d'état" in Front of the Presidential Palace]. *Aktuality.sk,* March 21, 2018. www.aktuality.sk/clanok/574774/pred-prezidentskym-palacom-bol-protest-proti-statnemu-prevratu/.
Bar-Tal, Daniel, Lily Chernyak-Hai, Noa Schori, and Ayelet Gundar. 2009. "A Sense of Self-perceived Collective Victimhood in Intractable Conflicts." *International Review of the Red Cross* 91 (874): 229–54.
Cagáň, Igor. 2013. "Modlitbová výzva pre všetkých katolíkov a slovenské katolícke farnosti 2013" [A Call to Prayer for all Catholics and Slovak Catholic Parishes]. *Jozeftiso.sk,*

202   *Zuzana Panczová*

March 14, 2013. http://jozeftiso.sk/jt/ludovy-kultus/modlitby/23-vyzva-vsetkym-katolikom-a-slovenskym-katolickym-farnostiam.

Droppa, Martin. 2018. "Zvláštny prípad Marián Kuffa" [The Strange Case of Marián Kuffa] (blog). *SME.sk*, published March 18, 2018. Accessed April 2, 2018. https://martindroppa.blog.sme.sk/c/479635/zvlastny-pripad-marian-kuffa.html.

Fabricius Miroslav, and Katarína Hradská, eds. 2007. *Jozef Tiso – Prejavy a články* (1938–1944) [Jozef Tiso – Speeches and Articles (1938–1944)]. Bratislava: AEPress.

Gdovin, Samuel. 2018. "Stojí George Soros za súčasnou krízou na Slovensku? Fico vôbec nemusí byť konšpirátor" [Is George Soros behind the Current Crisis in Slovakia? Fico is not Necessarily a Conspiracy Theorist.] *Hlavné správy*, March 7, 2018. www.hlavne spravy.sk/stoji-george-soros-za-sucasnou-krizou-na-slovensku-fico-vobec-nemusi-byt-konspirator/1335068.

Gödl, Doris. 2007. "Challenging the Past: Serbian and Croatian Aggressor-Victim Narratives." *International Journal of Sociology* 37 (1): 43–57.

Grečo, Peter. 2018. "Obetný baránok a vzrušujúca príčina" [Scapegoat and Instigating Cause]. *Zem a vek*, March 24, 2018. https://zemavek.sk/obetny-baranok-a-vzrusujuca-pricina/.

Grišinas, Arvydas. 2017. "Central Marginality: Minorities, Images, and Victimhood in Central-Eastern Europe." *Nationalism and Ethnic Politics* 23 (1): 66–80.

HNOnline. 2018a. "Fico tvrdí, že Kiska bol za Sorosom bez zástupcu ministerstva. Nie je to pravda, odkazuje prezident" [Fico Claims that Kiska visited Soros without a Representative of the Ministry. That is not True, the President Declares]. *HNOnline*, March 5, 2018. https://slovensko.hnonline.sk/1705654-fico-tvrdi-ze-kiska-bol-za-sorosom-bez-zastupcu-ministerstva-nie-je-to-pravda-odkazuje-prezident.

———. 2018b. "Kocky, ktoré dnes vyplašili Fica, nechal pred Úradom vlády v lete reštaurátor" [The Paving Stones that Frightened Fico Today were Left in Front of Government Buildings by Repair Workers during the Summer]. *HNOnline*, March 9, 2018. https://slovensko.hnonline.sk/1707702-kocky-ktore-dnes-vyplasili-fica-nechal-pred-uradom-vlady-v-lete-restaurator.

Hruboň, Anton. 2017. "Budovanie kultu Jozefa Tisa" [Building up the Cult of Jozef Tiso]. *Kultúrne dejiny/Cultural History* 8 (2): 213–39.

Jalušič, Vlasta. 2004. "Gender and Victimization of the Nation as Pre- and Post-war Identity Discourse." In *The Violent Dissolution of Yugoslavia Causes, Dynamics and Effects*, edited by Miroslav Hadžić, 145–65. Belgrade: Osce Mission to SaM.

Jancura, Vladimír. 2017. "Tiso fašista a Tiso antifašista" [Tiso Fascist and Tiso Antifascist]. *Pravda.sk*, March 13, 2017. https://zurnal.pravda.sk/neznama-historia/clanok/422481-tiso-fasista-a-tiso-antifasista/.

Jaško, Ľubomír. 2018. "Komentár Ľubomíra Jaška: V prípade sklerózy budú predčasné voľby fiaskom" [Ľubomír Jaško's Commentary: Since it's a Case of Sclerosis, the Early Elections will be a Fiasco]. *Aktuality.sk*, March 13, 2018. www.aktuality.sk/clanok/572184/komentar-lubomira-jaska-v-pripade-sklerozy-budu-predcasne-volby-fiaskom/.

Jenne, Erin K. 2016. "How Populist Governments Rewrite Sovereignty and Why." *Seminar at Joint PolBeRG and Con-Sec Seminar on Populism and Automated Content Analysis*. Last modified April 29, 2016. www.ceu.edu/sites/default/files/attachment/event/15587/erinjennepolberg-con-sec-2016.pdf.

Johnson, Paul E. 2017. "The Art of Masculine Victimhood: Donald Trump's Demagoguery." *Women's Studies in Communication* 40 (3): 229–50.

Kelly, Casey R. 2020. "Donald J. Trump and the Rhetoric of Ressentiment." *Quarterly Journal of Speech* 106 (1): 2–24. https://doi.org/10.1080/00335630.2019.1698756.

Kern, Miro. 2018. "Fico vidí za tlakom na Kaliňáka pokus o prevrat a Sorosa" [Fico Sees an Attempted Coup d'état and Soros behind the Pressure on Kaliňák]. *DenníkN.sk*, March 5, 2018. https://dennikn.sk/1050737/fico-vidi-za-tlakom-na-kalinaka-pokus-o-prevrat-a-sorosa/.

Kováts, Eszter. 2017. "The Emergence of Powerful Anti-Gender Movements in Europe and the Crisis of Liberal Democracy." In *Gender and Far Right Politics in Europe*, edited by Michaela Köttig, Renate Bitzan, and Andrea Petö, 175–89. Basingstoke: Palgrave Macmillan.

Kuby, Gabriele. 2017. *The Global Sexual Revolution: The Destruction of Freedom in the Name of Freedom*. Brooklyn: LifeSite/Angelico Press.

Kyseľ, Tomáš. 2018. "Bratislavská ĽSNS o vražde Jána Kuciaka: V podstate popravili zločinca" [Bratislava People's Party Our Slovakia about the murder of Ján Kuciak: Essentially they executed a criminal]. *Aktuality.sk*, March 28, 2018. www.aktuality.sk/clanok/568336/bratislavska-lsns-o-vrazde-jana-kuciaka-v-podstate-popravili-zlocinca/.

Letz, Róbert. 2014. *Sedembolestná Panna Mária v slovenských dejinách* [Our Lady of the Seven Sorrows in Slovak History]. Bratislava: Post Scriptum.

Lewandowsky, Stephan, Elisabeth A. Lloyd, and Scott Brophy. 2018. "When THUNCing Trumps Thinking: What Distant Alternative Worlds Can Tell Us About the Real World." *Argumenta* 3 (2): 217–31.

Lim, Jie-Hyun. 2010. "Victimhood Nationalism and History Reconciliation in East Asia." *History Compass* 8 (1): 1–10.

Misiefilmom. 2018a. "O. Kuffa: Liberalizmus je hmla . . . horšia ako tma" [Fr. Kuffa: Liberalism is Fog . . . Worse than Darkness]. *YouTube*, March 14, 2018. Accessed March 20, 2018. Video 5:15. www.youtube.com/watch?v=BrjIskJtiwg.

———. 2018b. "Marian Kuffa – časť 1" [Marian Kuffa – Part 1]. *YouTube*, December 12, 2018. Accessed December 15, 2018. Video 29:19. www.youtube.com/watch?v=fF5vpD9l4fQ&feature=youtu.be.

Ocilková, Renáta. 2015. "Istanbulský dohovor ako trójsky kôň?" [The Istanbul Convention as a Trojan Horse]. *Konzervatívny denník Postoj*, July 3, 2015. https://blog.postoj.sk/7046/istanbulsky-dohovor-ako-trojsky-kon.

Panczová, Zuzana. 2017. "The Image of the West in Conspiracy Theories in Slovakia and Its Historical Context." *Folklore. Electronic Journal of Folklore* 69: 49–68.

Panczová, Zuzana, and Petr Janeček. 2015. "Théories du complote et rumeurs en Slovaque et en Tchéque" [Conspiracy Theories and Rumoursin Slovakia and the Czech Republic]. *Diogène. Les théories du complot aujourd'hui* 249–50: 150–67.

Pavkovic, Alexandar, and Kelem, Christopher. 2015. *Anthems and the Making of Nation States: Identity and Nationalism in the Balkans*. London: Bloomsbury Publishing.

Prezident.sk. 2018. "Prezident Kiska: Vidím dve možnosti, rekonštrukciu vlády alebo nové voľby" [President Kiska: I See Two Options, Reconstruction of the Government or New Elections]. Published March 4, 2018. Accessed March 8, 2018. www.prezident.sk/article/prezident-kiska-vidim-dve-moznosti-rekonstrukciu-vlady-alebo-nove-volby/.

Rašla, Anton and Ernest Žabkay. 1990. *Proces s dr. J. Tisom* [The Trial of Dr. Jozef Tiso]. Bratislava: Tatrapress.

Rončáková, Terézia. 2013. "Aktuálne: Gabriele Kuby: Po fašizme a komunizme nastupuje gender" [Actual: Gabriele Kuby: Gender Follows After Fascism and Communism]. *Konzervatívny denník Postoj*, published March 13, 2013. www.postoj.sk/3401/aktualne-gabriele-kuby-po-fasizme-a-komunizme-nastupuje-gender.

Rybar, Marek and Anna Sovcikova. 2016. "The 2015 Referendum in Slovakia." *East European Quarterly* 44 (1–2): 79–88.

Sdzr. 2018. "O. Kuffa: prednáška k udalostiam posledných dní" [Fr. Kuffa: A Lecture on the Events of Recent Days]. *YouTube*, March 10, 2018. Accessed March 14, 2018. Video 29:14. www.youtube.com/watch?v=a23GxSY9Jp4.

SME. 2018. "Z novodobých dejín vyzdvihujú Slováci najviac SNP" [In Modern History Slovaks Are Proud of the Slovak National Uprising]. *SME*.sk, June 11, 2018. Accessed June 12, 2018. https://domov.sme.sk/c/20847038/z-novodobych-dejin-vyzdvihuju-slovaci-najviac-snp-ukazal-prieskum.html.

Szilágyi, A. 2017. "A Linguist Explains How Trump Is Using the Language of Victimhood to Position Himself As America's Savior." *Quartz*, February 2, 2017. https://qz.com/900800/donald-trumps-language-use-is-using-the-verbiage-of-victimhood-to-position-himself-as-americas-savior/.

The Slovak Spectator. 2019. "Marian Kočner has been Charged in the Case of Kuciak's Murder." *The Slovak Spectator*, March 14, 2019. https://spectator.sme.sk/c/22074905/kuciak-kusnirova-murder-kocner-charges.html.

Učeň, Peter. 2004. "Centrist Populism as a New Competitive and Mobilization Strategy in Slovak Politics." In *Party Government in Slovakia: Experience and Perspectives*, edited by Oľga Gyárfášová and Grigorij Mesežnikov, 45–73. Bratislava: Institute for Public Affairs.

van Prooijen, Jan-Willem. 2018. *The Psychology of Conspiracy Theories* [The Psychology of Everything]. London and New York: Taylor and Francis. Kindle edition.

Part IV

Eastern Europe goes global

Conspiracy theories and the rise
of populism

10 Soros conspiracy theories and the rise of populism in post-socialist Hungary and Romania

Corneliu Pintilescu and Attila Kustán Magyari

Introduction

In the context of the European migrant crisis, Hungary's prime minister Viktor Orbán argued on October 30, 2015, in one of his weekly radio interviews, that the migrants flooding Hungary were assisted by a network of NGO activists. In his view, these activists were supporting "anything and everything that could or will weaken nation states" and undermining what he called "the established European way of life" (Orbán 2015).[1] According to Orbán, "the most iconic" figure of this network was the Hungarian born Jewish-American billionaire George Soros (ibid.). This interview illustrates how the migration issue and anti-Soros discourse became entangled in Hungary, to emerge as the dominant conspiratorial narrative within the Hungarian public sphere after 2015. The anti-Soros campaign reached a high point in the months leading up to the national consultation on the so-called Soros Plan in October 2017, when Orbán's party Fidesz portrayed Soros as the "puppet master" behind a broad conspiracy to bring millions of Muslim migrants to Europe.

In neighboring Romania, in January 2017, the Sorin Grindeanu Cabinet, dominated by the Social-Democratic Party (PSD), planned to issue an emergency ordinance to amend the country's criminal code with a view to decriminalizing official misconduct. Despite public outrage, Government Emergency Ordinance no. 13 was ultimately issued on the eve of February 1, 2017. Over the following weeks, in several major cities across the country, hundreds of thousands of Romanians took to the streets in protest against the ordinance, the government, and corruption. Consequently, the cabinet was forced to back down and withdraw the ordinance. Another consequence was that the leadership of the ruling PSD, tightly controlled by its chairman Liviu Dragnea, started to disseminate through the government-friendly media a Soros-related conspiracy theory that to some extent was eerily similar to Orbán's pre-2015 conspiratorial narratives. Between 2017 and 2018, in several interviews published in leading Romanian newspapers and on talk shows, Dragnea suggested that the protests had been the result of a conspiracy involving Soros.

These two snapshots are illustrative of a phenomenon involving various forms of conspiratorial tropes featuring George Soros, which spread globally from

208 *Corneliu Pintilescu et al.*

Eastern Europe to the USA and to the Middle East after 2013. While Trump's allegations against Soros brought these conspiratorial narratives into the US mainstream following the 2016 elections, Israeli Prime Minister Benjamin Netanyahu and Turkish President Recep Tayyip Erdoğan turned anti-Soros conspiracy theories into effective weapons in their conflict with local civil societies after 2017.

Despite their worldwide spread, however, Soros-related conspiracy theories found a particularly fertile ground in many Eastern European countries. This is where, as early as the 1990s, the first such conspiracy theories were developed as a reaction of nationalist circles to the values advocated by Soros's foundations. However, most contemporary versions of Soros-related conspiracy theories were put forward in Eastern Europe after 2013 and spread from one country of the region to another. Essentially, they portray Soros as the main financial backer of protests, NGOs, and media outlets with a view to promoting a hidden agenda. Within the East European far-right circles of the early 1990s, these allegations became part of the New World Order–inspired conspiracy theory in which Soros was the epitome of evil global financial interests intent on undermining national sovereignty by interfering with national economies and politics. Among other examples, this was the case of the so-called Stop Operation Soros campaign in North Macedonia, initiated in January 2017 (Marusic 2017); the statement made by Slovak prime minister Robert Fico in March 2018, in which he blamed Soros for conspiring to destabilize his country (Gabrizova 2018); and the staunch opposition of the Polish ruling party Law and Justice (PiS) to the purchase of one of the main Polish Radio stations by a media trust and a fund backed by Soros in 2019 (Harper 2019).

According to Jacek Kucharczyk, a Polish sociologist and head of the Institute of Public Affairs in Warsaw, the protests and Vladimir Putin's repressive policy toward NGOs that followed the 2012 presidential elections in Russia were a significant turn in the Eastern European landscape of conspiracy theories (VOA 2017). In 2014, the Euromaidan movement in Ukraine prompted Putin to tighten his repressive policies toward Russian civil society, and Soros became part of the allegations that NGOs were an instrument of foreign powers aiming to undermine national security. The Soros-related conspiracy theories disseminated by the state-controlled mass media in Putin's Russia and Orbán's Hungary are key elements in the legitimization of abusive measures against civil society, as they were introduced by regimes that perceived protests as a main threat. These conspiracy theories have been widely disseminated in Eastern Europe via the Russian government–funded media outlets *Sputnik* and *Russia Today*. For instance, *Sputnik Romania* has an editorial section titled "This is who Soros is," which disseminates a mixture of local and imported conspiratorial narratives (Sputnik 2019). One main narrative strand in this section is that various protest movements, including the colored revolutions in Ukraine (2004) and Georgia (2009), were financed by Soros, who aims to destabilize the world (Sputnik 2016).

However, Russia's contribution to the spread of anti-Soros conspiracy theories in East-Central Europe should not be overestimated. The substantial financial support that Soros provided to civil society in Eastern Europe made him a convenient

Soros conspiracy theories 209

scapegoat for governments confronted with mass protests against their human rights abuses and corruption. After 2013, from Hungary to the USA, Soros became a highly useful archenemy, and the related conspiracy theories work as a key element in the articulation of populist discourses (The Associated Press 2017) in the context of what Rogers Brubaker calls "an extraordinary pan-European and trans-Atlantic populist moment" (2019, 27). Such conspiracy theories would not have become so influential without their extraordinary use value in constructing a variety of populist discourses.

From an analysis of various forms of Soros-related conspiracist narratives, it is obvious that they share similar tropes that are nonetheless adjusted to the different national contexts. These tropes were transferred and reshaped by both mainstream and far-right political circles and mass media that adopted populist discursive strategies. The electoral successes of politicians like Donald Trump and Viktor Orbán fueled this trend. Starting from this premise, this chapter aims to analyze the anti-Soros conspiracist narratives disseminated by both the Hungarian and Romanian governments and their friendly mass media after 2013, with a focus on how these narratives have been employed in articulating populist discourses and delegitimizing the activity of civil society. Thus, we attempt to answer the following questions: (1) When did the first Soros-related conspiracy theories emerge in both countries, and how have these conspiratorial narratives evolved? (2) What is the role of these conspiracist narratives in articulating the populist discourse during the 2010s? (3) What are the similarities and specificities of Soros-related conspiracy narratives in Hungary and Romania, and how can these features be explained? (4) Did transnational transfers of conspiratorial narratives actually take place? (5) If yes, what tropes have been transferred and how?

The reasons behind choosing these two cases is that they are appropriate for testing several hypotheses on the relationship between populism and conspiracy theories in Eastern Europe and beyond. Until 2015, the Soros-related conspiracist narratives in these two countries were very similar. Since then, however, their evolution has diverged, as they have been expressed and received differently. Although both Hungary and Romania share the use of negative electoral campaign strategies imported with the help of foreign political consultants in the 2000s and 2010s (in which Soros conspiracy theories play a key role), they also illustrate different patterns with regard to the emergence and development of populist discourses and their impact.

We also believe that by focusing on Orbán's and Dragnea's conspiracist narratives about Soros (within the broader context of conspiracy culture in the two countries), we can provide some answers as to how conspiratorial tropes and their use are imported and adjusted to various national audiences. Thus, the analysis will mainly deal with a corpus of official speeches given by the two leaders and their close collaborators as well as with several of their TV/radio interventions. From 2013 to 2019, these were all instrumental in disseminating anti-Soros conspiracy theories. Finally, we shall approach comparatively current conspiracy theories by looking back at similar conspiracist narratives rampant in the 1990s and early 2000s.

210 *Corneliu Pintilescu et al.*

Of these two cases, the Hungarian version of Soros conspiracy theories has received much more attention from both the Western press and academia. With the exception of Robert Swanson (2018), scholars such as Emilia Palonen (2018), Péter Krekó and Zsolt Enyedi (Krekó 2018; Krekó and Enyedi 2018), and Ivan Kalmar, Christopher Stevens, and Nich Worby (2018) focus on Hungary, especially on how the anti-Soros conspiracist narratives have been manipulated as a key component of the "Orbán laboratory of illiberalism" (Krekó and Enyedi 2018). Among the studies on Romania, those authored by George Voicu (2000) and by Onoriu Colăcel and Corneliu Pintilescu (2017) deal mainly with conspiracy culture in post-socialist Romania and its historical background.

This paper draws on Barkun's typology that divides conspiracy theories into "event conspiracies," "systemic conspiracies," and "superconspiracies" (2003, 6). To explain the relationship between conspiracy theories and populism, the analysis will resort to studies pertaining to what Brubaker calls the "discursive and stylistic turn in the study of populism" (2019, 29). Among these, studies authored by Ernesto Laclau (1977, 2005), Francisco Panizza (2005), Ruth Wodak (2015), Emilia Palonen (2018), and Rogers Brubaker (2019) provide the conceptual background of this research. Laclau argues that populism is "a particular *mode of articulation* of whatever social, political or ideological contents" (2005, 34). Panizza, in his attempt to develop Laclau's contribution on populism, describes it as "an anti-status quo discourse that simplifies the political space by symbolically dividing society between 'the people' (as the 'underdogs') and its 'other'" (Panizza 2005, 3). According to this approach, "the people" and "the other" are constructed by relations of antagonism (ibid., 3). In his view, both "the people as signifier" and "its content"—namely, "the people as signified"—are drawn as a reverse mirror image by constructing "the enemies of the people" (ibid., 3). By drawing on these contributions, we understand populism as a "discursive strategy" that constructs political identities by using antagonisms (the people vs. financial elites/the EU/migrants) and conspiracy theories as highly useful components of various populist discourses. According to Ruth Wodak, "the discursive strategies of 'victim-perpetrator reversal,' 'scapegoating' and the 'construction of conspiracy theories'" are among the main tools of the "right-wing populist rhetoric" (2015, 4).

The forgotten past: populism and Soros-related conspiracy theories in the 1990s and early 2000s

In order to understand the rise of populist discourse and its relation to conspiracy theories in Hungary and Romania, an insight into how these countries experienced Socialism and the post-socialist transition is necessary. While Hungary went through a smooth and quick transition from János Kádár's soft dictatorship to liberal democracy from the very late 1980s until the early 1990s, Romania experienced the violent fall of Nicolae Ceaușescu's regime in December 1989 and a tumultuous democratization process in the early 1990s. In Hungary, following the Polish model, Communist leaders agreed to negotiate with the opposition a gradual transition to democracy during the so-called Round Table Talks

Soros conspiracy theories 211

(Ripp 2002, 5–6). In Romania, however, the Ceauşescu regime kept an iron grip on the country, suppressing all forms of opposition, thus making a peaceful transition to democracy virtually impossible.

The different patterns of post-socialist transition can be partially explained by the distinct types of State Socialism that emerged in the two countries in the 1970s and 1980s. While Ceauşescu's Romania experienced a return to Stalinist practices in the 1970s, Hungary was labeled during the Kádár era as "the happiest barrack in the camp" (Kornai 2000, 133). This label mirrored the regime's reduced use of coercive measures, tolerance of a degree of intellectual freedom, and introduction of market-orientated economic reforms in the late 1980s. As opposed to this reformist trend in neighboring Hungary, the Ceauşescu regime became increasingly coercive, constantly rejecting any economic reforms and resorting to nationalism as a main legitimizing tool after the short period of liberalization from the late 1960s to the early 1970s (Petrescu 2009). Finally, Ceauşescu's cult of personality and despotic rule epitomized his regime's anachronism in the Eastern Bloc of the late 1980s.

After 1989, while Hungary was viewed alongside Poland as a "trendsetter" in the transition to liberal democracy and a market economy (Ágh 2016, 16), Romania's transition was slower and more turbulent. However, both countries experienced the profound social effects of the gradual dismantling of their respective state-controlled economies, especially a rise in unemployment and high social disparities. The social and economic effects of transition fueled the rise of extremist political parties that resorted to populist discourses as "fantasies of salvation" (Tismăneanu 1998). In Romania, these parties (namely, The Greater Romania Party, PRM, and the Romanian National Unity Party, PUNR) gained significant ground in the 1992, 1996, and 2000 general elections. Following Romania's integration into the EU in 2007, however, they lost much of their popular support and ultimately failed to win seats in parliament in the 2008 general elections.

The dramatic political, economic, and social changes and the legacy of former dictatorships, and especially of the secret police, created a fertile ground for the dissemination of conspiracy theories and shaped an audience eager to believe them. As Matthew Dentith argues in his chapter in this edited volume, it is historical experience that made these conspiracy theories appear believable and rational to many people in Eastern Europe. The legacy of the former secret police institutions and their files created an atmosphere of suspicion and distrust in post-socialist Eastern Europe. In the meantime, the fall of the Eastern European dictatorships allowed a latent and repressed former conspiracy culture to resurface. In Romania, most prominent among the conspiracy theories that resurfaced post-1989 were antisemitic ones (the Jewish-Bolshevik conspiracy and that of Jews controlling world finance—that is, the IMF and the World Bank) and those pertaining to Freemasons (Voicu 2000). The afterlife of the 1989 Romanian revolution, as the landmark event of post-socialist Romania, is the focus of a broad variety of conspiracy theories presenting it as the result of a conspiracy of the great powers and of foreign and domestic secret services (Roth 2016).

212   *Corneliu Pintilescu et al.*

Although the Western audience has been struck by the recent emergence of anti-Soros conspiracy theories in the US mainstream media, these conspiratorial tropes are not a novelty within the conspiracy culture of certain Eastern European countries. In the 1990s, Soros became the target of a wide range of allegations mainly emanating from extremist political circles in Hungary and Romania. In their narratives, Soros was portrayed as an agent of globalization and corrosive force acting against national interests and values (Colăcel and Pintilescu 2017, 35). Thus, the Soros-related conspiracy theories developed in the 1990s are closely connected to that part of the East European conspiracy culture that portrays Jews as the epitome of global financial capitalism (Michlic 2006, 263).

Soros's strong involvement in the post-socialist transition provided his enemies, eager to portray him as the puppet master behind various conspiracies, with plenty of ammunition. His financial support played a key role in the emergence of civil societies, in the democratization process, in the protection of minority rights, and in the promotion of liberal values in post-socialist countries—in other words, in the advancement of all the values that the far-right despised. Indeed, over the last three decades, Soros has spent $12 billion on supporting democratization and social causes in various parts of the world, with Eastern Europe being one of the main beneficiaries. For example, Hungary alone has received more than $400 million since the late 1980s (OSF 2019). In 1991, Soros founded the Central European University (CEU) in Budapest, an academic institution that enabled Eastern European scholars to connect with Western academic life (VOA 2017). The main vehicle for his support of civil society was the Open Society Foundations (OSF), a network of foundations that started its activity in Eastern European countries in the 1980s and early 1990s.

Born in 1930 in Hungary, from where he fled to the West in 1947, George Soros is a Holocaust survivor. His personal experience of Nazism marked his worldview and served as a motivation for the substantial financial support that he later offered to civil societies (VOA 2017). In this respect, Soros's activity is underpinned by Karl Popper's concept of "open society" and its intellectual tradition defined in opposition to the "closed societies" and "totalitarian movements" that caused many of the tragedies that occurred in the twentieth century (2012, 161–69).

Although they flourished in the 1990s, the origins of the conspiratorial narratives about Soros can be traced to before 1989. In Hungary, where the OSF launched its operations in 1984, János Kádár, who ruled Hungary from 1956 to 1988, viewed Soros as an enemy of his regime due to the latter's support for the democratic opposition (Hamvay 2017). However, rather than repressing the OSF's activity, Kádár preferred to legalize it in order to better handle it and avoid pushing it underground. Ironically, Viktor Orbán, at that time co-founder of an opposition party, was one of those who benefited from the grants offered by Soros to study at Pembroke College in Oxford in the late 1980s.

During the 1990s, Soros-related conspiracy theories emerged both in the mainstream rightist media (such as *Magyar Fórum*) and in far-right newspapers, such as *Riadó* (Alert). At that time, besides Hungarian far-right subcultures, the nationalist wing within the Hungarian Democratic Forum (*Magyar Demokrata Fórum*,

Soros conspiracy theories 213

MDF) represented one of the main disseminators of conspiratorial narratives about Soros through its voice in the media: the newspaper *Magyar Demokrata*. For example, in 1994, István Csurka, the Hungarian nationalist politician and intellectual who led the nationalist wing of the MDF, stated that of all countries, Hungary was the most "infected" by Soros (Csurka 1994). Rumors were spread about the alleged secret aims behind Soros's support for local civil society. According to the antisemitic remarks made by Gyula Zacsek, one of the MPs representing the MDF in the newly elected parliament, Soros was creating a dubious "empire," and people should not be so naive to believe that a Jewish fundholder would be altruistic when spending his money (Zacsek 1993). These conspiracist suspicions regarding Soros's hidden agenda were common in Hungary in the 1990s. For instance, an article published in 1993 in the far-right newspaper *Riadó* claimed to reveal some of Soros's secret aims in Hungary, such as to take hold of all strategically important positions, to destroy societies "built on national values, traditions, and ethnic specificities" and "to seize" the press, radio, and TV in order to destroy "Hungarian national consciousness" (Riadó 1993).

A similar discourse on Soros was disseminated by the Greater Romania Party (PRM) and its president, Corneliu Vadim Tudor, in Romania in the 1990s and early 2000s. Vadim Tudor had been one of the intellectuals involved in promoting Ceaușescu's personality cult and nationalistic cultural policies in the 1980s. Articles published in the cultural magazine bearing the same name as the party, *România Mare*, portrayed Soros as part of a New World Order–inspired conspiracy that included a broad network of conspirators ("Jewish capital," the IMF, and the World Bank) bent on subjugating Romania. *România Mare* also portrayed Soros as the epitome of Jewish and Hungarian conspiracies to dismantle the country. Therefore, in both Hungary and Romania, in the 1990s and early 2000s, anti-Soros conspiracy theories were mainly disseminated by extremist groups and included a strong and open antisemitic component.

Although the anti-Soros discourse was virulent in both countries throughout the 1990s, the Romanian extremist party PRM had a prominent position in the political landscape, while in Hungary far-right groups were more marginal at that time. The PRM was part of the government coalition from 1992 to 1996, and its leader reached the second round of the presidential elections in 2000. After Hungary and Romania joined NATO (in 1999 and 2004, respectively) and the EU (in 2004 and 2007, respectively), Soros-related conspiracy theories became less and less frequent for almost a decade. This might be partially explained by Soros's decreasing involvement in East-Central European civil society after 2007. From this perspective, the prominent reemergence of anti-Soros conspiracy theories in the 2010s seems paradoxical.

Refueling the populist discourse: Soros-related conspiracy theories and the anti-immigration campaign in Hungary

In August 2013, an article in the pro-government Hungarian newspaper *Heti Válasz* claimed that in 2012 George Soros had spent more than €1.5 billion on

214 *Corneliu Pintilescu et al.*

supporting what the author called "the 'civil' left wing," mentioning 11 NGOs that had allegedly received funding from the OSF (Válasz 2013; HHC 2017, 1–2). Moreover, in his famous speech held at Băile Tușnad/Tusnádfürdő in Romania on July 26, 2014, Orbán not only defined his vision of the "illiberal state" that he was building in Hungary but also argued that his "efforts" were "obstructed by civil society organizations" that were in his view "paid political activists" intent on advancing "foreign interests" (Orbán 2014; HHC 2017, 7–8). This shows that the Orbán government's anti-Soros discourse was right from the start closely tied to his attacks on civil society. At that time, Fidesz's discourse portrayed Soros as part of a wider conspiracy that was manipulating civil society to undermine Hungary's national interests. This discourse played a key role in delegitimizing criticism coming from civil society. It was accompanied by a campaign of harassment of those NGOs perceived as hostile to Fidesz, which included police raids and criminal investigations against several NGOs involved in administering the distribution in the country of EEA and Norway Grants funding (HHC 2017, 1). These measures culminated in attacks against several NGOs that had received financial support from the OSF. In 2017, Fidesz introduced the "Bill on the Transparency of Organizations Receiving Foreign Funds" (passed into law by the Hungarian parliament in June 2017), which stipulated that NGOs that received more than 7.2 million HUF (approx. €23,000) from abroad had to register for the purpose in court and acknowledge the receipt of foreign funds on their websites (ibid., 1). Orbán government's policies regarding civil society during his third term (2014–18) followed a similar path to Putin's after his reelection in 2012 (Krekó 2016). Another key source of inspiration for Orbán was Benjamin Netanyahu's government's discourse and policies regarding Israeli civil society, especially NGOs working on human rights protection. These NGOs heavily criticized the policies of Netanyahu's government, dominated by the right-wing Likud party, in the occupied Palestinian territories. The Israeli pro-government press often labeled them "traitors" and "foreign agents," while the Israeli national legislature, dominated by a right-wing coalition led by Likud, adopted in July 2016 a bill that required them to inform the state authorities about financial support received from abroad (Young 2016; Amnesty International 2019, 7). Netanyahu also introduced Orbán to Arthur Finkelstein—"master of the dark arts of negative campaigning"—who played a key role in defining the strategies of Fidesz's electoral campaigns from 2008 to 2017 (Pfeffer 2018). The fact that the influences worked in both directions is perfectly illustrated by Netanyahu's embrace in 2018 of conspiracy narratives about Soros and the migrant issue similar to those disseminated by the Orbán government (Keinon 2018).

However, Orbán's conspiracy narratives on Soros can only be understood by placing them in the broader context of Hungary's socioeconomic situation, Fidesz's authoritarian turn after its landslide victory in the 2010 general elections, and the role of Orbán's populist discursive strategies in consolidating his power. Hungary experienced severe economic difficulties in the mid- to late 2000s due to relatively high public debt and the impact of the 2008 financial crisis. These economic difficulties, coupled with the 2006 scandal of the leaked statements

Soros conspiracy theories 215

made by PM Ferenc Gyurcsány (who headed a left-wing government from 2004 to 2009) in which he admitted, among other matters, lying to the people about the real economic situation of the country, were capitalized on by Fidesz. The leak was followed by massive anti-government protests in which hundreds of civilians and police officers were injured. In this context, Fidesz managed to mobilize the Hungarian electorate and won the 2010 parliamentary elections by a substantial margin. Drawing on a strong majority in parliament, Fidesz succeeded in adopting a new constitution in April 2011 and new electoral legislation between 2012 and 2013. In this way Fidesz secured the legal basis for consolidating its power and seizing control of key state institutions.

Moreover, the party gradually tightened its grip on the mass media. Fidesz's strategy regarding the mass media led to "government-organized media" shaped by the Orbán regime's propaganda campaigns through its increasing economic dependence on government funds (Krekó and Enyedi 2018, 46). In 2017 alone, the Orbán government spent €40 million from public funds on the anti-Soros campaign by distributing money to pro-government media outlets (Erdélyi 2018a). Orbán's initiatives turned Hungary into a model for other leaders with authoritarian tendencies in the region, such as Fico and Dragnea (Krekó and Enyedi 2018).

As we shall elaborate below, Soros-related conspiracy theories played a key role in the success of Orbán's populist strategies, especially after 2015 when the anti-Soros discourse in Hungary took a radical turn during the migration crisis. By invoking the assistance provided to the migrants by several NGOs, Orbán connected two elements essential to his anti-immigration discourse: the so-called treason of "the 'civil' left wing" and the "migrant invasion." In February 2015, Orbán stated that his government intended to reveal the financial support that local NGOs received from Soros (HHC 2017). Later, the Hungarian government legitimized investigations into and attacks against various NGOs by invoking their alleged unlawful support for migrants. According to Orbán, Soros's goal was "to impose his opinions concerning the migration problems" through the NGOs he financed (ibid., 16). Furthermore, Soros's constant emphasis on the need to provide humanitarian help to asylum seekers offered Orbán some real facts that he could manipulate in his anti-Soros discourse (Soros 2015). In June 2018, the Fidesz-dominated Hungarian parliament passed the so-called Stop Soros legislation package, which criminalized assistance to asylum seekers. As a result, it severely limited the activity of NGOs and forced the OSF to move its regional office from Hungary to Germany (Krekó and Enyedi 2018, 47).

Another component of the anti-Soros campaign was the so-called Lex CEU passed in April 2017 and intended to abolish what the government called the "unjust privileges" of the "Soros University" (Kovács 2017). This measure was closely connected to Orbán's attacks on Soros and his broader anti-intellectual policy of harassing what he perceived as a bastion of liberal and left-wing thought in Hungary. In this respect, there are many similarities between Orbán's conspiracy theories concerning the Central European University (CEU) and those disseminated by the Hungarian far-right in the 1990s, in which the CEU was depicted as a nest of dangerous liberal and cosmopolitan values (Forisek 2018).

216 *Corneliu Pintilescu et al.*

Finally, Fidesz came up with an ingenious strategy to disseminate effectively its conspiratorial narratives on Soros and migration. It organized several national consultations and a referendum. The resort to national consultations by the Orbán government after 2010 in order to prove broad public support led the political scientist Hans-Georg Heinrich to label it a "plebiscitary government" (2019, 119). This strategy managed to turn the Hungarian adult citizens who took part in the consultations and the referendum into active participants in the propaganda campaigns that the government financed with public funds without, however, breaking the law. Legitimized by the national consultations, the anti-migration, anti-EU, and anti-Soros campaigns received approximately €169 million in 2017 and 2018 (Hungarian Spectrum 2019a).

The questions on these issues proposed by the four national consultations and one national referendum organized between 2015 and 2019 skillfully played on the collective fear of asylum seekers, while promoting a conspiratorial world-view. For instance, in the April 2015 national consultation, citizens were asked for their opinion on migration and terrorism by presenting migrants as a source of terrorism (Kiss 2016). During and after the national consultation, the government carried out a so-called information campaign filled with messages such as: "Hungarians have decided: they do not want illegal migrants" (ibid.). The state-controlled media, however, failed to mention that Hungary was merely a transit country for migrants on their way to Western European countries with better welfare policies.

In the meantime, Orbán launched a virulent anti-Soros propaganda campaign by disseminating conspiracy theories linking Soros's activities with the migrants. The EU refugee quota policy provided Orbán with the opportunity to expand his conspiratorial discourse to include Brussels too. As a result, in February 2016, the Hungarian government decided to call a referendum on the "compulsory reset-tlement quotas"—the name it gave to the EU refugee quotas (MTI 2016). The same month, the state ordered yet another national consultation named "Let's Stop Brussels," which, in addition to including an anti-migrant message, claimed to "regulate the transparency of international organizations" (Rogán 2017). The government also launched a poster campaign with Soros's face on it and the message "Let's not allow Soros to have the last laugh!" According to Péter Krekó and Zsolt Enyedi "the image of a Jewish financier running a worldwide conspiracy is a familiar anti-Semitic trope," and the Orbán government was "fully aware" of the possible reactions of the population (2018, 47). Orbán's government displays an ambivalent attitude toward Jews. On the one hand, antisemitism is involved not only in Orbán's anti-Soros discourse but also in his policy of rehabilitating the wartime Hungarian dictator Miklós Horthy, who passed antisemitic legisla-tion and allied the country with Nazi Germany (Lipstadt 2019, 215). On the other hand, Orbán cultivated a close collaboration with Israeli prime minister Benjamin Netanyahu and his party.

The anti-Soros campaign reached its climax in September 2017 when the Hun-garian government organized another national consultation on the so-called Soros Plan (Novak 2017). After the consultation, Fidesz supported the so-called Stop

Soros conspiracy theories 217

Soros legislation package, which was legitimized by invoking the "Soros network" made up of organizations that allegedly supported illegal immigration to Europe.

These national consultations and the referendum, together with the accompanying state-sponsored propaganda campaigns, helped the Orbán government to achieve several aims. First, the propaganda campaigns proved very effective in spreading fear among citizens by warning of a "migrant invasion" and of a vast network of enemies of the Hungarian nation led by Soros, who, according to Orbán, had declared that "at least one million Muslims should be let into Europe every year" (Orbán 2016). Collective fear is a key ingredient in the success of both populist discourses and top-down disseminated conspiracy theories. Politicians construct or manipulate conspiracy theories so that they fuel collective fears and make people eager to believe them (Bergmann 2018, 173), while belief in conspiracy theories is associated with an increase in extremist attitudes (Inglehart 1987, 243; van Prooijen et al. 2015). The relation between extremist political attitudes and belief in conspiracy theories is "bidirectional and self-reinforcing" (van Prooijen et al. 2015, 7).

Thus, in Hungary, anti-Soros conspiracy theories became intertwined with the Eurabia narrative. As Enzo Traverso argues, the so-called Eurabia conspiracy theories would have us believe that Muslims have replaced Jews as destroyers of European Christian values (2019, 65–66). Orbán's discourse not only was influenced by but also fueled pan-European nationalist anti-Muslim conspiracy theories, such as "the great replacement" conspiracy theory proposed by the French writer Renaud Camus (Hungarian Spectrum. 2019b). According to this conspiracy theory, a "replacist" power is conspiring to replace the Christian population in Europe with non-European populations, especially with Muslims (Camus and Lebourg 2017, 206–7). Second, this strategy actively involved citizens in government rhetoric and substantially contributed to Fidesz's success in the 2018 general elections and the 2019 European elections.

Third, the national consultations and the referendum provided the Orbán government with the ideal opportunity to promote the populist scenario of a radical antagonism between the Hungarian nation and its enemies—migrants, EU bureaucrats, global finance, and Soros as an umbrella for this global network of conspiracy theories. By conflating the Soros conspiracy theories with the migration issue, Orbán successfully refueled his populist discursive strategy. Furthermore, because the Hungarian opposition proved weak and unable to counter these populist narratives effectively, Orbán managed constantly to replenish his pool of foreign and domestic enemies within his discourse. The political scientist Emilia Palonen argues that Fidesz has discursively constructed several lines of polarization since the 1990s, such as those defined by the " 'anti-communist-anti-liberal' and the 'anti-nationalist' camps" (2018, 314–15). Fidesz contrasted its own illiberal ideology with the opposition's decadent liberal values, its own anti-leftist stance with the allegedly "communist" stance of its competitors, its own national values with the opposition's betrayal of these values, its own Christian values with those allegedly supporting the "Muslim invasion" (ibid., 316–17). Orbán's

218 *Corneliu Pintilescu et al.*

intensive instrumentation of conspiracy theories became a key factor in reshaping and reinventing populist antagonisms in the 2010s (ibid., 318).

In fact, some of these antagonisms constructed by Orbán's populist discourse emerged strongly intertwined with the multilayered networks of conspirators depicted in his speeches. While before 2015, the Soros-related conspiracy theories disseminated by Orbán's regime mainly focused on Hungary's internal affairs, starting from that year they gradually grew in complexity and scope. Soros was seen to become the puppeteer behind EU policies.

A high point of these developments was reached in March 2018 when the Hungarian government launched an information campaign on the UN's migration package, claiming that it coincided with the so-called Soros Plan (Szijjártó 2018). The anti-Soros conspiracist narratives morphed into a "superconspiracy" (Barkun 2003, 6). Soros became its keystone and the incarnation of an entire network of foreign and domestic "enemies" of the Hungarian nation. This "superconspiracy" fueled both the "vertical" and "horizontal" components of the populist antagonism (Brubaker 2019, 30). The first component includes the elite in Brussels bought by Soros's money versus the Hungarian nation, while the second sets the Hungarian nation in opposition to Muslim migrants—namely, the danger from outside.

A speech given by Orbán in March 2018 perfectly illustrates this role assigned to Soros, who "embodied" in the view of the Hungarian prime minister: "Media outlets maintained by foreign concerns and domestic oligarchs, professional hired activists, troublemaking protest organizers, and a chain of NGOs" (Orbán 2018). These narratives helped Orbán to build his image as the protector of the Hungarian nation against this vast "superconspiracy." Ernesto Laclau argues that "the leader" has a key role in the populist "mode of articulation" because he embodies "the unity of the group" (2005, 100). While Orbán symbolizes the "unity" of the discursively constructed Hungarian nation, Soros, as the counter-hero, embodies the conspiratorial enemies of the nation. As the portrayal of Soros in the campaign that targeted him after 2015 shows, the counter-hero is also very useful in presenting competitors or those criticizing the government "as enemies of the people" (Bergmann 2018, 173). Without Soros, various levels of the antagonism built by Orbán would have been too abstract and less appealing to broad audiences. By using him, the various enemies defined through Orbán's antagonisms mentioned above are given an easily identifiable face.

Against the stream: the outcome of the populist drive and Soros-related conspiracy theories in Romania after 2013

In the late 2000s, the anti-Soros conspiracy theories that had emerged in 1990s Romania became marginal following the failure of the nationalist parties to enter parliament. However, populist discursive strategies were occasionally used by mainstream politicians from both the right and the left. For example, Traian Băsescu, the leader of a center-right coalition who won the presidential elections in 2004 and 2009, managed to mobilize his electorate by criticizing the corrupt

Soros conspiracy theories 219

Romanian political elite, although he himself had been part of that elite since the early 1990s.

As in Hungary, the economic and social effects of the 2008 financial crisis caused political instability in Romania and fueled populist rhetoric. Between 2009 and 2012, the drastic austerity measures of center-right governments led to the victory of a center-left coalition, the Social Liberal Union (USL), made up of both center-left and center-right parties. This managed to bring down the government of Mihai-Răzvan Ungureanu by a no-confidence motion in May 2012, to win the 2012 parliamentary elections, and to appoint the government led by Prime Minister Victor Ponta, leader of the Social-Democratic Party (PSD). The PSD was the senior partner in the government coalitions from May 2012 to November 2015, when Ponta resigned due to protests against corruption following a disastrous fire, resulting in 64 deaths, at the Colectiv nightclub in Bucharest. The protesters accused the government that widespread corruption had caused the tragedy and invoked the fact that the nightclub had been allowed to operate without mandatory fire safety clearance. Dacian Cioloș followed Ponta as prime minister, leading a government dominated by technocrats. He stayed in office from November 2015 to January 2017. In 2016, the PSD won the parliamentary elections with a program that promised consistent wage and pension rises. From 2017 to 2019, successive PSD-dominated governments were often accused by the Romanian and Western press of replicating the populist drift of Fidesz in Hungary and Law and Justice in Poland. This had to do with their attempts to amend the legislation regarding corruption and their conflicts with Brussels on this issue.

Following the 2013 protests against the Roșia Montană gold mining project in the Western Carpathians, Soros's conspiratorial narratives surfaced in a new form compared to those of the 1990s. In this context of populist revival, these protests were driven by the damage likely to be caused to the natural and historical heritage. For example, the mining project entailed the building of a huge lake of cyanide near the planned gold mine in Roșia Montană. At the time of writing this chapter (September 2019), the protests have succeeded in stopping the project.

Since 2013, several politicians and mainstream newspapers have launched a conspiratorial interpretation of these protests, arguing that Soros has financed the NGOs organizing them. The same allegations have been made concerning the protests against corruption arising from the Colectiv nightclub fire. Several articles published in the mainstream press supported these allegations concerning the Roșia Montană and Colectiv protests by providing lists of NGOs benefitting from OSF projects. Romanian intellectuals who had received scholarships from Soros-financed institutions were placed on blacklists (Șomănescu 2015). For example, in September 2013, one of the main Romanian newspapers *Evenimentul Zilei* (The News of the Day) published an article arguing that the NGOs involved in organizing the Roșia Montană protests were financed by Soros and that they served his hidden agenda (Bot 2013). In fact, a wide variety of Soros-related conspiracy theories concerning Roșia Montană were released both by local far-right news outlets and in the mainstream media.

220   *Corneliu Pintilescu et al.*

A turning point in the advance of the anti-Soros conspiracy narratives was the 2015 Colectiv nightclub fire and the ensuing protests, which forced the PSD-dominated government to resign. Following pressure from civil society, President Klaus Iohannis nominated Dacian Cioloş to head a technocratic government, many of whose members were close collaborators of centrist and right-wing political parties that had supported Iohannis in the presidential campaign of 2014. In November 2016, *Evenimentul Zilei*, published an article titled "The Soros Network," which allegedly disclosed the source of financial support of NGOs and civil activists involved in the protests. The article concluded that behind the ascent to power of the Cioloş government lay NGOs financed by Soros (Ionescu 2016). The conspiracist narratives disseminated by *Evenimentul Zilei* after 2013 became very similar to those previously circulated in the extremist press, such as the magazine *România Mare* (Militaru 2015). The NGOs responded to these accusations by emphasizing that although some of them did carry out projects funded by OSF grants, this financial support was already in the open as acknowledgments regarding funding were duly noted in the first place by all concerned parties (Toma 2013). Besides, no one, including the staff of the NGOs, had been paid to take part in the protests; taking to the streets was the personal choice of the people involved.

The dissemination of anti-Soros conspiracy theories reached a height during the February 2017 anti-corruption protests against Emergency Ordinance no. 13 issued by the PSD-dominated coalition. At that time, the pro-government press asserted that Soros and multinational companies were inciting the people through the NGOs they controlled. According to news disseminated by a government-friendly TV channel in February 2017, Soros allegedly paid the protesters $24 each to attend the protests and even more if they brought their children or pets (Tamkin 2017). Additionally, in August 2018, during a talk show on the Antena 3 TV channel, Liviu Dragnea, the head of the PSD, stated that four paid assassins had followed him a year before and that he had narrowly escaped death. Asked about who was behind them, he blamed none other than Soros, whom he labeled as one of those who "have fed evil in Romania" (VOA 2017). Thus, Dragnea's discourse sought to place him in the position of the victim of a broad conspiracy, with Soros as the grand puppeteer who had triggered the attempt on his life. People reacted humorously to these accusations on social media, and they became the topic of jokes among the younger generation.

Soros-related conspiracy theories of this time recycle to a certain extent tropes already present in the anti-Soros conspiracist narratives of the 1990s and early 2000s. They point to the same hidden agenda behind Open Society's engagement with local civil society. However, there is also something new: namely, the accusations targeting Soros as the evil mind behind the protests aimed at destabilizing the government put in place by Dragnea. *Sputnik* and *Russia Today*, in particular, now came to constitute a platform for recirculating anti-Soros conspiracy theories from one country to another across Eastern Europe. For example, *Sputnik Romania* disseminates a mixture of local and imported conspiratorial narratives (Sputnik 2019). Although the Romanian audience is much less open to Russian

Soros conspiracy theories 221

mass media than is the case in Hungary, mostly due to the Russophobe feelings of a significant part of the Romanian population (Kalmar, Stevens, and Worby 2018), *Sputnik Romania* has played a role in mediating and developing close relationships between the Russian Federation and nationalist as well as radical Orthodox circles in Romania. Some of their key local contributors have previously asserted themselves as promoters of conspiratorial narratives once highlighted by the extremist press of nationalist parties such as PRM and PUNR.

Although the anti-Soros conspiracy theories were a main component of the conspiracist discourse backed by the PSD leadership and the pro-government mass media after 2013, 2018 brought a shift in these narratives. A new trope surfaced—namely, the so-called parallel state (*statul paralel* in Romanian) conspiracy theory, a locally adjusted version of the American deep state conspiracy theory (Blanuša 2018). This new conspiracy theory did not replace Soros-related conspiracy theories but reintegrated them into an updated conspiratorial framework.

Already convicted of election fraud and under investigation at the time for official misconduct and corruption-related offences, Dragnea organized a huge meeting in Bucharest in June 2018. He gathered more than 180,000 citizens, most of them bused from various parts of the country. This event, labeled by the PSD leaders as "a mass protest," was deemed to be the perfect scenography for charging the Romanian secret services and the Public Prosecutor's Office with having built the "parallel state." Dragnea also accused the EU of "encouraging and also financing" it (Santora and Gillet 2018). The catchphrase of the meeting was "We want prosperity, NOT security! [*securitate* in Romanian]." In this choice of words, Dragnea assimilated the anti-corruption campaigns in Romania, in which the secret services indeed played a key role in providing evidence by means of wiretapping, to the Stalinist terror enforced by the secret police, the Securitate.

In contrast to the Soros-related conspiracy theories, Dragnea's "parallel state" conspiracy theory found a propitious audience because of the Romanian conspiracy culture that had developed in connection with the Securitate and its legacy after 1989. In his attacks on the "parallel state," Dragnea invoked two facts as arguments: (1) the 2005 Supreme Council of National Defense decision concerning collaboration between the Romanian Intelligence Service (SRI) and the Public Prosecutor's Office, which focused on establishing a systemic policy of clamping down on corruption, together with other secret agreements between these two institutions (Stoiciu 2018); and (2) the inflated budgets of the Romanian secret services. Indeed, the Romanian secret services have very high budgets. For example, in 2018, the SRI had a higher budget than its French counterpart (the DGSI), €500 million in the case of the SRI and €300 million in the case of the DGSI (Davidescu 2018).

Dragnea's conspiratorial narratives tried to merge various conspiracy theories and evoked a broad network of conspirators aimed at undermining the national interest. Soros, foreign and local secret services, the Romanian Public Prosecutor's Office and the National Anti-Corruption Directorate (DNA), the EU, and multinational corporations operating in Romania come together as the enemy

222 *Corneliu Pintilescu et al.*

within. Essentially, the "parallel state" became an umbrella term for a vague bunch of local and global conspirators.

The conspiracist narratives focusing either on Soros or on the "parallel state" were not Dragnea's original contributions. In fact, both of them were globally circulating conspiracy tropes. Some of them were inspired by successful populist discourses in the USA and Turkey. Effectively, they made their way into the Romanian public sphere via the activity of foreign political consultants. In this connection, it is worth mentioning the article published in December 2016 by the Israeli newspaper *Jerusalem Post* about the successful careers of two political advisers, Moshe Klughaft and Sefi Shaked. They staged Benjamin Netanyahu's attack on local NGOs, which were depicted as undercover networks for foreign secret services, in a manner very similar to Dragnea's discourse about Romanian civil society. The article disclosed that the two political advisers also worked for the PSD in the 2016 parliamentary electoral campaign in Romania (Hoffman 2016; Grosereanu 2017). Although sharing some common features with US deep state conspiracy theories, the term "parallel state" seems to be an import from Erdoğan's rhetoric and his accusations that the Gülenist movement was creating a "parallel state" in Turkey. These accusations legitimized the repressive measures against the movement's members after the 2013 protests in Turkey and the failed coup d'état (Söyler 2015, 3).

In contrast with Fidesz's success in Hungary, in Romania Soros-related conspiracy theories were less effective. The fact that Dragnea made little effort to adjust some of these tropes to the local context led some Romanian journalists to consider his campaign of spreading Soros-related conspiracy theories as artificial and unable to gain enough traction with the public (Rogozanu 2019). However, due to the intense media coverage of Soros-related conspiracy theories by some government-friendly TV channels, a part of the Romanian audience became receptive to these conspiratorial narratives. According to a survey carried out by the Romanian Institute for Evaluation and Strategy in 2018, 36% of respondents said they agreed with the statement: "Soros has done a lot of evil to Romania," while 39% disagreed, and 25% refused to answer or did not know (IRES 2018). Moreover, Soros-related conspiracy theories failed to mobilize the electorate in Romania. While in Hungary he was a public figure long before 2013, Soros was little known in Romania. Taking into account the country's problems with corruption, many Romanians actually considered that the protests accused by the pro-government press of being staged by Soros were legitimate. Another factor playing a key role in the success of Soros-related conspiracy theories in Hungary was the structure of the mass media. While the pro-Fidesz mass media in Hungary covers "77.8% of the entire news and public affairs segment" (Mérték Médiaelemző Műhely 2019), Romanian mass media is more fragmented.

Although investing a lot of energy in spreading "parallel state" or Soros-related conspiracy theories, Dragnea failed to make them a tool of political success. Through his anti-EU discourse and his attacks on the justice system, he managed to antagonize the greater part of Romanians as well as the EU and local civil society. The PSD's defeat in the 2019 European elections illustrates the failure of his

Soros conspiracy theories 223

cliché-ridden conspiracist narratives in Romania. Finally, Dragnea's conviction for official misconduct in May 2019 seems to have marked the end of his political career.

Soros-related conspiracy theories and populist discursive strategies in Hungary and Romania: a comparative approach

In both Hungary and Romania, the post-2013 anti-Soros conspiracy theories were built on similar narratives. Essentially, they looked back to the 1990s and early 2000s. Both the old and the more recent versions of conspiracy theories dealing with Soros claim to expose the Jewish-Hungarian-American billionaire as the interface of a vast New World Order–inspired conspiracy theory, in which evil global financial interests are opposed to national sovereignty and cultural values. Thus, after 2013, a part of the Hungarian and Romanian audience was already acquainted with conspiracies about Soros. However, while in the 1990s, Soros-related conspiracy theories were from the ground up, and mostly circulated by extremist political groups on the fringes, in the 2010s these conspiratorial stories became mainstream and were disseminated top-down. During the 1990s and early 2000s, the antisemitism of the Soros-related conspiracy theories was openly stated; in contrast, the post-2013 conspiracy theories about Soros manipulate latent antisemitism, and their antisemitic component is implicit rather than explicit (Palonen 2018, 317).

The most successful conspiratorial narratives in Hungary and Romania after 2013 portray Soros as an essentially evil mind plotting to bring down the government through machinating protests in order to impose his hidden agenda. This trope was heavily used by various governments in the region in order to delegitimize protests coming from civil society. For example, the PSD leaders and the government-friendly mass media called the protesters "Sorosists" (*soroşisti*), while in Hungary Fidesz labeled them "Soros mercenaries," and in Slovakia PM Robert Fico dubbed them "Soros children" (Meseznikov 2019). In this respect, Eastern Europe heavily contributed to launching a global trend in the field of conspiracy theories. The Soros-related conspiracy theories in the USA that took the world by storm during Trump's presidential term are a case in point. However, this influence was not unidirectional. The spread of Soros-related conspiracy theories in the USA legitimized the resort to Soros-related conspiracy theories by various politicians in Eastern Europe and made them acceptable for mainstream media.

Conspiracy theories that feature Soros were circulated through various channels such as the increasingly globalized mass media, social media, foreign political consultants promoting negative campaign strategies, and collaboration among authoritarian leaders and far-right movements in Europe. The Kremlin-controlled media played also an important role in these transfers across Eastern Europe by reshaping Soros-related conspiracy theories (and not only these) and fueling their spread in the region. In both Hungary and Romania, the Russian mass media established close collaboration with nationalist groups, with whom Putin's

224 *Corneliu Pintilescu et al.*

propaganda apparatus found common interests such as combating liberal values, minority rights, and foreign-backed NGOs.

The transfers were mediated also with the help of foreign political consultants working with Fidesz and the PSD after 2013. They advanced the instrumentalization of Soros conspiracy theories within broader strategies of negative electoral campaigns. In an interview granted in 2019, the political consultant George Eli Birnbaum said that "his former mentor and friend" Arthur Finkelstein had planned the negative campaigns focused on Soros as Hungary's archenemy (Grassegge 2019). According to Birnbaum's statements, Finkelstein realized that Orbán needed for the 2014 parliamentary elections an imagined enemy who could "make sure that on Election Day they have a reason to go out and vote" (ibid.). Because the opposition was weak in Hungary after 2010, they decided to focus the campaign on Soros (ibid.). As the aforementioned article published in 2016 by the *Jerusalem Post* shows, the political advisers Moshe Klughaft and Sefi Shaked, who staged Benjamin Netanyahu's attack on local NGOs, also worked for the PSD during the 2016 parliamentary electoral campaign (Hoffman 2016). Klughaft and Shaked collaborated closely with George Eli Birnbaum as well.

The close collaboration between far-right movements in Europe, together with the emulation between authoritarian leaders such as Orbán, Putin, and Erdoğan, also encouraged the transfer of some populist discursive strategies from one country to another. Dragnea tried to emulate Fidesz's strategies, such as its anti-EU rhetoric and its conspiracist narratives, in the hope of similar electoral results (Ioniță 2019).

From 2013 to 2018, the complexity of Orbán's conspiracist narratives increased, and a world-explanatory role was ascribed to them. When looking at the conspiracy theories circulated within the Hungarian printed and online press, as early as 2013, the pro-Fidesz press fabricated a "systemic" conspiracy theory in which NGOs were the main target of the attacks because they were allegedly part of a secret network (Barkun 2003, 6). After 2015, Soros gradually became the evil mind behind most of the UN or EU decisions. The Soros-related conspiratorial narratives evolved toward a "superconspiracy" in Barkun's typology (ibid.), which was filled up with a jigsaw puzzle of smaller-scale conspiracy theories.

In comparison, the Romanian versions of the Soros-related conspiracy theories never reached the same complexity. Soros was alleged to be behind local protests, but he was seldom presented as the great puppeteer enforcing EU policies. In Dragnea's conspiracist narratives, Soros became a secondary component in a larger conspiracy that included Romanian secret services, the Public Prosecutor's Office, Brussels, and multinational corporations, as a local version of the US deep state conspiracy theory.

The Hungarian case, rather than the Romanian one, shows how conspiratorial narratives became a key component of an effective populist discursive strategy. In Hungary, Soros became the hate figure through which Orbán aimed "to avoid bursting the bubble of populist life-cycle" (Palonen 2018, 314–15). However, the results of the 2019 local elections in Hungary, in which Fidesz lost in Budapest and several of the main cities, might be a clue that the instrumentalization of anti-Soros conspiracy theories had also run out of steam.

While Orbán succeeded in the 2018 parliamentary elections, Dragnea's populist discourse led to different results. Dragnea's vocal attacks on Soros, the EU, and multinational corporations had a disastrous outcome for the PSD in the 2019 European elections. Due to the obvious opportunities created by the EU for Romanians, not least the fact that more than 3 million Romanians work in Western Europe, the anti-EU discourse was hardly believable. Moreover, recent history also worked against Dragnea's populist drive. The image of an authoritarian leader fighting for the national interest against foreign forces was very similar to the propaganda of Ceaușescu's regime during the 1980s.

By developing Laclau's theory, Panizza argues that populism involves "radical redrawing of social borders" and constitutes "new identities" (2005, 9). Thus, in both countries, the anti-Soros conspiracist discourse entailed vertical and horizontal components (Brubaker 2019, 30). On the one hand, Soros was an enemy from above, who epitomized the power of global capital and supranational structures such as the EU or the IMF. The vertical antagonism was developed on the opposition between global and national. On the other hand, the anti-Soros discourse also materialized the antagonisms working inside the societies of Hungary and Romania: liberal *versus* conservative values, the agenda of the NGO activists *versus* alleged national interest, native citizens *versus* immigrants, and so on.

Conclusion

In both Hungary and Romania, the post-2010 Soros-related conspiracy theories are not a novelty. They have been built on similar narratives that emerged in the local nationalist circles of the 1990s. The older and newer anti-Soros conspiracy theories have a common trope: namely, they both present Soros as the epitome of evil global financial forces conspiring to undermine national sovereignty and traditional values. There are also differences: in the 1990s, these conspiracy theories were rather perceived as being disseminated by extremist political groups on the fringes, while in the 2010s, the stories became mainstream and their dissemination involved a vast system of pro-government press, especially in Hungary. If in the 1990s their antisemitism was explicit, in the 2010s, conspiracy theories about Soros rather manipulated a latent antisemitism in the two countries. Whereas the Soros-related conspiracy theories of the 1990s originated more in the local political and cultural context, those emerging after 2013 reflect to a higher degree global trends and transfers. Thus, the post-2013 anti-Soros conspiracy theories entail new tropes, such as Soros's alleged plans to bring millions of Muslims to Europe (in Hungary). Besides benefiting from the increasingly globalized media market, these transfers took place via emulation among authoritarian leaders, collaboration between far-right groups in Europe, and the input of foreign political consultants.

The two cases also illustrate how the Soros conspiracy theories worked in two different national political contexts. In both countries, Soros-related conspiracy

226 *Corneliu Pintilescu et al.*

theories played a key role in articulating populist discourses, by providing a tangible symbol for a wide variety of foes both inside and outside the country. The conspiratorial tropes proved to be very flexible, able to accommodate the different culture-bound projections of enemy figures across many Eastern European countries (and not only there). If in Hungary Soros conspiracy theories brought together the fight against global financial capitalism, EU bureaucracy, local NGOs, Muslim immigrants, and liberal ideologies, in Romania, Soros was able to synthesize both recent foes such as NGOs and multinational corporations and the traditional "archenemies" of the Romanian far right: the Hungarians and the Jewish capital. While in Romania, these conspiracist narratives were less successful and became a secondary component of the Romanian version of the deep state conspiracy theory, in Hungary they evolved toward a "superconspiracy" that unified various webs of alleged conspirators and gained a world-explanatory role.

Acknowledgments

I would like to acknowledge and thank the members of the COST Action COMPACT ("Comparative Analysis of Conspiracy Theories") attending the meeting in Huelva (May 2019) for their feedback to an early version of this chapter; to the coeditors of this edited volume Anastasiya Astapova, Tamás Scheibner, Onoriu Colăcel; and to James Brown and Lindsay Porter for their very useful suggestions and comments.

Note

1 All translations from Hungarian and Romanian by authors, unless otherwise noted.

Bibliography

Ágh, Attila. 2016. "The Deconsolidation of Democracy in East-Central Europe: The New World Order and the EU's Geopolitical Crisis." *Politics in Central Europe* 12 (3): 7–36.

Amnesty International. 2019. "Elected But Restricted: Shrinking Space For Palestinian Parliamentarians in Israel's Knesset." Accessed September 27, 2019. www.amnesty.org/download/Documents/MDE1508822019ENGLISH.PDF.

Barkun, Michael. 2003. *A Culture of Conspiracy: Apocalyptic Visions in Contemporary America*. Berkeley, CA: University of California Press.

Bergmann, Eirikur. 2018. *Conspiracy & Populism: The Politics of Misinformation*. Cham: Palgrave Macmillan.

Blanuša, Nebojša. 2018. "The Deep State between the (Un)Warranted Conspiracy Theory and Structural Element of Political Regimes?" *Critique and Humanism* 49 (1): 369–84.

Bot, Mădălin. 2013. "Cum manipulează șmecherii din ONG-uri Piața Universității și cât de toxică e dezinformarea" [The Wise Guys of the NGOs are Lying by Engaging in Disinformation]. *Evenimentul Zilei*. September 14, 2013.

Brubaker, Rogers. 2019. "Why Populism?" In *Populism and the Crisis of Democracy: Volume 1: Concepts and Theory*, edited by Gregor Fitzi, Juergen Mackert, and Bryan S. Turner, 27–46. London: Routledge.

Soros conspiracy theories 227

Cabinet Office of the Prime Minister (MTI). 2016. "Hungarian Government Decides to Call Referendum on Compulsory Resettlement Quotas." *Cabinet Office of the Prime Minister*, February 24, 2016. Accessed July 23, 2019. www.miniszterelnok.hu/hungarian-government-decides-to-call-referendum-on-compulsory-resettlement-quotas/.

Camus, Jean-Yves, and Nicolas Lebourg. [2015] 2017. *Far-right Politics in Europe*. Translated by Jane Marie Todd. Cambridge, MA: The Belknap Press of Harvard University Press.

Colăcel, Onoriu, and Corneliu Pintilescu. 2017. "From Literary Culture to Post-communist Media. Romanian Conspiracism." *Messages, Sages and Ages* 4 (2): 31–40.

Csurka, István. 1994. "A médiaháború Soros-fejezete" [The Soros-chapter of the Media War]. *Függetlenség*, January 31, 2014 [originally published in 1994]. www.eredetimiep.hu/fuggetlenseg/2014/januar/31/14.htm.

Davidescu, Lucian. 2018. "Știați că bugetul SRI e mai mare decât al serviciului secret din Germania?"[Did You Know that the Budget of the Romanian Intelligence Service is Higher than the One of the German Secret Service?] *România curată*, August 6, 2018. www.romaniacurata.ro/stiati-ca-bugetul-sri-e-mai-mare-decat-al-serviciului-secret-din-germania/.

Erdélyi, Katalin. 2018a. "Hungarian Government Spent €40 Million on Anti-Soros Propaganda in 2017." *Atlatszo.hu*, February 4, 2018. https://english.atlatszo.hu/2018/02/04/hungarian-government-spent-e40-million-on-anti-soros-propaganda-in-2017/.

Forisek, Ádám. 2018. "The Truth about Soros' University." *888.hu*, December 8, 2018. https://888.hu/amerika-london-parizs/the-truth-about-soros-university-4164033/.

Gabrizova, Zuzana. 2018. "Fico Blames Soros for Provoking Instability in Slovakia." *Euractiv*, March 6, 2018. www.euractiv.com/section/elections/news/fico-blames-soros-|for-provoking-instability-in-slovakia/.

Grassegger, Hannes. 2019. "The Unbelievable Story Of The Plot Against George Soros." *BuzzFeed News*, January 20, 2019. www.buzzfeednews.com/article/hnsgrassegger/george-soros-conspiracy-finkelstein-birnbaum-orban-netanyahu.

Grosereanu, Bogdan. 2017. " 'Soroșismul', inventat în laborator de consilierii israelieni ai lui Dragnea? ["Sorosism" was Invented in the Laboratories of the Israeli Political Consultants Working for Dragnea?]. *România Curată*, February 21, 2017. www.romaniacurata.ro/sorosismul-inventat-in-laborator-de-consilierii-israelieni-ai-lui-dragnea/.

Hamvay, Péter. 2017. "Megszereztük Orbán 1988-as beszédét Soros Györgyről. Előadja: Kádár János" [We Aquired Orbán's Speech from 1988 about George Soros. Performer: János Kádár]. *HVG*, April 21, 2017.

Harper, Jo. 2019. "Related Subjects Media Freedom, Poland, Jaroslaw Kaczynski." *Deutsche Welle*, February 26, 2019. www.dw.com/en/soros-boosts-anti-pis-media-ahead-of-crucial-polish-polls/a-47686631

Heinrich, Hans-Georg. 2019. "From Horthy to Orbán: Neo-Authoritarianism in Hungary." In *New Authoritarianism: Challenges to Democracy in the 21st century*, edited by Jerzy J. Wiatr, 100–28. Leverkusen: Verlag Barbara Budrich.

Hoffman, Gil. 2016. "Israeli Strategists Win Romanian Election." *jpost.com* [Jerusalem Post], December 18, 2016. www.jpost.com/Israel-News/Politics-And-Diplomacy/Israeli-strategists-win-Romanian-election-475699

Hungarian Helsinki Committee (HHC). 2017. "Timeline of Governmental Attacks against Hungarian Civil Society Organisations." November 17, 2017. Accessed April 11, 2019. www.helsinki.hu/wp-content/uploads/Timeline_of_gov_attacks_against_HU_NGOs_short_17112017.pdf.

Hungarian Spectrum. 2019a. "Government-generated Anti-EU Propaganda in Hungary." *Hungarian Spectrum*, February 20, 2019. https://hungarianspectrum.org/2019/02/20/government-generated-anti-eu-propaganda-in-hungary/.

228 *Corneliu Pintilescu et al.*

———. 2019b. "Viktor Orbán and the Great Replacement Theory." *Hungarian Spectrum*, March 16, 2019. https://hungarianspectrum.org/2019/03/16/viktor-orban-and-the-great-replacement-theory/.

Inglehart, Ronald. 1987. "Extremist Political Positions and Perceptions of Conspiracy: Even Paranoids Have Real Enemies." In *Changing Conceptions of Conspiracy*, edited by edited by Carl F. Graumann and Serge Moscovici, 231–44. New York: Springer-Verlag.

Institutul Roman pentru Evaluare si Strategie (IRES). 2018. "Sondaj de opinie la nivel naţional privind nivelul discriminării în România şi percepţiile actuale asupra infacţiunilor motivate de ură" [National Level Opinion Poll Concerning the Discrimination in Romania and the Current Perceptions Motivated by Hate]. Accessed July 11, 2019. www.ires.com.ro/uploads/articole/ires_cncd_discriminarea-in-romania_2018.pdf.

Ionescu, Simona. 2016. "Reţeaua Soros. Bani 'albi' pentru politicienii şi ONG-urile care se implică în viaţa politică din România" [Soros Network: "White" Money for Politicians and NGOs Involved in the Romanian Political Scene]. *Evenimentul Zilei*, November 7, 2016. http://evz.ro/reteaua-soros-bani-pentru-organizatiile-civice-1.htm.

Ioniţă, Sorin. 2019. "PSD-Dragnea, pătlăgeaua 'cu chimicale' şi neofascismul românesc" [PSD-Dragnea, the chemical tomatoes and the Romanian neo-fascism]. *Revista 22*, April 14, 2019. https://revista22.ro/opinii/sorin-ionita/psd-dragnea-patlageaua-cu-chimicale-si-neofascismul-romanesc.

Kalmar, Ivan, Christopher Stevens, and Nicholas Worby. 2018. "Twitter, Gab, and Racism: The Case of the Soros Myth." *SMSociety '18*, [July 18–20, 2018, Proceedings of the 9th International Conference on Social Media and Society, Copenhagen]: 330–34.

Keinon, Herb. 2018. "Netanyahu Blames Soros for Israel Anti-deportation Campaign." *jpost.com* [The Jerusalem Post], February 4, 2018. www.jpost.com/Israel-News/Netanyahu-blames-Soros-for-Israel-anti-deportation-campaign-540640.

Kiss, Eszter. 2016. " 'The Hungarians Have Decided: They Do Not Want Illegal Migrants:' Media Representation of the Hungarian Governmental Anti-Immigration Campaign." *Acta Humana – Emberi jogi közlemények* 6: 45–77. Accessed July 23, 2019. https://folyoiratok.uni-nke.hu/document/nkeszolgaltato-uni-nke-hu/03_AH_2016_6_Kiss_Eszter.pdf.

Kornai, János. 2000. *Evolution of the Hungarian Economy 1848–1998, Volume II. Paying the Bill for the Goulash Communism*. New York: Columbia University Press.

Kovács, Zoltán. 2017. "CEU: Facts versus Frenzy." *About Hungary*, April 6, 2017. http://abouthungary.hu/blog/ceu-facts-versus-frenzy/.

Krekó, Péter. 2016. "Closing Space in Hungary with a Russian Cookbook." October 28, 2016. Accessed April 7, 2019. www.opendemocracy.net/en/openglobalrights-openpage/closing-space-in-hungary-with-russian-cookbook/.

———. 2018. *Tömegparanoia* [Mass Paranoia]. Budapest: Athenaeum Kiadó.

Krekó, Péter, and Zsolt Enyedi. 2018. "Explaining Eastern Europe: Orbán's Laboratory of Illiberalism." *Journal of Democracy* 29 (3): 39–51.

Laclau, Ernesto. 1977. *Politics and Ideology in Marxist Theory: Capitalism, Fascism, Populism*. London: Verso.

———. 2005. *On Populist Reason*. London: Verso.

Laclau, Ernesto, and Chantal Mouffe. 1985. *Hegemony and Socialist Strategy Towards a Radical Democratic Politics*. London: Verso.

Lipstadt, Deborah E. 2019. *Antisemitism: Here and Now*. New York: Schocken.

Marusic, Sinisa-Javov. 2017. "New 'Stop Soros' Movement Unveiled in Macedonia." *Balkan Insight*, January 18, 2017. https://balkaninsight.com/2017/01/18/macedonia-forms-anti-soros-movement-01-18-2017/.

Soros conspiracy theories 229

Mérték Médiaelemző Műhely. 2019. "Fidesz-friendly Media Dominate Everywhere." *Mérték Médiaelemző Műhely*, May 2, 2019.

Meseznikov, Grigorij. 2019. "The EU, Russia, Ukraine in Slovak Pro-Russian Media." *4liberty.eu* [news outlet], March 25, 2019. http://4liberty.eu/the-eu-russia-ukraine-in-slovak-pro-russian-media/.

Michlic, Joanna Beata. 2006. *Poland's Threatening Other: The Image of the Jew from 1880 to the Present*. Lincoln, NE: University of Nebraska Press.

Militaru, George. 2015. "Guvernul Ciolos egal Soros" [Cioloş Government is in Fact Soros Government]. *România Mare*, October 30, 2015. http://romaniamare.info/guvernul-ciolos-egal-guvernul-soros/.

Novak, Benjamin. 2017. "Here are the 'Soros Plan' National Consultation Questions!" *The Budapest Beacon*, September 28, 2017. https://budapestbeacon.com/soros-plan-national-consultation-questions/.

Open Society Foundations (OSF). 2019. "Open Society in Hungary." Accessed July 28, 2019. www.opensocietyfoundations.org/uploads/0a3e7c4b-b236-45eb-b3e2-dc62009900c6/factsheet-osf-hungary-en-20180514.pdf.

Orbán, Viktor. 2014. "A munkaalapú állam korszaka következik" [The Era of the Labor-Based State Follows]. *Magyarország Kormánya*, July 26, 2014. www.kormany.hu/hu/a-miniszterelnok/hirek/a-munkaalapu-allam-korszaka-kovetkezik.

———. 2015. "Interview with Viktor Orbán on the '180 minutes' Programme on Kossuth Radio." Interview by Éva Kocsis. *Miniszterelnok.hu*, October 30, 2015. http://2010-2015.miniszterelnok.hu/in_english_article/interview_with_viktor_Orbán_on_the_180_minutes_programme_on_kossuth_radio.

———. 2016. "Interview with Prime Minister Viktor Orbán on the Kossuth Rádióprogramme '180 Minutes'." *Website of the Hungarian Government*, May 22, 2016. Accessed July 23, 2019. www.kormany.hu/en/the-prime-minister/the-prime-minister-s-speeches/interview-with-prime-minister-viktor-orban-on-the-kossuth-radio-programme-180-minutes-20160520.

———. 2018. "Orbán Viktor's Ceremonial Speech on the 170th Anniversary of the Hungarian Revolution of 1848." March 16, 2018. Accessed July 13, 2019. www.kormany.hu/en/the-prime-minister/the-prime-minister-s-speeches/orban-viktor-s-ceremonial-speech-on-the-170th-anniversary-of-the-hungarian-revolution-of-1848.

Palonen, Emilia. 2018. "Performing the Nation: the Janus-faced Populist Foundations of Illiberalism in Hungary." *Journal of Contemporary European Studies* 26 (3): 308–21.

Panizza, Francisco. 2005. "Introduction: Populism and the Mirror of Democracy." In *Populism and the Mirror of Democracy*, edited by Francisco Panizza, 1–31. London: Verso.

Petrescu, Dragoş. 2009. "Building the Nation, Instrumentalizing Nationalism: Revisiting Romanian National-Communism, 1956–1989." *Nationalities Papers* 37 (4): 523–44.

Pfeffer, Anshel. 2018. "Netanyahu and Orban: An Illiberal Bromance Spanning From D.C. to Jerusalem." *Haaretz.com*, July 18, 2018. Accessed September 4, 2019. www.haaretz.com/israel-news/.premium-the-netanyahu-orban-bromance-that-is-shaking-up-europe-and-d-c-1.6290691.

Popper, Karl. 2012. *The Open Society and Its Enemies, Volume 1: The Spell of Plato*. 7th ed. London: Routledge.

Riadó. 1993. "Egy Amerikában élő újságírónő leleplezi a Soros Alapítványt" [A Journalist Living in the USA Exposes the Soros Foundation]. *Riadó*, February 24, 1993.

Ripp, Zoltán. 2002. "Unity and Division: The Opposition Roundtable and Its Relationship to the Communist Party." In *The Roundtable Talks of 1989: The Genesis of Hungarian Democracy*, edited by András Bozóki, 3–39, Budapest: CEU Press.

230 *Corneliu Pintilescu et al.*

Rogán, Antal. 2017. "The National Consultation Has Begun." *Website of the Hungarian Government,* April 3, 2017. Accessed July 23, 2019. www.korman y.hu/en/cabinet-office-of-the-prime-minister/news/the-national-consultation-has-begun.

Rogozanu, Cristi. 2019. "Alegeri 2019. Concluzii. Și o notiță despre închiderea lui Dragnea" [The 2019 European Parliament Elections in Romania: Conclusion and a Note about Dragnea's Conviction]. *Criticatac* [news outlet], May 28, 2019. www.criticatac.ro/alegeri-2019-concluzii-si-o-notita-despre-inchiderea-lui-dragnea/.

Roth, Eduard Rudolf. 2016. "The Romanian Revolution of 1989 and the Veracity of the External Subversion Theory." *Journal of Contemporary Central and Eastern Europe* 24 (1): 37–50.

Santora, Marc, and Kit Gillet. 2018. "Claiming 'Parallel State' Cabal, Romania's Leaders Target Anti-Corruption Prosecutor." *The New York Times*, June 17, 2018. www.nytimes.com/2018/06/17/world/europe/romania-corruption-prosecutors.html.

Șomănescu, Mihai. 2015. "Lista lui Soros. Cine sunt oamenii care au schimbat România, cu sau fără voia noastră: miniștri, demnitari de rang înalt, jurnaliști" [Soros' List: People Who Changed Romania with or without Our Will]. *Activenews.ro*, May 18, 2015. www.activenews.ro/stiri-politic/Lista-lui-Soros.-Cine-sunt-oamenii-care-au-schimbat-Romania-cu-sau-fara-voia-noastra-ministri-demnitari-de-rang-inalt-jurnalisti-112622.

Soros, George. 2015. "Rebuilding the Asylum System." *Project-Syndicate*, September 26, 2015.Accessed June 17, 2019. www.project-syndicate.org/commentary/rebuilding-refugee-asylum-system-by-george-soros-2015-09.

Söyler, Mehtap. 2015. *The Turkish Deep State: State Consolidation, Civil-Military Relations and Democracy.* Abingdon: Routledge.

Sputnik. 2016. "How Soros-Funded NGOs Disrupt Real Democracy Around Russia's Borders." *Sputnik International,* April 17, 2016. https://sputniknews.com/politics/201604171 038155629-soros-georgia-latvia-investigation/

———. 2019. "Cine este Soros" [Who is Soros]. *Sputnik.md.* Accessed August 24, 2019. https://ro.sputnik.md/trend/george-soros/.

Stoiciu, Victoria. 2018. "Raportul paralel" al comisiei SRI și elefantul din cameră" [The Parallel Report of the SRI Commission and the Elephant in the Room]. *România curate*, July 31, 2018. www.romaniacurata.ro/raportul-paralel-al-comisiei-sri-si-elefantul-din-camera/.

Swanson, Robert C. R. 2018. "Two Case Studies of Russian Propaganda in Romania and Hungary." *International Affairs Review* 26 (1): 1–23.

Szijjártó, Péter. 2018. "Government to Launch Information Campaign on the UN Migration Package." *Website of the Hungarian Government,* February 28, 2018. Accessed July 23, 2019. www.kormany.hu/en/ministry-of-foreign-affairs-and-trade/news/government-to-launch-information-campaign-on-the-un-migration-package.

Tamkin, Emily. 2017. "Who's Afraid of George Soros? How an Octogenarian Businessman Became the Bogeyman of Europe." *Foreign Policy*, October 10, 2017. https://foreignpolicy.com/2017/10/10/whos-afraid-of-george-soros/.

The Associated Press. 2017. "Demonization of George Soros Throughout Europe Recalls anti-Semitic Conspiracy Theories of Yore." July 10, 2017. www.haaretz.com/world-news/europe/demonization-of-soros-recalls-anti-semitic-conspiracies-1.5472319.

Tismăneanu, Vladimir. 1998. *Fantasies of Salvation: Post-communist Political Mythologies.* Princeton: Princeton University Press.

Toma, Mircea. 2013. "Finanțările primite de ActiveWatch de la fundațiile Soros" [The Financial Support Granted to ActiveWatch by Soros]. *ActiveWatch*, September 16, 2013. Accessed July 11, 2019. http://blog.activewatch.ro/diverse/un-raspuns-pentru-domnul-stelian-negrea/.

Soros conspiracy theories 231

Traverso, Enzo. 2019. *The New Faces of Fascism: Populism and the Far Right.* London: Verso.

Válasz. 2013. "Soros félmilliárdot adott Orbán ellenfeleinek" [Soros Gave Half a Billion to Orbán's Opponents]. *Válasz*, August 14, 2013. Accessed July 23, 2019. http://valasz.hu/itthon/soros-felmilliardot-adott-orban-ellenfeleinek-67174

van Prooijen, Jan-Willem, André P. M. Krouwel, and Thomas V. Pollet. 2015. "Political Extremism Predicts Belief in Conspiracy Theories." *Social Psychological and Personality Science* 6 (5): 570–78.

Voice of America (VOA). 2017. "Demonization of Soros Recalls Old Anti-Semitic Conspiracies." *Voice of America*, May 15, 2017. www.voanews.com/europe/demonization-soros-recalls-old-anti-semitic-conspiracies

Voicu, George. 2000. *Zeii cei răi. Cultura conspirației în România postcomunistă* [The Evil Gods: Conspiracy Culture in Postcommunist Romania]. Iași: Polirom.

Wodak, Ruth. 2015. *The Politics of Fear: What Right-Wing Populist Discourses Mean.* London: Sage.

Young, Holly. 2016. "Israel: 'Some NGOs Are Seen as the Enemy From the Inside.'" *The Guardian*, May 11, 2016. www.theguardian.com/global-development-professionals-network/2016/may/11/israel-some-ngos-are-seen-as-the-enemy-from-the-inside

Zacsek, Gyula. 1993. ""Termeszek rágják a nemzetet, avagy gondolatok a Soros-kurzusról, és a Soros-birodalomról" [Termites are Chewing the Nation, or Thoughts on the Soros-Course, and the Soros-Empire]. *Magyar Fórum*, September 3, 1993.

11 Conspiracy theories on Moldovan commercial TV

Onoriu Colăcel

Introduction

Together with the Baltic republics, "Ukraine, a country central to the recent tensions between Russia and Western states" (Szostek 2017a, 380), is commonly the subject of debate when it comes to Russian information war. In contrast, Ukraine's much smaller neighbor, the Republic of Moldova, has remained largely under the radar despite having already faced similar crises to those being experienced by Ukraine. It had an armed conflict with Moscow-backed rebels in the 1990s, now frozen (the war broke out in 1992). Like Ukraine, it is home to large Russian-speaking communities. Its media landscape, although changed since the fall of the USSR, was largely Russian for a long time, with some Romanian influence. The present-day Republic of Moldova (RM) mostly refers to the land between the rivers Prut and Dniester, which used to be known as the eastern half of the medieval principality of Moldavia up to the moment it was annexed by the Russian Empire in 1812. Importantly, the so-called Pridnestrovian Moldavian Soviet Socialist Republic (Transdniester, a narrow strip of land between the river Dniester and the border with Ukraine) is officially part of the Republic of Moldova although Russia has exercised effective control over its territory ever since the end of the USSR.

The recent history of the post-Soviet republic has been shaped by the frozen conflict in the east of the country. Effectively, competing nation-building projects postulate "the existence of a multicultural and bilingual Moldovan people" (Țîcu 2016, 57). These nation-building policies have been deployed by local and foreign elites in order to replace regional self-identification patterns rooted in the shared heritage of the Moldavian Principality, which is very much alive in the eastern part of present-day Romania, also widely known under the name "Moldova."

A poor country, the Republic of Moldova is torn between two political words, the EU and Russia, and likely to fall back to pro-Russian parties. Over $1 billion stolen under the watch of pro-EU political parties, which governed the country from 2009 to 2019, caused widespread political disenfranchisement among the Moldovan people. Ultimately, ethnic divisions and socioeconomic problems are a breeding ground for populism and conspiracy theories, which are woven deeply into the popular culture of the multilingual Republic of Moldova. Since its independence in 1991, the country has searched for ways to revive its economy and

Moldovan commercial TV conspiracy theories 233

political fortune. The Moldovan political elites looked at the close and distant neighbors of the country (Popescu 2006, 42), which have embarked on different political paths after the fall of the Eastern Bloc. For a long time, Ukraine remained close to Russia. Meanwhile, Romania had become a NATO and EU member. On the other hand, Russia has maintained a strong presence across Russian-speaking areas and among those self-identifying with the Soviet past. Once the Moldovan Communist Party was ousted from power in 2009, self-avowed pro-EU coalitions ruled for more than a decade. Often, they promised to crack down on the Kremlin's propaganda. The government in office at the time of writing (first half of 2019), headed by Maia Sandu and backed by both pro-EU and pro-Russian parties, took over from the prime minister, Pavel Filip, a proxy of Vlad Plahotniuc, who fled the country in June 2019. Allegedly, his past in the Russian mafia helped Plahotniuc to gain effective control of all political decision-making in the Republic of Moldova, not to mention most economic assets and major media groups.

The Republic of Moldova is a media battleground that both the East and the West are willing to fight over. A case study right on the doorstep of the EU, the media of the Republic of Moldova can help us understand some of the timeliest issues about the Kremlin's propaganda for Russian-speaking audiences abroad as well as Western countermeasures. Moreover, the response of Brussels to Russian-sponsored news and opinion in the Republic of Moldova is gradually becoming more robust.

On TV, conspiracy theories originating from the Kremlin elucidate why things always seem to go wrong for the average Moldovan. Standing up for the little man comes with the territory of Moldovan politics. As such, conspiracy thinking and populism make perfect sense together. On the one hand, the conspiracy theories that have gained currency in Moldovan society are steeped in notions of "conspiratorial distrust of both the government and those outside the in group" (Knight 2003, xi). On the other hand, populism in the Republic of Moldova is indeed a "thin-centered ideology" (Mudde 2004, 543), possibly more so than in other (Eastern European) countries. It has "a restricted morphology, which necessarily appears attached to—and sometimes is even assimilated into—other ideologies" (Mudde and Kaltwasser 2017, 6). Explicitly, opportunism in Moldovan politics attributes demographic and economic crises to traditional ideologies, from right to left. Having failed to deliver on their promises, local politicians resort to mudslinging and scapegoating: extolling the Orthodox Church borders on xenophobia, while EU integration, union with Romania, or the return to the *Russkiy Mir* (Russian world) ultimately illustrate a deep-seated mistrust in local elites. Essentially, Moldovan populism is linked to Romanian nationalism, Soviet nostalgia—alongside fascination with the Russian world—Moldovan civic identity, pervasive corruption, and state capture by foreign interests. For the Moldovan public, conspiracy theories coming from abroad are an effective way of constructing identity relations (Armstrong 2009) at home: conspiracism is the major narrative strand of an emerging national tradition marked by "rival strategic narratives" (Szostek 2017a, 380). Much like "exclusionary populism" (Mudde and Kaltwasser 2013), conspiracy theories on Moldovan television feature agents

234 *Onoriu Colăcel*

that are essentially different only according to their target audience. Otherwise, common purpose in safeguarding one's culture against the perceived intrusion of other communities is the grand narrative that tells the story of the nation for all. Conspiracy theories play into the widespread suspicion that the country is a testing ground for Russian disinformation campaigns and counter-campaigns run by EU-backed news outlets. They are all aimed at both hostile and friendly audiences living in former Soviet republics (Szostek 2017b, 3).

Finally, the history of the Republic of Moldova and the language most of its citizens share with the Romanian people help conspiracy theories make their way across the border and into Romania. *Sputnik International* and *Russia Today*, the official media outlets of the Russian government, operate online and broadcast news in Romanian/Moldovan as well. Both Sputnik Moldova and Sputnik Romania share the same headquarters in Chişinău, the capital city of the Republic of Moldova.

Research questions and methodology

My reading of conspiracy theory and populist narratives draws on the media representation of political events in the buildup to the fall of Vladimir Plahotniuc who "was the richest man in Europe's poorest country" (Nemtsova 2019). Plahotniuc, the head of the ruling coalition in power from January 2016 to June 2019, has lately become embroiled in most Moldovan conspiracy theories. Essentially, he hijacked power in the Republic of Moldova, as his proxies managed to buy out most of the country's major media companies. Although a self-declared enemy of the Kremlin, his media empire sold Russian content to Moldovan audiences, often conspiracy theories originating from Russia. The TV stations of the General Media Group (GMG), his media holding, used to rebroadcast quite a number of Russian news and entertainment programs. On a regular basis, stories that followed the agenda of the Kremlin were supplied to both Russian and Romanian-speaking audiences. Consequently, the struggle to sway their views on the future of the Republic of Moldova is known to have given rise to competing visions of the past. Moldovan talk shows experiment with story forms that push conspiracy theories about the EU or the Kremlin. Explicitly, distinctive narrative features are consistently used in order to reduce political events to evil intentionality. Most of them mix conspiracy narratives with news and criminal reporting.

My qualitative content analysis looks at media frames (Gamson and Modigliani 1987) in order to trace patterns shared by mainstream local conspiracy theories. Essentially, they are interpretive frames (Entman 1993), sensemaking narratives that develop explanatory models of political agency for the public, particularly so at times of heightened anxiety about the future. I approach them as a discursive phenomenon (Hofstadter 1967; Melley 2002; Barkun 2013), revealing of the depths of suspicion stirred up by the establishment, mainstream media channels, and (alleged) government cover-ups (Knight 2008). The conspiracy narratives of Moldovan media are "a productive challenge to an existing order—albeit one that can excessively simplify complex political and historical events" (Fenster

2008, 90). Basically, conspiracy theories work as populist theories about political power; they reawaken a sense of dissent against political elites (i.e., the "other"), thus giving audiences a say in the redistribution of power (Yablokov 2015).

Most Moldovan media pundits and politicians seem to concur that politics is about revealing conspiracies against their target audience. The political TV format consists of different styles of talk (McNair 2011, 70–82), with the anchor addressing the camera and extensive one-on-one interviews. I have in mind *În Profunzime* ("In Depth," hosted by Lorena Bogza on ProTV Chişinău), *Important* ("Important," with Gheorghe Gonţa, TVC21), *Megafon* ("Megaphone," hosted by Iurie Roşca on NTV Moldova), *Cabinetul din Umbră* ("The Shadow Cabinet," Val Butnaru on JurnalTV) and *Politica* (as of early May 2018, "*Natalia Morari's Politics*," aired on TV8). Often, they have guests who use both Russian and Romanian in the same sentence; some TV shows are bilingual, like *Important*, *Megafon*, and *Politica*. Throughout the first six months of 2018, *Important*, *Megafon*, and *Politica* were each aired 24 times (once a week). Averaging three weekly broadcasts, *Politica* (as of early May 2018, *Natalia Morari's Politics*, TV8), had significantly more air time.

I approach political TV shows from a comparative perspective on media-created frames and themes. These TV broadcasts are "a source for conspiratorial expression" (Evans 2003, 435), which make the most out of the fact that conspiracy theories have a long history in the Republic of Moldova. "With the advent of the Cold War and the rise of collective security organizations . . . geopolitical conspiracy theories and narratives" (Gulyas 2016, 44) became a staple of Moldovan culture. Anti-Western conspiracy theories in the USSR (Kuzio 2011) were deemed useful in achieving political goals. As a socialist republic in the USSR, the country had its share of conspiracy theories that entered the mainstream of Moldovan life: they were related to Russian-speaking migration into urban areas, the status of the native population, and the Russian ascendency over all other ethnic groups. In the long run, they paved the way for present-day conspiracism.

The research question that challenges previous ones about the use of conspiracy theories across Eastern Europe is whether they are actually conspiracy theories after all. Ultimately, Moldovan conspiracism is an instance of a "*wider class of conspiratorial explanations*, which includes both warranted *and* unwarranted conspiracy theories" (Dentith 2014, 38). The gap between conspiracies and conspiracy theories is increasingly smaller in Moldovan media. Conspiracies, as "the joining together of two or more individuals and their acting in collusion to achieve a desired outcome," shed light on local conspiracy theories; they are "an explanation, either speculative or evidence-based, which attributes the causes of an event to a conspiracy or a plot" (Byford 2011, 20–21). Commonly, both conspiracies and conspiracy theories are nurtured by geopolitical tensions and Moldovan history throughout the twentieth century. Nowadays, the proximity of Russia and the EU prompts most Moldovans to call conspiracy theories either examples of disinformation techniques or attempts at debunking conspiratorial thinking. However, conspiracy theories on Moldovan TV conflate right and left wing populisms by identifying the people both in socioeconomic (i.e., the exploited working classes

236 *Onoriu Colăcel*

versus a small number of profiteers) and ethnic terms (the autochthonous population versus Russian-speaking communities emerging from policies of tsarist and Soviet colonization). This translates into stereotypical media representations that challenge traditional understandings of conspiracy theories and conspiracies proper. One way or another, conspiracy theories in the Republic of Moldova are, in fact, telltale signs of a culture of fear that has a long history in its relationship with close (Romania) and distant (Russia) neighbors.

Post-Soviet Moldovan media

The notion of a Cold War–like standoff is embedded in the political culture of the Republic of Moldova, and the frozen conflict of Transdniester has catalyzed the growth of such public narratives. The media features endless debates over the geopolitical orientation of the country, and there is no shortage of spokespersons for the cause of the Eurasian Economic Union (EEU) as much as for that of the EU. Moldovan politics relates to wider historical and cultural factors despite the fact that the genre of the political talk show is highly mediatized, a form of self-referential journalism. Essentially, the mediatization of politics occurs at the expense of political reporting. Mutual distrust is rife between most Eastern European neighbors of Russia and the Kremlin (Besemeres 2016). Effectively, the two sides have long engaged in a "new Cold War" (Ciută and Klinke 2010) that, as far as media representation is concerned, mostly translates former ideologies into nativism and dangerous national "others." As such, the Moldovan conspiratorial landscape is shaped by the "current US-Russia relationship" (Smith 2019), with the EU (and Romania) in the background. The media contest between the two sides unfolds on the Moldovan screens in order to highlight threat perceptions. Yet, the multipolar world of the present owes most of its plotlines in the media to the old "two superpower" world order. As there is a long history across Eastern Europe of borders being changed by use of force, exclusionary forms of representation in the media promote values long formalized in institutionalized narratives of identity and literary cultures.

Consequently, even the sinister secret societies feared by TV show hosts are believed to be headquartered in the home countries of the Russian and Romanian news outlets operating in the Republic of Moldova. The local industry has lately become increasingly competitive, as Romanian-language media organizations have entered the Moldovan market. Consequently, the Russian media lost its monopoly on the news. Even now, Russian and Romanian-speaking outlets are unevenly distributed in favor of the former; all in all, their respective biases seem to be equally transparent in a country where television viewing is more instrumental in shaping public opinion (Vukanović 2016, 172) than in other Eastern European countries. The relative newcomers in the Moldovan media space—that is, the Romanian-language news outlets—come across as a European answer to the challenges coming from Russia.

Thanks to funding by the European Endowment for Democracy, the media war over the former Soviet republic is gaining momentum. Local commercial

Moldovan commercial TV conspiracy theories 237

TV broadcasters (i.e., JurnalTV and TV8) benefited from European money in order to stay afloat (Butnaru 2018). Alongside ProTV Chişinău, associated with the Romanian TV station ProTV, they take a stand against threats coming from the EEU—that is, Russia. Prior to Plahotniuc's flight from the RM in June 2019, he owned "about 70 percent of Moldova's television market" (Gotişan 2016, 7). Few non-Plahotniuc-aligned broadcasters are still on air, although they have been denied national coverage—that is, ProTV Chişinău, JurnalTV, and TV8, which are mostly Romanian-language commercial TV stations committed to EU integration. TVC21, AccentTV, ExclusivTV–TNT Russia, and NTV Moldova are Russian-language/pro-Kremlin broadcasters, quite friendly with Igor Dodon, the president of the Republic of Moldova. However, two advertising agencies, Casa Media and Exclusive Sales House, teamed together to create a near-monopoly in the media market. The former belongs to the same Vladimir Plahotniuc, while the latter is close to Corneliu Furculiţă, a member of the parliament for the Socialist Party (Newsmaker.md 2017). The media empire of Vladimir Plahotniuc was not so much a cheerleader for the main government party, the Democratic Party of Moldova, as much as a mouthpiece of the government that maligns the opposition. Specifically, the talk shows of the GMG's flagship television stations, PrimeTV and PublikaTV, target the reputation of other political parties. Much like the other TV channels (Canal2, Canal3) and radio stations (PublikaFM, MuzFM, MaestroFM) of GMG, they sling insults at the leaders of the opposition and the owners of competing news organizations.

Conspiracy theories: exclusionary narratives of belonging

Narratives of belonging and exclusion run through political arguments on television over the past and the future of the Republic of Moldova; they reveal conspiracy theories about perceived enemies of the Moldovan people. The conspiratorial-minded produce a judgmental discourse on various ethnolinguistic groups. Local conspiracism seeks to marginalize citizens whose allegiance to one's own imagined community can be questioned. All public behavior is believed to be purposeful, and such assumptions reinforce populist narratives that politicize crises in order to save the people from corrupt elites (Laclau 2005) and foreign encroachment.

Based on their experience, most Moldovans on camera act as if conspiracy theories, as well as political conspiracies, reveal the truth behind the smoke screen of politics. For example, even though no evidence emerged about the alleged international agreement that ousted Plahotniuc from power in June 2019, there is no doubt that the people alone had failed to do so. As the envoys of the EU, Russia, and the USA convened in Chişinău to negotiate (Creţu 2019), the 2019 election deadlock ended with the decision of the pro-Russian Socialist Party and the pro-EU *Acum* bloc to form the ruling coalition that toppled Plahotniuc's political proxy, Prime Minister Pavel Filip.

The most influential conspiracy theories aired on political talk shows look back on the Romanian and the Soviet past of the multiethnic Republic of Moldova—that

238 *Onoriu Colăcel*

is, both the Romanians and the Russians have conspired against the Moldovan people and statehood. On the one hand, there is the legacy of Russian imperialism; the "managed democracy" of the Putin regime (Colton and McFaul 2003); and the energy wars that crop up in news stories, events, and editorials. On the other hand, the consensus-driven politics of Brussels, the enlargement of the union to the east, and the Romanian roots of most Moldovan citizens underlie analysis of daily events that border on conspiracist thinking. Collective anxieties around historical events are exacerbated by the feeling that even history textbooks are not to be trusted. Several conspiratorial story lines have become common on Moldovan TV; they revolve around anti-EU and anti-Russian narratives with xenophobic twists. Corruption-related issues feature prominently on the Moldovan conspiracist agenda as well. Real and perceived conspiracy theories further develop into several other narrative strands: genderism, Soros, and anti-Romanian conspiracy theories. Often, politicians and media pundits expose conspiracies and conspiracy theories, which makes it difficult to pinpoint where one ends and the other begins.

Anti-Russian conspiracy theories

For the average Moldovan, the prevalence of conspiracism in the media comes with the territory of politics. The moment threats from the East or the West become headline news, TV talk shows draw on them. Ultimately, they are a way of expressing "a European-Eurasian battle between democracy and autocracy" (Scott 2017, 30). For example, Moldovan media is very aware of developments in neighboring Eastern Ukraine. It reminds the public of the frozen conflict between the Russian-backed troops of the Pridnestrovian Moldavian Republic and the central government in Chişinău. Although this foothold of the Kremlin in the east of Europe has obviously lost some of its relevance (especially after the 2014 crisis in Ukraine and with the Crimean Peninsula firmly in the grip of Russia), the debate over the threat posed by the so-called Russian peacekeepers stationed in the breakaway region of the Republic of Moldova is instrumental to the future of the country. It turns out that the "mediatization of [the] war" (Müür et al. 2016, 29) in Eastern Ukraine makes the point that, for the Moldovan public, everything is connected through political and military action.

Years after the annexation of Crimea, the approach to Russia is nevertheless clichéd. Essentially, it is a failed attempt to come up with answers to questions that arise from Russian narratives for foreign audiences. Among the great variety of talk shows available, the ones that I approach address the state of Moldovan perpetual crisis in a way that can potentially be read through the lens of conspiracy theories involving Russia. The interpretive frames commonly employed by politicians and media pundits are indicative of ethno-national conspiracy theories as well as corruption-related ones. They are sensemaking devices meant to distinguish true and false claims about Russian plans over the Republic of Moldova. Essentially, they push anti-Russian conspiracy theories by relying on affective communication. Media pundits and politicians show commitment to the EU, European know-how, and occasionally to the Romanian heritage of the Republic

Moldovan commercial TV conspiracy theories 239

of Moldova. My focus is on attempts at debunking Russian conspiracy theories. The pro-EU media stages anti-Russian conspiracy theories that have reemerged ever since 2014, with the Kremlin's propaganda over the "fascist Ukraine" (NRT24.ru 2017). The Kremlin's maneuvers are put in the spotlight: the politicians committed to EU membership are being replaced by the Russian-friendly ones. Aided and abetted by Russian secret services and media, the Russian-speaking media is plotting the subversion of democracy in the Republic of Moldova. According to local pro-EU political figures, the weakness of Putin's regime is what makes and breaks conspiracy theories as "a Russian public diplomacy tool" (Yablokov 2015).

Val Butnaru's *Shadow Cabinet* on May 18, 2018, is a case in point of how Plahotniuc-centered conspiracy theories function, set against the backdrop of narratives that touch on Russia. Although a self-professed Europhile, Plahotniuc was believed to have mimicked the methods of the Kremlin in order to take full control of the country. This installment of the show is titled "The recording that reveals the true colors of the Plahotniuc Dodon regime." Val Butnaru's guests argued that the enemy abroad (Russia) subsidizes traitors within (the Socialist Party and the president of the republic, Igor Dodon). The host and his guests attempted to spot patterns in the behavior of President Dodon, referring to his countless visits to Vladimir Putin and his vows of allegiance to the Kremlin. This further catalyzed the belief in a Russian conspiracy against the Republic of Moldova. Like elsewhere in the post-Soviet space, the master narrative spread by *The Shadow Cabinet* comes back to the internal enemies (Ortmann and Heathershaw 2012) of the pro-EU, Romanian-speaking Moldovan citizens. This is seen as a case of the little man fighting against the oligarch and his people, who have captured the state. Various media holdings (the GMG and the pro-socialist television stations) are in the spotlight as possibly the most sinister organizations that operate in the Republic of Moldova on behalf of the Kremlin. The show propagates both conspiracies and conspiracy theories, while exposing quite a number of them. Namely, such narratives point out specific instances of Russian meddling in Moldovan politics. The ban on agricultural exports (allegedly one of the conspiracies meant to weaken the resolve of the pro-EU Moldovans to stay on the European course) or the Kremlin's financial support for local politicians (Igor Dodon is only one of them) is showcased as part of the Kremlin's scheme to keep the Republic of Moldova within the Russian world.

When aired on television, the anti-Russian conspiracy theories (that allege Russian agents at work in the Republic of Moldova) actually grow into even broader explanations of geopolitical issues. As a matter of fact, the Moldovan people are actually asked to work together against Russian imperialism. Strengthening a sense of confusion among audiences and scholars of conspiracy theories, the staunch supporters of the EU literally narrate theories of conspiracy in order to advance their agenda. Political campaigning is carried out with the help of such narratives meant to expose plots against European values and democracy. Awareness of such conspiratorial thinking adds a second level of discourse to most of the conspiracy theories coming from abroad. As such, they thoroughly explain

240   *Onoriu Colăcel*

the world the Moldovan people live in, a world of threats coming from both east and west.

Aired on May 5, 2018, Natalia Morari's talk show, *Politics*, tackled the big questions of media concentration and propaganda wars. Supposedly, local media was abandoned to the devious maneuvers of Russian politics, and such debates perpetuate the concern for such developments. Professionals working in media or media-related fields make painfully clear a new kind of media polarization. According to Morari's guests, the media landscape is sharply divided on the question of news as public service. On the one hand, there is the public good ethos of EU-backed commercial TV (TV8 JurnalTV) and ProTV Chişinău. On the other hand, there is what Morari calls the "questionable ethics" promoted by the media arms of the Democratic (PrimeTV, PublikaTV, Canal2, Canal3) and the Socialist Parties (TVC21, AccentTV, ExclusivTV, and NTV). The show ensures that audiences find out that the campaigns run by the media affiliated to the Democrats and the Socialists are indebted to Russian-like disinformation tactics. In other words, journalists are in the service of their employer, not of the people. Even if the pro-EU political elites have failed to live up to both European standards and the expectations of the Moldovans, some news organizations have not. The guests of Natalia Morari tend to paint a rather strange image of all those who report for the TV stations of Plahotniuc and the Socialist Party. They seem perfectly happy to follow the lead of the government, at the expense of media freedom. Having "to pay their mortgages," journalists go along with the government or the presidential administration. The fact that the media empire of Vladimir Plahotniuc and the emerging one of Igor Dodon work together—under the cartel agreement between the two advertising agencies, Casa Media and Exclusive Sales House—is seen as proof that they have been pooling resources for a long time already. For Morari, the way out is the advent of new technologies and EU backing for the principles that underlie reputable journalism.

However, most of those present acknowledge the shortcomings of online communication. As consumers of media that boast strong ties to one political side or another, Moldovan citizens seem to be caught in an information loop. They naturally gravitate to news and opinion sources that fit their political interests and more or less seem to disregard everything else. According to Morari, most of them are likely to end up in media bubbles of "collective narcissism" (Bilewicz et al. 2015, 45). Furthermore, political journalism on TV reinforces one's own opinion on ethnic relations. If one is to believe her, the media industry seeks to create chaos for the sake of foreign interests, particularly Russian ones.

On April 19, 2018, Gheorghe Gonţa had as a guest on his talk show, *Important*, the chairman of the Communist Party of Moldova, Vladimir Voronin. Having lost political hegemony in 2009, his party had gradually lost its support base to the Socialist Party. According to Voronin, all Moldovan citizens are right to feel angry: the Republic of Moldova does not live up to the standards of either Eastern or Western blocs, while Soviet nostalgia is fully justified by the state of affairs in the country. Voronin quickly made clear that commitment to the values of the EU or the EEU is more than a political option, while his own lies with the East.

Ultimately, the two political unions stand for belief systems. Voronin, the president of the republic from 2001–9, argues that the pro-EU public are invested in anti-Russian conspiracy theories. He stated that Kremlin involvement with politics in the Republic of Moldova is a matter of legitimate concern for Russian citizens living here. Once again, Voronin confirms the people's belief that the elites, irrespective of their mother tongue, are not to be trusted. Yet, this became obvious once the country signed various agreements with the EU—the proof that Russia is right in defending its interests in the Republic of Moldova. It follows that (European, Russian, and Romanian) agents, hidden in plain sight, populate the media and the political establishment. As a matter of fact, Voronin continued, this broad-based conspiracy, able to explain the inner workings of all political operations in the Republic of Moldova, is the reason why Voronin and his party fell from grace. He does not shy away from references to the supposed "herd behavior" of the Moldovan people. His main allegation against the former electorate of the Communists is that most of them are too gullible to understand they are constantly being lied to by everyone else but the Communists. Effectively, Moldovan political shows call out conspiracy theories originating from Russian media. In doing so, they attribute Russian policy in the Republic of Moldova to plots hatched by the Kremlin in order to steer the former Soviet republic toward the EEU (rather than to the EU or Romania). Ultimately, confronting Russian conspiracy theories on Moldovan TV becomes nothing more than another conspiracy theory. Such public discourses aim for confusion, if not fear, and develop into several narrative strands: genderism, Soros-related, and anti-Romanian conspiracy theories.

The European Endowment for Democracy's money—coming in for local commercial TV broadcasters that debunk Russian conspiracies and, consequently, push anti-Russian conspiracy theories—is further proof that whatever happens in the Republic of Moldova is of concern to Brussels. The history that most Moldovan citizens share with the Romanian people, not to mention the same language, allows for real-world testing of audiences' responses both to conspiracy theories originating from the Russian media and to Brussels-sponsored countermeasures.

Anti-EU conspiracy theories

For a long time now, the Russian-speaking media has delivered comparatively more favorably received media products among Moldovan citizens than the Romanian-speaking media (Milewski 2013, 252). However, Russian news is not necessarily a big audience puller. Then again, the Russia-produced quiz show *Pole Chudes* ("Field of Miracles"), the talk show *Pust Govoryat* ("Let Them Talk"), and various Russian film series definitely are bringing in droves of viewers (AGB-Nielsen Media Research 2017).

Iurie Roşca's talk show, *Megaphone*, aired on NTV Moldova, a Kremlin mouthpiece in the Republic of Moldova (Russia's NTV is owned by Gazprom) argues on behalf of a Moldovan civic nation, now in the making. On January 22, 2018, he approached the topical events of early January 2018, such as the mass protests in neighboring Romania and the latest developments in the USA. The Trump

242 *Onoriu Colăcel*

administration is an opportunity for the pro-Kremlin host to disclose the truth about the way Western democracies "really" work. He is positive that the so-called deep state rules over all Western democracies, not to mention that Donald Trump himself does his best not to yield to the dark side of American democracy—the CIA, FBI, and even NATO. The narrative put together by the show is riddled with inconsistencies and paradoxical references to the USA, Russia, Hungary, and Romania. Much like the financial system and Christian values, the survival of the Republic of Moldova itself comes under threat because of the association agreement with the EU, NATO, impending war, and demographic meltdown. According to the show's host, the supporters of the EU are paid by George Soros and Brussels. Moreover, waves of Syrian refugees were about to flood the Republic of Moldova because of the politicians who side with the EU. Actually, the association agreement is an invasion against the sovereignty of the Republic of Moldova; against the average Moldovan citizens; and ultimately against peaceful, law-abiding Christian people. Whether such fears are unfounded or not, the Russian Orthodox Church in the Republic of Moldova, by far the largest community of Orthodox believers in the country, stokes the flames of anti-EU sentiments among the Russian-speaking Moldovans. Equally so, it speaks against the Metropolitanate of Bessarabia, established by the Romanian Orthodox Church in 1992, as a means to reclaim its former place in the mainstream of Moldovan life. Ultimately, the Russian-speaking clergy on TV are adamant about the perils of modern life and the deadly threat posed to the Russian world by the USA, NATO, and the EU. Moreover, the infatuation with Putin is widespread in the Republic of Moldova as well as in Europe (Hungary, France, the UK). Moldovan politics are increasingly personality driven: the president of the republic is a look-alike of Vladimir Putin himself. Eventually, pro-Russian stands on political matters in the Republic of Moldova reveal the lengths that the Kremlin has gone to win hearts and minds. The Socialist Party of Moldova opposes the EU's "colonial rule"; its followers are not necessarily brainwashed into submission by the propaganda machine of Russian media. Instead, they self-identify as belonging to the Russian world for reasons that range from nostalgia for the Soviet period to everyday use of the Russian language.

The framing devices of the political talk show genre can be traced back to specific comparisons and metaphors. Particularly, Moldovan political TV shows foment paranoia, which comes in the wake of the many scandals that have rocked the country: namely, an internationally famous case of bank fraud worth $1 billion, passing legislation on a new electoral system susceptible to vote rigging, the clampdown on corruption that has seen only the leaders of the political opposition detained, and an anti-Russian propaganda law. This is why the timing of the vote on the bill "banning Russian propaganda" (Interfax 2017), passed on December 7, 2017, by the Moldovan parliament, caused outrage across the political spectrum. Except for the largely government-controlled media, everyone else found preposterous the claim that the political elites had finally decided to crack down on Russian propaganda. The ban was passed off as an anti-propaganda campaign, while being a tactical move in Vladimir Plahotniuc's conspiracy to secure his position for one more electoral cycle. Such a view of politics can be simply a belief or even

Moldovan commercial TV conspiracy theories 243

the truth. With the evidence available to the public, there is no way of knowing for sure whether political wrangling in the Republic of Moldova is conducted within the context of what might be termed "conspiracy" or "conspiracy theory."

As everywhere else, local conspiracy theories posit a cause-and-effect relationship where none can say for a fact that this is the case. Even if such an explanation of events is plausible, there is no solid proof that the alleged puppeteers and their puppets actually work together. Often, the leaders of the opposition are branded as puppets or tools of external propaganda. The ambassadors of the EU and the USA to the Republic of Moldova and even by Vladimir Putin himself make the shortlist for the title of the grand puppeteer. In other words, all politicians are being manipulated by local or international big players.

Questions about the future of the Republic of Moldova elicit emotional responses from the audience. Feelings of dejection among the electorate have led to widespread political disengagement, with voter turnout at just over 49% in the last parliamentary elections (OSCE ODIHR 2019, 29). According to local conspiracy theories, the low turnout is engineered by world powers, which have benefited from Moldovan emigration. The local political elites have brought the country to the brink of falling apart because they have allowed if not encouraged migration, which "is the eleventh highest in the world" (Liller 2018).

Positive self-description is a means of dealing with complex issues pertaining to Romanian nationalism (brought about by the Romanian Kingdom in the interwar years and rekindled to some extent following the collapse of the USSR), Moldovan civic identity (rooted in tsarist and later Soviet policies of Moldovan nation-building), and Soviet nostalgia. As the political squabble over the mayorship of the capital city in 2018 was to be settled in favor of the same Vladimir Plahotniuc, these narrative strands are interwoven to follow either Plahotniuc or Dodon. A web of plots and conspiracies against the people of Moldova was revealed by the guests of the talk show of Lorena Bogza, *InPROfunzime*, aired on April 12, 2018. They confirmed that the speech of Moldovan politicians essentially quoted Russian or Romanian conspiracy theory tropes, but with a Moldovan twist. Socialist and Democrat officials disclosed the extent of each other's essentially weak positions (as proponents of opposing views on the future of the country). The Socialists were pro-Russian, while the Democrats were self-avowed supporters of EU integration. However, their arguments were often one and the same, except for the depth of their devotion to either the EU or the EEU. Effectively, this revealed some of the normative functions of political talk in the Republic of Moldova. The image of Romania in the Republic of Moldova is associated with the EU, while Russia effectively stands for the EEU. The fact that significant segments of the public assume a critical attitude toward Romania or Russia is highly consequential for the consumption of conspiracy theories coming from abroad. This shapes a negative perception of either the East or the West (and of their respective supporters), if not of both the East and West. "A feature of conspiracy theories is their negative, distrustful representation of other people and groups" (Douglas, Sutton, and Cichocka 2017, 540), which is self-evident for most Moldovans in front of the camera. Of course, the EU comes under criticism mainly for

244   *Onoriu Colăcel*

other issues than Romania's membership in it. Moral decay, multiculturalism, and the question of a pan-European identity at odds with national self-identification are the charges commonly found in anti-EU conspiracy theories. The open border policy versus an authoritarian regime, the so-called deep state versus Christian-influenced culture, and the energy war between Russia and the EU are the most salient aspects of the Moldovan debates on foreign affairs.

Whatever the topic of the day (e.g., the 2018 snap elections in the capital city, Chișinău), placing it in context makes the difference for the Moldovan public. Plahotniuc; the EU bureaucrats; the elites of Russia and Romania; or international moneylenders such as the International Monetary Fund, the World Bank, or the European Bank for Reconstruction and Development are mentioned most often. They are all actors in innumerable conspiracies against the Republic of Moldova and come under scrutiny whenever Moldovan authorities take action with regard to politics. Conspiracy theorizing advances the idea that Moldovan politics is mostly a game of false moves, which are being made by real or perceived grand puppeteers. The currency of Moldovan politics is suspicion: the assumption that someone is always plotting every last detail of a campaign to rule the Republic of Moldova for another electoral cycle is taken for granted.

Ultimately, Moldovan talk shows prove that received wisdom about the West and Russia frames the discursive space within which reporting on the EU and the EEU takes place. Specifically, television journalism resorts to generally accepted views of the East-West divide. The USA and the EU are the enemy of the Russian world. Both sides come across as distinct entities, once again in a standoff. Perceived primarily as a clash of civilizations, this reductionist view of the world of politics is nevertheless proven wrong. The Moldovan media landscape shows that the belief in a divide between Eastern and Western interests is increasingly challenged by complex story lines that reveal the many entanglements between various identities located across Europe, with the Republic of Moldova at the forefront of international politics. Moldovan talk shows explore *Russkiy Mir* as a means to showcase political ideas that dovetail with the current concerns of the EU and the Kremlin's foreign policy.

Irrespective of their ideology, most local TV pundits argue that the Republic of Moldova has no other choice than to take sides in the tug of war over Eastern Europe. In the long run, the EU and EEU give ready answers to this predicament. For the Moldovan people, the answers are steeped in a need for validation; essentially, the demand for recognition of one's own group identification (Dahlgren 2006) fuels debates over the future. Russian- and Romanian-language talk shows make clear that all ethnic groups seek to gain the recognition of the other communities living in the former Soviet republic. Simply put, antagonistic portrayals of various ethnolinguistic communities are constantly being used to affirm national and cultural boundaries on TV. Most of the time, the argument trotted out by talk shows is that grand puppeteers prevent the country from pursuing integration with either the EU or the EEU. Even if one does not share such a view on the nature of Moldovan politics, the local TV audiences are told that political power in Chișinău is wielded by interest groups always far removed from the public spotlight.

Moldovan commercial TV conspiracy theories   245

As far as political TV shows in the Republic of Moldova are concerned, there is more to conspiracy theories coming from abroad than "conspirational politics" (Bale 2007, 54). The base of conspiracy theory believers is unlikely to be reduced to one demographic or another. Political programming relies on conspiracy theorizing activities irrespective of the specific target audience; the universal appeal of conspiracy theories goes beyond national cultures and brings the Moldovan people together as one community in front of the TV set.

Conclusion

Media-disseminated conspiracy theories in the Republic of Moldova come across as anti-Russian or anti-EU narratives that subsume all other conspiracy-related topics (such as anti-vaccination, genderism, the deep state). They pose a methodological challenge to models of inquiry that bring together Western knowledge and practice (mainly from the EU and the US) and the post-Soviet space. Moldovan conspiracy theories are (1) instrumental in political campaigning; (2) coming from abroad; and finally, (3) as forms of knowledge, they are the least stigmatized. The proximity of Russia and of the EU prompts journalists and politicians to label everything related to conspiracy theories either (crude) disinformation techniques or attempts at debunking conspiratorial thinking. This points to the fact that most of the Moldovan people use the words EU and EEU to stand for opposing worldviews or belief systems. Historically, the shifting national borders of their community means that confirmation bias and cognitive closure, brought about by the plots of conspiracy theories, make conspiracy thinking useful to the average TV watcher in the Republic of Moldova. As a matter of fact, the political TV shows feature media pundits impervious to expert opinions and even facts that might hurt the perceived interests of their respective community.

Ever since the Russian annexation of 1812, awareness of a stand-alone and mostly regional identity, growing out of various nation-building attempts, has gained some traction among the people living on the territory of the present-day Republic of Moldova. In fact, this imaginative glue that keeps many media stories together is of a conservative nature, despite the fact that consensus on what needs to be preserved (i.e., the independent Republic of Moldova or the ties with the Russian world or with Romania) is definitely lacking.

The conspiracy theories that have gained traction in the media of the Republic of Moldova can simultaneously be conspiracies proper and conspiracy theories. It is quite possible that events related to the local elites, Russia, and the EU and Romania or the USA have caused the current state of affairs in this former Soviet republic. Against a background of growing social inequality, the presidency of Igor Dodon proves that local political leaders try to ride populist waves to power. Despite poor political mobilization, political change is a consequence of politicians jumping on the bandwagon of promises to make living in this former Soviet republic nothing less than a dream come true. Paradoxically, the trends toward democratic change go hand in hand with discourses on Soviet-style egalitarianism and fairness. A brand of restorative populism—advocating the return either to

246 *Onoriu Colăcel*

Russia or Romania, the idea of medieval statehood represented by the principality of Moldavia—that confounds external observers elicits clumsy rewritings of history on television. The average Moldovan is likely to assume that all those in front of the camera may very well serve hidden masters. On TV, politics is stripped back to its most basic ingredient: self-promotion and evil intentionality. Ultimately, the interpretive frames of xenophobia, anti-immigration, and corruption tie in with wider public discourses on the morally decadent West and Russian imperialism. As instances of the clash between the East and West, gender, and Soros-related conspiracy theories, alongside anti-vaccination stories, are in the tool kit of every local conspiracy theorist, they reveal the use value of conspiratorial beliefs rather than their intrinsic worth and are instilled in the Moldovan people so as to change or reinforce their political attitudes.

While acknowledging that those at the very top of the political chain play one Moldovan community against another, both journalists and politicians, as they are exposing conspiracy theories, indulge in the same bigoted behavior themselves. Effectively, everyone sees puppeteers and puppets everywhere. In a public sphere where disagreement reigns supreme, all sides are resolute that everyone else is to blame for anything and everything. While making use of binary oppositions, conspiracy thinking effectively estimates the consequences of one's actions and reveals the limited knowledge of the conspiracists themselves.

The conspiracy theories with a focus on the EU and Russia are a major part of the disinformation campaigns within the media of the Republic of Moldova. Tried and tested with the help of media that serves both the Romanian- and Russian-speaking communities, the conspiracy theories make their way across the border with Romania and on to other post-Communist countries. Particularly, Moldovan political journalism on TV is the trial ground for conspiracy theories that are likely to be used across Europe and the Russian Federation.

Most conspiracy theories with a Moldovan twist have to do with one and the same assumption: namely, the Republic of Moldova is on the brink of collapse and the culture of the Moldovan people is on the wane. Everything happens because of sinister organizations that threaten the moral fiber of society. Plots against the nation and the church are the main concerns for local conspiracy theorists. This is plain fearmongering that revolves around matters of military security and religious faith. Ultimately, there is not much to learn from Moldovan political shows on the border between conspiracy theories and conspiracies proper. Other than widespread suspicion that media content is paid-for public relations, television-mediated conspiracy theories in the Republic of Moldova are telltale signs of a culture of fear that has a long history in the Moldovan relationship with close (Romania) and distant (Russia) neighbors.

Bibliography

AGB Nielsen Media Research. 2017. "Obzor televizionoi auditorii za dekabr' 2017 goda" [December Television Survey 2017]. Accessed May 20, 2019. http://agb.md/article/2017/Обзор%20телевизионной%20аудитории%20(декабрь%202017).pdf.

Armstrong, Sean. 2009. "Stalin's Witch-hunt Magical Thinking in the Great Terror." *Totalitarian Movements and Political Religions* 10 (3–4): 221–40.

Bale, Jeffrey. M. 2007. "Political Paranoia v. Political Realism: on Distinguishing between Bogus Conspiracy Theories and Genuine Conspiratorial Politics." *Patterns of Prejudice* 41 (1): 45–60.

Barkun, Michael. 2013. *A Culture of Conspiracy. Apocalyptic Visions in Contemporary America*. Berkeley: University of California Press.

Besemeres, John. 2016. *A Difficult Neighbourhood: Essays on Russia and East-Central Europe since World War II*. Canberra: Australian National University Press.

Bilewicz, Michal, Aleksandra Cichocka, and Wiktor Soral. 2015. *The Psychology of Conspiracy*. London: Routledge.

Butnaru, Val. 2018. "Replică lui Plahotniuc" [A Retort to Plahotniuc]. *Jurnalul.md*, January 26, 2018. Accessed July 5, 2019. http://jurnal.md/ro/politic/2018/1/26/val-butnaru-replica-lui-plahotniuc-e-infuriat-ca-ue-finanteaza-unele-proiecte-pe-care-le-aplicam-astfel-dandu-ne-dreptate/.

Byford, Jovan. 2011. *Conspiracy Theories: A Critical Introduction*. Hampshire: Palgrave McMillan.

Ciută, Felix, Ian Klinke. 2010. "Lost in Conceptualization: Reading the 'new Cold War' with Critical Geopolitics." *Political Geography* 29 (6): 323–32.

Colton, Timothy J., and Michael McFaul. 2003. *Popular Choice and Managed Democracy: The Russian Elections of 1999 and 2000*. Washington, DC: Brookings Institution Press.

Crețu, Felicia. 2019. "EU, Russia, US Send Envoys to Moldova as Possible Pro-Russian Coalition Emerges." *Euroactiv*. Accessed December 11, 2019. www.euractiv.com/section/enlargement/news/eu-russia-us-send-envoys-to-moldova-as-possible-pro-russian-coalition-emerges/.

Dahlgren, Peter. 2006. "Doing Citizenship: The Cultural Origins of Civic Agency in the Public Sphere." *European Journal of Cultural Studies* 9 (3): 267–86.

Dentith, Matthew R. X. 2014. *The Philosophy of Conspiracy Theories*. New York: Palgrave Macmillan.

Douglas, Karen, Robbie M. Sutton, and Aleksandra Cichocka. 2017. "The Psychology of Conspiracy Theories." *Current Directions in Psychological Science* 26 (6): 538–42.

Entman, Robert M. 1993. "Framing: Toward Clarification of a Fractured Paradigm." *Journal of Communication* 43 (4): 51–58.

Evans, C. Wyatt. 2003. "Lincoln, Abraham, Assassination of." In *Conspiracy Theories in American History: An Encyclopedia*, edited by Peter Knight, 435–41. Santa Barbara, CA: ABC-CLIO.

Fenster, Michael. 2008. *Conspiracy Theories. Secrecy and Power in American Culture*. Minneapolis: University of Minnesota Press.

Gamson, William A., and Andre Modigliani. 1987. "The Changing Culture of Affirmative Action." In *Equal Employment Opportunity: Labor Market Discrimination and Public Policy*, edited by Paul Burstein, 373–94. Piscataway, NJ: Transaction Publishers.

Gotișan, Victor. 2016. "Nations in Transit Moldova." *Freedom House*. Accessed May 11, 2019. https://freedomhouse.org/report/nations-transit/2017/moldova.

Gulyas, Aaron John. 2016. *Conspiracy Theories: The Roots, Themes and Propagation of Paranoid Political and Cultural Narratives*. Jefferson, NC: McFarland.

Hofstadter, Richard. 1967. "The Paranoid Style in American Politics." In *The Paranoid Style in American Politics and Other Essays*, 1–40. New York: Vintage Books.

JurnalTV. 2018. "Înregistrarea ce demască binomul PlahoDon" [Video evidence showing that Plahotniuc and Dodon are in cahoots]. Accessed June 20, 2019. www.jurnaltv.md/news/19b6022ad5da299b/cabinetul-din-umbra-17-mai.html.

Knight, Peter. 2003. *Conspiracy Theories in American History: An Encyclopedia*. Santa Barbara, CA: ABC-Clio.

248 *Onoriu Colăcel*

———. 2008. "Outrageous Conspiracy Theories: Popular and Official Responses to 9/11 in Germany and The United States." *New German Critique* 1: 165–95.

Kuzio, Taras. 2011. "Soviet Conspiracy Theories and Political Culture in Ukraine: Understanding Viktor Yanukovych and the Party of Regions." *Communist and Post-Communist Studies* 44 (3): 221–32.

Laclau, Ernesto. 2005. *On Populist Reason*. London: Verso.

Liller, Stefan. 2018. "Making the Most of Emigration. Moldova is Losing its People through Migration. How Can We Tap the Potential of the Diaspora?" *UNDP Moldova*. Accessed November 28, 2019. www.md.undp.org/content/moldova/en/home/blog/2018/making-the-most-of-emigration.html.

McNair, Brian. 2011. *An Introduction to Political Communication*. Oxon: Routledge.

Melley, Timothy. 2002. "Agency, Panic and the Culture of Conspiracies." In *Empire of Conspiracy: The Culture of Paranoia in the Postwar America*, edited by Peter Knight, 57–81. New York: Cornell University Press.

Milewski, Natalia. 2013. "Mapping the Moldovan Media System and Journalism Culture." *Central European Journal of Communication* 2: 249–61.

"Moldovan Parliament Passes Bill Banning 'Russian propaganda'." 2017. *Interfax.* Accessed February 12, 2019. www.interfax.com/newsinf.asp?y=2010&m=1&d=18&pg=6&id=796122.

Mudde, Cas. 2004. "The Populist Zeitgeist." *Government & Opposition* 39 (3): 541–63.

Mudde, Cas, and Cristobal Rovira Kaltwasser. 2013. "Exclusionary vs. Inclusionary Populism: Comparing the Contemporary Europe and Latin America." *Government and Opposition* 48 (2): 147–74.

———. 2017. *Populism. A Very Short Introduction*. Oxford: Oxford University Press.

Müür, Kristina Holger Mölder, Vladimir Sazonov, and Pille Pruulmann-Vengerfeldt. 2016. "Russian Information Operations against the Ukrainian State and Defence Forces: April-December 2014 in Online News." *Journal on Baltic Security* 2 (1): 28–71.

Nemtsova, Anna. 2019. "By Pushing Out Filthy Rich Vladimir Plahotniuc, Moldova Takes the Lead in Ending the Era of the Oligarchs." Accessed December 29, 2019. www.thedailybeast.com/by-pushing-out-filthy-rich-vladimir-plahotniuc-moldova-takes-the-lead-in-de-oligarchization.

Newsmaker. 2017. "Deputat socialist Corneliu Furculiță și-a creat propria casă" [Corneliu Furculiță, the Socialist MP who has his own media business]. Accessed December 17, 2019. http://newsmaker.md/rom/noutati/deputat-socialist-corneliu-furculita-si-a-creat-propria-casa-de-publicitate-34683

NRT24.ru. 2017. "There Is No Stopping the Nazi Poroshenko Regime, Gorlovka Hit Hard, Civilian Severely Wounded and One Has Been Murdered Last Night!" 2018. Accessed May 17, 2019. http://nrt24.ru/en/news/there-no-stopping-nazi-poroshenko-regime-gorlovka-hit-hard-civilian-severely-wounded-and-one.

NTV.md. 2018. "Megafon." January 22, 2018. Accessed December 15, 2019. http://ntv.md/news/15852.

Ortmann, Stefanie, and John Heathershaw. 2012. "Conspiracy Theories in the Post-Soviet Space." *The Russian Review* 71 (4): 551–64.

OSCE ODIHR Election Observation Mission Final Report. 2019. Accessed December 4, 2019. www.osce.org/odihr/elections/moldova/420452?download=true.

Popescu, Gabriel. 2006. "Geopolitics of Scale and Cross-border Cooperation in Eastern Europe: The Case of the Romanian-Ukrainian-Moldovan Borderlands." In *EU Enlargement, Region Building and Shifting Borders of Inclusion and Exclusion*, edited by James Wesley Scott, 35–51. Aldershot: Ashgate.

Moldovan commercial TV conspiracy theories 249

PROTV Chișinău. 2018. "In Profunzime" [In Depth]. Accessed November 29, 2019. http://inprofunzime.protv.md/stiri/politic/urmareste-live-campania-pentru-alegerile-locale-din-balti-si-chisinau.html.

Scott, James Wesley. 2017. "Reconceptualizing European Neighbourhood Beyond Geopolitics." In *Neighbourhood Perceptions of the Ukraine Crisis. From the Soviet Union into Eurasia?* edited by Gerhard Besier and Katarzyna Stoklosa, 24–38. London and New York: Routledge.

Smith, Nicholas Ross. 2019. *A New Cold War. Assessing the Current US-Russia Relationship*. Cham: Palgrave.

Szostek, Joanna. 2017a. "The Power and Limits of Russia's Strategic Narrative in Ukraine: The Role of Linkage." *American Political Science Association* 15 (2): 379–95.

———. 2017b. "Nothing Is True? The Credibility of News and Conflicting Narratives during 'Information War' in Ukraine." *The International Journal of Press/Politics* (November 29): 1–20.

Țîcu, Octavian. 2016. "Borders and Nation-Building in Post-Soviet Space: A Glance from the Republic of Moldova." In *The EU's Eastern Neighbourhood: Migration, Borders and Regional Stability*, edited by Ilkka Liikanen, James W. Scott, and Tiina Sotkasiira, 50–64. New York: Routledge.

TV8.md. 2018. "Politica cu Natalia Morari: Despre presa liberă care a mai rămas 03/05/2018." [Politics with Natalia Morari: What's Left of the Free Media]. Accessed September 7, 2019. http://tv8.md/tv8-show/politica-cu-natalia-morari-despre-presa-libera-care-a-mai-ramas/.

TVC21. 2018. "Important with Gheorghe Gonța, 19/04/2018" [Important with Gheorghe Gonța]. Accessed July 11, 2018. www.youtube.com/watch?v=mcEnK6kEohU.

Vukanović, Zvezdan. 2016. *Foreign Direct Investment Inflows into the South East European Media Market. Towards A Hybrid Business Model*. Springer International Publishing.

Yablokov, Ilya. 2015. "Conspiracy Theories as a Russian Public Diplomacy Tool: The Case of Russia Today (RT)." *Politics* 35 (3–4): 301–15.

12 North Macedonia goes global

Pro-EU aspiration and anti-EU sentiment as a basis for EU-related conspiracy theories

Biljana Gjoneska, Kristijan Fidanovski, and André Krouwel

Ever since declaring independence in 1991, the Republic of North Macedonia (MK) has viewed integration into the European Union (EU) as its single biggest geostrategic priority. Aspirations to join the EU have stood the test of time and have been largely unaltered by a series of tumultuous events in the country's post-socialist transition. These include the wars in much of the neighboring post-Yugoslav region throughout the 1990s and also North Macedonia's own internal armed conflict in 2001.

By submitting its application for membership (in 2004) and becoming a candidate member (in 2005), the country began its long and still ongoing sojourn in "Brussels' waiting room."[1] However, 14 years since becoming a candidate member, North Macedonia has still not opened any of the 35 accession chapters of the European Union's Acquis Communautaire (i.e., complete legislative framework), the full closure of which constitutes a mandatory prerequisite for accession. In fact, at the time of writing (2019), the date for the start of accession talks remains to be set. North Macedonia has long been overtaken in the accession race by Montenegro and Serbia, both of which became candidate members as many as six years after North Macedonia (European Commission Progress Report 2018).

However, North Macedonia's delayed accession to the EU has not prompted the Macedonian people to reconsider their biggest geostrategic objective. On the contrary, during the last decade, support for EU accession has consistently equaled or exceeded a high 71% of the population according to the International Republican Institute (2018, 68). This number does not just indicate pragmatic support for EU membership, based on hopes for a higher living standard. Beyond the potential privileges and future perspectives, the favorable statistics also extend to signify favorable attitudes toward the EU and its values. Indeed, three separate public opinion surveys, conducted on representative samples throughout 2018, have consistently demonstrated that a decidedly positive (as opposed to negative) view of the EU was held by a majority of respondents, as follows: 59% positive versus 11% negative attitudes (Regional Cooperation Council 2018, 49); 59% versus 19% (Standard Eurobarometer 2019, 89); 49% versus 18% (National Democratic Institute 2018, 10), with the rest categorized as either neutral or undecided. Hence, at first glance, North Macedonia seems to provide little fertile ground for the emergence of anti-EU conspiracy theories.

North Macedonia goes global 251

Yet, such conspiracy theories exist and should not be ignored even in cases when the initial supporters or the target audiences are rather small, because their potential impact may nevertheless be very strong. This chapter demonstrates that even the smallest decrease in support for EU membership might coincide with a significant increase in anti-EU conspiracy theories. So far, the conspiracy theories have failed to shatter the predominant pro-EU consensus in the country, yet the narratives' formidable diversity and creativity, along with their abrupt emergence, are certainly influential and deserve adequate attention. One can observe this in many European and non-European countries, where expanded internet access and the increased use of social media platforms have helped to divert public attention toward provocative speculation or fast-spreading controversial theories (for a famous case of disinformation spread and dissemination via MK digital platforms refer to Subramanian 2017, 70–79).

Moreover, the consistent strength of pro-EU sentiments in North Macedonia should not be overemphasized. While the country remains strongly pro-EU by the standards of the Western Balkans, and even by those of most EU member states, this trend is not immune to future reversals. The 2013 case of the accession of Croatia—a country with similar geostrategic objectives as North Macedonia—provides an important cautionary tale on the impact of delayed accession on domestic support for EU membership. The massive drop in EU support (from the low 70s to the mid-40s percentage range) experienced by Croatia hints at the significant negative impact of the continued postponement of accession talks on pro-EU sentiments. In fact, a study by Belloni (2016) reports a similar decline in support of European integration in most of the Western Balkan countries (except Kosovo and Albania) through a period of 10 years (2006–15), which happened in parallel to the delays in their accession talks. Interestingly, in the case of Croatia, this effect was only exacerbated by the eventual opening of accession talks (Štulhofer 2006, 146). Thus, paradoxically, the potential end of North Macedonia's 14-year-long wait for accession talks might also put an end to the near-unanimous support for membership and divide Macedonian citizens. In fact, the protracted and delicate nature of these talks might conceivably harm pro-EU sentiments *even if* these remain strong—unlike in Croatia—all the way to the beginning of accession talks. This is especially true, when considered in the light of the fact that Euroskepticism is omnipresent and inherent both for the member countries and candidate countries alike (with 15.75% and 23.46% of expressed support for Euroskeptic parties in each group, respectively), as reported by Taggart and Szczerbiak (2002, 7–8). Given that many European countries (regardless of their status in the EU) are not immune to this phenomenon, and anticipating the potential consequences from the rise of anti-EU conspiracy theories, we aim in this chapter to contribute to the scholarly literature about the phenomena by offering critical analysis of the present Macedonian sociopolitical context.

This chapter is organized into three main parts. The first part portrays the general sociopolitical landscape (with an overview of past events) and the psychosocial determinants (the collective mindset), in order to answer the question: *What contributes to the appeal of EU-related conspiracy theories in North Macedonia?* The second part speculates about the specific conditions and actors that

252 *Biljana Gjoneska et al.*

enabled the recent emergence of anti-EU narratives. It identifies key domestic or foreign political figures and parties, expands on their mutual interplay around recent events, and outlines the resulting conspiracy theories. It aims to answer the question: *Who are the main enablers of recent EU-related conspiracy theories?* The third part builds on the previous theoretical considerations about the possible enforcers in order to postulate the research hypotheses and offer empirical evidence about possible conspiracy believers in North Macedonia today. It aims to answer the question: *Who are the main believers in recent EU-related conspiracy theories?*

What contributes to the appeal of EU-related conspiracy theories in North Macedonia?

North Macedonia is one of the seven former Yugoslav republics, located centrally in the Balkans. The region is burdened with images of historical turbulence and violence, complemented by orientalizing discourses from outside states (Todorova 1994, 453–82; Bakić-Hayden 1995, 917–31) and augmented by actual memories of societal breakdown in the aftermath of the collapse of Yugoslavia. As a result, most of the former republics underwent turbulent political and economical transition, governed by weak institutions and opportunistic parties that proved unable to secure a scandal-free political climate.

The effects of a past societal trauma (1991–2006)

Despite the fact that North Macedonia managed to peacefully secede from former Yugoslavia, the memory of recent wars in neighboring countries (during the 1990s), along with experienced trauma from internal armed conflict (in 2001), has endured in the minds of Macedonian citizens. The negative political developments marked by security concerns were also coupled with a protracted and thorny economic transition from a largely state-controlled system to a market economy (all throughout the 2000s) and the stagnation in the EU accession process. Together, these events have cast a long shadow on people's sense of stability, shattered their internal sense of control, and shaken the very foundations of their peaceful existence. Thus, it is natural to assume that the space for premeditated, rational, and analytical observations of ongoing political events may have become limited with time. If this is the case, then the floor was certainly opened to various speculations about internal and external enemies (including the EU) who conspire to harm the country.

Human history offers numerous examples of conspiratorial narratives emerging in response to societal crises, like powerful and impactful events that question the existing order, norms, standards, even groups or entire populations in a society (van Prooijen and Douglas 2017, 322–33). This is because crises create the hardest of times, which makes them more difficult to grasp, so conspiracy theories serve to provide simplistic explanations for complex events and direct causal interpretations of otherwise intricate and interconnected happenings (Hofstadter

North Macedonia goes global   253

1966). The need for this particular kind of sensemaking and rationalization (Lantian, Wood, and Gjoneska 2020, 156–67) is grounded on the following:

a)   *Fast regulation of the stress* experienced in the face of traumatic events and the lingering *anxiety* that remains long after (Swami et al. 2016, 72–76). In this regard, *conspiracy theories act as coping strategies* in dealing with negative emotions in the aftermath of wars, conflicts, or disasters. Previously, Grzesiak-Feldman (2013, 110–18) has demonstrated that the levels of both trait anxiety (which is inherent to the personality) and state anxiety (which is a product of the circumstances) are positively associated with conspiratorial thinking. Therefore, anxiety born as a result of crisis and massive societal changes should particularly increase the proneness toward conspiracy theories, which in turn serve to strengthen one's sense of agency and maintain one's self-esteem (Robins and Post 1997).

b)   *Efficient restoration of feelings of certainty and predictability* that diminish in times of sudden, unexpected, and unfavorable events. In this regard, *conspiracy theories serve a compensatory function*, as they reinstall a sense of order and control over the situation and reduce feelings of powerlessness (Hofstadter 1966; Abalakina-Paap et al. 1999, 637–47). There is ample evidence in support of the fact that a decreased sense of certainty combined with a lack of perceived control over the situation can increase conspiratorial thinking: McCauley and Jacques (1979, 637) showed that stories with unfavorable and uncontrollable endings (like the successful assassination of a president) increased the proneness for conspiratorial explanations in tested subjects. In a similar line of reasoning, van Prooijen and Jostmann (2013, 109–15) demonstrated that scenarios accompanied by increased levels of personal uncertainty among the participants influence the extent to which they interpret intentions of concerned authorities as (a)moral and judge their actions as conspiratorial. Finally, Sullivan, Landau, and Rothschild (2010, 434) evidenced that people attribute exaggerated influence to perceived enemies "in order to compensate for perceptions of reduced control over their environment" (see also Rothschild et al. 2012, 1148).

In summary, conspiracy theories ultimately serve to strengthen a sense of agency. With the reintroduction of causality through straightforward narratives about difficult events and the reinstallation of their sense of agency, people are secured "from perceiving themselves to be at the mercy of capricious and arbitrary forces" and as being powerless agents (LeBoeuf and Norton 2011, 139). Simply put, if they believe that they can predict effectively the causes of the traumatic events, they can feel empowered, steady, and ready to act in order to prevent such events from recurring in the future. The mentality of modern Macedonian citizens in the years since the country's independence was undoubtedly molded both by their fears (of succumbing to the surrounding threats) and by their striving to maintain control, order, and balance (within the confines of their country's borders), increasing their susceptibility to various conspiracy theories.

254   *Biljana Gjoneska et al.*

The consequences of VMRO-DPMNE's long governance (2006–17)

The persistence of societal fears for security of the nation long after the conflicts, enabled the decade-long endurance of a coalition government led by the right-wing party "VMRO-DPMNE" ("Internal Macedonian Revolutionary Organization–Democratic Party for Macedonian National Unity"). Throughout this period, the party was mostly dominated by—and associated with—the strongman prime minister, Nikola Gruevski. His populist and technocratic leadership style, along with his public image as a strong-willed and charismatic leader (Nai, Martínez i Coma, and Maier 2019), yielded the capture of various official institutions, such as "judicial bodies, regulatory agencies, and media outlets" (European Commission Progress Report 2016). His long-lasting rule eventually led to a "state capture" characterized by the "manipulation of elections, closure of critical media, pressure on journalists and independent institutions" (Bieber 2018, 342). This was accompanied by the open embrace of ethno-nationalism in an attempt to "reconstruct Macedonian ethnic identification through educational and cultural policies and elite framing" (Vangeli 2011, 13–32; Vangelov 2019, 221). In 2015, however, Gruevski was faced with a major wiretapping scandal, as the opposition at the time released a series of recordings with highly incriminating phone conversations, between top-level government officials. The scandal revealed "a massive invasion of fundamental rights including: the right to participate in public affairs and to vote; the right of equal access to public services; the right to privacy and the protection of personal data, as well as the right to an independent and impartial judiciary" (Priebe Report 2015). Leaked by whistleblowers in the national intelligence agency and illegally tapped by the government itself, the conversations revealed the full extent of the corruption of the governing regime.

In line with the definition of a political scandal (Einstein and Glick 2013), the wiretapping incident can be regarded as a political scandal of massive proportions, since it involved an intricate network of collaborators (from the highest echelons in politics), who deviated from expected societal norms and bridged the basic privacy rights of about 20,000 citizens by listening in on their conversations. Einstein and Glick (2013, 2015) hypothesized that a scandal-filled political climate perpetuates the so-called vicious circle of cynicism, where scandals diminish the trust in government and give rise to conspiracy theories while the conspiracy theories further diminish the trust in the governing structures and so on. Thus, scandals can reinforce the conspiratorial mindset and vice versa. At the core of conspiracy theories generated as a result of political scandals, there always lies a lack of trust in the system. Indeed, feelings of distrust (toward political figures, official authorities, and governmental institutions and representatives) act as a driving force behind the tendency to believe in conspiracy theories, regardless of whether they are generated from situational constrains or are dispositional characteristics. The inherent distrust in society can be extended to a perception that the "social and political conditions are crumbling" (Teymoori et al. 2016) or that "society's fundamental, defining values are under siege" (Federico, Williams, and Vitriol 2018, 936), with a consequent rejection of social norms known

North Macedonia goes global 255

as "anomie" (Goertzel 1994, 731–42; Abalakina-Paap et al. 1999, 637–47). Such resentment and resignation among Macedonian citizens is yet another explanation as to why they became more prone to conspiracy theories in order to rationalize the machinations in the society and restore their sense of power.

Who are the main enablers of recent EU-related conspiracy theories?

VMRO-DPMNE's decade-long rule, culminating with the wiretapping scandal, unfurled a chain of events that ultimately resulted in a change of government. However, what is of interest here, is the test of character that the wiretapping scandal posed for the EU, Gruevski's establishment, and himself, as well as his supporters. In the following section, we will provide an overview of their mutual interplay, in an attempt to answer the question of who instigated the anti-EU narratives, surfacing and still circulating in the country at present.

Having tolerated Gruevski by providing largely positive assessments of his rule in its annual progress reports on North Macedonia as late as 2014 (European Commission Progress Report 2009, 2010, 2014), Brussels had good reason to suspect that Gruevski's eventual demise might also undermine the EU's own credibility in the eyes of Macedonian citizens. In fact, the EU's reputation may well have been one of the biggest victims of the wiretapping scandal. This momentous event in North Macedonia's political history prompted a major—albeit not immediate—shift in EU policy toward the country. As Macedonians began to take to the streets, and while the government was still denying the authenticity of the recordings, the EU took it upon itself to mediate between Gruevski and the opposition and facilitate the holding of fair elections (European Commission Progress Report 2015). At first glance, the EU's decision to become closely involved in North Macedonia's internal affairs was a commendable act in the interest of Macedonian democracy, which should have only enhanced the EU's popularity in the country. Yet, the EU's hitherto policy toward the country—and the refusal of the disgraced government to go down without a fight—were both so strong that the scandal caused damage to pro-EU sentiments in North Macedonia from two different and logically opposed standpoints. Suddenly, the EU found itself on: a) the proverbial "black list" of Gruevski's opponents (most of them EU supporters) for having tolerated Gruevski *before* the scandal; b) the proverbial "black list" of Gruevski's supporters (many of them EU skeptics) for defying him *after* the scandal.

a)   The logic of Gruevski's opponents: *"The EU likes Gruevski = We don't like the EU"*

According to a poll conducted by the International Republican Institute, support for EU membership in North Macedonia dropped from 84% in November 2012 to 76% in February 2014 (International Republican Institute 2018, 48). This 8% decline is outside of the margin of error. Of course, in and of itself, this statistic

256   *Biljana Gjoneska et al.*

does not constitute concrete evidence for the claim that the EU's tacit support for Gruevski before the wiretapping scandal diminished pro-EU sentiments in the country. After all, the statistic stems from a single specific poll, albeit conducted on a nationally representative sample with 1,100 respondents. Another reason why it cannot be used as a means of establishing causality is the possibility for an alternative explanation: Macedonians might have simply grown tired with the delayed accession of their country. This might have prompted them to turn against the EU, *regardless of* their view on Brussels' good relationship with Gruevski. Yet, the 76% in February 2014 was the lowest-ever level of EU support in the country by this point, and it was followed by continued decline to an all-time-lowest 71% in April 2016, after the wiretapping scandal (ibid.). The findings reported by IRI are also supported by data from other public surveys (Belloni 2016), throughout the period of Gruevski's rule (for the years 2006, 2010, and 2015 consecutively), showing continual decline in the positive attitudes of Macedonian citizens toward the EU (76%, 60%, and 40%, respectively). Taken together, these data suggest the EU's declining popularity could be due in part to Brussels' toleration of Gruevski.

The reasons for the EU's decision to tolerate Gruevski before the wiretapping scandal fall outside of the scope of this chapter, but they can be largely reduced to a strategy of keeping a popular pro-EU leader in power regardless of the nature of his rule, in order to keep the country on its European integration path. In the long run, this policy of "stabilitocracy" or prioritizing short-term stability over democracy and "according external legitimacy to competitive authoritarian regimes" proved to be unsustainable (Bieber 2018, 345). The EU's appeal in North Macedonia has suffered from Brussels' "admission of guilt" and sudden policy reversal in 2015, as well as by the open confirmation of Gruevski's regime (evidenced in the recordings). For a moment, North Macedonia served as an example of how the "transformative effect [of the EU] has indeed made a difference, but in the wrong direction" (Dimitrov, Jordanovska, and Taleski 2016, 3). Thus, it is unsurprising that many genuine local believers in European values began to lose faith after seeing those very values undermined in their own country for years. That said, it is difficult to draw a direct causal link between the emergence of anti-EU conspiracy theories in North Macedonia and Brussels' politics of "stabilitocracy" toward Gruevski. The claim that the EU's policy toward the country prior to the wiretapping scandal cost Brussels more than 10% of North Macedonia's pro-EU sentiments rests upon the assumption that the people who turned against the EU because of this were still supportive of the EU *in principle*. Their opposition was directed merely toward the current outlook of the EU—probably personified by commissioner for Neighborhood Policy and Enlargement Johannes Hahn—which they thought violated their principles as well as its own.

This temporary shift against the EU—with its context-specific causes—can hardly be seen as fertile ground for conspiratorial thinking vis-à-vis the EU. This was a shift motivated by demands for *more, not less* respect for EU values. Therefore, it can be helpful to analyze the motives of citizens whose EU-related attitudes were *not* altered by recent circumstances, but whose long-standing resentment toward Brussels and the West was merely vindicated by them. As hypothesized in

North Macedonia goes global 257

the latter sections of this chapter, the portion of the population who supported—and were influenced by—the regime that sought to secure its own survival were the ones who were eager to capitalize on anti-EU sentiments. Hence, members or supporters of Gruevski's regime constituted the likeliest "suspects" for the appearance of anti-EU conspiracy theories in North Macedonia.

b)   The logic of Gruevski's supporters: *"The EU Doesn't Like Gruevski = We Don't Like the EU"*

Paradoxically, Gruevski's strategy in dealing with the aftermath of the wiretapping scandal was to turn against his main supporter for almost a decade: the EU. As soon as Brussels got involved in facilitating the free parliamentary elections that could (and eventually did) bring an end of the state capture, the incumbents resorted to what was a textbook rallying-around-the-flag scenario. For a regime that had lost its legitimacy, the only recourse was to paint an existential threat facing the country—and to portray itself as the sole protector against it. This sudden and vociferous turn against the EU in a number of public narratives advanced by the government-controlled media indicates a considerable degree of instilled nationalism behind the abrupt emergence of anti-EU conspiracy theories in light of the wiretapping scandal. Yet, it would be inaccurate to characterize this shift as a fully top-down phenomenon, imposed by a government in distress on its otherwise unwilling subjects. The considerably high support for EU membership before 2015 does capture the (low) likelihood for the average Macedonian citizen to oppose EU accession. However, it says nothing about the *salience* of anti-EU sentiments among the small portion of the population who harbor them. These sentiments are fueled by nationalistic scaremongering, as well as *foreign-based* disinformation campaigns against the EU and the West, mostly published in Russian outlets indirectly influencing the information and political landscape (but also marked by Chinese and Turkish interference in the business and the educational sector) of the country (Chrzová et al. 2019). As a result, the existing Euroskepticism among this portion of the population indeed served as a fertile ground for anti-EU conspiracy theories, which blossomed as soon as another enabling condition emerged: the 2018 name-change referendum. On September 30, 2018, Macedonian citizens were asked the following referendum question: "Are you in favor of European Union and NATO membership, by accepting the agreement between the Republic of Macedonia and the Republic of Greece?" The agreement, signed in June 2018, mandated the replacement of the hitherto name "Republic of Macedonia" with what is now the "Republic of North Macedonia" as a means of solving a decades-long naming dispute and opening the path to EU-accession talks (Prespa agreement 2018). The referendum was non-binding in nature (i.e., not a necessary precondition for the eventual ratification of the name proposal by the Macedonian parliament in January 2019) and proved unsuccessful, as it failed to meet the minimum turnout requirement of 50% (the actual turnout was 36.91% of registered voters). However, the results of those who did vote revealed overwhelming support for the agreement (94%). In any case, the polarizing mood

258 *Biljana Gjoneska et al.*

that was fostered during the referendum campaign provided fertile ground for the emergence of anti-EU conspiracy theories, and not necessarily just among the marginal anti-EU fractions of the population. VMRO-DPMNE, now in opposition, as well as several far-right and, to a lesser extent, pro-Russian factions, decided to oppose the long-overdue resolution of the naming dispute by spreading charged narratives about the name-change agreement being an unacceptably costly sacrifice for EU accession. As a result, dissociating the name change from EU accession proved to be cognitively impossible for some Macedonian voters, as EU integration was included in the referendum question itself. Due to the EU's policy of unanimous ratification of the acceptance of new members by existing member states, Greece had the power to block North Macedonia's accession process (Fidanovski 2018, 26), and the EU was seen as its enabler. In this climate, numerous instances of anti-EU conspiracy theories emerged, so in the following section we present the most prominent examples.

North Macedonia: (In)fertile ground of anti-EU conspiracy theories

Even though the referendum question regarding the name change did not encroach on the identity of Macedonian citizens, opponents of the agreement seized the opportunity to engage in identity-based scaremongering. To name just one prominent example, a wealthy Russian-Greek businessman was accused of providing €300,000 to paid demonstrators in Skopje to protest against the name change as well as against North Macedonia's integration into Western institutions (Cvetkovska 2018).

Broadly speaking, several different manipulative, conspiratorial narratives were present ever since the wiretapping scandal. They were positioning a range of actors—from ethnic Albanians to George Soros and ultimately the EU—as inimical to North Macedonia's existence. With regard to the EU, some of the most striking narratives emphasized the pivotal role of Germany in contemporary EU policymaking, especially in approving the opening of the accession talks. This was used to advance a narrative of a century of continuous German domination and ultimately to draw unsubstantiated parallels with Nazi Germany. Such narratives aimed to depict the EU as a threat to national security. More common, however, were conspiracy theories that aimed to portray the EU as a threat to societal values. These narratives framed the EU as a vehicle for imposing allegedly alien social norms (such as freedom of sexual orientation) to new member states. Interestingly, in all the scenarios, the EU was painted as a malevolent actor that aimed to dissolve the country, or the moral fabric of society, while the Gruevski regime was framed as "the only safeguard against the change of Macedonia's name and identity" (Vangelov 2019, 221). That the campaign was effective became evident immediately after the subsequent transfer of power to the opposition and was reflected in the low turnout at the referendum. In fact, the spread of a distinctly anti-Western mood prompted some real security concerns as soon as the 2016 election took place. During this period many ambassadors of EU member states found their photographs on ominous-looking posters in obituary formats, which could reasonably be interpreted as death threats. While none of these ambassadors experienced violent encounters of any kind, the nature and timing of these events points to the dangers posed by an abrupt increase in anti-EU sentiments, encouraged by Gruevski's establishment and supporters, and consistently incorporating conspiratorial narratives.

Who are the main believers of EU-related conspiracy theories?

Having considered the recent political context and the contemporary mindset of Macedonian citizens, both shaped by major societal shifts, we now turn to empirical evidence. Specifically, we will analyze the ideological determinants of Macedonians' support (or lack thereof) for the EU-integration processes as well as their beliefs in general and in EU-related conspiracy theories. In the next segment, we present the list of posed/tested hypotheses:

a) First, we hypothesize that the period coinciding with the change of government and the loss of power of the right-wing coalition (2016–18) will be marked by an overall decrease in the support for EU integration. More importantly, we expect a significantly different level of support between the main political camps, with the right-wing (RW) group being less supportive of EU accession than the left-wing (LW) group of voters. This reasoning is based on our previous theoretical considerations about the most likely actors to enforce anti-EU sentiments and narratives.

b) Following the same line of reasoning, we further postulate that in the period surrounding the referendum (September–October 2018), the level of anti-EU conspiracy endorsement will also be marked by a significant difference between the two groups of voters. Again, we presume that the RW group will express higher levels of endorsement of anti-EU directed conspiratorial narratives (as compared to the LW group).

c) Next, we hypothesize that the general susceptibility to conspiracy theories or so-called conspiracy mentality (Imhoff and Bruder 2014, 25–43) will be positively associated with the belief in EU-specific conspiracy theories. Moreover, we postulate that the conspiracy mentality will predict the belief in anti-EU/anti-West theories (at least to a degree). In their most basic form, conspiracy beliefs typically rely on the presumption that *a powerful group* is at the backdrop of some experienced/expected harmful event. The EU is typically perceived as a high-power and high-status community, so it is natural to assume that the existence of such a relationship is possible and statistically verifiable.

We were able to test the postulated hypotheses across three different studies performed within the framework of COST Action for comparative analysis of conspiracy theories[2] and in collaboration with KiesKompas's Macedonian Voting Advice Application (2016–18) for the purpose of this chapter. They scanned

260   *Biljana Gjoneska et al.*

EU-related attitudes and anti-EU conspiracy beliefs of Macedonian citizens at crucial points in the recent past—immediately/considerably after the state capture. Specifically, the studies were conducted: immediately before/after the parliamentary elections in 2016 (December 2016–January 2017 for Study 1), after the Macedonian referendum (October 2018 for Study 2), and right before the referendum (September 2018 for Study 3). Study 3 was conducted at a time when polarization was expected to be highest, so it was extended to employ specific examples of anti-EU conspiracy theories.

Participants and methods

An online recruitment method was employed in all studies, by sending solicitation emails to a pool of respondents who had agreed to participate in KiesKompas surveys (i.e., a database with participants in earlier studies who signed up as volunteers in future ones). However, the principal analyses in Study 3 were conducted on an enlarged sample, obtained with an additional snowball recruitment method via social networks, by posting open calls on public groups of RW/LW supporters.

In Study 1, a total of 217 adult Macedonian citizens completed the surveys on a voluntary basis, while 266 and 755 respondents were recruited for Studies 2 and 3, respectively. After exempting those who self-declared as belonging to a political center, the final samples for statistical analyses in each of the studies consisted of the following number of subjects: 192 participants in Study 1, 261 participants in Study 2, and 602 participants in Study 3.

In all three studies, participants' political orientation was measured via direct question, asking for self-placement on a finer-grained 11-point Likert scale (Study 1) or a coarser-grained 9-point Likert-type item (Studies 2 and 3). The responses were always coded to start with "1" signifying "extremely left," while end-numbers corresponded to "extremely right" political orientation. Based on their responses, participants were then split into two groups, with the LW group consisting of voters who ranked themselves in the first half and the RW group of voters with self-assigned scores in the second half of the scale. Those who belonged to the political center (i.e., selected "6" in Study 1 or "5" in Studies 2 and 3) were not included in the analysis since their political orientation was not explicitly aligned with any ideology.

Additionally, in Study 1 participants were asked to rate the following question "Do you support Macedonia's efforts to become an EU member state?" A 5-point Likert scale offered five possible options: "1" = "completely agree," "2" = "agree," "3" = "neither agree nor disagree," "4" = "disagree," "5"= "completely disagree." On the other hand, for Study 2, respondents were given questions regarding their referendum-related vote: "How did you vote on the referendum?" The options were the following: "1" = "I voted in favor," "2" = "I voted against," "3" = "I didn't vote," "4" = "I refuse to answer." In both studies, after excluding the non-answers (e.g., "I refuse to answer" or "neither agree nor disagree"), based on the rest of responses, the participants were then split into anti-oriented (coded as "1") and pro-oriented group (coded as "2"),

North Macedonia goes global 261

which were against or in favor of the posed statement, and this grouping variable was used for further analysis.

Finally, in Study 3, participants were requested to complete the Conspiracy Mentality Questionnaire (Imhoff and Bruder 2014) by indicating on 11-point Likert scales how likely they thought each of the five statements was to be true, from "0" (0% = "certainly not") to "10" (100% = "certainly yes"). They were also presented with two additional statements: "The European Union is a conspiracy of big business that aims to destroy national states" (portraying the EU as an enemy of the national economy and security) and "The destiny of Balkan nations and countries always fell prey to the secret plots of the imperial forces" (portraying the international community as an ideological enemy to the Balkan people and countries). The statements were rated on 5-point Likert scales, where "1" signified "I completely disagree" while "5" signified "I completely agree."

Results

Studies 1 and 2: Of the total, a portion of *153 participants (79.68%)* in Study 1 and *171 participants (64.28%)* in Study 2 provided favorable answers to the statements that were directly/indirectly related to the pro-EU aspirations of the Macedonian government. Our next test (Chi-square) relied on the analysis of the Political Group (LW/RW) in relation to the expressed attitudes (Pro/Anti) on each of the statements. Statistically significant results were found in Study 1, $\chi2(1, N = 171) = 19.42$, p < 0.001, with a lower amount of support for EU-integration aspiration (72.92%) among RW group, than in the LW group (95.93% of left-leaning respondents). In a similar fashion, the findings in Study 2, $\chi2$ (1, N = 261) = 36.04, p < 0.001, reflected a lower amount of support for the referendum (38.87%) in the RW group, than in the LW group (75.38% of left-leaning respondents).

Study 3: First, we ran a simple linear regression analysis where the mean scores from participants' responses to the statements from the Conspiracy Mentality Questionnaire were used as a predictor variable, while their responses to each of the additional statements against the EU/West were employed as dependent variables. The analyses returned statistically significant results in both cases (anti-EU F(1, 553) = 120.22, $p < 0.001$; anti-West F(1, 559) = 118.67, $p < 0.001$), meaning that there existed a positive linear relationship between the tested variables. The effect was rather small (explaining about 18% of the variance in the data responses), but reliable in both cases (anti-EU $R^2 = 0.177$; anti-West $R^2 = 0.174$, respectively). Hence, the general conspiracy mentality can be taken as a predictor for the belief in the specific theories that targeted the EU and the Western international community as national enemies.

Next, we performed ANOVA's with the group (LW/RW) as a between-subjects factor and the scores on each of the anti-EU/anti-West statements (separately) as dependent variables. Both analyses revealed significant levels of interaction (anti-EU F (1, 566) = 79.96, $p < 0.001$; anti-West F (1, 573) = 23.99, $p < 0.001$), meaning that there was a meaningful difference between the groups in their ratings of

262 *Biljana Gjoneska et al.*

the statements. Specifically, for each of the statements, the RW group (N = 128) always ascribed higher average scores (anti-West RW/LW = 2.84/1.75; anti-West RW/LW = 3.88/3.29), thus expressing a stronger conviction in the truthfulness of the conspiratorial statements.

Interpretation of the results

In order to interpret our findings from all three studies, we should return to the original hypotheses and pose them as questions. First, are we able to show that the period coinciding with the change of the government and the loss of power of the RW coalition (2016–18) was indeed marked by an overall decrease in the support for EU integration processes? According to our findings from Study 1, in 2016 the support for EU accession was 79.68% (differing slightly—in absolute percentage values—from the all-time-lowest score of 71% as registered by IRI for the same year). In comparison, the scores obtained from 2018 on our post-referendum survey (in Study 2), showed that a lower percentage (i.e., 64.28%) of respondents provided unequivocal support for the name-change in function of the EU-accession process. More importantly, are we able to confirm that the level of EU support was significantly different between the two political camps, with the RW group being less supportive of EU accession than the LW group of voters? Our analyses indeed returned corresponding findings regardless of the period, with the RW group expressing lower EU support (as compared to the LW group), both in 2016 and 2018. Second, are we able to claim that the level of anti-EU conspiracy endorsement was marked with significant difference between the political camps, with the RW group showing a higher level of support for anti-EU narratives (as compared to the LW group)? In line with our expectations, the RW group (seeking to reclaim the power of their party or position of their former leader) indeed proved to be more susceptible to conspiracy theories that target the international community.

Finally, our findings on the conspiracy mentality confirmed our initial hypothesis that general susceptibility to conspiracy theories can predict the belief in EU-specific conspiracy theories (i.e., theories directed against high-power and high-status groups). Future studies employing additional scales/measures (see in the discussion) can help disentangle the causes and point to specific groups, responsible for the registered tendencies.

Discussion and conclusion

The literature offers evidence that the right-wing electoral body typically comprises voters who endorse "group-centrism" principles (Kruglanski et al. 2006, 84). In addition to conservatism, regarded as proneness to resist social change (in MK evidenced through the glorification of the past and "antiquization" of the country), group-centrism is also marked by the following principles: conformism with pressure for uniformity of opinion (in MK evidenced in a decade-long rule by the same party); conventionalism with perpetuation of group norms and

North Macedonia goes global   263

rejection of deviates (in MK present through the narratives and subsequent attacks on the LGBTI community); in-group favoritism with out-group derogation (in MK reflected in the prejudiced stories against Syrian refugees); and adherence to in-group authorities. The latter tendency is especially important for the purposes of this chapter, as it constitutes the so-called Right-Wing Authoritarianism (RWA) tendency and is accentuated in right-wing followers. Namely, people who score high on RWA tend to be submissive toward their in-group authorities, insomuch as they also justify authoritarian aggression (toward out-groups) and endorse authoritarian norms, principles, and conventions (Altemeyer 1996). Hence, it is logical to assume that people with right-wing authoritarian tendencies were the most passionate supporters of a single conservative leader, since they aimed to secure his long, unquestioned, and uninterrupted rule in the country. Also, they were the most likely to believe in his narratives (or those of the party in general) without questioning their motives and most likely to support the subsequent conspiracy theories. Indeed, literature shows that RWA tends to be robustly and positively associated with beliefs in conspiracy theories (Imhoff and Bruder 2014, 25–34; Wood and Gray 2019, 163–66; for a review, refer to Grzesiak-Feldman 2015, 117–39). According to the dual-process motivational model by Duckitt (2001; Sibley and Duckitt 2013, 448–66; Wilson and Rose 2014, 273–91), people who tend to stick to their group under the guidance of a strong leader also tend to perceive the world as "a dangerous place" where there is only "black or white" and the bad threaten to exploit the good. Such a Manichean worldview that goes hand in hand with the preference for far-right ideologies is also associated with a tendency to believe in conspiracy theories (where beliefs arise from the feelings of threat and insecurity, while ideology provides a sense of security and stability).

To the best of the authors' awareness, no study has yet tackled the current Macedonian sociopolitical context in order to directly test these claims. In our chapter we did not provide a direct link between the RWA or dual-process model with conspiratorial tendencies, but we did offer a broader perspective on the topic. Namely, we used the space of the chapter to theorize about the sociopolitical circumstances and psychosocial determinants of susceptibility to conspiratorial beliefs present among Macedonian citizens (in the first part); to speculate about the possible enablers/enforcers of recent anti-EU directed conspiratorial narratives (in the second part); and to offer empirical clues for the possible believers, emphasizing the relationship between conservative ideology and the tendency to believe in anti-EU conspiracy theories (in the third part). Regarding the latter, it is important to highlight that we also examine the link between the general conspiracy mentality and the tendency to believe in specific anti-EU conspiracy theories as two very related concepts for the MK national context. Namely, the general conspiracy mentality understands high-power groups as malicious actors with hidden and harmful intentions. In the case of North Macedonia, this especially comes to light in the conspiracy theories that target the EU and West, because they are regarded as both powerful and crucial to Macedonian interests and progress. Therefore, through exploration of EU-specific narratives, we also provide a more general understanding of the tendency to believe in conspiracy theories as a whole.

264 Biljana Gjoneska et al.

In summary, recent developments (when the state was captured by a right-wing leader striving to maintain his rule) and ongoing events (when the conservative party seeks to restore its rule) are marked with political and public discourse that is increasingly populated with anti-EU conspiracy theories. In all likelihood, they stem from a combination of factors: implications of the traumatic past and a climate saturated by political scandals (situational variables) as well as unconditional support for a conservative party and leaders (dispositional characteristics). We believe that our findings provide a meaningful contribution to the scientific understanding of explored topics, which may improve the overall European perspectives of the country.

Notes

1 A term used by the Minister of Foreign Affairs of North Macedonia, Nikola Dimitrov, in an address to the High Representative of the Union for Foreign Affairs and Security Policy, Federica Mogherini, on March 7, 2018 (retrieved from www.mfa.gov.mk).
2 The COST COMPACT Action can be accessed at: https://conspiracytheories.eu/.

Bibliography

Abalakina-Paap, Marina, Walter G. Stephan, Traci Craig, and W. Larry Gregory. 1999. "Beliefs in Conspiracies." *Political Psychology* 20 (3): 637–47.

Altemeyer, Bob. 1996. *The Authoritarian Specter*. Cambridge: Harvard University Press.

Bakić-Hayden, Milica. 1995. "Nesting Orientalisms: The Case of Former Yugoslavia." *Slavic Review* 54 (4): 917–31.

Belloni, Roberto. 2016. "The European Union Blowback? Euroscepticism and its Consequences in the Western Balkans." *Journal of Intervention and Statebuilding* 10 (4): 530–47.

Bieber, Florian. 2018. "Patterns of Competitive Authoritarianism in the Western Balkans." *East European Politics* 34 (3): 337–54.

Chrzová, Barbora, Anja Grabovac, Martin Hála, and Jan Lalić. 2019. *Western Balkans at the Crossroads: Assessing Influences of Non-Western External Actors*. Prague: Prague Security Studies Institute.

Cvetkovska, Saska. 2018. "Russian Businessman behind Unrest in Macedonia." *Organized Crime and Corruption Reporting Project*, July 16, 2018. Accessed June 5, 2019. www.occrp.org/en/28-ccwatch/cc-watch-indepth/8329-russian-businessman-behind-unrest-in-macedonia.

Dimitrov, Nikola, Ivana Jordanovska, and Dane Taleski. 2016. "Ending the Crisis in Macedonia: Who Is in the Driver's Seat?" *Policy Brief*. Accessed May 10, 2019. www.balkanfund.org/publib/biepag/Ending-the-Crisis-in-Macedonia-Who-is-in-the-driving-seat-web.pdf.

Duckitt, John. 2001. "A Dual-process Cognitive-motivational Theory of Ideology and Prejudice." *Advances in Experimental Social Psychology* 33: 41–113.

Einstein, Katherine Levine, and David M. Glick. 2013. "Scandals, Conspiracies and the Vicious Cycle of Cynicism." Paper presented at the *Annual Meeting of the American Political Science Association*. Chicago, IL. Accessed February 28, 2020. http://sites.bu.edu/dmglick/files/2014/01/BLS-IRSv5.pdf

———. 2015. "Do I Think BLS Data are BS? The Consequences of Conspiracy Theories." *Political Behavior* 37 (3): 679–701.

European Commission. 2019. *Standard Eurobarometer 89*. Accessed October 11, 2019. https://ec.europa.eu/commfrontoffice/publicopinion/index.cfm/Survey/getSurvey Detail/instruments/STANDARD/surveyKy/2180.

European Commission Progress Report. 2009. *The Former Yugoslav Republic of Macedonia Progress Report, COM (2009)533*. Brussels. Accessed May 10, 2019. https://ec.europa.eu/neighbourhood-enlargement/sites/near/files/pdf/key_documents/2009/mk_rapport_2009_en.pdf.

———. 2010. *The Former Yugoslav Republic of Macedonia Progress Report, COM (2010)660*. Brussels. Accessed May 10, 2019. https://ec.europa.eu/neighbourhood-enlargement/sites/near/files/pdf/key_documents/2010/package/mk_rapport_2010_en.pdf.

———. 2014. *The Former Yugoslav Republic of Macedonia Progress Report, COM (2014)*. Brussels. Accessed May 10, 2019. https://ec.europa.eu/neighbourhood-enlargement/sites/near/files/pdf/key_documents/2014/20141008-the-former-yugoslav-republic-of-macedonia-progress-report_en.pdf.

———. 2015. *Statement by Commissioner Hahn and MEPs Vajgl, Howitt and Kukan: Agreement in Skopje to Overcome Political Crisis*. Accessed May 11, 2019. http://europa.eu/rapid/press-release_STATEMENT-15-5372_en.htm.

———. 2016. *The Former Yugoslav Republic of Macedonia Progress Report, SWD (2016)*. Brussels. Accessed May 12, 2019. https://ec.europa.eu/neighbourhood-enlargement/sites/near/files/pdf/key_documents/2016/20161109_report_the_former_yugoslav_republic_of_macedonia.pdf.

———. 2018. *The Former Yugoslav Republic of Macedonia Progress Report, SWD (2018)*. Brussels. Accessed May 11, 2019. www.sobranie.mk/content/republic-of-macedonia-report%2017.4.18.pdf.

Federico, Christopher M., Allison L. Williams, and Joseph A. Vitriol. 2018. "The Role of System Identity Threat in Conspiracy Theory Endorsement." *European Journal of Social Psychology* 48 (7): 927–38.

Fidanovski, Kristijan. 2018. "What's in a Name? Possible Ways Forward in the Macedonian Name Dispute." *Slovo* 31 (1): 18–44.

Goertzel, Ted. 1994. "Belief in Conspiracy Theories." *Political Psychology* 15 (4): 731–42.

Grzesiak-Feldman, Monika. 2013. "The Effect of High-anxiety Situations on Conspiracy Thinking." *Current Psychology* 32 (1): 100–18.

———. 2015. "Are the High Authoritarians More Prone to Adopt Conspiracy Theories? The Role of Right-wing Authoritarianism in Conspiratorial Thinking." In *The Psychology of Conspiracy*, edited by Michal Bilewicz, Aleksandra Cichocka, and Wiktor Soral, 117–39. London: Routledge.

Hofstadter, Richard. 1966. *The Paranoid Style in American Politics and Other Essays*. Cambridge: Harvard University Press.

Imhoff, Roland, and Martin Bruder. 2014. "Speaking (Un-) Truth to Power: Conspiracy Mentality as a Generalised Political Attitude." *European Journal of Personality* 28 (1): 25–43.

International Republican Institute. 2018. "Macedonia National Public Opinion Poll." Center for Insights in Survey Research, Skopje. Accessed May 10, 2019. www.iri.org/sites/default/files/iri_macedonia_july_2018_poll_public_final.pdf.

Kieskompas, Amsterdam, NL. *Macedonian Voting Advice Application (Izboren Kompas) and Survey Data*. 2016–18.

266 *Biljana Gjoneska et al.*

Kruglanski, Arie W., Antonio Pierro, Lucia Mannetti, and Eraldo De Grada. 2006. "Groups as Epistemic Providers: Need for Closure and the Unfolding of Group-centrism." *Psychological Review* 113 (1): 84–100.

Lantian, Anthony, Michael J. Wood, and Biljana Gjoneska. 2020. "Personality Traits, Cognitive Styles, and Worldviews Associated with Beliefs in Conspiracy Theories." In *Routledge Handbook of Conspiracy Theories*, edited by Michael Butter and Peter Knight, 155–67. London: Routledge.

LeBoeuf, Robyn A., and Michael I. Norton. 2011. "Consequence-cause Matching: Looking to the Consequences of Events to Infer Their Causes." *Journal of Consumer Research* 39 (1): 128–41.

McCauley, Clark, and Susan Jacques. 1979. "The Popularity of Conspiracy Theories of Presidential Assassination: A Bayesian Analysis." *Journal of Personality and Social Psychology* 37 (5): 637–44.

Nai, Alessandro, Ferran Martínez i Coma, and Jürgen Maier. 2019. "Donald Trump, Populism, and the Age of Extremes: Comparing the Personality Traits and Campaigning Styles of Trump and Other Leaders Worldwide." *Presidential Studies Quarterly* 49 (3): 609–43.

National Democratic Institute. 2018. *Between East and West: Public Opinion & Media Disinformation in the Western Balkans*. USA. Accessed May 10, 2019. www.ndi.org/sites/default/files/Download%20Report_0.pdf.

Prespa Agreement. 2018. "Final Agreement for the Settlement of the Differences as Described in the United Nations Security Council Resolutions 817 (1993) and 845 (1993), the Termination of the Interim Accord of 1995, and the Establishment of a Strategic Partnership between the Parties." *Prespa*. Accessed June 5, 2019. https://vlada.mk/sites/default/files/dokumenti/spogodba-en.pdf.

Priebe Report. 2015. *The Former Yugoslav Republic of Macedonia: Recommendations of the Senior Experts' Group on Systemic Rule of Law Issues Relating to the Communications Interception Revealed in Spring 2015*. Brussels. Accessed May 10, 2019. https://ec.europa.eu/neighbourhood-enlargement/sites/near/files/news_corner/news/news-files/20150619_recommendations_of_the_senior_experts_group.pdf.

Regional Cooperation Council. 2018. *Balkan Barometer: Public Opinion Survey Analytical Report*. Sarajevo: Regional Cooperation Council Secretariat. Accessed May 10, 2019. www.rcc.int/pubs/66/balkan-barometer-2018-public-opinion-survey.

Robins, Robert Sidwar, and Jerrold M. Post. 1997. *Political Paranoia: The Psychopolitics of Hatred*. London: Yale University Press.

Rothschild, Zachary K., Mark J. Landau, Daniel Sullivan, and Lucas A. Keefer. 2012. "A Dual-motive Model of Scapegoating: Displacing Blame to Reduce Guilt or Increase Control." *Journal of Personality and Social Psychology* 102 (6): 1148–63.

Sibley, Chris G., and John Duckitt. 2013. "The Dual Process Model of Ideology and Prejudice: A Longitudinal Test During a Global Recession." *The Journal of Social Psychology* 153 (4): 448–66.

Štulhofer, Aleksandar. 2006. "Euroscepticism in Croatia: On the Far Side of Rationality?" In *Croatian Accession to the European Union*, edited by Katarina Ott, 141–60. Zagreb: Friedrich-Ebert-Stiftung. Accessed May 2019. www.ssoar.info/ssoar/bitstream/handle/document/6130/ssoar-2006-stulhofer-euroscepticism_in_croatia_on_the.pdf?sequence=1&isAllowed=y&lnkname=ssoar-2006-stulhofer-euroscepticism_in_croatia_on_the.pdf.

Subramanian, Samanth. 2017. "Inside the Macedonian Fake-news Complex." *Wired Magazine,* February 15, 2017. Accessed May 10, 2019. www.wired.com/2017/02/veles-macedonia-fake-news/.

Sullivan, Daniel, Mark J. Landau, and Zachary K. Rothschild. 2010. "An Existential Function of Enemy Ship: Evidence that People Attribute Influence to Personal and Political Enemies to Compensate for Threats to Control." *Journal of Personality and Social Psychology* 98 (3): 434–49.

Swami, Viren, Adrian Furnham, Nina Smyth, Laura Weis, Alixe Lay, and Angela Clow. 2016. "Putting the Stress on Conspiracy Theories: Examining Associations Between Psychological Stress, Anxiety, and Belief in Conspiracy Theories." *Personality and Individual Differences* 99: 72–76.

Taggart, Paul, and Aleks Szczerbiak. 2002. "The Party Politics of Euroscepticism in EU Member and Candidate States." Brighton: Sussex European Institute. Accessed May 10, 2109. www.sussex.ac.uk/webteam/gateway/file.php?name=sei-working-paper-no-51.pdf&site=266.

Teymoori, Ali, Jolanda Jetten, Brock Bastian, Amarina Ariyanto, Frédérique Autin, Nadia Ayub, Constantina Badea et al. 2016. "Revisiting the Measurement of Anomie." *PloS One* 11 (7): e0158370.

Todorova, Maria. 1994. "The Balkans: From Discovery to Invention." *Slavic Review* 53 (2): 453–82.

Vangeli, Anastas. 2011. "Nation-building Ancient Macedonian Style: The Origins and the Effects of the So-called Antiquization in Macedonia." *Nationalities Papers* 39 (1): 13–32.

Vangelov, Ognen. 2019. "The Primordialisation of Ethnic Nationalism in Macedonia." *Europe-Asia Studies* 71 (2): 1–22.

van Prooijen, Jan-Willem, and Karen M. Douglas. 2017. "Conspiracy Theories as Part of History: The Role of Societal Crisis Situations." *Memory Studies* 10 (3): 323–33.

van Prooijen, Jan-Willem, and Nils B. Jostmann. 2013. "Belief in Conspiracy Theories: The Influence of Uncertainty and Perceived Morality." *European Journal of Social Psychology* 43 (1): 109–15.

Wilson, Marc Steward, and Chelsea Rose. 2014. "The Role of Paranoia in a Dual-Process Motivational Model of Conspiracy Belief." In *Power, Politics, and Paranoia: Why People Are Suspicious of Their Leaders*, edited by Jan-Willem van Prooijen, 273–91. Cambridge: Cambridge University Press.

Wood, Michael J., and Debra Gray. 2019. "Right-wing Authoritarianism as a Predictor of Pro-establishment versus Anti-establishment Conspiracy Theories." *Personality and Individual Differences* 138: 163–66.

13 Conspiracy theory, epistemology, and Eastern Europe

M R. X. Dentith

Introduction

Conspiracy theory theory—the scholarly study of conspiracy theory—examines both what conspiracy theory is and what constitutes belief in said theories. Over the last 10 years or so, there has been an explosion of academic interest in what are known as "conspiracy theories," and conspiracy theory theorists—the scholars who engage in conspiracy theory theory—have taken a variety of approaches, most of which stem from the theoretical background of the researchers. Cultural theorists, for example, have been interested in the cultural underpinnings of conspiracy theory both as a general phenomenon and also with respect to particular conspiracy theories themselves. Sociologists have taken a similar tack. Psychologists have been interested in what drives people to become conspiracy theorists or endorse conspiracy theories and have related belief in conspiracy theories to other kinds of weird beliefs. Philosophers have tended to be interested in conspiracy theories *as theories*, asking what makes them warranted or unwarranted, as well as how are they argued for or against.

All these approaches—if they are to be commensurate in some form—need to agree on at least two things: the first is that there are these things called "conspiracy theories." The second is that there are people who believe such theories, the "conspiracy theorists."

Yet there is a problem at the heart of conspiracy theory theory: while a lot of conspiracy theory theorists study conspiracy theories, it often seems that the scholars of conspiracy theory more often than not talk past each other rather than with one another; it turns out that these things called "conspiracy theories" are a surprisingly contentious topic, and—as we will see—our opinion on what counts as a "conspiracy theory" subsequently informs who we think the "conspiracy theorists" are.

This problem—one of definitions and the operationalization of such definitions—has meant that the research programs of psychologists, sociologists, philosophers (and the like) have all branched out separately as a result of various attempts to resolve the apparent problems of conspiracy theory. I argue this is a particularly vexatious problem, of special interest to readers of this volume: when we talk about conspiracy theories in Eastern Europe (especially those of the Communist

Conspiracy theory 269

and post-Communist era), the way in which we characterize what conspiracy theories are, and who believe or espouse them, is much trickier than it is for scholars working in or on the West.

Issues of definition

To situate talk of conspiracy theory, we need to define what we mean both by "conspiracy" and "conspiracy theory." What counts as a "conspiracy" should be simple to define. After all, we know conspiracies have occurred. As such, we can define them with respect to what falls under the class of known conspiratorial activity.

A conspiracy is an activity undertaken in secret by two or more people toward some end. There are numerous examples of these in history, from the plot to assassinate Caesar in the Roman Republic, the engineering of the guilty verdicts in the Moscow show trials in Soviet Russia, and the Watergate scandal in the United States. In each case, a group of plotters worked together toward some goal (an assassination in the Roman case, a perversion of justice in the Russian example, and a cover-up of what the president knew in the US case) and did so in secret to avoid outsiders working out what was *really* going on.

Such a definition captures the basic parts of "conspiracy." We might be tempted to add to such a definition some additional claims, such as the intended goal of the plotters being sinister or suspicious in nature. This would have the effect of narrowing the scope of the definition: if we say conspiracies are sinister states of affairs, then certain activities that would otherwise qualify as being conspiratorial under the general definition would be ruled out under the narrower one.

For example, the organization of a surprise party requires that people work together and keep the organization of the party secret from at least one person (the one you want to surprise). That is, it looks conspiratorial under the general definition. However, given that surprise parties are not typically suspicious or sinister activities, under the narrower definition, the organization of a surprise party would not be an example of a conspiracy. You might also restrict talk of *proper* conspiratorial activity to large-scale conspiracies (which might also rule out surprise parties in some cases but not in others).[1]

Various scholars have advocated for different restrictions when it comes to the proper subject of a conspiracy, and most of these align with the notion that the kind of conspiratorial activity we ought to be interested in are political conspiracies. But no matter our view on what counts as a "conspiracy," the more interesting definitional question is "How do we define 'conspiracy theory'?" That is: what is it to theorize about a conspiracy? Herein lies the difficulty: in the existing literature there are—in essence—two competing definitions of "conspiracy theory."

One definition takes it that they are *merely* theories about conspiracies. The other posits that they are typically *unwarranted* theories about conspiracy: they are theories that are suspect for epistemic or psychological reasons.

This choice between these different definitions (as well as whether or not we should work with a general definition of "conspiracy") is a topic I have discussed

270 *M. R. X. Dentith*

at length elsewhere (see Dentith 2014; M R. X. Dentith 2018a). However, what is important to our discussion about conspiracy theories *in Eastern Europe* is that the history of Eastern Europe—particularly the way in which Communist governments and the resistance movements to those governments worked—typically invokes discussion of actual conspiracies, many of which were labeled as *"mere conspiracy theories"* at the time. This means that our choice of definition as to what counts as a conspiracy theory has a direct effect on how we understand talk about the history of conspiracy and conspiracy theory in the region. Let us, then, look at the arguments for or against these two types of definitions.

Conspiracy theory as merely theory

We could just define a "conspiracy theory" as a proposed explanation of some event that cites a conspiracy as a salient cause. "Proposed" here plays an important role: if a conspiracy theory is just a theory about a conspiracy, then as a theory, it will need to be assessed on the evidence and arguments for and against it. That is, we would end up treating conspiracy theories like we would any other kind of theory: only some scientific or historical theories end up being warranted according to the evidence, after all, and the work we find in the sciences and the social sciences tends to be based around working out which theoretical constructs survive such scrutiny.

This definition is very general. It is also (and this is notable) non-pejorative in that it does not automatically mark out conspiracy theories as problematic. Any theory that cites a conspiracy as a salient cause of an event turns out to be a conspiracy theory according to this definition, whether that be Hungarian prime minister Viktor Orbán's conspiracy theory about George Soros seeking the downfall of the European Union or conspiracy theories about the Russian Federation trying to sway elections in other countries.

Proponents of this kind of general definition are rife in philosophy: see, for example, Brian L. Keeley (2007), Charles Pigden (2016), David Coady (2006), Lee Basham (2018b), and myself (Dentith 2016). This is likely due to philosophers being interested in the arguments for or against certain views rather than being interested in the psychological disposition of believers of such theories. Our interest to date has been epistemic in nature: we are concerned with the epistemology of conspiracy theory.

However, you might consider that this definition does not match common usage, in that defining a conspiracy theory as *merely* a proposed explanation that cites a conspiracy as a salient cause of some event does not reflect the often pejorative way in which we talk about conspiracy theories. However, common usage is not fixed: conspiracy theory is sometimes used pejoratively, and sometimes not. The academic work of Michael J. Wood (2016) and Petar Lukić, Iris Žeželj, and Biljana Stanković (2019), suggests that in common or ordinary language it is not clear that the public treats the term "conspiracy theory" as something that is *prima facie* irrational to believe. Similar arguments are to be found in the work of Ginna Husting and Martin Orr (2007), Mathijs Pelkmans and Rhys Machold (2011), and Ole Bjerg and Thomas Presskorn-Thygesen (2016).

Conspiracy theory 271

As such, it is even possible that the pejorative implication of "conspiracy theory" is, in the words of Charles Pigden, a "modern superstition" (2006). Even if it did turn out the term was pejorative in common usage, for the purpose of an academic analysis, we are not required to adhere to such usage anyway. We do not, for example, require that physicists or political scientists work with technical terms as they are understood by the lay public. Sometimes it is even preferable for scholars to stipulate definitions as, while they may not match common usage, they end up being the most fruitful construal for future research. We will come back to this after discussing our second definitional option.

Conspiracy theory *as* prima facie *suspicious*

Some conspiracy theory theorists believe there is something more to a conspiracy theory than it being just a theory about a conspiracy. Rather, they argue that such theories are *prima facie* suspicious: either belief in conspiracy theories is psychologically suspect, or conspiracy theories are typically epistemically faulty. Either way, anything that is a conspiracy theory is a theory we typically ought not to believe.

Some scholars have defined conspiracy theories as theories that are *prima facie* false—see the work of Viren Swami et al. (2014) and Daniel Pipes (1997), for example—but it should be clear this option is a non-starter. Such a definition rules out the possibility of something that had been labeled a "conspiracy theory" as ever being warranted, and this is a problem. Some conspiratorial explanations—such as that of the Moscow show trials of the 1930s and the Watergate scandal of the 1970s—were labeled "conspiracy theories" *at the time* but turned out to be warranted to believe all along. If conspiracy theories are false by fiat, then either these labeled "conspiracy theories" were never conspiracy theories to begin with (which complicates things linguistically) or theorists like Swami et al. and Pipes have to explain how things that were conspiracy theories (read: unwarranted theories) somehow became non-conspiracy theories (read: warranted theories) later (which complicates things metaphysically).

Most conspiracy theory theorists who reject an open and non-pejorative definition argue that *typically* conspiracy theories are unwarranted (but not necessarily false), and this is the reason why we have grounds to be suspicious of such theories generally.

Some of this stems from the pioneering work of Richard Hofstadter, who argued belief in conspiracy theories *resembles* paranoid ideation, and that if we think paranoia is irrational, then *by analogy* belief in conspiracy theories will be irrational as well (1965). Hofstadter did not think that conspiracy theorists were paranoid. Rather, they suffered from something akin to, but not exactly like, paranoia: he called this the "paranoid style." This tendency to point the finger at the mental lives of conspiracy theorists continues to this day. Karen Douglas and Robbie Sutton, for example, have argued that conspiracy theorists are the kind of people who are likely themselves to conspire, and thus see conspiracies everywhere as a result (2011).

272   *M R. X. Dentith*

Other scholars have argued that conspiracy theorists overstate the incidence of successful conspiracies—a point argued by Karl Popper (1969) back in the 1940s and followed up by Peter Lipton (2004) and Bradley Franks, Adrian Bangerter, and Martin W. Bauer (2013).

Yet the kinds of examples such conspiracy theory theorists use to show that conspiracies are unsuccessful or implausible end up being examples of unsuccessful or implausible conspiracies. That is, such arguments implicitly assume the conclusion belief in conspiracy theories is problematic and then use selected examples to show their definitional choice was the right one all along. This, however, begs the question about the rationality of belief in conspiracy theories in the first place.

Some scholars argue that the problem with conspiracy theories is the negative consequences associated with such beliefs. Sander van der Linden, for example, has argued that exposure (even potential exposure) to conspiracy theories can lead to undesirable social consequences (2015).[2] Jan-Willem van Prooijen has argued that belief in conspiracy theories can lead to detrimental implications, like a loss of trust in political authority and the like (2016).[3] Yet this kind of argument assumes such a loss of trust is itself unwarranted. However, in a variety of cases—as I will argue at some length in the last half of this chapter—a loss of trust in political authority and the like may well develop out of knowing conspiracies do occur (or have recently occurred) in your polity. Not just that, but there can be positive and desirable consequences to belief in some conspiracy theories, such as increased political oversight of suspected corrupt governments, a tendency to not take propaganda at face value, and the like.

Some scholars have even argued that we have reasons to prefer official (read: non-conspiratorial) theories over rival conspiracy theories. Michael Barkun (2016), Alessandro Bessi, Mauro Coletto, George Alexandru Davidescu, Antonio Scala, Guido Caldarelli, and Walter Quattrociocchi (2015), as well as Neil Levy (2007), all argue that official stories (or theories) should be preferred over rival *conspiracy* theories.

Yet what is called an "official theory" may well turn out to be a "conspiracy theory" at some other time or place. Often, this leads to the following problem: theories labeled "conspiracy theories" at one time turned out to be warranted all along. For example, the Watergate, Iran-Contra, and Tuskegee syphilis scandals were disbelieved by some *merely* because they were not considered official or endorsed by the authorities at the time. This then leads to the odd problem of having to explain what makes a *former* conspiracy theory an official theory today and whether it was ever really a conspiracy theory in the first place. Add to this the problem that what was a conspiracy theory in one place might well be recognized as official in another. In late 1930s and 1940s Germany, for example, the theory of a Jewish plot to destroy society was the official theory despite it being considered a conspiracy theory in other nations. Therefore, any such demarcation between official theories and conspiracy theories is a very problematic way to talk about the supposed irrationality of conspiracy theories in general.

Other conspiracy theory theorists have argued that the problem is epistemic. Cass Sunstein (along with Adrian Vermeule) has argued that conspiracy theorists are epistemically crippled: conspiracy theorists see conspiracy theories where there are none (Sunstein and Vermeule 2009) and tend to echo information from other conspiracy theorists uncritically (Sunstein 2009). Quassim Cassam ascribes to conspiracy theorists' epistemic vices: defects of epistemic character that preclude them from acting rationally toward claims of conspiracy (2016). Yet Cassam, in particular, has to invent a conspiracy theorist (named "Oliver") in order to justify the view that conspiracy theorists, like the fictional Oliver, suffer from an epistemic vice with respect to belief in conspiracy theories. Yet if a conspiracy theory is the kind of thing we typically ought not to believe, how, once again, do we deal with theories that had been labeled "conspiracy theories" but that, nonetheless, turned out to be true, or conspiracy theorists who turned out to have been right the entire time?[4]

Now, one response is to hold to the conditional claim of "typically unwarranted." We can admit *some* conspiracy theories end up being true, but hold that most do not, thus justifying skepticism of such theories generally. But that is an empirical matter: no one actually knows the ratio of how many conspiracy theories are true compared to false. But this sidesteps the issue anyway: by building into the definition of "conspiracy theory" that such theories typically ought not to be believed, we are building into the definition a pejorative aspect that ends up being self-serving. Conspiracy theories that—on investigation—turn out to be unwarranted confirm the definition, while those that—also on investigation—end up being warranted are the "exceptions." But these exceptions are only exceptional because of the choice of definition in the first place.

The problem with generalism

The view that belief in conspiracy theories is typically problematic is a *generalist* view, and part and parcel of the problem with such generalist approaches to talk of conspiracy theory is a tendency to think of conspiracies as both rare and unusual *in Western polities*.[5]

As a Westerner, I too have tended to focus on examples from my own political sphere (Australasia). However, as someone who also lived in Romania, I also have a newfound appreciation of just how sensible[6] it can be *in certain contexts* to theorize about conspiracies, especially given the history of how conspired a society has or turns out to be.

While I do not want to overly generalize, the politics and history of former Communist (now post-Communist) countries often show up the supposed irrationality of theorizing that conspiracies might be behind certain kinds of political events. Indeed, in certain contexts not thinking that conspiracies are a factor in the politics of your society sometimes means you may not be paying attention to your own history. This is to say that while there may well be psychological reasons as to why *some* people are more susceptible to belief in conspiracy theories than others, sometimes the suspicion that conspiracies are behind events in politics is not something akin to paranoia but, rather, a view based upon the evidence. Belief in conspiracy theories can be the result of a well-formed epistemic attitude toward

274   *M. R. X. Dentith*

particular kinds of evidence, and theoretical positions that ignore this often run counter to the lived experiences of a dazzling array of peoples.

Take, for example, Douglas and Sutton's argument that people who suspect conspiracy theories typically turn out to be the kind of person who think they, too, would conspire in a similar situation. If you grew up in a society where conspiracies were evident (or had been raised by people who had lived in a conspiratorial regime), you might very well consider conspiracy as a viable social or political strategy. We might also consider Sunstein and Cassam's claim that there is something irrational about theorizing about conspiracies. Under a regime that operates conspiratorially, surely to not suspect conspiracies is to suffer from an epistemic vice, or—in Sunstein's words—to epistemically cripple oneself.

The problem with generalism is that it is often a view that trumps evidence, which is to say that the particulars of belief (or suspicion) in the existence of conspiracies is valued less than a skeptical attitude toward conspiracy theories. Sometimes this is justified by the argument that belief in conspiracy theories leads to negative social consequences. Yet in a society that is ridden with conspiracies, is a loss of trust really all that negative a consequence? For the politician, yes. But that trust is uneasy at best if conspiracies turn out to be common (or even normal). Meanwhile, for the citizen, a lack of trust in political authority might well lead to greater oversight of the political class (and maybe even revolution). Indeed, in such situations non-conspiracy theories will not be obviously preferable to theories that suggest a conspiracy is occurring because there will be a lingering suspicion—in a range of cases—that the official theories emanating from the government might be propaganda. As such, suspecting there is something else at work is neither irrational nor pathological in these situations: it is just sensible.

Indeed, as I have argued elsewhere,[7] showing some particular conspiracy theory is warranted or justified to believe requires we show that not only has a conspiracy occurred but also it is the most likely explanation for the event in question. We need to show two or more people worked together in secret toward some end and that the resultant conspiracy is the salient cause of the event we are seeking to explain.[8]

Assessing conspiracy theories on the available evidence is no trivial task. After all, conspiracy theories are typically complex: they not only deal with "the facts" but also claims about how we should best interpret those facts. Sorting out plausible conspiracy theories from those we ought not to believe is tricky.[9] This is a *particularist* position, in that we ought to be interested both in particular conspiracy theories (rather than just the class of theories labeled as conspiratorial) along with the particular evidence used to support or dismiss those theories.

Think of it this way: if you come from a society where conspiracies are or have recently been relatively common, suspecting the existence of conspiracies here and now is not irrational. This affects what we might call the "prior probability" calculation. In terms of inferential reasoning, we can talk about the way in which evidence lends credence toward some explanatory hypothesis. When we think

Conspiracy theory 275

about how conspired or unconspired a society is when asking "Could there be a conspiracy occurring now?" we are considering the prior probability that conspiracies occur and how this affects our understanding of the possibility conspiracies might be occurring now. After all, politicians or their parties are often judged on their past behavior, with ministers who are known to be liberal with the truth less likely to be trusted when they say "There is nothing to see here!"

We then tend to weigh that consideration with the available evidence in the here and now, which is to say that we are considering the "posterior probability." For example, if someone has been shot, and we see a smoking gun in someone's hand, then this evidence lends credence to the idea that the person with the gun is the shooter. In the same respect, if there is a political scandal, and the person at the center of the scandal is caught lying about their role in it, then that lends credence to the idea that a cover-up is going on.

Once we have considered the prior and posterior probabilities, we then have to—in a situation where there turns out to be more than one plausible explanatory hypothesis on offer—compare the various potential explanations. That is, we have to judge their relative probabilities. After all, to show that some conspiracy theory is the best explanation, we need to demonstrate that the conspiracy theory is more likely than some plausible rival.[10]

That some conspiracy theories might turn out, then, to be warranted on such reasoning should not be an issue. Yet there is a persistent belief by some that belief in conspiracy theories is typically irrational. Given the focus on Western polities in the conspiracy theory theory literature, I think it is fair to say the kind of analyses that underpin the generalist and pejorative analyses come from polities that—while not totally unconspired—have a lengthy history of open, liberal governance. However, given the focus on Eastern Europe in this volume, and the lengthy history of conspiracy in the politics of former Soviet Bloc nations, what philosopher Charles Pigden, as previously mentioned, calls a "modern superstition" about conspiracy theories can be challenged.

My contention is that in a society that has a recent history of conspiracy, people are still likely to suspect conspiracies now. This is not *prima facie* suspect psychologically or epistemically. Rather, the problem with belief in such associated conspiracy theories will be predicated on the available evidence.

Conspiracy theories in Eastern Europe

As I alluded to earlier, a fault common to much conspiracy theory theory is a (implicit or explicit) focus on Western European and US examples. That is, many conspiracy theory theorists form their approach toward conspiracy theory from the perspective of what *at least appear to* be relatively unconspired societies. But once we look outside of Western polities, the story we should be telling about conspiracy theory needs to change.

On the face of it, this point of view might be seen as an overreaction. After all, as recent work covering Eastern Europe has shown, the region is neither unique

276   *M R. X. Dentith*

nor exceptional when it comes to belief in the kind of famous or well-known conspiracy theories we find worldwide. As Péter Kréko notes in an interview about Hungarian conspiracy theories:

> [W]hat we are seeing is a general phenomenon. Hungary may stick out but conspiracy theories are gaining traction all across the globe. That has a lot to do with the prevailing mood of the day, which shows how little trust people have in international institutions and how changes in our world lead people to believe the craziest theories about their causes
>
> (Verseck 2018).

Kréko has made a study of belief in conspiracy theories, particularly Hungarian ones. Hungary is often put forward as an example of a country where conspiracy theory has become part of official government policy. Its prime minister (at time of writing), Viktor Orbán, and his party, Fidesz, have not just promoted a raft of conspiracy theories but also used them to justify governmental policies and priorities. From claims about Hungarian-American billionaire and philanthropist George Soros undermining the traditions of Hungary and the European Union generally via his Open Society Foundations, the Central European University fomenting opposition to the Hungarian government,[11] and the refugee crisis being manipulated to weaken Europe as a whole, the Hungarian government has effectively weaponized certain conspiracy theories in order to justify policies that might seem—from the outside—contrary to the evidence.

Hungary has often been singled out as being relatively unique in this regard and often lumped in with Italy and Brazil as outlier polities where conspiracy theories are promoted by the government of the day. However, as we have seen in the last few years, these outlier countries have been joined by larger polities such as the United States and the United Kingdom, where conspiracy theories have also been endorsed and weaponized by their respective governments. The United States under President Donald J. Trump, for example, has talked up a supposed refugee crisis along its southern border to justify changes to immigration policy and has made numerous (and contrary) claims about election interference, which seem to rest upon political lines rather than the evidence. The government of the United Kingdom, at least with respect to the Brexit process, has blamed both internal and external conspiracies in order to explain what some might consider to be simply a haphazard negotiation process with the European Union by the British government. All of this is to say that even supposedly outlier polities in Eastern Europe—like Hungary—are not all that exceptional when it comes to belief in conspiracy theories if we consider them in context.

Indeed, as a 2013 study showed, belief in conspiracy theories in Eastern European countries (like Hungary and Slovenia) is not all that different from that of Western European nations like France (Gyárfášová et al. 2013). The French context here is important, as it shows that Eastern European polities are not all that different to what we might consider to be a "mainstream" country of "sensible" people.

Conspiracy theory 277

This all might speak to the idea—despite my earlier claim—that there should be no problem theorizing about conspiracy theory from the perspective of the West.[12] Yet I think we need to be careful. It is true that we do not have good grounds to think that Eastern Europe is awash in belief in conspiracy theories compared to Western nations. But we must also remember that much of the work on belief in conspiracy theories here comes from a *generalist* perspective: these analyses assume to some degree that there is something inherently suspicious to anything that has been labeled a "conspiracy theory." For example, the aforementioned 2013 report admits we should not automatically assume that when people agree with the statement "Actually, it is not the government that runs the country: we don't know who pulls the strings" that this means the respondent is necessarily endorsing a conspiracy theory. The authors argue that while endorsing such a claim does not necessarily mean the respondent believes some conspiracy theory, at the very least it suggests they are committed to making some claim about covert control from behind the scenes (Gyárfášová et al. 2013, 9). Yet another way to look at such a claim is to say that "behind the scenes" can also mean "via non-democratic means" (or some such formulation): respondents might think corporations or rich individuals, for example, have additional leverage when it comes to swaying governments. This does not even need to be covert; it simply needs to be identified as operating beyond the usual means of representative democratic governance to count as "behind the scenes." People know that backroom deals go on, for example, which means these things happen out of sight without necessarily making them conspiratorial.

What is probably more important for the kind of analyses we want to do in establishing conspiracy theory theory is working with prior probabilities, and it is here that Eastern European polities provide us with some truly interesting material, because even if Eastern Europe shares many of the same conspiracy theories with its Western neighbors, Eastern Europe also has a history (a recent one at that) of actual conspiracies that people theorized about at the time.

The Romanian example

My interest, as a conspiracy theory theorist, in Eastern European conspiracy theories stems largely from living and working in Romania for almost two years. As we see in the rest of Eastern Europe, many of the conspiracy theories we find elsewhere in the world—from anti-vaccine conspiracy theories, stories about the so-called real reason population demographics/fertility rates are falling in the EU, and crypto antisemitic banking conspiracy theories—are also present in Romania.

Unfortunately, being no different from the rest of the world means that, like other nations, we can also point toward the sometimes disastrous consequences belief in these garden-variety conspiracy theories leads to in a country like Romania. Take, for example, anti-vaccine conspiracy theories. After the release of a free online book in 2015 by Christei Todea-Gross—which concerned the apparent dangers of the MMR vaccine schedule—there was an associated measles outbreak that was predicated on a drop in the number of people vaccinated (a drop from 95% of children in 2013 to 80% in 2016). This led to the death of at least 24 people (Herriman 2017).[13]

Conspiracy theories like these have obvious negative social consequences, which is one of the main reasons why a generalist approach toward conspiracy theory has been so prevalent in the literature: it seems hard to defend the possibility that some belief in conspiracy theories can be rational when faced with situations just like this.[14] Yet, to reiterate once again, if our focus is solely on conspiracy theories we have already defined as irrational to believe, then it just follows *by definition* that there will be negative consequences to belief in such theories.

But, as I argued earlier, it is far better to take the particularist approach and analyze the *broader class* of conspiratorial theories and activities that come from working with a non-pejorative take on conspiracy theory. After all, it was the contrast between my home country of Aotearoa New Zealand and Romania—at least politically—that was startling from the perspective of conspiracy theory theory.

If we are really interested in the epistemology of conspiracy theory, we should be interested in how people conceive of their society and its politics. Politics in Aotearoa New Zealand is seen—both internally and externally—as benign and largely open and uncorrupt. Politics in Romania, however, seems to be viewed through the lens of significant distrust by the populace toward their elected representatives.

Such perceptions are measurable, as we can see from the work of such organizations like Transparency International (TI), who regularly produce a Corruption Perceptions Index (CPI) (Transparency International 2018). The CPI considers *perceptions of corruption* in a given society, which are mostly elicited from business members and the members of other large organizations. It is important to note that the CPI does not measure corruption itself. Rather, it measures the perception of corruption and then compares that to other nation-states.[15] However, perceptions of corruption do tend to correlate with the actual incidence of corruption, and so we can use the CPI to analyze the notion that governmental corruption tends to go hand in hand with low- and high-level conspiratorial activity.[16]

Out of 176 countries, Romania is, according to the metrics of the CPI, relatively *but not entirely corrupt*, scoring 47 out of 100, at least as of the 2018 report. As such, Romania compares well to its neighbors of Hungary (46), Bulgaria (42), and the Republic of Moldova (33), which are considered to be more corrupt (a lower score means more perceived corruption).

Perceived corruption suggests a lack of trust in governmental (and other large) organizations. That is, in relatively corrupt societies, there is good reason to suspect that corrupt practices, like conspiracies, are happening here and now, especially in cases where you know that corrupt practices—once again, like conspiracies—have occurred not just recently but systemically for quite some time in your polity. That is, *perceived corruption* affects our judgment about the prior probability that certain kinds of events or states of affair are normal in a particular context.[17]

Conspiracy theory 279

Perceptions do not, of course, come out of nowhere. People perceive corruption not only because they encounter it in their day-to-day lives but also because sometimes recent history supports the idea that people live (or have lived in) corrupt polities. For post-Communist countries in Eastern Europe, how the state functioned during the Communist period, as well as the transitional period post the fall of their Communist regimes, is often perceived as corrupt and conspiratorial. As we will see in our discussion of the Securitate (the Romanian secret police of the Communist period) later in this chapter, for many the perception of corruption in Eastern European polities is a legacy of both the Communist period and the failure to deal with that legacy in the post-Communist period. While Romania will be the focus of our discussion here, it is fair to say that the kind of issues Romanians grappled with during and after the Communist regime is illustrative of the Eastern European situation generally.

Romania has a rich history of recent scandals and examples of corruption: a former prime minister, Victor Ponta, who plagiarized significant sections of his PhD (a minor scandal) (Marinas 2014); various members of the government engaging in electoral fraud (a major scandal) (Barbu 2019); and an attempt to rewrite the criminal code in order to make it harder to prosecute some forms of corruption (which was itself presented to the public as *merely* being a way to reduce the prison muster, a major scandal that was also admittedly, a botched conspiracy) (John 2017).

All this is important because history, along with the perception of corruption, affects our beliefs about the kind of behavior the members of influential institutions are likely to be engaging in now. That is, said beliefs are part of the way in which we consider the prior probability of conspiracy in a given society, which in turns affects our judgment of how likely we think conspiracies are now.

Perceptions may not necessarily be absolute evidence of corruption (or relative corruption, given we are comparing countries) now, but they do influence our views about the likelihood of corrupt practices in a given nation-state here and now.[18]

So, as argued earlier, when we judge the plausibility of a conspiracy theory, we need to ask "Just how common is conspiratorial activity *in this society*?" Beliefs about how corrupt or uncorrupt polities are in turn affect our beliefs about putative claims about corruption here and now. For example, in a society that is considered relatively uncorrupt, an expenses scandal is more likely to be put down to stupidity or incompetence than it is to greed or malice. If, however, we live in a world where conspiracies are commonplace, then we ought to consider conspiracy theories among the pool of potential explanations for certain kinds of events.

The post-Communist period in Romania

Over the course of the twentieth century, Romania went through a period of far-right dictatorships, a Communist regime, and then a pivot to (and some would say only ostensibly) a modern Western democracy.

280   *M R. X. Dentith*

The Communist government and its last (and most famous) leader, Nicolae Ceauşescu, is still in living memory for a great many Romanians. The Romanian Revolution occurred in December 1989, which means any Romanian older than 30 lived under Communist rule, and most Romanians younger than 30 grew up in households where talk of the previous Communist regime was still very much alive and well.

It is fair to say that life under Communist regimes in Eastern Europe was rife with conspiracies and conspiracy theories. From suspicions about party officials living lives of luxury to worries about government surveillance of citizenry and propaganda on state television, life under such regimes featured official narratives of thwarted conspiracies against the state and unofficial conspiracy theories about the state itself.

There are, of course, numerous conspiracy theories about the December Revolution of 1989, which saw the end of the Communist regime in Romania.[19] After all, there is—at least to some—a perceived strangeness about the events of the revolution, which might only be explained by reference to a conspiracy. The protest in what is nowadays Revolution Square in Bucharest, which precipitated the fall of the dictator Ceauşescu, was not, on the face of it, all that different from similar protests. Yet on this day, things panned out differently. For this reason alone, people suspect that there was something more to the events of that day than a simple protest that escalated to a revolution. Why, these various conspiracy theories suppose, did the authorities not act that day? Why did the armed forces decide not to back Ceauşescu as he tried to take back control? This has led some people to suspect the protest was planned and stage-managed or, at the very least, the peoples' protest ended up being subverted by Ceauşescu's political opponents. Or was Ceauşescu a lost cause, which led his former collaborators to join the protestors?

Now, regime changes are often the topic of conspiracy theories, especially dramatic and seemingly unexpected ones like the December Revolution of 1989. This is especially the case when the narrative of a regime change is made up of contradictory stories that flourish due to a lack of accurate or, in some cases, no concrete information. Given what happened afterward, including the quick execution of the dictator Nicolae Ceauşescu and the formation of a temporary transitional government made up of members of the Communist Party, which—contrary to expectations—contested and won the new elections, is taken by some as sufficient evidence to suggest that the revolution was orchestrated by Communist Party elites who were simply tired of Ceauşescu's leadership.

Now, the suspiciousness of the event does not, of course, mean that it is *prima facie* likely that the event unfolded the way it did because of a conspiracy. The full story of that day may well be a combination of unrest by the people and some amount of forethought and contingency planning by members of the second echelon of the Romanian Communist Party. Yet the nature of how Romania was governed under the Communist Party means that it is understandable to think of the revolution as potentially the result of a Communist conspiracy. Indeed, this has been leveraged by opposition MPs in Romania even to this day, presenting the current government and its predicaments as the natural extension of the same old regime, with the only change being the color of the MPs' ties.

Conspiracy theory 281

These considerations are based upon judging the available evidence *at the time*—that is, evidence that speaks to the posterior probabilities as well as what happened afterward. That is, such conspiracy theories reflect an understanding of the available evidence that takes into account the purported motivations of the political actors involved. This then speaks to one part of the calculus when it comes to judging claims of just how conspired you think your society is (a consideration of how we establish the prior probability of conspiracy in a given society). If you live in a society that was heavily conspired, a regime change is the kind of event you are likely to think is the result of a conspiracy.

The legacy of the Securitate

Another example is how Romania dealt with its secret police after the December Revolution. The role of secret police services in Eastern European polities throughout the twentieth century[20]—the Committee for State Security in Bulgaria and the State Protection Authority in Hungary, for example—had a chilling effect on political discourse and created an air of suspicion. Officers of said organizations kept their identities secret, so you could not be sure who was listening in on your conversations in public, and said officers would surveil targets secretly, which meant you could not be sure that your private conversations were not being listened to. Add to this the use of collaborators and informants—whose identities were also kept secret—and you had a situation where the public were justified in their suspicion that they were being spied upon.

Worse still, however, was the fact that you could not be sure of (and had no appeal against) what exactly it was that might get you placed onto a watch list in the first place, which was—in the end—the purpose of a secret police: keeping the population worried, and thus, less likely to foment revolution.

Following the December 1989 Revolution, the Securitate, Romania's secret police, became a problem in search of a solution. As Lavinia Stan has described (2002, 2004), after 1989, the Securitate was ostensibly replaced or reformed with the Romanian Intelligence Service, which was—at least according to the new government that established it—an organization that was untainted by association with the Securitate. However, the idea that the Romanian Intelligence Service was not just the Securitate by any other name was confounded by their refusal to open the Securitate archives to the public, as well as its attempts to destroy Securitate-related information.

Part of the problem was that the Romanian Intelligence Service was created by the very people who had held control during the Communist period. While in other similar countries, political power moved away from the Communist party to the opposition in the wake of their revolutions, Romania simply changed hats, not regimes.[21] As Stan writes:

> [I]t changed hands from a closed sycophantic coterie surrounding the Ceausescu family to second-echelon communist officials disgruntled not with the

282 *M R. X. Dentith*

official ideology but with the president's betrayal of core Marxist-Leninist principles.

(2002, 146)

As such, Romanians were late (compared to other countries who had been in similar situations) in gaining access to the files held by the secret police. This was due to a number of issues and resulted in some fairly undesirable consequences.

For example, it was assumed that former Securitate officials and their collaborators were now part of the post-revolution government. The Securitate (like the Stasi) had relied on collaborators not just to collect information on persons of interest but also to alert the Securitate to people they ought to have under surveillance. During the Communist period, this had led to (and, it seems, justifiably) paranoia between private citizens, who could not be entirely sure that their friends, families, and neighbors were surveilling or informing on them. With the archives closed to the public despite the apparent change of regime, it seemed that perhaps this was to protect those former collaborators with the Communist regime. This, then, was taken to be one reason why there was resistance to opening up the Securitate archives to the public.

It did not help, either, that the public was suspicious of the number of supposedly missing files, and there were rumors about leaked Securitate material being used for blackmail purposes. This issue was compounded by the suspicion that post the revolution, former Securitate officers were manufacturing or modifying records in order to tarnish the reputations of their political enemies. Whether or not this was true, when it was discovered that some political candidates were named in the archives as either officers or informants, one defense raised was that this had to be the result of malicious tampering.[22] Thus, the history of the Securitate and the reluctance of the state to deal with that legacy is the kind of evidence that supports the claim "If this has happened before, what is to stop it from happening again?"

Examples like these should give us pause when performing our analysis of conspiracy theory, at least in a generalist mode. Sometimes positing the idea that conspiracies occur is a rational response to knowing your own history.

Conclusion

If we are historically or politically literate, then we should know not only that conspiracies occur but also that conspiracy theories turn out to be warranted on the evidence. As such, whether or not we think there are psychological factors that contribute toward belief in *some* conspiracy theories or we think that conspiracy theories are—on the whole—unlikely, we should still reject a generalist analysis of conspiracy theory in favor of particularism: we should be appraising conspiracy theories on the evidence rather than making assumptions about them just because they have been labeled "conspiracy theories."

Conspiracy theory 283

The problem with generalist analyses of conspiracy theory is that marking out belief in conspiracy theories as *prima facie* irrational runs counter to the evidence and often ignores the context under which conspiracy theorizing occurs.

Part and parcel of this problem of definitions—as I argued in the first part of this chapter—is the unfortunate result of an undue focus in the conspiracy theory theory literature on the West and its particular historical and political context. In the face of open and largely transparent governments over the course of the twentieth century, Western conspiracy theory theorists have (rightly or wrongly) been confident that while some conspiracies occur in their polities, generally, conspiracy theories are rarely ever warranted.[23] However, once we broaden our horizons and admit, among other regions, Eastern Europe into the conversation, the generalist position faces the problem of evidence.

We think of this as the lesson of Eastern Europe when it comes to conspiracy theory theory: the way in which we label "conspiracy theories" as *prima facie* problematic flies in the face of history as well as what we know of politics (and particular political regimes). Of course, as Charles Pigden has argued, we should already know this: anyone who is historically or politically literate knows not only that conspiracies occur but that many conspiracy theories have turned out to be warranted (Pigden, in press). That is, we should not need to look to Eastern Europe to learn this lesson.

Perhaps, however, the real lesson here is that we should be worried that the pejorative aspect associated with such theories—if it remains unquestioned and is used uncritically—will lend itself to the very suppression of the kinds of questions we might think are essential to a well-formed, functioning democracy. As we saw in the lead-up to the invasion of Iraq in 2003, and the current political crisis in the United States (as well as the rhetoric around the United Kingdom's Brexit referendum), people in positions of power have tried to quash questions about corruption and collusion by claiming that these are *mere* conspiracy theories that we ought to ignore simply because they have been pejoratively labeled as such.

Yet for people who grew up under closed governments or oppressive regimes, or are dealing with corrupt governments now, this rhetorical move turns out to be no surprise. As academics interested in not just the theory of conspiracy theory but also its practical implications and extensions, we really ought to pay attention to both how we define what counts as a "conspiracy theory" and the historical and political context that conspiracy theorizing occurs under—a context that often ignores the Eastern European situation. As we saw in the second half of this chapter, Eastern Europe is not an outlier when it comes to belief in pejoratively labeled "conspiracy theories." However, given the recent history of conspiracies in the region, it seems that Eastern Europeans take the threat of conspiracy more seriously because they are more cognizant of the dangers that come with people in positions of power conspiring against the public.

This is not to say that all conspiracy theories must be treated as *prima facie* warranted. That, too, would suffer from being too broad a generalization. Rather, what this points to is the need to take conspiracy theory seriously and—rather

284 *M. R. X. Dentith*

than dismiss conspiracy theories *as a class*—investigate them on a case-by-case basis.[24] Such a reappraisal of conspiracy theory, however, requires that we resist definitions of both "conspiracy theory" and "conspiracy theorist," which preemptively say belief in conspiracy theories is *prima facie* problematic. Sometimes—indeed, oftentimes—the political or historical context under which many of us live informs how we judge the rationality of the particular conspiracy theories we encounter. Some of us, it turns out, have been underestimating the problem.

Acknowledgments

I would like to acknowledge both Corneliu Pintilescu and Onoriu Colăcel and the rest of the panel members and attendees at the COST Action at the Hotel de Bilderberg in 2018 for their feedback on a very early version of this chapter. I also want to acknowledge my colleagues and friends at the Institute for Research in the Humanities of the University of Bucharest (IRH-ICUB), all of whom helped me come to grips with conspiracy theory in Romania.

Notes

1 For example, a surprise party for Stalin might well have encompassed the entire state and thus be the proper subject of a conspiracy.
2 This point has also been made by Robert Brotherton and Christopher French (Brotherton and French 2014).
3 Similar arguments have been proposed by Michael Barkun (Barkun 2003), Viren Swami, Martin Voracek, Stefan Stieger, Ulrich S. Tran, and Adrian Furnham (Swami et al. 2014).
4 For further details of this criticism of both Sunstein and Cassam, see "The Problem of Conspiracism" (Matthew R. X. Dentith 2018).
5 This has been noted by other scholars, such as Joseph Uscinksi (Uscinski 2018).
6 I use this word advisedly here: "sensible" here refers to the idea that at least entertaining conspiracy theories about political events is not out of the ordinary.
7 See both my book (Dentith 2014) and the article "When Inferring to a Conspiracy Theory Might Be the Best Explanation" (Dentith 2016).
8 Conspiracies can fail, and for a number of reasons: sometimes the conspirators have a falling out; the existence of the conspiracy is leaked out before any work toward the desired end is ever completed; or the conspirators never get around to doing anything, despite an express desire to do so.
9 Many of the evidential issues concerning conspiracy theories are covered in my article "Conspiracy Theories on the Basis of the Evidence" (Dentith 2019).
10 In some cases, the only available explanations might turn out to be conspiracy theories: the September 11 attacks in New York, of 2001, for example, are conspiratorial no matter which rival explanation you favor. The terrorist plot explanation features people working in secret toward some end (thus, a conspiracy) while the claim it was an inside job orchestrated by the US government is obviously a conspiracy theory as well.
11 The consequence of this conspiracy theory being promoted by the Hungarian government has been that the CEU was forced to relocate its campus from Budapest to Vienna in 2019.
12 If, for example, you either think attitudes toward conspiracy theories are not unique to particular polities, or that no matter the social consequence to some belief in such theories, we should still be particularists.

Conspiracy theory 285

13 See also this article for more details of the issues surrounding vaccination rates and the role of the anti-vax movement in Romania (Kakissis and Coman 2018). There have also been, in recent years, similar conspiracy theories about the HPV (Human papillomavirus) vaccine in Romania.

14 For a nuanced debate on why we might be epistemic particularists but generalists of an *ethical persuasion* with respect to conspiracy theory, see the debate between Patrick Stokes (Stokes 2018), Lee Basham (Basham 2018a), and myself (M. R. X. Dentith 2018c) in the volume *Taking Conspiracy Theories Seriously*.

15 There are also other measures we can look at, such as the 2017 Digital News Report, which looks at digital news consumption in 37 countries, focusing on issues of trust and misinformation. According to the report, "Trust in Romanian media is low in international comparison, with evidence of political and economic interference in the news agenda" (Radu 2017).

16 Low-level conspiratorial activity in this case will simply be backroom deals; high-level conspiratorial activity will be massive cover-ups and the like.

17 For more on this, see Grigorij Mesežnikov's chapter in *Conspiracy Theories in Europe: A Compilation* (Mesežnikov 2014).

18 There is also the question of the role the Romanian diaspora plays in framing those perceptions, given that not only does Romania have one of the largest diasporas in the world but also the most significant part of the diaspora happened in the early years post the December 1989 Revolution. Many of the members of this diaspora live in polities considered to be *less corrupt* than Romania. Does the existence of such a large expatriate population—one that arguably is in a position to see how politics works in their host nations—lead to cases of Romanians in Romania being more likely to perceive corruption in Romania? If so, this lends credence to the notion that in a society that has a history of conspiracy, and is still dealing with the transition from a closed- to open-style of governance, suspecting corruption and conspiracy is not itself irrational.

19 See, for example, Eduard Rudolf Roth's article "The Romanian Revolution of 1989 and the Veracity of the External Subversion Theory" (Roth 2016).

20 For example, Romania had a secret police service prior to the Communist period, the *Siguranța*.

21 This is not in itself an unusual claim: the Bonn Republic of Western Germany (1949–90) featured many former Nazis in high-ranked positions, leading some to claim that while the Nazis had been ostensibly defeated in World War II, the Nazi regime simply quietly moved into the background of political life in the new republic.

22 Although being either former Securitate or a collaborator did not preclude one from public office. Rather, the system relied upon an honor system: it was assumed that former Securitate officers and collaborators would not stand for public office.

23 Such generalism in the West might also come across as historical, given the history of conspiracy there, but the seeming open and transparent governments of most Western nations are taken as evidence that the era of abundant conspiring is past. Whether this is true or not is open to debate; for example, Kathryn S. Olmsted's book on US conspiracy theories of the twentieth century suggests conspiracies in the US over the course of the twentieth century have been more common than scholars tend to think (Olmsted 2009).

24 I have outlined one way in which we can systematically investigate particular conspiracy theories here (M. R. X. Dentith 2018b).

Bibliography

Barbu, Paul. 2019. "Romanian Political Leader Convicted After His Party Loses European Elections." Accessed November 14, 2019. https://web.archive.org/web/20191114022729/http://business-review.eu/news/romanian-political-lider-convicted-201453.

286   M R. X. Dentith

Barkun, Michael. 2003. *A Culture of Conspiracy: Apocalyptic Visions in Contemporary America*. Berkeley, CA: University of California Press.

———. 2016. "Conspiracy Theories as Stigmatized Knowledge." *Diogenes*. https://doi.org/10.1177/0392192116669288.

Basham, Lee. 2018a. "Conspiracy Theory Particularism, Both Epistemic and Moral, Versus Generalism." In *Taking Conspiracy Theories Seriously*, edited by M R. X. Dentith, 39–58. London: Rowman & Littlefield Publishers, Inc.

———. 2018b. "Joining the Conspiracy." *Argumenta* 3 (2): 271–90.

Bessi, Alessandro, Mauro Coletto, George Alexandru Davidescu, Antonio Scala, Guido Caldarelli, and Walter Quattrociocchi. 2015. "Science Vs Conspiracy: Collective Narratives in the Age of Misinformation." *PLOS One*, 1–17. https://doi.org/10.1371/journal.pone.0118093.

Bjerg, Ole, and Thomas Presskorn-Thygesen. 2016. "Conspiracy Theory: Truth Claim or Language Game?" *Theory, Culture & Society* 34 (1): 137–59.

Brotherton, Robert, and Christopher C. French. 2014. "Belief in Conspiracy Theories and Susceptibility to the Conjunction Fallacy." *Applied Cognitive Psychology* 28 (2): 238–48.

Cassam, Quassim. 2016. "Vice Epistemology." *The Monist* 99: 159–80.

Coady, David. 2006. "The Pragmatic Rejection of Conspiracy Theories." In *Conspiracy Theories: The Philosophical Debate*, edited by David Coady. Hampshire, UK: Ashgate.

Dentith, M R. X. 2018a. "Conspiracy Theories and Philosophy – Bringing the Epistemology of a Freighted Term into the Social Sciences." In *Conspiracy Theories & the People Who Believe Them*, edited by Joseph E. Uscinski, 94–108. New York: Oxford University Press.

———. 2018b. "Taking Conspiracy Theories Seriously and Investigating Them." In *Taking Conspiracy Theories Seriously*, edited by M R. X. Dentith, 217–25. London: Rowman & Littlefield Publishers, Inc.

———. 2018c. "What Particularism About Conspiracy Theories Entails." In *Taking Conspiracy Theories Seriously*, edited by M R. X. Dentith, 59–69. London: Rowman & Littlefield Publishers, Inc.

———. 2019. "Conspiracy Theories on the Basis of the Evidence." *Synthese* 6: 2243–61.

Dentith, Matthew R. X. 2014. *The Philosophy of Conspiracy Theories*. London: Palgrave Macmillan.

———. 2016. "When Inferring to a Conspiracy Might Be the Best Explanation." *Social Epistemology* 30 (5–6): 572–91.

———. 2018. "The Problem of Conspiracism." *Argumenta* 3 (2): 327–43.

Douglas, Karen M., and Robbie M. Sutton. 2011. "Does It Take One to Know One? Endorsement of Conspiracy Theories Is Influenced by Personal Willingness to Conspire." *British Journal of Social Psychology* 50: 544–52.

Franks, Bradley, Adrian Bangerter, and Martin W. Bauer. 2013. "Conspiracy Theories as Quasi-Religious Mentality: An Integrated Account from Cognitive Science, Social Representations Theory, and Frame Theory." *Frontiers in Psychology* 4 (242): 1–12.

Gyárfášová, Olga, Péter Kréko, Grigorij Mesežnikov, Csaba Molnár, and Marley Morris. 2013. "The Conspiratorial Mindset in an Age of Transition: Conspiracy Theories in France, Hungary and Slovakia." Counterpoint; Political Capital: Policy Research & Consulting Institute; Institute for Public Affairs.

Herriman, Robert. 2017. "Romania: Anti-Vaxxer Movement Results in Huge Measles Surge in 2016." Accessed November 14, 2019. https://web.archive.org/web/20191114023029/

Conspiracy theory 287

http://outbreaknewstoday.com/romania-anti-vaxxer-movement-results-huge-measles-surge-2016/.

Hofstadter, Richard. 1965. *The Paranoid Style in American Politics, and Other Essays*. 1st ed. New York: Knopf.

John, Tara. 2017. "Everything to Know About Romania's Anti-Corruption Protests." Accessed November 14, 2019. https://web.archive.org/web/20191114023229/https://time.com/4660860/romania-protests-corruption-problem/.

Kakissis, Joanna, and Octavian Coman. 2018. "The Story Behind the Worst Measles Outbreak in the European Union." *NPR*. Accessed November 14, 2019. https://web.archive.org/web/20191114023414/www.npr.org/sections/goatsandsoda/2018/11/24/669228140/the-story-behind-the-worst-measles-outbreak-in-the-european-union.

Keeley, Brian L. 2007. "God as the Ultimate Conspiracy Theorist." *Episteme* 4 (2): 135–49.

Levy, Neil. 2007. "Radically Socialized Knowledge and Conspiracy Theories." *Episteme* 4 (2): 181–92.

Linden, Sander van der. 2015. "The Surprising Power of Conspiracy Theories." Edited by Kaja Perina. 2015. Accessed November 14, 2019. www.psychologytoday.com/blog/socially-relevant/201508/the-surprising-power-conspiracy-theories.

Lipton, Peter. 2004. *Inference to the Best Explanation*. 2nd ed. London: Routledge.

Lukić, Petar, Iris Žeželj, and Biljana Stanković. 2019. "How (Ir)rational Is It to Believe in Contradictory Conspiracy Theories?" *Europe's Journal of Psychology* 15 (1): 94–107.

Marinas, Radu-Sorin. 2014. "Romanian Pm Gives up Doctorate After Years of Plagiarism Allegations." Accessed November 14, 2019. www.reuters.com/article/us-romania-ponta-idUSKBN0JU1N520141216.

Mesežnikov, Grigorij. 2014. "Conspiracy Theories in Slovakia: State of Affairs, Shifts and Contexts." In *Conspiracy Theories in Europe: A Compilation*, 27–32. Counterpoint; Political Capital.

Olmsted, Kathryn S. 2009. *Real Enemies: Conspiracy Theories and American Democracy, World War I to 9/11*. New York: Oxford University Press.

Orr, Martin, and Ginna Husting. 2007. "Dangerous Machinery: 'Conspiracy Theorist' as a Transpersonal Strategy of Exclusion." *Symbolic Interaction* 30 (2): 127–50.

Pelkmans, Mathijs, and Rhys Machold. 2011. "Conspiracy Theories and Their Truth Trajectories." *Focaal – Journal of Global and Historical Anthropology* 59: 66–80.

Pigden, Charles R. 2006. "Complots of Mischief." In *Conspiracy Theories: The Philosophical Debate*, edited by David Coady. Hampshire, UK: Ashgate.

———. 2016. "Are Conspiracy Theorists Epistemically Vicious?" In *A Companion to Applied Philosophy*, edited by David Coady, Kimberley Brownlee, and Kasper Lipper-Rasmussen, 120–32. Chichester: John Wiley & Sons, Ltd.

———. In press. "Conspiracy Theories and the Conventional Wisdom Revisited." In *Secrets and Conspiracies*, edited by Olli Loukola. Rodopi.

Pipes, Daniel. 1997. *Conspiracy: How the Paranoid Style Flourishes and Where It Comes from*. New York: Free Press.

Popper, Karl Raimond. 1969. *The Open Society and Its Enemies*. 5th ed. Vol. 2. London; Henley: Routledge; Kegan Paul.

Prooijen, Jan-Willem van. 2016. "Why Education Predicts Decreased Belief in Conspiracy Theories." *Applied Cognitive Psychology* 31: 50–58.

Radu, Raluca. 2017. "Digital News Report – Romania." Edited by Nic Newman, Richard Fletcher, Antonis Kalogeropoulos, David A. L. Levy, and Rasmus Kleis Nielsen. 2017. https://web.archive.org/web/20180729222820/www.digitalnewsreport.org/survey/2017/romania-2017/.

288 *M R. X. Dentith*

Roth, Eduard Rudolf. 2016. "The Romanian Revolution of 1989 and the Veracity of the External Subversion Theory." *Journal of Contemporary Central and Eastern Europe* 24 (1): 37–50.

Stan, Lavinia. 2002. "Access to Securitate Files: The Trials and Tribulations of a Romanian Law." *East European Politics and Societies* 16 (1): 145–81.

———. 2004. "Spies, Files and Lies: Explaining the Failure of Access to Securitate Files." *Communist and Post-Communist Studies* 37: 341–59.

Stokes, Patrick. 2018. "Conspiracy Theory and the Perils of Pure Particularism." In *Taking Conspiracy Theories Seriously*, edited by M R. X. Dentith, 25–37. London: Rowman & Littlefield Publishers, Inc.

Sunstein, Cass R. 2009. *Going to Extremes: How Like Minds Unite and Divide*. Oxford University Press.

Sunstein, Cass R., and Adrian Vermeule. 2009. "Conspiracy Theories: Causes and Cures." *Journal of Political Philosophy* 17 (2): 202–27.

Swami, Viren, Martin Voracek, Stefan Stieger, Ulrich S. Tran, and Adrian Furnham. 2014. "Analytic Thinking Reduces Belief in Conspiracy Theories." *Cognition* 133: 572–85.

Transparency International. 2018. "Corruption Perceptions Index." 2018. Accessed November 11, 2019. www.transparency.org/cpi2018.

Uscinski, Joseph E. 2018. "How Do Conspiracy Theorists and Non-Conspiracy Theorists Interact?" In *Conspiracy Theories & the People Who Believe Them*, edited by Joseph E. Uscinski, 109–10. New York: Oxford University Press.

Verseck, Keno. 2018. "Hungary: Europe's Champion of Conspiracy Theories." *Deutsche Welle*. Accessed November 14, 2019. www.dw.com/en/hungary-europes-champion-of-conspiracy-theories/a-46689822.

Wood, Michael J. 2016. "Some Dare Call It Conspiracy: Labeling Something a Conspiracy Theory Does Not Reduce Belief in It." *Political Psychology* 37 (5): 695–705.

Index

1+1 (Ukrainian television channel) 173, 175
1789 French Revolution 6
1917 Bolshevik Revolution 100
1918 Aster Revolution 100
1919 Hungarian Bolshevik Revolution 94
1956 uprising 102
1989 Romanian Revolution 211, 280
1990 democratic elections 104

Act 447 125
Aeronet 193
Agency for Fundamental Rights 134
Alexievich, S. 30–3, 34, 35, 40, 41
alternative medicine 32
Amalrik, A. A. 79
Ancient and Accepted Scottish Rite of Freemasonry 112
"anomie" 255
anti-capitalism 97
anti-colonialism 151
anti-Communism 9, 12, 48, 54, 55, 60, 69, 82, 89, 102–3, 106, 217
Anti-Defamation League 133
anti-Fascist Partisan movement 150
anti-immigration discourse 213, 215, 246
anti-imperialism 13, 151, 154
anti-liberalism 17, 195, 197, 217
antisemitism 1, 2, 8–9, 12–13, 15, 17–19, 49, 57, 67, 73, 74, 89, 91, 92, 93, 95–100, 102, 103–7, 125–30, 133, 136, 137–9, 211, 213, 216, 223, 225, 277; and anti-modernism 17; and anti-Nazism 99; and freemasonry 7, 9, 12, 15, 17, 95, 104, 106, 110, 111–13, 114, 115, 116, 117, 118, 120, 121, 188, 211; and worker's movement 92
Arbuzov, S. 184
Ashton, C. 176
assimilation 8, 99, 103, 104, 127, 159

Austria 6, 70, 89, 126, 148, 149, 155, 162
A zsidók rémuralma Magyarországon (The Terror of the Jews in Hungary) 91

Balkans 110, 147, 148, 151, 152, 164, 251, 252, 261
Bar-Tal, D. 187
Belarus 11, 29, 30, 34, 35, 37–8, 40, 42, 43, 44
Benedek, I. 103
Benedek, M. 104
Benedek, S. 104
"black, green, and yellow devils" 163
"Black Hand" conspiracy 148
blacklists 50, 51, 56, 219
blood-libel accusations 4, 126
Bolchevistes de Hongrie 93
Bosnia and Herzegovina 159, 160, 161, 163, 164
Breivik, A. 37
Brexit 276, 283
brotherhood and unity 150, 155, 164
Bujdosó könyv (An Outlaw's Diary) 94
Bulgarian Agrarian Popular Union 113
Budapest 105, 152, 212, 224, 284
Bukovsky, V. K. 79, 82
Bulgarian Freemasonry 111, 112
Bulgarian judiciary 111, 114, 116, 118, 120, 121

Cassam, Q. 273, 274, 284
Catholicism, political 90, 100
Ceaușescu, N. 11, 281
Ceaușescu regime 210–11, 225
censor 12
Central Committee of the Communist Party 71, 76, 79
Central European University (Budapest) 212, 215, 276
Central Powers 149

290   *Index*

Chernobyl conspiracy theories 29, 30, 37, 38, 43, 44
Chernobyl, HBO mini-series 41, 43
Chetniks 150, 151, 155, 156
Cioloş, D. 219, 220
Churchill, W. 92, 93, 151, 152
climate change 38, 43
Cold War 9, 10, 15–16, 18, 20, 33, 35, 42, 44, 48, 55, 61, 69, 153, 235, 236
Colectiv nightclub fire 219, 220
collective victimhood 138, 187
Cominform 54, 55, 57, 59, 152, 155, 158, 159, 160, 162
Comintern, Third International 50, 51
Communism 9, 10, 12, 16, 17, 34, 36, 38, 42, 48, 50, 51, 52, 53, 54, 55, 56, 57, 58, 59, 60, 61, 68, 69, 71, 73, 80, 81, 89, 90, 91, 93, 96, 98, 99, 100, 103, 105–7, 110, 111, 113, 119, 129, 136, 147, 150, 151, 152, 154, 156, 157, 159, 160, 161, 162, 190, 191, 193, 195, 196, 197, 210, 217, 233, 240, 241, 270, 279, 280, 281, 282
conservative revolution 97, 101
conspiracy, surprise party (as an example of a conspiracy) 269, 284
conspiracy theory(ies): and antisemitism 1, 2, 8, 9, 12, 13, 15, 17, 18, 19, 49, 57, 67, 73, 74, 89, 91, 92, 93, 95, 96, 97, 98, 99, 100, 102, 103, 104, 105, 106, 107, 125, 126, 127, 128, 129, 130, 133, 136, 137, 138, 139, 211, 213, 216, 223, 225, 277; around CIA 32, 33, 34, 41, 42, 43, 44, 75, 242; around KGB 16, 33, 35, 36, 38, 67, 68, 70, 71, 72, 73, 75, 76, 78, 79, 80, 81; around the USA 33, 34, 35, 40, 41, 42, 43, 44, 55, 60, 68, 71, 73, 74, 79, 93, 130, 149, 152, 154, 162, 167, 200, 208, 209, 221, 222, 223, 237, 241, 242, 243, 244, 245; conspiracism 2, 3, 4, 6, 7, 8, 12, 13, 14, 16, 19, 20, 57, 58, 59, 90, 93, 99, 103, 104, 106, 107, 150, 154, 155, 156, 157, 163, 164, 167, 233, 235, 237, 238; conspiracy theories and disaster 14, 30, 32, 34, 36, 39, 41, 42, 43, 44, 139, 219, 253; and cultural exchange 107; and cultural heritage 91, 101; in France 48, 50, 52, 54, 56–7, 59, 60; and Gothic literature 95; and humor 31, 220; in Hungary 9, 19, 89, 93, 102, 105, 133, 207, 209, 210, 213, 215, 217, 219, 221, 223, 224, 225–6; and internal enemies 7, 49, 50, 113, 128, 239; in the

interwar period 9, 90, 95, 98, 103, 111; and jokes 32, 42, 117, 118, 194, 220; in literature 6, 8, 55, 90, 95, 97, 100, 102, 236; mentality 132, 136, 259, 261, 262, 263; and national character 98; pejorative definitions 4, 270, 271, 273, 275, 283; as political tools 7, 10, 20, 55; in post-Soviet space 16, 34, 40, 43, 44, 67, 93, 178, 232, 236, 239, 245; and racial debility 96; social consequences of belief in 272, 274, 278; in the Soviet Union 1, 5, 10, 11, 13, 15, 29, 32, 33, 34, 35, 36, 37, 41, 42, 44, 48, 50, 51, 55, 56, 57, 60, 61, 67, 68, 69, 70, 71, 72, 73, 75, 76, 78, 79, 80, 81, 151, 152, 154, 232, 235, 243; and tourism 43; in the United Kingdom 2, 89, 136, 276, 283; and worker's movement 92
conspiracy theory theory 268, 275, 277, 278, 283
control deprivation 136, 137
corruption 30, 55, 60, 113, 114, 116, 117, 119, 173, 174, 175, 187, 191, 193, 207, 209, 219, 221, 222, 233, 238, 242, 246, 254, 278, 279, 283, 285; probability, prior 274–5, 278, 279, 281
Council of Europe 171, 172, 177, 180
Croatia 147, 149, 150, 155, 156, 158, 159, 160, 161, 162, 163, 164, 251
Cserny, J. 92
Csizmadia, S. 92
Csoóri, S. 103, 104, 106
Csurka, I. 104, 213
cultural transfer 50, 61
Czechoslovakia 9, 154, 169, 188, 193

Daudet, L. 93
Davison, C.-M. 95
December Revolution 280, 281
deep state conspiracy theory 7, 11, 221, 222, 224, 226, 242, 244, 245
democratic transition 1, 6, 11, 12, 13, 14, 17, 34, 97, 102, 110, 120, 137, 210, 211, 212, 250, 252, 279, 280, 285
Dentith, M R. X. 3, 20, 211, 235, 269, 270
Der Tat 97
Dimitrov, G. 111
discrimination 103, 128, 133, 154, 158, 159, 179
Dmowski, R. 128
doctors' plot 57
Domagalska, M. 127
Doncheva, T. 116, 118

Index 291

Dragnea, L. 1, 19, 207, 209, 215, 220, 221, 222, 223, 224, 225
dual-process model 263

eco-nationalism 37, 38
Erdoğan, R. T. 208, 222, 224
ethnicism 91
Eurabia conspiracy theory 14, 217
Euromaidan 18, 38, 168, 208
European migrant crisis 207, 214, 215, 217
external enemies 7, 19, 67, 68, 70, 71, 72, 79, 162, 163, 164, 188, 191, 252
extreme-right 2, 11, 19, 37, 48, 49, 52, 53, 54, 55, 56, 89, 91, 92, 95, 96, 97, 101, 194, 105, 106, 107, 117, 125, 128, 130, 131, 160, 163, 178, 208, 209, 210, 212, 213, 214, 215, 219, 220, 223, 224, 225, 254, 258, 272, 263, 264, 279

fake 14, 43, 52, 94, 175, 177
fear 11, 14, 18, 35, 39, 49, 51, 59, 60, 95, 147, 148, 150, 153, 162, 167, 168, 170, 173, 178, 179, 193, 216, 217, 236, 241, 242, 246, 253, 254
Fekete, G. 104
Fico, R. 191, 192, 193, 194, 200, 208, 215, 223
Fidesz 104, 105, 208, 214, 215, 216, 217, 219, 222, 223, 224, 276
Fifth Column 53, 60, 156
Finkelstein, A. 214, 224
folklore 15, 30, 32, 76
Food Program 80
framing 173, 242, 254, 285
French Communist Party 52, 53, 55, 56, 57, 58
Fried, F. 97, 98

Gati, C. 105
gender, ideology 132, 133, 192, 195, 196, 197, 198
generalism 273, 274
German conservative revolution 97
Germany 1, 5, 6, 9, 11, 15, 18, 51, 53, 73, 89, 90, 92, 93, 95, 97, 97, 112, 126, 129, 147, 148, 150, 161, 162, 163, 189, 215, 216, 258, 272
Gerrits, A. 8, 89, 90, 106
glasnost 36, 42
globalization 13, 14, 15, 19, 212
Goldman, E. 92
Gömbös, G. 95
Gorbachev, M. 30, 33, 34, 42

Gordon 171, 173, 175
Great Britain 59, 93, 151, 188
Greater Romania Party (PRM) 211, 213, 221
Greater Serbia 160, 163
great powers 1, 6, 7, 12, 13, 15, 151, 153, 163, 200, 211
"great replacement" conspiracy theory 217
Great Terror 67, 78
Grindeanu, S. 207
Gross, J. T. 129
group-centrism 262
Gruevski, N. 19, 254, 255, 256, 257, 258, 259
Gyurcsány, F. 215

Haskalah 127
Hegedűs, L. Jr. 105
Hegedűs, L. (Mrs.) 105
Helsinki Accords 69, 74
Helsinki Watch groups 73
Heti Válasz 213
Hlinka, A. 188, 189
hoax 29, 38, 39, 40, 43
Hofstadter, R. 3, 4, 12, 234, 252, 253, 271
Horthy, M. regime 89, 91, 92, 94, 97, 98, 216
Holocaust 38, 96, 125, 126, 128, 129, 130, 137, 139, 194, 212
Hoxha, E. 152
Hrytsenko, A. 176
Hungarian Democratic Forum (MDF) 104, 213
Hungarian Revolution 58, 153
Hungarian Soviet Republic 89, 90, 91, 92, 93, 95, 96, 97, 99, 100, 103, 107
Hungary 9, 12, 14, 17, 18, 19, 58, 89, 91, 92, 93, 94, 95, 96, 99, 100, 102, 103, 104, 105, 133, 134, 150, 152, 155, 162, 169, 188, 189, 207, 208, 209, 210–19, 221–6, 242, 276, 278, 281

ICTV 173, 175, 176
ICTY 161, 163
identity 7, 13, 15, 18, 21, 38, 61, 77, 78, 81, 82, 89, 91, 92, 105, 114, 135, 137, 138, 139, 159, 170, 173, 175, 177, 186, 187, 189, 200, 210, 225, 232, 233, 236, 242, 243, 244, 245, 254, 258, 281
IMF 156, 211, 213, 225
information warfare 44, 68, 69, 71, 72, 73, 76, 81
international Zionism 129

292   *Index*

Italian Communist Party 51, 55, 58, 60
Italy 18, 49, 51, 55–60, 134, 148, 150,
   155, 162, 276
Ivanov, H. 116, 117

Jánošík, J. 188
Jewish Communism 49, 89, 90, 94, 95,
   103, 128; *see also* Judeo-Bolshevik
   conspiracy
*Jewish Question in Hungary after 1944,
   The* 102
Judeo-Bolshevik conspiracy 9, 17, 89, 90,
   91, 93, 94, 95, 96, 98, 101, 106, 211
Judeo-Polonia 125, 127
Juriga, F. 188
Justice for Everyone 117, 118

Kádár, J. 102, 210, 211, 212
Karasev, V. 178
Kertész, I. 103
Kisebbségben (In Minority) 100, 102,
   103, 106
Kiska, A. 191, 192, 195
Kočner, M. 191, 201
Kofta, M. 133
koloradi 172, 173
Komsomol 41, 76
Kosovar Albanians 156, 157, 159
Kosovo 149, 158, 160, 162, 251
Kotleba–Ľudová strana Naše Slovensko
   194, 199
Kréko, P. 210, 216, 276
Kuby, G. 196
Kuciak, J. 19, 186, 191, 192, 194, 195,
   198, 199, 200
Kun, B. 92, 93
Kušnírová, M. 186, 191, 198, 200

Lechner, K. 96, 108
Leymarie, M. 93, 108
Lezsák, S. 104
liberalism 61, 99, 102, 190, 195, 196, 197,
   198, 200
literary culture 236
Lukács, G. 94, 99, 100, 105, 106
Luxembourg, R. 92

Macedonian citizens 163, 251, 252, 253,
   255–60, 263
Magyar Fórum 212, 231
Manichean worldview 61, 190, 263
March 1968 129, 141
Marx, K. 92
Mečiar, V. 190, 191

Memorandum of the Serbian Academy of
   Science and Arts 157
Mészöly, M. 103
Milošević, S. 156, 159, 161, 163
MMR vaccine conspiracy theory 277
Moldavia 232, 246
Moldova, republic of 19, 232–46, 278
Moscovici, S. 132, 135
Most-Híd party 192

Napkelet (Orient) 93
Nappali hold (Moon at Daylight) 103,
   104, 107
National Anti-Corruption Directorate
   (DNA, Romania) 221
nationalism 12, 18, 98, 102, 106, 126, 155,
   159, 187, 199, 211, 233, 243, 254, 257
nationalist conspiracism 157
nation-building 36, 232, 243, 245
NATO 5, 147, 154, 162, 195, 213, 233,
   242, 257
Neighbours 129
Németh, L. 90, 97–104, 106
Nemzetiség és kisebbség (Nationality and
   Minority) 103
neofascism, MSI 51, 55
Netanyahu, B. 208, 214, 216
New Age 32, 37, 43
New Zealand 278
Niemcewicz, J. U. 127
Non-Alignment Movement 153, 154
North Macedonia 19, 20, 148, 208, 250,
   251–8, 263, 264

Obozrevatel 173, 175
Obóz Wielkiej Polski 128
Odessa 18, 167, 168, 171–9
Oleinyk, V. 176
Open Society Foundations (OSF) 212, 214,
   215, 219, 220
Orbán, V. 1, 13, 19, 104, 105, 194, 207,
   209, 210, 212, 214–18, 224, 225
Order of the Knights Templar 112,
   114, 117
overdetermination 17, 110, 120, 121

"parallel state" 221, 222
paranoid style 271
particularism 282
Pashinsky, S. 176
Plahotniuc, V. 233, 234, 237, 239, 240,
   243, 244
"plebiscitary government" 216
Polish Prejudice Surveys 130

Index   293

political culture 2, 10, 48, 50, 55, 58, 59, 60, 61, 102, 161, 236
political scandal 254, 275
Ponta, V. 219, 279
Popper, K. 212
populism 1, 15, 16, 17, 18, 19, 21, 22, 90, 161, 167, 178, 179, 190, 200, 202, 207, 209, 210, 225, 232, 233, 245
populist "mode of articulation" 218
Postoj 196
post-socialist transition 6, 12, 14, 17, 110, 120, 210, 211, 212, 250
Prespa agreement 257
Princip, G. 148
"Priština-Zagreb-Ljubljana Axis" 159
probability 193; perceptions of corruption 278; posterior 275; prior 274, 275, 278, 279, 281; relative 275
progressivism 97, 101
Prohászka, O. 90, 100
Protestantism 100, 101
Protocols of the Elders of Zion, The 102
prototype of conspiring group 130, 133
Putin, V. 168, 170, 176, 208, 224, 238, 239, 242, 243

Quand Israël est roi (When Israel Is King) 93

Radić, S. 149
Rákosi, M. 94, 102
Revue des Deux Mondes 93
rhizome 121
Right-Wing Authoritarianism 130, 263
"right-wing populist rhetoric" 210
Rola 127
Romania 9, 11, 12, 19, 20, 72, 134, 152, 154, 155, 169, 207, 209, 210–26, 232, 233, 234, 236, 241, 242, 243, 245, 246, 273, 277, 278, 279, 280, 281, 284
Romanian Communist Party 280
Romanian Intelligence Service (SRI) 221, 281
Romanian National Unity Party (PUNR) 211
Roşia Montană 219
rumor 31, 35, 192
Russia 1, 5, 6, 8, 10, 13, 14, 15, 16, 18, 29, 34, 35, 37, 38, 48, 56, 67, 80, 89, 92, 126, 127, 132, 135, 168, 169, 170, 171, 174, 175, 176, 177, 178, 179, 195, 208, 220, 232, 233, 234, 235, 236, 237, 238, 239, 241, 242, 243, 244, 245, 246, 269

sabotage 29, 32, 33, 34, 35, 43, 44, 53, 71, 72, 82, 117, 152
St. Vitus's Day Constitution 149
scapegoat(-ing) 80, 135, 137, 209
secret society 111, 112, 116, 122
Securitate 72, 82, 221, 279, 281, 282, 285
Segodnya 173, 175, 176, 177
self-victimization 18, 39, 187, 188
separatism 149, 171, 172, 173, 174, 175
Serbia 147, 148, 149, 155, 156, 157, 158, 159, 160, 162, 163, 164, 250
Simmel, G. 111, 112, 113
Slovak Catholic Church 189
Slovakia 9, 186, 188–201, 223
SMER-SD 191
Social-Democratic Party (PSD, Romania) 207, 219, 220–5
socialist conspiracism 156
Soros, G. 2, 13, 19, 104, 105, 192, 193, 194, 195, 196, 200, 207, 208–10, 212–26, 238, 241, 242, 246, 258, 270, 276
Soviet Union 1, 5, 10, 11, 13, 15, 29, 32, 33, 34, 35, 36, 37, 41, 42, 44, 48, 50, 51, 55, 56, 57, 60, 61, 69, 72, 151, 152, 154
Spartacus 92
Sputnik 34, 208, 220, 234
Sputnik Romania 208, 220, 221, 234
stabilitocracy 256
"Stagnation era" 78
Stalinism 10, 50, 67, 73, 78, 102, 136
Stalin, J. V. 10, 11, 34, 50, 57, 78, 80, 81, 151, 152, 284
Stan, L. 281
Steed, H. W. 93
Štefánik, M. R. 188
Steinmeier, F-W. 176
suffering rivalry 125, 129, 139
"superconspiracy" 218, 218, 224, 226
Szabó, D. 99, 103, 104
Szamuely, T. 92
Szekfű, G. 98
Szemere, B. 95, 96
Szerb, A. 95
Sztójay, D. 96
Szülőföldünk (Our Homeland) 102

Tharaud, Jean 93
Tharaud, Jérôme 93
Thorez, M. 51, 54, 59
Times (London) 92, 93
"Tirana-Belgrade-Bucharest axis" 154
Tiso, J. 187, 188, 189, 190, 194
Titoism 57

294   Index

Tito, J. B. 147, 148, 150, 151, 152, 153, 154, 155, 156, 158, 159, 161
Tito-Stalin split 151, 152
Togliatti, P. 51, 54, 56
Tormay, C. 93, 94, 100
Transparency International 278
Tripartite Pact 150
Trotskyist conspiracy 49, 50, 56, 57
Trotsky, L. 92, 94
Tsacheva, T. 117, 118
Tuđman, F. 163
Tudor, C. V. 213
Turchynov, O. 175
Tymoshenko, Y. 176

Ukraine 18, 29, 30, 35–9, 42–4
UN 162, 170, 171, 177, 196, 224
United Grand Lodge of Bulgaria 111, 112, 113
USA 40, 71, 73, 74, 147, 162, 200, 208, 209, 222, 223, 237, 241, 242, 243, 244, 245
Ustasha 150, 151, 155, 156, 159

victimhood 7, 13, 15, 18, 138, 161, 186, 187, 190, 199, 200, 201

victimization 18, 39, 186, 187, 188, 195, 199, 200, 201
Vienna 284

Webster, N. 93
Weishaupt, A. 92
women's movement 93, 94, 95
World Jewish Congress 105
World Revolution: The Plot Against Civilization 93
World War I 9, 89, 94, 111, 113, 126, 148, 188
World War II 1, 9, 31, 35, 40, 44, 51, 59, 79, 90, 95, 96, 125, 128, 129, 130, 136, 147, 150, 152, 155, 156, 158, 159, 161, 169, 285

Yatsenyuk, A. 176
Yugoslav Committee 148, 149
Yugoslavia 6, 18, 57, 147–64, 252
Yugoslav People's Army 160, 161

Zacsek, G. 213
żydokomuna 128